Panic Disorder

An Einstein Psychiatry Publication

Publication Series of the Department of Psychiatry
Albert Einstein College of Medicine of Yeshiva University
New York, NY

1. CONTEMPORARY APPROACHES TO PSYCHOLOGICAL ASSESSMENT
Edited by Scott Wetzler, Ph.D. & Martin M. Katz, Ph.D.
2. COMPUTER APPLICATIONS IN PSYCHIATRY AND PSYCHOLOGY
Edited by David Baskin, Ph.D.
3. VIOLENCE AND SUICIDALITY: PERSPECTIVES IN CLINICAL
AND PSYCHOBIOLOGICAL RESEARCH
*Edited by Herman M. van Praag, M.D., Ph.D.,
Robert Plutchik, Ph.D., & Alan Apter, M.D.*
4. THE ROLE OF SEROTONIN IN PSYCHIATRIC DISORDERS
*Edited by Serena-Lynn Brown, M.D., Ph.D.
& Herman M. van Praag, M.D., Ph.D.*
5. POSITIVE AND NEGATIVE SYNDROMES IN SCHIZOPHRENIA:
ASSESSMENT AND RESEARCH
by Stanley R. Kay, Ph.D.
6. NEW BIOLOGICAL VISTAS ON SCHIZOPHRENIA
*Edited by Jean-Pierre Lindenmayer, M.D.
& Stanley R. Kay, Ph.D.*
7. "MAKE-BELIEVES" IN PSYCHIATRY, OR THE PERILS OF PROGRESS
by Herman M. van Praag, M.D., Ph.D.
8. GENETIC STUDIES IN AFFECTIVE DISORDERS: BASIC METHODS,
CURRENT DIRECTIONS, AND CRITICAL RESEARCH ISSUES
*Edited by Demitri F. Papolos, M.D.
& Herbert M. Lachman, M.D.*
9. PSYCHIATRIC-LEGAL DECISION MAKING BY THE MENTAL HEALTH PRACTITIONER:
THE CLINICIAN AS DE FACTO MAGISTRATE
*Edited by Harvey Bluestone, M.D.,
Sheldon Travin, M.D., & Douglas B. Marlowe, J.D., Ph.D.*
10. EGO DEFENSES: THEORY AND MEASUREMENT
Edited by Hope R. Conte, Ph.D. & Robert Plutchik, Ph.D.
11. TREATMENT APPROACHES WITH SUICIDAL ADOLESCENTS
Edited by James K. Zimmerman, Ph.D. & Gregory M. Asnis, M.D.
12. PANIC DISORDER: CLINICAL, BIOLOGICAL, AND TREATMENT ASPECTS
Edited by Gregory M. Asnis, M.D. & Herman M. van Praag, M.D., Ph.D.

Panic Disorder
Clinical, Biological, and Treatment Aspects

Edited by

GREGORY M. ASNIS

HERMAN M. VAN PRAAG

A Wiley-Interscience Publication

John Wiley & Sons, Inc.

New York • Chichester • Brisbane • Toronto • Singapore

Library of Congress Cataloging-in-Publication Data:

Panic disorder : clinical, biological, and treatment aspects / edited
   by Gregory M. Asnis, Herman M. van Praag.
      p.   cm. — (An Einstein psychiatry publication ; 12)
   Includes index.
   ISBN 0-471-08999-0 (cloth : alk. paper)
   1. Panic disorders. I. Asnis, Gregory M. II. Praag, Herman M.
van (Herman Meïr), 1929-   . III. Series.
   [DNLM: 1. Panic Disorder. W1 EI535 v.12 1995 / WM 172 P1926
1995]
   RC535.P356   1995
   616.85'223—dc20
   DNLM/DLC
                                     95-980

Printed in the United States of America

10 9 8 7 6 5 4 3 2 1

Contributors

David H. Arnold, Ph.D. Assistant Professor, Department of Psychology, Tobin Hall, University of Massachusetts, Amherst, Massachusetts.

Gregory M. Asnis, M.D. Professor and Director of the Affective Disorders Program, Department of Psychiatry, Albert Einstein College of Medicine, Montefiore Medical Center; Director of the Adult Psychiatry Outpatient Department, Montefiore Medical Center, Bronx, New York.

Aaron T. Beck, M.D. University Professor, Center for Cognitive Therapy, University of Pennsylvania, Philadelphia, Pennsylvania.

Jacques Bradwejn, M.D., FRCPC Professor, Department of Psychiatry, University of Toronto; Head, Psychobiology and Clinical Trials Research Unit in Anxiety, The Clarke Institute of Psychiatry, Toronto, Canada.

Deborah S. Cowley, M.D. Associate Professor, Department of Psychiatry and Behavioral Sciences, University of Washington, School of Medicine, Seattle, Washington.

Raymond R. Crowe, M.D. Professor, Department of Psychiatry, University of Iowa, College of Medicine, Iowa City, Iowa.

Stephen R. Dager, M.D. Associate Professor, Department of Psychiatry and Behavioral Sciences and Bioengineering, University of Washington, School of Medicine, Seattle, Washington.

David L. Dunner, M.D. Professor, Department of Psychiatry, University of Washington, School of Medicine; Director, Outpatient Psychiatry; Co-Director, Center for Anxiety and Depression; Vice-Chairman for Clinical Services, University of Washington, Seattle, Washington.

William W. Eaton, Ph.D. Professor, Department of Mental Hygiene, John Hopkins University, School of Hygiene and Public Health, Baltimore, Maryland.

Jack M. Gorman, M.D. Professor of Psychiatry, Columbia University, College of Physicians and Surgeons; Chief, Department of Clinical Psychiatry, New York State Psychiatric Institute, New York, New York.

René S. Kahn, Ph.D. Professor and Chairman, Department of Psychiatry, University Hospital Utrecht, Utrecht, The Netherlands.

Penelope M. Keyl, Ph.D. Assistant Professor, Department of Epidemiology, John Hopkins University, School of Public Health, Baltimore, Maryland.

Diana Koszycki, Ph.D. Research Coordinator, Psychobiology and Clinical Trials Research Unit in Anxiety and Department of Psychiatry, The Clarke Institute of Psychiatry, Toronto, Canada.

Clare Moore, M.S. Research Coordinator, Department of Psychiatry, Bronx VA Medical Center, Bronx, New York.

Laszlo A. Papp, M.D. Associate Professor of Clinical Psychiatry, Columbia University, College of Physicians and Surgeons; Director, Phobia, Anxiety and Stress Disorders Clinic, Hillside Hospital, New York, New York.

B. Ashok Raj, M.D. Associate Professor, Department of Psychiatry, University of South Florida, College of Medicine, Tampa, Florida.

Jill H. Rathus, Ph.D. Instructor, Department of Psychiatry, Albert Einstein College of Medicine, Montefiore Medical Center, Bronx, New York.

William C. Sanderson, Ph.D. Associate Professor, Department of Psychiatry and Director, Cognitive Behavior Therapy Program, Albert Einstein College of Medicine, Montefiore Medical Center, Bronx, New York.

David V. Sheehan, M.D. Professor of Psychiatry, University of South Florida, College of Medicine; Institute for Research in Psychiatry, Clinical Research Center, Tampa, Florida.

Thomas W. Uhde, M.D. Professor and Chairman, Department of Psychiatry, Wayne State University School of Medicine, Detroit, Michigan.

Herman M. van Praag, M.D., Ph.D. Professor and Chairman, Academic Psychiatric Center and University of Limburg, Maastricht, The Netherlands.

Herman G. M. Westenberg, Ph.D. Associate Professor, Department of Psychiatry, University Hospital Utrecht, Utrecht, The Netherlands.

Scott Wetzler, Ph.D. Chief, Division of Psychology, Associate Professor, Department of Psychiatry, Albert Einstein College of Medicine, Montefiore Medical Center, Bronx, New York.

Catherine L. Woodman, M.D. Assistant Professor of Psychiatry, University of Iowa, College of Medicine, Iowa City, Iowa.

A Note on the Series

Psychiatry is in a state of flux. The excitement springs in part from internal changes, such as the development and official acceptance (at least in the United States) of an operationalized, multi-axial classification system of behavioral disorders (the DSM-IV), the increasing sophistication of methods to measure abnormal human behavior, and the impressive expansion of biological and psychological treatment modalities. Exciting developments are also taking place in fields relating to psychiatry; in molecular (brain) biology, genetics, brain imaging, drug development, epidemiology, experimental psychology, to mention only a few striking examples.

More generally speaking, psychiatry is moving, still relatively slowly, but irresistibly from a more philosophical, contemplative orientation to that of an empirical science. From the 1950s on, biological psychiatry has been a major catalyst of that process. It provided the mother discipline with a third cornerstone, that is, neurobiology, the other two being psychology and medical sociology. In addition, it forced the profession into the direction of standardization of diagnoses and of assessment of abnormal behavior. Biological psychiatry provided psychiatry not only with a new basic science and with new treatment modalities, but also with the tools, the methodology, and the mentality to operate within the confines of an empirical science, the only framework in which a medical discipline can survive.

In other fields of psychiatry, too, one discerns a gradual trend toward scientification. Psychological treatment techniques are standardized and manuals developed to make these skills more easily transferable. Methods registering treatment outcome—traditionally used in the behavioral/cognitive field—are now more and more requested and, hence, developed for dynamic forms of psychotherapy as well. Social and community psychiatry, until the 1960s were more firmly rooted in humanitarian ideals and social awareness than in empirical studies, profited greatly from its liaison with the social sciences and the expansion of psychiatric epidemiology.

Let there be no misunderstanding: Empiricism does *not imply* that it is only the measurable that counts. Psychiatry would be mutilated if it would neglect that which cannot be captured by numbers. It *does imply* that what is measurable should be measured. Progress in psychiatry is dependent on ideas and on experiment. Their linkage is inseparable.

This Series, published under the auspices of the Department of Psychiatry of the Albert Einstein College of Medicine, Montefiore Medical Center, is meant to keep track of important developments in our profession, to summarize what has been achieved in particular fields, and to bring together the viewpoints obtained from disparate vantage points—in short, to capture some of the ongoing excitement in modern psychiatry, both in its clinical and experimental dimensions. The Department of Psychiatry at Albert Einstein College of Medicine hosts the Series, but naturally welcomes contributions from others.

Bernie Mazel originally generated the idea for the series—an ambitious plan which we all felt was worthy of pursuit. The edifice of psychiatry is impressive, but still somewhat flawed in its foundations. May this Series contribute to consolidation of its infrastructure.

—HERMAN M. VAN PRAAG, M.D., PH.D.
Professor and Chairman
Academic Psychiatric Center
University of Limburg
Maastricht
The Netherlands

Preface

Panic disorder is frequently undiagnosed or misdiagnosed, yet it is acknowledged as a distinct psychiatric disorder that is increasingly being recognized. The National Institute of Health and the National Institute of Mental Health recently initiated a number of educational programs on panic disorder for the public, family practitioners, and mental health professionals.

In this book, we provide a comprehensive review of what is known about panic disorder, focusing on the psychological, clinical, and biological aspects of this anxiety disorder. The book provides both clinicians and academicians with a resource to better understand, study, and diagnose this illness.

Important developments in a specific illness may take years to be disseminated and appreciated. This book attempts to make the important information on panic disorder more immediately available. Mood disorders, especially major depressive disorder, have received great attention. Yet even here, clinical, biological, and treatment issues are poorly disseminated and frequently misunderstood.

It is time for panic disorder to receive adequate attention. This book should be an important resource for all interested parties and assist in the quality of knowledge, care, and future studies of panic disorder.

GREGORY M. ASNIS
HERMAN M. VAN PRAAG

Acknowledgments

We would like to thank our wives, Lauren and Nelleke for their support. Ms. Nancy Ruiz-Mejia, secretary of the Anxiety and Depression Clinic at Montefiore Medical Center provided excellent secretarial services. We want to thank our contributors who responded promptly and graciously to the numerous requests for revisions and updates of their manuscripts.

Contents

Introduction   1

PART I   CLINICAL ASPECTS OF PANIC DISORDER

1. Panic Disorder: *Phenomenology and Differential Diagnosis*   15
   JILL H. RATHUS AND
   GREGORY M. ASNIS

2. The Epidemiology of Panic   50
   WILLIAM W. EATON AND
   PENELOPE M. KEYL

3. The Genetics of Panic Disorder   66
   CATHERINE L. WOODMAN AND
   RAYMOND R. CROWE

4. Comorbidity of Panic Disorder   80
   SCOTT WETZLER AND
   WILLIAM C. SANDERSON

5. Panic Disorder and Suicidal Behavior   99
   DAVID H. ARNOLD,
   WILLIAM C. SANDERSON, AND
   AARON T. BECK

PART II   BIOLOGICAL UNDERPINNINGS OF PANIC DISORDER

6. The Norepinephrine System in Panic Disorder   119
   GREGORY M. ASNIS AND
   HERMAN M. VAN PRAAG

7. Increased Serotonin Function and Panic Disorder   151
   RENÉ S. KAHN,
   HERMAN G. M. WESTENBERG, AND
   CLARE MOORE

8. Caffeine-Induced Anxiety: *An Ideal Chemical Model of Panic Disorder?*   181
   THOMAS W. UHDE

9. The Lactate Infusion Challenge   206
   DEBORAH S. COWLEY,
   STEPHEN R. DAGER, AND
   DAVID L. DUNNER

10. Cholecystokinin and Panic Disorder   233
    JACQUES BRADWEJN AND
    DIANA KOSZYCKI

11. Respiratory Neurobiology of Panic   255
    LASZLO A. PAPP AND
    JACK M. GORMAN

PART III   TREATMENTS OF PANIC DISORDER

12. Somatic Treatment Strategies in Panic Disorder   279
    B. ASHOK RAJ AND
    DAVID V. SHEEHAN

13. Cognitive Behavioral Treatment of Panic Disorder   314
    WILLIAM C. SANDERSON AND
    SCOTT WETZLER

Author Index   337

Subject Index   352

Introduction

Panic disorder is a relatively new diagnostic category spanning approximately two decades. Its conception arose out of clinical observations by Klein (1964) that a subgroup of anxious patients who had panic attacks tended to do well when treated with imipramine in contrast to those with other anxiety disorders. Panic disorder was first formally recognized by the Feighner Criteria (Feighner et al., 1972) and Research Diagnostic Criteria (Spitzer, Endicott & Robins, 1978), finally entering the official American Psychiatric Association (APA) nomenclature—the *Diagnostic and Statistical Manual of Mental Disorders,* third edition (DSM-III) and third edition, revised (III-R) (APA, 1980 and 1987 respectively) and now the fourth edition (DSM-IV) (APA, 1994).

Panic disorder, which was previously subsumed under various anxiety syndromes, such as anxiety neurosis, neurocirculatory asthenia, and DaCosta's Syndrome, is a distinct anxiety disorder with specific phenomenology, treatment response, genetics, family history, and epidemiology. Originally thought to be a rare illness, panic disorder is a prevalent mental disorder. It is the most common presenting problem among people seeking mental health treatment as well as the fifth most common clinical profile that primary care physicians encounter (Klerman, Weissman, Ovellette, Johnson, & Greenwald, 1991). Although earlier thought to be a mild disorder, panic disorder is now recognized to be associated with a significant degree of dysfunction in social, occupational, and family activities comparable to depressive disorders (Markowitz, Weissman, Ovellette, & Liek, 1989). Of particular concern are recent reports suggesting that panic disorder is associated with a high prevalence of suicidal behaviors (Weissman, Klerman, Markowitz, & Ovellette, 1989).

1

Since panic disorder is readily treatable by both somatic and pyschological therapies, it is imperative to make an early and correct diagnosis to ensure that appropriate treatments are administered. Unfortunately, panic disorder is frequently undiagnosed or misdiagnosed, leading to inadequate or incorrect treatments. The National Institute of Health and National Institute of Mental Health have recently initiated a number of educational programs on panic disorder for the public, family practitioners, and mental health professionals to help remedy this health problem. In fact, an 800 telephone line has been established, inviting concerned others to seek information (1-800-64-PANIC).

The purpose of this book is to provide, in one volume, a comprehensive review of what is known about panic disorder. It has focused on psychological, clinical, and biological aspects of this anxiety disorder, providing both clinicians and academicians a resource to better understand, study, and treat this illness.

This book, composed of 13 chapters, is organized into three parts: Part I, Clinical Aspects of Panic Disorder, Part II, Biological Underpinnings of Panic Disorder, and Part III, Treatments of Panic Disorder. The contributors were carefully selected, representing the leading clinical and academic authorities in their areas of specialization.

PART I CLINICAL ASPECTS OF PANIC DISORDER

Chapter 1, "Panic Disorder: Phenomenology and Differential Diagnosis," by Jill H. Rathus and Gregory M. Asnis, brings into clinical focus the complicated nature of panic disorder. It not only emphasizes the importance of panic attacks per se, which are central to the diagnosis, but also describes other aspects of the disorder, such as anticipatory anxiety and phobic avoidance, which contribute significantly to the patients' functional impairment. The chapter provides a structure for the clinician to comprehensively evaluate a patient with panic disorder and differentiate the disorder from a vast number of other diagnostic categories and clinical conditions that may share symptoms or mimic its presentation. In addition, a number of biopsychosocial stressors that can precipitate or exacerbate the disorder are discussed (e.g., childbirth, loss, illness, and interpersonal stressors). Finally, the authors provide an update of the recent DSM-IV criteria (APA, 1994) for panic disorder, noting the significant changes from the previous diagnostic classificatory system, DSM-III-R (APA, 1987).

Chapter 2, "The Epidemiology of Panic," by William W. Eaton and Penelope M. Keyl, presents a summary of the epidemiology and course of panic attacks and panic disorder. The authors address these epidemiological questions by reviewing the most extensive relevant data bases available, the epidemiological catchment area (ECA) studies, and the National Comorbidity Survey. What is most striking is the high prevalence of the disorder, 1.5 to 3.5 percent, with even a higher prevalence of panic attacks, 10 to 15 percent, which do not fulfill criteria for panic disorder. The authors review the role of sex and ethnicity on prevalence and symptom profile. They note that females have twice the prevalence as males across all ethnic groups, and that blacks and Hispanics have a lower lifetime prevalence than whites. The authors also review different symptom profiles of specific cultures. Last, they review the course of panic, risk factors, and sequelae. It is clear that patients with panic disorder have an increased number of health problems as well as a high prevalence of alcohol/drug abuse and depression.

Chapter 3, "The Genetics of Panic Disorder," by Catherine L. Woodman and Raymond R. Crowe, reviews the etiology of this illness, evaluating the age-old question of whether nature or nurture predominates. The authors review both family and twin studies. It is clear that although genetic factors are present, they make only a modest contribution to the occurrence of panic disorder. The authors suggest a model that includes both genes and environment. The mode of inheritance is also explored by reviewing monogenic versus polygenic inheritance. At this point, the mode of inheritance is unclear. A search for specific genes that may further clarify the genetics of panic disorder is presented with a review of ongoing linkage studies.

Chapter 4, "Comorbidity of Panic Disorder," by Scott Wetzler and William C. Sanderson, reviews a topic that has not been given the attention that it deserves. Comorbidity refers to the presence of independent psychiatric diagnoses. The authors point out that comorbidity in panic disorder is very common, citing ECA data indicating that two-thirds of patients with panic disorder have co-occurring major psychiatric disorders. According to the authors' review, approximately 40 percent of panic disorder patients have a comorbid personality disorder. Patients with panic disorder who have comorbidity have a worse symptom profile course, prognosis, and response to treatment. The authors strongly recommend that clinicians evaluate all panic patients for Axis I and II disorders so that adequate treatment can be provided for each problem.

Chapter 5, "Panic Disorder and Suicidal Behavior," by David H. Arnold, William C. Sanderson, and Aaron T. Beck, reviews a highly controversial topic. Originally Weissman and colleagues presented data that patients with panic disorder have a high prevalence of suicidal behaviors, comparable to patients with major depression. Although some studies have replicated this finding, others have not. This important issue is reviewed in depth. Since severity of illness in panic disorder, depression, substance abuse, and comorbid personality disorder appear to be important factors contributing to suicidal behaviors in panic disorder, the authors suggest that future studies must evaluate all of these areas including all comorbid Axis I and II disorders, in order to fully understand the relationship of suicidal behaviors in panic disorder.

PART II BIOLOGICAL UNDERPINNINGS OF PANIC DISORDER

Chapter 6 through 10 review the biology of panic disorder, evaluating the role of various neurotransmitters and peptides. Although each chapter focuses predominately on a particular system, references within each chapter suggest a complicated integration of many of these biological systems to best explain the biology of panic.

Chapter 6, "The Norepinephrine System in Panic Disorder," by Gregory M. Asnis, reviews the role of the neurotransmitter norepinephrine in panic disorder. The most popular biological hypothesis in panic disorder is the norepinephrine hypothesis, which suggests that hyperactivity of the norepinephrine system and dysfunction at the locus coeruleus are associated with this disorder. Various paradigms of norepinephrine functioning are reviewed, including basal levels of norepinephrine output, behaviorally evoked panic attacks, peripheral adrenoceptor assessments, and selective noradrenergic challenge tests (to provoke neuroendocrine and behavioral responses) in order to assess the validity of this hypothesis. Although the chapter suggests some inconsistencies, particularly regarding the baseline norepinephrine output studies, most data have supported a dysfunction of the norepinephrine system, especially from the noradrenergic challenge tests. Yohimbine, an alpha-2-adrenoceptor antagonist, has been the most reliable and meaningful challenge test, demonstrating an exaggerated response in anxiety, blood pressure, pulse, cortisol, and 3-methoxy-4-hydroxyphenylethylene glycol (MHPG). These yohimbine responses have been highly specific for panic disorder normalizing after clinical recovery. This data is supportive of presynaptic alpha-2-adrenoceptor hyposensitivity (MHPG data) and alpha-2-adrenoceptor dysregulation in general (e.g., increased anxiety response). Other noradrenergic challenges also have found selective abnormalities of the norepinephrine system, but they have been nonspecific for panic disorder (a blunted human growth hormone response to clonidine, an alpha-2-adrenoceptor agonist, suggesting postsynaptic alpha-2-adrenoceptor hyposensitivity; a blunted cortisol response to the desipramine, a norepinephrine reuptake inhibitor, suggesting alpha-1-adrenoceptor hyposensitivity; an increased anxiogenic response and a decreased heart rate and lymphocyte cyclic AMP response to isoproteronol, a beta-adrenoceptor agonist, suggesting central nervous system beta-adrenoceptor hypersensitivity and peripheral beta-adrenoceptor hyposensitivity respectively). Thus, there is strong evidence of a dysfunction of the norepinephrine system involving hypersensitivity and hyposensitivity of various adrenoceptor subtypes depending on what area of the brain and nervous system that these adrenoceptors are located. Further investigations of the norepinephrine system as well as other potentially interrelated neurotransmitters and peptides are recommended in panic disorder to help clarify the pathophysiology of this illness.

Chapter 7, "Increased Serotonin Function and Panic Disorder," by René S. Kahn, Herman G. Westenberg, and Clare M. Moore, reviews the evidence available concerning the function of serotonin (5-hydroxytryptamine, 5HT) in panic disorder. The authors first summarize animal studies, suggesting a role of 5HT in anxiety. Although animal studies may not be directly relevant to humans, they suggest that increased 5HT activity is correlated with increased anxiety, while decreased 5HT function has an anxiolytic effect. Most of the chapter then explores 5HT functions in panic disorder through the use of 5HT neuroendocrine and behavior studies (5HT challenges) as well as via treatment studies affecting 5HT function. The summary of this work suggests that panic disorder is associated with postsynaptic 5HT hypersensitivity. This hypersensitivity is responsible for exaggerated behavioral (anxiogenic) and neuroendocrine (cortisol, ACTH, and prolactin) responses to acute challenges with selective 5HT agonists (e.g., fenfluramine and m-chlorophenylpiperazine). The treatment studies using serotonin-potentiating agents such as selective serotonin reuptake inhibitors appears to have antipanic efficacy, and thus support the 5HT hypothesis of panic disorder. Interestingly, the authors suggest that the initial worsening of symptoms that may occur in the early stages of treatment (10 to 14 days) is a result of overstimulation of hypersensitive receptors by the increased amount of 5HT resulting from treatment. Continuation of treatment then allows the postsynaptic 5HT receptors to down-regulate, resulting in a therapeutic clinical response in two to four weeks. The authors propose that a presynaptic 5HT deficiency actually may be the initial neurotransmitter dysfunction in panic disorder. Finally they review related symptomatology (e.g., aggression and suicide) that is also associated with 5HT dysfunction, as well as the effect of 5HT on other neurotransmitter systems.

Chapter 8, "Caffeine-Induced Anxiety: An Ideal Chemical Model of Panic Disorder?" by Thomas W. Uhde, reviews one of the most widely used models for panic disorder. Uhde presents indirect evidence suggesting that caffeine is strongly associated with panic disorder, including a significant overlap of symptoms of caffeine intoxication with panic disorder. In addition, it is well known that panic patients themselves realize that caffeine exacerbates or provokes their condition and cut back voluntarily on coffee consumption. The use of caffeine as a challenge in panic disorder is extensively reviewed, revealing that caffeine-induced behavioral and biochemical changes differentiate patients with panic disorder from nonpanic disorder patient groups and normal controls. In summary, there were greater increases in cortisol and lactate levels in panic disorder with approximately 50 percent having a panic attack. Uhde suggests that this model has clinical validity for the following reasons.

1. The threshold for caffeine induced changes is significantly lower for panic disorder.
2. Caffeine-induced attacks approximate naturally occurring attacks.
3. Treatment with alprazolam normalizes caffeine sensitivity in panic disorder, although imipramine has been only partially successful in blocking these chemically provoked attacks.
4. Last, this chemically induced panic attack can be replicated, although some habituation does take place between provocations.

Uhde suggests that although caffeine is not necessarily an ideal model to study panic disorder (no chemical model is in fact ideal, he suggests), it is a useful one. The yohimbine model will add to the understanding of the neurobiology and pathophysiology of panic disorder. The author also suggests multiple pathways that may explain the action of caffeine, such as antagonism of adenosinergic receptors and interaction with noradrenergic , dopaminergic, and benzodiazepine-gaba-ergic systems.

Chapter 9, "The Lactate Infusion Challenge," by Deborah S. Cowley, Stephen R. Dager, and David L. Dunner, reviews in detail the role of lactate and lactate infusions in panic disorder. Earlier interest in lactate was stimulated by findings of Pitts and McClure (1967) that panic disorder patients had higher lactate levels after exercise than normal controls, suggesting that lactate may be important in the pathogenesis of panic disorder. This led to the study of lactate infusions over the last 20 years. Overall, the authors find that lactate-induced panic attacks are moderately sensitive and specific for panic disorder, occurring in 67 percent of patients with panic disorder and 13 percent of controls. Recent work has suggested that lactate vulnerability is specific for the presence of panic attacks whether they are a part of panic disorder or some other diagnosis, such as major depression or bulimia. A question now exists whether even a past history or a family history of panic attacks also is associated with vulnerability to lactate-induced panics; like any good chemical model of panic disorder, lactate infusions induce panic attacks that are similar to naturally occurring ones. Furthermore, treatment with antipanic medications or cognitive therapy decreases lactate vulnerability. Although the mechanism of action of lactate is unclear, the stimulation of hyperventilation is clearly provoked and may be an important factor in panic induction. To increase our understanding of spontaneous panic attacks, the authors encouraged continued efforts to understand how lactate works.

Chapter 10, "Cholecystokinin and Panic Disorder," by Jacques Bradwejn and Diane Koszycki, reviews the role of this novel peptide in the pathophysiology of panic disorder. Although originally found in the gastrointestinal tract (and possessing enzymatic activity), cholecystokinin (CCK) subsequently has been found in various areas of the brain and is believed to be a neurotransmitter/neuromodulator. Based on laboratory evidence that CCK antagonizes a number of benzodiazepine-induced behaviors in the animal model, the authors proceed to review clinical and research studies exploring whether CCK was anxiogenic in humans. CCK was found to induce panic attacks in normal controls and patients with panic disorder, but clearly panic patients had an increased sensitivity. The authors found that CCK satisfies the criteria for an ideal panicogenic agent, since (1) it is safe; (2) it provokes attacks that are similar to a patients' naturally occurring attacks; (3) was specific for patients with panic disorder versus normal controls, with approximately 91 percent of panic patients having a panic attack to 25 μg injection of CCK, versus 17 percent of normal controls; (4) it is reliable, that is, its behavioral responses can be replicated on a second challenge with no habituation; (5) antipanic drugs such as imipramine decrease the paniogenic effect of CCK, and (6) drugs that are ineffective antipanic agents fail to alter the CCK response. In reviewing possible mechanisms of action for CCK, the authors explore potential effects of CCK on benzodiazepine, noradrenergic, serotonergic, and adenosinergic receptors. They review the development of CCK receptor antagonists that partially block the anxiogenic effect of CCK in humans. Currently, various CCK antagonists are being developed and tested in the treatment of panic disorder. This recent demonstration that CCK is related to the pathophysiology of panic disorder appears to have opened up new directions for the understanding and treatment of the disorder.

Chapter 11, "Respiratory Neurobiology of Panic," by Laszlo A. Papp and Jack M. Gorman, proposes a new theory to explain the underlying vulnerability and neurobiology of panic disorder. The authors suggest that patients with panic disorder have "hypersensitive central nervous system respiratory regulators." Normally when carbon dioxide (CO_2) levels reach a critical concentration, breathing is triggered. Papp and Gorman suggest that in panic, the threshold for CO_2 detection is significantly lowered, representing an organic abnormality. Thus, when this CO_2 center is triggered by rising CO_2 levels or directly by certain challenge agents such as caffeine, a "suffocation false alarm" mechanism goes off, resulting in a hyperventilation response. The authors dispel the idea that hyperventilation triggers panics, but instead propose that hyperventilation is a result of the respiratory-driven panic response. Panic symptoms are a result of this false air suffocation alarm, resulting in shortness of breath and secondary symptoms of hyperventilation such as dizziness, chest pain, and so on. The authors review previous studies that consistently demonstrate a panicogenic response to CO_2 challenges (inhalations), supporting an increased sensitivity to CO_2 in panic disorder. They suggest that most other panicogenic stimuli either induce anxiety also by increasing CO_2 levels (e.g., lactate) or by directly stimulating the hypothesized supersensitive respiratory center (e.g., caffeine). Interestingly, the authors point out that many successful treatments for panic disorder result in normalization of this respiratory sensitivity. This major new hypothesis of the neurobiology of panic disorder will surely lead to further advances in this field.

PART III TREATMENTS OF PANIC DISORDER

Chapter 12, "Somatic Treatment Strategies in Panic Disorder," by B. Ashor Raj and David V. Sheehan, provides an overview of the effectiveness of various pharmacological interventions in the treatment of panic disorder. Although alprazolam, a triazalobenzodiazepine, is the only medication approved by the Food and Drug Administration for panic disorder, the authors acknowledge the efficacy of a number of medications of different pharmacological classes, such as cyclic antidepressants, monoamine oxidase inhibitors, selective serotonin uptake inhibitors, and combinations of various medications. Alternate treatment strategies also are reviewed, such as the use of anticonvulsants. For each drug class, the authors review dosing issues, side effect profiles, and use of bloods levels. Furthermore, Raj and Sheehan propose a rational strategy of drug administration for the clinician, with recommendations of which drugs to initiate treatment, dosing issues, when to use other classes of medications, and so on. Most important, the authors update clinicians on new recommendations regarding treatment duration. It appears that, as with major depression, there should be an acute phase of treatment lasting approximately eight weeks as well as a continuation phase ranging from six months to one year. Since panic disorder is frequently a chronic illness, some patients will relapse when taken off medications and will in fact need maintenance medication beyond a year.

Chapter 13, "Cognitive Behavioral Treatment of Panic Disorder," by William C. Sanderson and Scott Wetzler, reviews several controlled studies that have demonstrated that cognitive behavior therapy (CBT) is an effective treatment for panic disorder with and without agoraphobia. During a consensus conference sponsored by the National Institute of Mental Health on the treatment of panic disorder, CBT, along with several specific medications, was recommended as a treatment of choice—the only psychotherapeutic treatment to receive this endorsement. During the past decade, CBT for panic disorder has changed dramatically. The state-of-the-art version is designed to address the entire configuration of panic disorder: panic attacks, anticipatory anxiety, and agoraphobia. In their clinically oriented, how-to chapter, Sanderson and Wetzler describe the treatment strategies employed in protocols that have been validated empirically. CBT treatment strategies such as cognitive restructuring, breathing training, progressive muscle relaxation, psychoeducation, visualization, and exposure are detailed, and case examples are presented to illustrate their use. Self-monitoring forms used in the treatment also are included. In addition to outlining the treatment strategies, the authors suggest mechanisms of action of CBT and make several recommendations regarding the use of medication in conjunction with CBT.

SUMMARY

Panic disorder is now clearly recognized to be an important anxiety disorder, being highly prevalent with specific symptomatology, course, epidemiology, genetics, and treatment response. Focused attention is now revealing how significant and disabling the disorder can be, as well as the specific neurotransmitters/neuropeptides that may underlie its pathophysiology.

Clinicians and even academicians frequently are shielded from important developments in a specific illness that may take years to be disseminated and appreciated. Mood disorders, especially major depressive disorder, have received great attention in recent years. Yet even with this great attention, it is unfortunately evident that clinical, biological, and treatment issues are poorly disseminated and are frequently misunderstood. Through concentrated national efforts, these problems have been increasingly addressed with positive results (Regier et al., 1988). It is now time for panic disorder to receive the attention it merits. The message must be broadcast to all mental health professionals, family physicians (who probably see and treat the majority of these patients), and the public. We hope this book will become an important resource for all interested parties and assist in the quality of knowledge, care, and future studies of panic disorder. Unusually rapid strides in understanding the pathophysiology of this disorder and identifying effective treatments. Further mastery of this illness, including better understanding of etiology, treatment, and perhaps even prevention, is imminent.

REFERENCES

American Psychiatric Association (1980). *Diagnostic and statistical manual of mental disorders* (3rd ed.). Washington, DC: Author.

American Psychiatric Association (1987). *Diagnostic and statistical manual of mental disorders* (3rd ed., revised). Washington, DC: Author.

American Psychiatric Association (1994). *Diagnostic and statistical manual of mental disorders* (4th ed.). Washington, DC: Author.

Feighner, J. P., Robins, E., Guze, S. B., Woodruff, R. A., Winokur, G., & Munoz, R. (1972). Diagnostic criteria for use in psychiatric research. *Archives of General Psychiatry, 38*, 57–63.

Klein, D. F. (1964). Detineation of two drug responsive anxiety syndromes. *Psychopharmacology, 5*, 397–408.

Klerman, G. L., Weissman, M., Ovellette, R., Johnson, J., & Greenwald, S. (1991). Panic attacks in the community: Social morbidity and health care utilization. *Journal of the American Medical Association, 265*, 742–746.

Markowitz, J., Weissman, M. M., Ovellette, R., & Liek, J. (1989). Quality of life in panic disorder. *Archives of General Psychiatry, 46*, 984–992.

Pitts, F. N., Jr., & McClure, J. N., Jr. (1967). Lactate metabolism in anxiety neurosis. *New England Journal of Medicine, 277*, 1329–1336.

Regier, D. A., Hirschfeld, R. M. A., Goodwin, F. K., Burke, J. D., Jr., Lazar, J. B., & Judd, L. L. (1988). The NIMH Depression Awareness, Recognition, and Treatment Program: Structures, aims, and scientific basis. *American Journal of Psychiatry, 145*, 1351–1357.

Spitzer, R. L., Endicott, J., Robins, E. (1978). Research diagnostic: Rationale and reliability. *Archives of General Psychiatry, 35*, 773–782.

Weissman, M. M., Klerman, G. L., Markowitz, J. S., & Ovellette, S. (1989). Suicidal ideation and suicide attempts in panic disorder and attacks. *New England Journal of Medicine, 321*, 1209–1218.

PART I
Clinical Aspects of
Panic Disorder

1

Panic Disorder
Phenomenology and Differential Diagnosis

JILL H. RATHUS AND
GREGORY M. ASNIS

As early as 1872, Charles Darwin provided a vivid depiction of the terrifying fear state we now label panic:

> The heart beats quickly and violently, so that it palpitates or knocks against the ribs . . . the skin instantly becomes pale, as during incipient faintness. This paleness of the surface, however, is probably in large part, or exclusively, due to the vasomotor centre being affected in such manner as to cause the contraction of the small arteries of the skin. That the skin is much affected under the sense of great fear, we see in the marvelous and inexplicable manner in which perspiration immediately exudes from it. This exudation is all the more remarkable, as the surface is then cold, and hence the term a cold sweat . . . The hairs on the skin also stand erect; and the superficial muscles shiver. In connection with the disturbed action of the heart, the breathing is hurried . . . One of the best-marked symptoms is the trembling of all the muscles of the body. (Darwin, 1872, p. 290)

The most common presenting problem among people seeking mental health treatment (Boyd, 1986; Klerman, Weissman, Ouellette, Johnson, & Greenwald, 1991), and the fifth most common complaint brought to the attention of primary care physicians (Beitman, Basha, & Flaker, 1987; Klerman et al., 1991); panic disorder overcomes its sufferers with sudden bursts of intense fear, surging physiologic symptoms, and horrifying sensations of losing control, going crazy, or dying (APA, 1994). Its characteristic features include increased arousal, symptoms of anxiety, and fear of the recurrence of such symptoms. This fear may become so paralyzing that it evolves into an inability to tolerate being alone or venturing into public places, for fear of another attack. Such fear, termed agoraphobia, often leads to greatly restricted travel and avoidance of an ever-increasing range of situations. This chapter describes the phenomenology of panic disorder, documents changes in diagnostic criteria from the *Diagnostic and Statistical Manual of Mental Disorders,* third edition, revised (DSM-III-R) (APA, 1987) to the fourth edition (DSM-IV), and highlights considerations for differential diagnosis of the disorder.

IMPAIRMENT AND PREVALENCE

Panic disorder can be associated with marked impairment in social, occupational, and family functioning (Markowitz, Weissman, Ouellette, & Leib, 1989; Nagy, Krystal, Woods, & Chang, 1989), at its best causing people to endure fear and discomfort in everyday situations, and at its worst leading people to relinquish their careers, withdraw from normal routines, and become unable to leave their homes (Klerman, et al., 1991). People with panic symptoms frequent emergency rooms and general medical practitioners (Beitman et al., 1987; Klerman et al., 1991), because of the intense somatic symptoms leading to the belief that they are seriously physically ill.

According to recent community-based studies, the lifetime prevalence of panic disorder is estimated at between 1.5 and 3.5 percent (APA, 1994), with 3 percent of the adult population reporting recurrent attacks (but not meeting criteria for the disorder) and a full 10 percent reporting occasional or isolated attacks (Weissman, 1988; Wittchen, 1986). Panic attacks, independent of the diagnosis of panic disorder, are highly prevalent among psychiatric patients, with reports of up to 83 percent among patients presenting with anxiety or mood disorders at an anxiety disorders clinic (Barlow, Vermilyea, Blanchard, Vermilyea, DiNardo, &

Cerny, 1985). The onset of panic disorder in treatment samples tends to occur in the latter teens through the late 20s (Barlow, 1988; Klerman et al., 1991; Marks, 1987; von Korff, Eaton, & Keyl, 1985).

MAKING THE DIAGNOSIS OF PANIC DISORDER

The typical presentation of panic disorder involves recurrent panic attacks, or discrete periods of intense fear or discomfort usually lasting minutes, with at least four associated symptoms (DSM-IV, 1994). Although the criteria allow for cases of discomfort rather than fear, fearless presentations of the disorder are relatively rare. (See "Atypical Presentations" below). Rather, the typical panic patient reports episodic bursts of extreme terror and lives in fear of future attacks.

Panic attacks most often occur *unexpectedly* in the initial phases of the disorder. To receive the diagnosis of panic disorder, the panic attacks must have occurred when not triggered by being the focus of other's attention (as in social phobia), by events or situations that normally trigger anxiety (as in simple phobia), or by organic factors. The unexpected nature of the attacks is a central feature, although later in the course of the disorder various feared situations (e.g., driving a car) may trigger the attacks. To meet diagnostic criteria for the disorder, recurrent unexpected panic attacks must occur, with one or more attacks followed by at least one month of one or more of the following: (1) persistent concern over future attacks, (2) worry about implications or consequences of the attack, or (3) significant behavior change related to the attacks. While the DSM-III-R required only one attack for the diagnosis if followed by at least one month of persistent fear, this presentation is extremely rare. According to the Cross National Panic Study, for example, the typical panic patient experienced one to two panic attacks per week before presenting for treatment (Ballenger et al., 1988).

The onset of a panic attack is typically marked by the sudden presence of intense fear, apprehension, or dread, frequently with the feeling of impending doom. The DSM-IV requires the development of at least four of 13 symptoms, which must develop suddenly and reach a peak in intensity within 10 minutes of the first symptom perceived. The distinction of escalating symptom intensity within 10 minutes highlights the sudden and episodic nature of panic, differentiating it from the more diffuse anxiety symptoms present in an anxiety condition such as generalized anxiety disorder. Panic symptoms include physiologic symptoms, such as palpitations, sweating, trembling, and shortness of breath; and cognitive symptoms, including derealization and fear of dying, going crazy, or losing control. (See Table 1–1.) Expressive-behavioral symptoms often include the urgent desire to flee or escape the situation at hand. The autonomic symptoms of panic transcend human systems and reflect biologically wired, primitive alarm reactions manifested across species, known as the fight-or-flight reaction to a feared stimulus, or what Barlow (1988) has termed the "true alarm." This response allows for mobilization under threat conditions through quick mental and physical action, and has important adaptive significance. Because initial panic attacks typically occur unexpectedly—in the absence of a recognizable threat cue—spontaneous panics have been labeled "false alarms" (Barlow, 1988). Explanations for the genesis of initial uncued attacks include diathesis-stress models and theories of biological dysregulation (cf. Barlow, 1988). Much of the terror during panic, as well as the residual fear of its recurrence, comes from the very absence of an identifiable threat. With no obvious trigger for their symptoms, panic sufferers understandably believe that an undiagnosed and likely dangerous physical or psychiatric illness has overcome them, and often live in a hypervigilant state fearing its (apparently unpredictable) recurrence.

TABLE 1–1
Summary of DSM-IV
Symptoms of Panic Attacks

Palpitations or accelerated heart rate
Sweating
Trembling or shaking
Shortness of breath/smothering sensations
Choking
Chest pain or discomfort
Nausea/abdominal distress
Dizziness or faintness
Depersonalization/derealization
Fear of losing control/going crazy
Fear of dying
Numbness or tingling (paresthesias)
Chills or flushes

Source: American Psychiatric Association, 1994.

Cued panic attacks are those that have become associated with any of a variety of triggers through the process of fear conditioning and have been called "learned alarms" (Barlow, 1988). That is, situations or internal cues not directly threatening but associated with the occurrence of panic attacks can themselves elicit attacks. These can take the form of situations or places, such as being in enclosed spaces from which escape might be difficult. They also can take the form of internal symptoms, such as a subtle increase in heart rate, which may occur outside of awareness yet trigger panic attacks through a process known as *interoceptive* conditioning. Such attacks may appear to develop "out of the blue," as in the case of a false alarm, but are in fact manifestations of learned alarms.

LIMITED SYMPTOM ATTACKS

If fewer than four of 13 panic symptoms occur, they are referred to as limited symptom attacks. Limited symptom attacks can produce symptoms similar to full panic attacks, but tend to be perceived as less intense and to be associated with less of a heart rate increase (Taylor et al., 1986). Reports of limited symptom attacks in the absence of any full panic attacks are relatively rare (Barlow, 1988). However, patients with full panic attacks commonly have limited symptom attacks as well. Klerman and colleagues (1991) have reported that patients with panic attacks who do not meet criteria for the disorder, while less severe than panic disorder patients, still show substantial impairment and are likely to seek treatment.

COURSE

Although the frequency and intensity of panic attacks vary widely, patients with panic disorder typically report attacks nearly every day and experience an average of seven symptoms during an attack (Klerman et al., 1991). An attack normally peaks within minutes, and residual symptoms (e.g., shakiness, weakness) last from minutes to hours longer. The disorder is thus characterized by short-lived bursts of intense symptoms followed by longer periods of less intense symptoms. The attacks may persist for weeks or months and then remit, and may recur at a later time. Untreated, the course is typically chronic, with fluctuations in the level of debilitation it imposes (Keller & Baker, 1992). In a review of studies of panic disorder conducted between 1950 and 1966, in which patients received treatments now considered ineffective (e.g., supportive psychotherapy), Marks and Lader (1973) concluded that between 41 and 50 percent of patients were recovered or significantly improved at follow-up evaluations. However, the remaining portion of just over half of the patients received little or no symptom reduction. In later studies using efficacious treatments, researchers have continued to report relatively high rates of chronicity. For example, after treatment with alprazolam and behavior therapy, Nagy and associates (1989) reported that over half of the patients reported continued symptoms on follow-up, with 38 percent reporting mild and 18 percent reporting moderate symptoms after one to four years. Similarly, Noyes, Garvey, and Cook (1989) reported that after treatment with imipramine, 38 percent of patients reported mild and 50 percent reported moderate symptoms after one to four years. Recent research following panic patients treated with a complete behavior therapy protocol suggests that while the majority of treated patients may continue to manifest selected symptoms of the disorder, the majority are recovered in terms of overall functional impairment (e.g., Barlow, Craske, Cerny, & Klosko, 1989).

AGORAPHOBIA

Patients for whom panic disorder persists commonly develop the associated condition of agoraphobia, or the fear of being in places from which escape might be difficult. According to the Epidemiologic Catchment Area (ECA) study, one-third of the general population with panic disorder also had agoraphobia (Klerman et al., 1991), although the rate is much higher in clinical samples. This condition develops when persistent panic attacks become associated with places or situations in which they have occurred previously, leading to the development of anticipatory anxiety when approaching such situations and increasing discomfort in or avoidance of them. The specific fears present in agoraphobia generally concern perceptions of catastrophes that might occur in the event of a panic attack, such as not being able to escape, being humiliated, or not having access to help. That is, the agoraphobic actually fears not the avoided situations themselves, but the onset of distressing symptoms in these situations. Because of this "fear of fear" (e.g., Goldstein & Chambless, 1978) a range of restrictions develop, such as need of a companion when traveling outside of the home, restricting travel to within a small radius of one's home, or, in more severe cases, not being able to leave one's home at all. In more mild cases of agoraphobia, feared situations are endured despite intense anxiety. For example, a mild agoraphobic may tremble and experience palpitations while driving over a bridge, and yet endure the symptoms rather than avoid the particular route. The most typically reported agoraphobic situations include increasing distance from home; being on a bus or train; driving in a car, particularly when in restrictive surroundings such as bridges, tunnels, or heavy traffic; or being in crowds, such as when shopping in malls or standing in line (e.g., Burns & Thorpe, 1977). Although patients with panic disorder without agoraphobia may suffer only limited impairment, those with agoraphobia by definition suffer impairment in many aspects of functioning. In severe cases, agoraphobics are unable to leave the home without a companion, or become housebound and must give up their jobs and social interactions.

The prevalence of agoraphobia among patients with panic disorder is much greater in clinic than community samples, occurring as an associated diagnosis in the vast majority of cases. For example, Sanderson, Rapee, and Barlow (1987) reported that of 56 patients presenting to an Anxiety Disorders Clinic, only one had pure panic disorder with no associated avoidance. Twenty-five of these patients had mild, 21 had moderate, and nine had severe agoraphobic avoidance. Panic disorder with agoraphobia occurs about three times as frequently in females as in males, although panic disorder without agoraphobia occurs at similar rates in both sexes (e.g., Sanderson et al., 1987).

Because substantial evidence has supported the etiological role of panic in the development of agoraphobia (e.g., Barlow et al., 1985; Klein & Gorman, 1987; Tearnan, Telch, & Keefe, 1984), the DSM-III-R changed the DSM-III classification of agoraphobia with panic attacks to panic disorder with agoraphobia (APA, 1987). Despite the demonstrated link between panic and agoraphobia, a substantial percentage of people with recurrent panic attacks do not develop avoidance behavior (Craske, Sanderson, & Barlow, 1987). The presentation of panic both with and without agoraphobia has led to consideration of whether the presence of agoraphobia simply indicates a more severe form of panic disorder, or whether it represents a qualitatively different disorder from uncomplicated panic disorder. Emerging evidence supports the notion that agoraphobia represents a disorder with distinct characteristics, rather than merely a more severe form of panic disorder. Several studies comparing agoraphobic and nonagoraphobic panic patients have cast doubt on the severity hypothesis by failing to find an association between avoidance and either frequency of panic attacks or severity of symptoms. (See Craske and Barlow, 1988, for review.) Additionally, the diagnosis of agoraphobia appears associated with lifetime comorbidity of other anxiety and mood disorders, suggesting greater overall psychopathology in agoraphobics (Noyes et al., 1990; Pollack et al., 1990; Starcevic, Uhlenhuth, Kellner, & Pathak, 1992). Further, several studies have demonstrated differences in the cognitive factors in those patients with avoidance, including differences in anticipated fear, expected likelihood of panic occurrence, appraisals of the consequences of panic, and perceived coping efficacy for managing panic symptoms (e.g., Craske, Rapee, & Barlow, 1988; Rachman & Lopatka, 1986; Telch, Brouillard, Telch, Agras, & Taylor, 1989). Thus, overall psychopathology and cognitive style, rather than the nature of the panic attacks themselves, appear to differentiate agoraphobics and nonagoraphobics.

STRESSORS RELATED TO THE ONSET OF PANIC DISORDER

Work on the origins of panic disorder has commonly focused on childhood separation anxiety as a precursor (Gittelman & Klein, 1985; Gittelman-Klein, 1975; Klein, 1964). However, several recent studies have refuted this hypothesis, noting that neither rates of early parental separation nor childhood separation anxiety differ in patients with panic disorder compared to patient controls with various other disorders (Thyer, Nesse, Cameron, & Curtis, 1985; Thyer, Nesse, Curtis, & Cameron, 1986; Van Der Molen, Van Den Hout, Van Dieren, & Griez, 1989).

More support has emerged for a general biopsychosocial model of the origins panic disorder. As already discussed, this model involves the interaction of the biologically wired alarm system with maladaptive cognitive appraisals and fear conditioning (cf. Barlow, 1988). One quite consistently observed precursor to the development of panic disorder and agoraphobia is the occurrence of negative life events prior to the first episode of panic (Tearnan et al., 1984). Although actual initial panic attacks seem to occur "out of the blue," when prompted, patients typically can identify at least one negative life event raising stress levels in the time period just prior to the first episode of panic (Barlow, 1988).

Several studies have examined the occurrence of stressful life events in the onset of panic disorder. Shalomskas and her colleagues (1993) reported that panic disorder onset occurred at greater than chance levels in the postpartum period following women's first childbirth. Other work also has linked panic onset with endocrinological or physiological changes, including childbirth, menopause, and gynecological surgery (Klein, 1964; Liebowitz & Klein, 1991). The link of panic onset with childbirth may of course be linked with psychosocial factors as well. For example, Doctor (1982) found that approximately 80 percent of a sample of 404 agoraphobic patients reported prior life stressors, the third most common of which involved taking on major new responsibilities. The two most common stressors were separation or loss and relationship difficulties.

Much other work has identified both psychosocial and health-related factors in the onset of panic disorder. In one of the earliest studies to employ a control group, Roth (1959) found life stressors in 96 percent of his sample of 135 agoraphobics, which was a significantly higher percentage than those found in 50 psychiatric and 50 medically ill controls. The most commonly reported stressors involved bereavement of or serious illness in a loved one, serious personal illness or danger, familial/domestic stress, and pregnancy or childbirth. Finlay-Jones and Brown (1981) interviewed female psychiatric outpatients using the Present State Examination (PSE) and found that stressors related to loss were more prominent in patients with depressive disorders, while those related to danger were more prominent in patients with various anxiety disorders. Last, Barlow, and O'Brein (1984) found that 81 percent of their sample of 58 agoraphobics reported negative life events prior to the onset of their disorder. These events fell roughly evenly into categories of interpersonal conflict or loss situations (e.g., marital difficulties, bereavement) and endocrine or physiological problems (e.g., hysterectomy, drug reaction). Craske, Miller, Rotunda, and Barlow (1990) examined features of initial panic attacks in 162 panic patients and found that they occurred following stressors in 72 percent of the cases. The most common stressors reported were major life changes, excessive drug or alcohol use, interpersonal difficulties, loss of significant others, health problems or injury, and problems at work or school. Faravelli (1985) and Faravelli and Pallanti (1989) found that compared with normal controls, panic disorder patients reported more stressful life events in general in the time period preceding the onset of their disorder. Breier, Charney, and Heninger (1986) evaluated 60 panic patients and found that 63 percent had experiences stressful life events temporally related to the onset of their disorder. Finally, in a study with contrary findings, Newman and Bland (1994) reported that in a community sample, in which over 3,000 respondents were interviewed using the Diagnostic Interview Schedule (DIS) and the Life Events Scale (LES), individuals with a diagnosis of panic disorder did not have elevated LES scores for the previous year compared with individuals without a diagnosis. Patients with major depression and generalized anxiety disorder, by contrast, had strongly elevated LES scores. However, this study measured life events for the previous year regardless of the time of onset of patients' disorders, so it cannot be considered conclusive regarding stressful events occurring *prior* to the onset of panic disorder. This study also had a very small number of panic disorder cases compared to diagnoses of major depression and generalized anxiety disorder.

Findings across studies, then, generally support the conclusion that for the majority of patients, increased stressful life events precede the onset of panic disorder. Life events involving loss, interpersonal conflict, and health-related/physiological stressors are especially common precipitants. However, despite these findings, the link between stressful life events and panic onset cannot yet be considered conclusive. First, these studies all rely on retrospective reports, and panic patients may be subject to mood-congruent memory distortions (cf. Barlow, 1988). Prospective studies are needed to clarify this issue. Further, although a few of the studies employ control groups (e.g., Roth, 1959), most focus exclusively on panic (or panic with agoraphobia) patients. More studies are emerging that link life stressors with a wide spectrum of both psychological (e.g., Depue & Monroe, 1986) and physical disorders (e.g., Flor, Turk, & Birbaumer, 1985), casting doubt on the notion of a unique link between life stressors and panic disorder. The data seem to best support a diathesis-stress model of psychopathology; individuals have dispositional or biological vulnerabilities that become expressed under conditions of stress (e.g., Hammen, Mayol, de Mayo, & Marks, 1986). Further support for this vulnerability model includes the finding that many people encounter stress without any resulting disorder, and many variables appear to moderate the effects of stress (e.g., Depue & Monroe, 1986). Thus, individuals may have characterological or biological vulnerabilities that contribute to the specific development of a panic disorder resulting from stress.

DIFFERENTIAL DIAGNOSIS

In addition to uncomplicated panic disorder and panic disorder with agoraphobia, panic attacks are prevalent in other disorders as well. (See Chapter 4.) The ubiquity of panic, in fact, has led to confusion regarding when to apply the term "panic attack" (Liebowitz, 1992). Although the DSM-III-R did not explicitly rule out its use in reference to disorders other than panic disorder, the manual subsumed the phenomenology of panic attacks within the section on panic disorder. This organization implicitly linked the attacks to the disorder, despite the common occurrence of these attacks in the context of other disorders. The DSM-IV Task Force (see Frances, Pincus, Widiger, Davis, & First, 1990) addressed this ambiguity by proposing a section outlining criteria for panic attacks separate from the section on panic disorder. (An extended discussion of changes in DSM-IV criteria for panic disorder follows.) Panic attacks thereby remain a phenomenon central to panic disorder, but clearly apply to other diagnostic presentations as well.

Within the anxiety disorders per se, many symptom presentations share features with panic disorder. Nonclinical panic states may be confused for the disorder as well. In addition, different diagnostic conditions, including other psychiatric disorders as well as organic conditions, contain overlapping features with panic disorder and may present a confusing diagnostic picture. Furthermore, panic disorder has a variety of atypical presentations that may steer the clinician off course in arriving at a diagnosis. The following sections, based on DSM-IV categorizations, address the various diagnoses sharing features with panic disorder, as well as variations of the disorder itself, and outline when the diagnosis of panic disorder is appropriate. These segments are preceded by a systematic discussion of changes in criteria from DSM-III-R to DSM-IV.

Changes in DSM-IV

The recently published DSM-IV contains a number of small, yet important, changes related to the differential diagnosis of panic disorder. The updated manual incorporates new developments in the field and offers enhanced compatibility with the *International Classification of Diseases*, 10th edition (ICD-10; World Health Organization, 1992), the statistical classification of diseases including but not limited to mental disorders.

While the DSM-IV contains a revamped collection of diagnostic criteria, based on extensive research (e.g., Frances et al., 1990), the wording of panic disorder criteria changes only slightly from DSM-III-R. However, based on field studies conducted by the DSM-IV work group on anxiety disorders, these small changes improve the empirical rationale for the criteria, increase the sensitivity of the diagnosis, and more closely describe the prototypical panic patient (Ballenger & Fyer, 1993).

As mentioned earlier, panic attacks are now classified separately from panic disorder and are then listed as the central feature of panic disorder and an associated feature of various other disorders. The definition of a panic attack as a discrete period of intense fear or discomfort with abrupt onset remains, with the slight change from the requirement of four symptoms increasing in intensity within 10 minutes to four symptoms *reaching a peak* within 10 minutes.

Although the symptoms listed in the DSM-III-R remain unchanged, they have been reordered in terms of their frequency of occurrence (Ballenger & Fyer, 1993). The new order of symptoms is: palpitations, pounding heart, or accelerated heart rate; sweating; trembling or shaking; sensations of shortness of breath or smothering; feeling of choking; chest pain or discomfort; nausea or abdominal distress; feeling dizzy, unsteady, lightheaded, or faint; derealization or depersonalization; fear of losing control or going crazy; fear of dying; parasthesias (numbness or tingling sensations); and chills or hot flushes.

To further specify the nature of panic attacks in different disorders, the DSM-IV highlights the difference between unexpected and cued panic attacks. Whereas in DSM-III-R diagnostic criteria for panic disorder included the description that at least one panic attack occurred that was unexpected, the DSM-IV criteria refer to *recurrent* unexpected panic attacks, in order to improve reliability of the diagnosis. The DSM-IV specifies that *uncued* panics are required for a diagnosis of panic disorder, while *situationally bound* panics are most commonly linked with social phobias and specific (the DSM-IV replacement for the term "simple") phobias.

While the DSM-III-R required four attacks within a four-week period or a minimum of one attack followed by at least one month of fear of another attack, DSM-IV criteria have expanded to involve the provisions that a minimum of one attack is followed by either (1) persistent concern about having additional attacks, (2) worry about the implications of the attack or its consequences (e.g., losing control, having a heart attack, "going crazy"), or (3) a significant change in behavior related to the attacks. As in DSM-III-R, the panic attacks must not be organically or substance-induced, and the anxiety symptoms must not be due to another disorder (e.g., fear of public humiliation in social phobia, fear of contamination in obsessive compulsive disorder).

DSM-IV, like DSM-III-R, contains the categories of panic disorder without agoraphobia, panic disorder with agoraphobia, and agoraphobia without history of panic disorder. The definition of agoraphobia is unchanged in the DSM-IV, but has the added specification that the anxiety and phobic avoidance of agoraphobia is not due to any medical condition (e.g., hyperthyroidism), substance (e.g., drugs, medication) or to another psychiatric disorder (e.g., post-traumatic stress disorder, social phobia, obsessive compulsive disorder).

The following sections detail various presentations of panic disorder and other DSM-IV diagnoses with overlapping symptoms, in order to outline diagnostic distinctions.

Nonclinical Panic Attacks

In addition to those patients who present to clinics with panic episodes, panic attacks occur in the normal population as well (e.g., Telch, Lucas, & Nelson, 1989), typically at lower levels of frequency or intensity. Some studies have reported extremely high prevalence rates of nonclinical panic (i.e., up to 50–60 percent in studies of university students); however, these results have likely been overestimations due to false positives on self-report measures and misinterpretations of general anxiety symptoms (c.f. Wilson et al., 1992). Community studies using the Diagnostic Interview Schedule have reported lifetime prevalence rates of panic attacks between 5.1 and 9.3 percent (Joyce, Bushnell, Oakley-Browne, Wells, & Hornblow, 1989; Weissman, Klerman, Markowitz, & Ouellette, 1989; Wittchen, 1986). Theorists have debated whether symptom occurrence in panic disorder differs in etiology and quality from those in nonclinical presentations. Research findings suggest that there are primarily quantitative, but few qualitative, differences in the two conditions. The diagnostician should query about subjective distress and impairment to distinguish the disorder from the nonclinical condition. Although the differential diagnosis of nonclinical panic may seem moot because these individuals would likely not seek treatment, it may be diagnostically important if a patient seeking treatment for another disorder relates a history of panic attacks.

Agoraphobia without History of Panic Disorder

This disorder involves the fear of being in places or situations from which escape might be difficult or might lead to embarrassment, or in which help might not be available in the case of the onset of a symptom or symptoms. As a result of this fear, the person restricts travel from home, depends on a companion when leaving the home, or endures agoraphobic situations with intense anxiety. The key point of differentiation is that the person must never have met criteria for panic disorder. The avoidance must also not be accounted for by another disorder.

DSM-IV specifies that agoraphobics without panic disorder most often fear the occurrence of either paniclike symptoms or limited symptom attacks (i.e., fewer than four symptoms) and may or may not have experienced such attacks in the past. Thus, it is misleading to envision patients with this disorder as merely avoidant but panic-free. Rather, they typically closely resemble panic disorder patients in terms of fearing symptom onset but simply have experienced subthreshold attacks or attacks with paniclike symptoms other than those meeting criteria for panic attacks (e.g., loss of bladder control). Of course, any prior full attacks rule out the diagnosis of agoraphobia without panic disorder. A history of full-blown panic attacks that have not occurred during the past six months receives a diagnosis of panic disorder with agoraphobia, panic attacks in full remission.

The diagnosis of agoraphobia without panic disorder has faced considerable controversy in terms of its prevalence and phenomenology. For instance, Klein and others espouse the view that agoraphobia represents a conditioned avoidance reaction to the aversive stimulus of panic attacks; this view represents skepticism of panic-free agoraphobic conditions (Klein, 1981; Klein & Gorman, 1987; Klein & Klein, 1989; Mendel & Klein, 1969). Others, however, implicate a variety of aversive events, as well as a general cognitive style, in the development of agoraphobia and believe its onset is unrelated to the occurrence of panic attacks (Lelliot, Marks, McNamee, & Tobena, 1989; Marks, 1987).

Great discrepancies have been reported between community and clinic samples in the percentages of agoraphobics without panic, with ranges of 29 to 85 percent in community studies and from 0 to 31 percent in clinical studies. (See Horwath, Lish, Johnson, Hornig, & Weissman, 1993, for review.) Such discrepancies reflect measurement, interviewer, and sample differences (i.e., clinic populations likely contain higher rates of comorbidity). In an effort to clarify the issue, Horwath and colleagues (1993) reinterviewed a subset of subjects from the Epidemiologic Catchment Area study, in which 68 percent of 961 subjects with agoraphobia had been found to have no history of panic disorder. In the ECA study, the Schedule for Affective Disorders and Schizophrenia-Lifetime Version Modified for the Study of Anxiety Disorders (SADS-LA; Fyer, Mannuzza, Klein, & Endicott, 1985) was administered by trained clinicians, in place of the originally used Diagnostic Interview Schedule (Robins, Helzer, Croughan, & Ratcliff, 1981), administered by lay interviewers. In this reappraisal of the initial findings, they found only one case (5 percent) out of 22 subjects to have probable agoraphobia without panic. The other 21 cases had been misclassified, due to both overdiagnosis of agoraphobia and underdiagnosis of panic attacks. These findings suggest an overestimation of prevalence rates of agoraphobia without a history of panic disorder from the ECA study as well as other community studies using the DIS and lay interviewers. They also support the position of Klein and colleagues regarding the course of the disorder as normally preceded by panic attacks.

Generalized Anxiety Disorder

Patients with panic disorder commonly develop some degree of apprehension or nervousness between attacks. Since anticipatory anxiety may be prolonged in panic disorder, or residual panic symptoms may linger for hours, the patient may report continuous anxiety states. The clinician may confuse this with generalized anxiety disorder, in which persistent anxiety is the predominant feature. If the patient reports a surge of autonomic arousal in which symptoms reach a crescendo and then slowly dissipate, or if periods of apprehension solely concern the development of additional panic attacks, the diagnosis of generalized anxiety disorder does not apply. However, if the onset of arousal occurs more gradually, and the patient's concern does not relate to the recurrence of panic symptoms, the diagnosis may be appropriate. The diagnosis further requires unrealistic and excessive worry, over at least two concerns not relating to panic attacks, for more days than not over a period of six months.

DSM-IV reduced the list of required associated anxiety symptoms for the diagnosis of generalized anxiety disorder to three out of six from the six out of 18 required in DSM-III-R. This revision eliminates the majority of autonomic hyperactivity symptoms listed, which were nearly identical to symptoms of panic attacks. For example, symptoms such as shortness of breath, palpitations, sweating, dizziness, nausea, and flushes have been eliminated in the DSM-IV generalized anxiety disorder criteria, and replaced with symptoms of restlessness or feeling keyed up, being easily fatigued, difficulty concentrating, irritability, muscle tension, and sleep disturbance. Although DSM-III-R specified that the 18 symptoms listed did not constitute a generalized anxiety disorder diagnosis if present only during panic attacks, the overlap in these symptoms with the phenomenology of panic attacks made this a nebulous distinction. The revised criteria alter the descriptive sense of the anxiety in generalized anxiety disorder to that of a more pervasive than contained and acute state, and should facilitate differentiating the two disorders. However, much overlap remains between these symptoms and anticipatory and residual anxiety states of panic; the clinician still must carefully determine the nature of symptom onset and the content of any apprehension.

Specific Phobia

Specific phobia (formerly *simple* phobia, in DSM-III-R) may be confused with panic disorder because its presentation may be very similar. Phobic patients experience abrupt onset of anxiety symptoms in the presence of a feared object or situation. They typically make great efforts to avoid phobic stimuli as well. Such patients may manifest their fear in the form of full-blown panic attacks, with surging autonomic arousal symptoms and the desperate urge to escape.

The extreme, persistent fear of phobic patients concerns a circumscribed stimulus, which is either avoided or endured with significant anxiety. Patients recognize the excessiveness of the fear and have either marked distress about the fear or significant impairment in normal routines because of it. To receive the diagnosis, the fears and avoidance may not be accounted for by another mental disorder, such as panic disorder (e.g., fear of panic symptoms), social phobia (e.g., fear of social humiliation), obsessive compulsive disorder (e.g., fear of contamination), or post-traumatic stress disorder (e.g., avoidance of stimuli reminiscent of the trauma). The most common specific phobias include fears of animals (especially dogs, snakes, insects, and mice), blood-injury phobia, claustrophobia (fear of closed spaces), acrophobia (fear of heights), and fear of flying (APA, 1987). The diagnostic criteria for the disorder were retained from DSM-III-R to DSM-IV, with the added specification in the newer manual that the fear must be objectively excessive and unreasonable, rather than only identified by the person as such.

The differential diagnosis of specific phobia from panic disorder involves, in part, the reliability of symptom development in the presence of the phobic stimulus. That is, people often develop panic symptoms in response to exposure to the phobic stimulus and avoid situations in which exposure to the stimulus is likely. In such patients, however, there is a direct relationship between exposure to a circumscribed feared stimulus and the anxiety response. Symptoms nearly invariably occur just before or upon exposure to the phobic stimulus, and their intensity increases and decreases with varied proximity to the feared situation or object. Most important, if the patient totally avoids the feared stimulus, attacks of anxiety are eliminated. Such circumscribed fears, cued by an anxiety response upon exposure to the normally avoided stimulus, constitutes a specific phobia diagnosis. In panic disorder, even if the attacks become associated with specific feared situations (e.g., driving), panic attacks do not occur reliably when presented with the situation, and attacks may occur unexpectedly, when away from the feared situation.

Further, persons with specific phobias fear the phobic object (e.g., snakes) or situation (e.g., riding in an airplane) itself, rather than fearing having a panic attack if exposed to the situation. Patients with both disorders may have topographically identical avoidance behavior and may present a confusing diagnostic picture. For example, the avoidance of flying may characterize the specific phobic or the agoraphobic, and these patients may be difficult to distinguish at first. In such a case the diagnostician should determine whether the patient fears the onset of panic symptoms or something specific to the avoided situation (e.g., plane crash), whether the fear began following a spontaneous panic attack, and whether the symptoms occur reliably with each flight (e.g., Liebowitz, 1992). These disorders can co-occur if symptoms for both disorders are met.

Social Phobia

In social phobia, the person persistently fears one or more situations with a risk of exposure to scrutiny by others and of doing something that will lead to embarrassment. The fear is recognized by the person as excessive or unreasonable, and causes either marked distress or functional impairment. In social phobia, being the focus of others' attention may trigger anxiety reactions in the form of panic attacks. Attacks triggered in this way by definition exclude a diagnosis of panic disorder, and if accompanied by fear of being embarrassed should be given a diagnosis of social phobia. DSM-IV has clearly articulated the criteria for this disorder to include the additional fear of performance situations and of exposure to unfamiliar people.

The social phobic may fear and avoid the same types of situations the panic patient with agoraphobia fears and avoids, but the motivation is to avoid the risk of acting in an embarrassing way, rather than to avoid the sudden development of symptoms. Even this clear-cut distinction can become blurry, however, because of overlap in phenomenology for the different disorders. Panickers may dread future attacks because of the fear that the symptoms (e.g., palpitations, dizziness, fear of dying) may lead them to do something embarrassing (faint, run away, act in an uncontrolled manner), or might make them the subject of public scrutiny; criteria for agoraphobia include fear of doing something from which escape might be embarrassing.

To arrive at the correct classification, the examiner can probe for additional fears elicited by the avoided situations (e.g., Is there fear of having a heart attack?), the history of onset (i.e., Did the onset follow a panic attack?), and the reliability of symptom onset when exposed to the feared situation. Social phobics, like those with specific phobias, experience an immediate fear reaction when exposed to phobic situations.

Post-Traumatic Stress Disorder

According to DSM-III-R classification, post-traumatic stress disorder (PTSD) involved the development of symptoms subsequent to a distressing event outside the range of usual human experience. The manual specified that the event typically would be experienced with extreme terror and helplessness, and would then be followed by reliving the traumatic event, numbing of emotions, avoiding stimuli associated with the event, and an increase in physiologic reactivity, particularly when exposed to situations symbolizing the original trauma.

In response to recognition of the variety of common precipitants of PTSD, DSM-IV has changed the requirement for an event "outside the range of usual human experience" (APA, 1987, p. 250) to exposure to traumatic events involving actual or threatened death or serious injury, or threat to the physical integrity of oneself or others, with a response of intense fear, helplessness, or horror. In addition, DSM-IV has added the category of acute stress disorder. For this diagnosis, the person must experience a traumatic event followed by at least three dissociative symptoms, along with marked avoidance and arousal symptoms. These symptoms must last between two days and four weeks and occur within four weeks of the trauma.

The associated increased arousal of a PTSD syndrome can, in fact, occur in the form of a full panic attack. Despite the similarities to symptoms of panic disorder (i.e., abrupt onset of increased arousal and avoidance of the feared event), the fear and avoidance in PTSD focus not on the recurrence of panic symptoms themselves but on cues relating to a particular traumatic event (e.g., combat, rape, destruction of one's home, witnessing a murder). Thus, even when full panic attacks and avoidance occur, they do not constitute panic disorder if they occur as responses to exposure to trauma cues. An additional diagnosis of panic disorder applies, however, if the patients meet criteria for this disorder as well.

Recently, investigators have begun to address the issue of whether panic attacks themselves qualify as traumatic stressors, evoking PTSD reactions (Lundy, 1993; McNally & Lukach, 1992). The rationale for this inquiry comes from observations that panic attacks, like PTSD stressors, are often experienced as sudden, terrifying, unpredictable, and life-threatening. Initial findings suggest that while a small percentage of panic disorder patients develop PTSD following their worst panic attack, such cases are rarer and less severe than would be expected from exposure to more objectively life-threatening traumas (e.g., gunfire, combat) (McNally & Lukach, 1992).

Obsessive Compulsive Disorder

Obsessive compulsive disorder (OCD) often includes subjective anxiety, physiologic arousal, phobic avoidance, and impairment in normal routine. The anxiety in OCD may build up to the intensity of a panic attack, and the constriction of activities may resemble agoraphobia. For example, a person fearing contamination may avoid public areas. A major difference is that while in panic disorder the triggers are often not obvious, and identified cues do not always evoke panic attacks, those triggers in OCD are obvious and consistently evoke panic attacks. Further, anxiety in OCD is most often evoked by recurrent, intrusive thoughts or impulses typically experienced as excessive or unreasonable at some point in the disorder. (However, clinical experience with these patients has yielded equivocal impressions on this issue, with some patients clearly viewing their rituals as necessary in preventing negative consequences [e.g., Insel & Akiskal, 1986].) Panic disorder patients, by contrast, view their fears about panic symptoms as necessary for their well-being or even survival (e.g., belief that allowing symptoms to occur could lead to heart attack).

Similarly, avoidance in OCD patients takes the form of repetitive or stereotyped behaviors (i.e., compulsions) intended to neutralize or prevent discomfort or a dreaded situation, is clearly excessive to the situation, and leads to a release of tension. In agoraphobics, avoidance also reduces anxiety, but takes the form of limiting exposure to the feared stimulus and may be realistically connected to the prevention of panic symptoms. DSM-IV makes the diagnosis of OCD more inclusive than in DSM-III-R by allowing for patients who do not necessarily recognize the excessiveness or senselessness of their obsessions or compulsions. In the newer manual, the person may recognize these features of his or her symptoms at any point in the course of the disorder, rather than only initially, as DSM-III-R specified. Further, the new specification of "Poor Insight Type" allows for the diagnosis in those patients who fail to recognize their symptoms are excessive or unreasonable for the preponderance of their disorder. Despite these distinctions, the two disorders can co-occur if criteria for both are met. (See Chapter 4.)

Major Depression

A major depressive episode involves at least a two-week period characterized by depressed mood or loss of interest or pleasure along with at least four associated symptoms, such as changes in sleep or appetite, guilt, or suicidal ideation. Major depression can present as an agitated state, with anxiety symptoms such as pacing, hand-wringing, general psychomotor agitation, and worrying. Additional anxiety symptoms can include recurrent and unexpected panic attacks. When a patient presents with such anxiety symptoms, depression may be ruled in or out by specifically questioning the presence and characteristics of a dysphoric mood state. Purely anxious patients report less sustained dysphoric periods and seldom show symptoms such as early-morning awakening, appetite loss, low self-worth, and thoughts of death. If criteria are met for both disorders of major depression and panic disorder, both diagnoses can be made.

The ability within DSM-IV and DSM-III-R classifications to diagnose an anxiety and a mood disorder concurrently reflects a change from DSM-III, in which a hierarchical classification system precluded an anxiety disorder diagnosis in the presence of a mood disorder. This change reflects, in part, conclusions from comorbidity and family studies suggesting that panic disorder is frequently the principal diagnosis when occurring with an affective disorder (c.f. Leckman, Clubb, & Pauls, 1990).

PREOCCUPATION WITH PHYSICAL HEALTH: HYPOCHONDRIASIS, DELUSIONAL DISORDER, AND SOMATIZATION DISORDER

Panic disorder patients typically are extremely concerned with their physical health, frequenting emergency rooms and visiting doctor after doctor, hoping to find a cure for their unexplainable but seemingly deadly physical symptoms. The unexpected occurrence of panic attacks leaves most panic patients terrified of the intense, mysterious physical state overcoming their bodies. For some, preoccupation with physical ailments reaches the severity of a somatic mental disorder, and should be diagnosed as such along with the panic disorder diagnosis. For others, a somatic preoccupation reflects a principal somatoform disorder that may resemble, but not meet criteria for, panic disorder. Here we address distinctions between panic disorder and three somatoform disorders: hypochondriasis; delusional disorder, somatic type; and somatization disorder.

Hypochondriasis

Patients with panic disorder commonly will report hypochondriacal concerns, such as the belief that they will die of a heart attack during a panic episode, despite numerous experiences to the contrary. Ongoing beliefs may include the certainty that their palpitations during panic attacks stem from a chronic heart ailment, despite physical evaluations attesting to cardiac health. Such preoccupation with illness indicates a diagnosis of hypochondriasis rather than panic disorder when several conditions are met. The beliefs must persist, despite medical reassurance, to the point of preoccupation with the fear that physical signs indicate the presence of a serious illness. Further, medical evaluation must reveal no physical disorder accounting for the physical signs, the symptoms must not be limited to those of panic attacks, and the beliefs must persist for six months. The preoccupation with fear of disease cannot occur exclusively as part of another disorder, such as panic disorder, GAD, OCD, or a depressive disorder. Both diagnoses can be assigned when criteria for both disorders are met.

Delusional Disorder, Somatic Type

Hypochondriasis may present in such a severe and persistent form that it reaches delusional intensity. In this case a diagnosis of delusional disorder, somatic type, is made to describe the unfounded beliefs in physical disorder or disease. In delusional disorder, the beliefs are nonbizarre (i.e., they involve situations that could realistically occur) fixed delusions, which have persisted for at least one month, that cannot be accounted for by another mental disorder or organic condition.

Somatization Disorder

Somatization disorder is characterized by a history of persistent (i.e., greater than six months) multiple somatic complaints, for which medical attention has been sought but for which no physical disorder has been found. In DSM-III-R, the diagnosis required 13 of 35 symptoms, grouped into six categories: gastrointestinal, cardiopulmonary, pain, conversion, sexual, and female reproductive symptoms. DSM-IV reduces the overlap of somatization with panic symptoms somewhat. Rather than any 13 of 35 listed symptoms, it requires four pain symptoms, two gastrointestinal symptoms, one sexual symptom, and one pseudoneurological symptom. Further, these symptoms cannot have occurred only during a panic attack. Thus, despite sharing some physical symptoms with panic disorder (i.e., gastrointestinal problems), this disorder involves a more ongoing focus on the belief in being sickly, rather than a persistent fear of sudden onset of the symptoms themselves. Both diagnoses should be made if recurrent panic attacks occur during the course of the somatization disorder.

DIFFERENTIAL DIAGNOSIS OF MEDICAL ILLNESS AND PSYCHOACTIVE SUBSTANCES

DSM-III-R classified mental disorders due to medical conditions and substance-induced disorders in a single section termed "organic disorders." This separate listing misleadingly implied that the "functional" mental disorders were free of biological or organic factors. DSM-IV thus eliminated the label *organic* and instead refers to mental disorders due to a general medical condition or to substance-induced mental disorders. Not only can a variety of both medical conditions and substance-induced states produce panic symptoms, but panic symptoms resemble a variety of medical conditions as well.

Medical Illnesses

Because the anticipatory, acute, and residual phases of anxiety associated with panic attacks involve many physiological systems, the symptoms resemble (and may be mistaken for) a wide variety of medical illnesses. For example, a patient with anxiety-induced palpitations may fear a cardiac ailment. Because panic symptoms mimic medical illnesses, panic patients notoriously seek medical consultations and frequent emergency rooms. One study reported that 100 percent of a sample of patients with panic disorder had sought medical attention for their panic symptoms (Sheehan, Ballenger, & Jacobsen, 1980), although Raj and Sheehan (1987) speculate that this number is decreasing with growing public awareness of panic disorder and its phenomenology.

Similarly, many medical conditions produce paniclike symptoms or even full-blown attacks. A patient reporting periods of dizziness and tremors, for example, may be unknowingly hypoglycemic; an individual experiencing episodes of tachycardia with depersonalization may have a seizure disorder. Although not focusing specifically on panic disorder, one study of 2,090 psychiatric outpatients found that 43 percent had a physical illness, and in nearly half of these cases the condition had gone undiagnosed (Koranyi, 1979). In fact, while a medical condition was simply co-occurring with the psychiatric condition in 13 percent of the patients, it actually caused the psychiatric condition in 8 percent of the cases and exacerbated it in an additional 22 percent. What remains unclear is how many patients with panic disorder have medical problems that either cause or exacerbate panic features in particular. Nonetheless, Raj and Sheehan (1987) identified highly associated medical conditions that must be evaluated in Panic Disorder patients. (See Table 1–2.)

Raj and Sheehan (1987) contend that because many more panic patients today are self-diagnosing and self-referring, they will directly seek panic treatment and may bypass a general physical evaluation. Although this may save on costly and unnecessary workups, true underlying

TABLE 1–2
Physical Disorders Associated with Anxiety

Cardiovascular	*Neurologic*
Cardiac arrhythmias	Collagen vascular disease
Congestive heart failure	Epilepsy
Coronary insufficiency	Huntington's disease
Hypertension	Multiple sclerosis
Mitral valve prolapse	Organic brain syndrome—delirium,
Myocardial infarction	dementia
	Vestibular dysfunction
Endocrine	Wilson's disease
Carcinoid	
Cushing's syndrome	*Substance-Related*
Hyperthyroidism	Intoxication
Hypothyroidism	Anticholinergic drugs
Hypoparathyroidism	Aspirin
Hypoglycemia	Caffeine
Menopause	Hallucinogens
Pheochromocytoma	Steroids
Premenstrual syndrome	Sympathomimetics
	Withdrawal
Respiratory	Alcohol
Asthma attacks	Narcotics
Chronic obstructive pulmonary disease	Sedative hypnotics
Hyperventilation syndrome	
Hypoxia	
Adrenal gland tumors	
Atypical chest pain	

Source: From Raj & Sheehan, 1987.

medical conditions may be more likely to be overlooked. It follows, then, that a thorough medical history should be taken from all patients to screen for signs of medical etiologies. Raj and Sheehan (1987) present guidelines for medical evaluation of the anxious patient, recommend routine physical examinations, and discuss the types of findings that warrant more sophisticated laboratory investigation.

The medical diagnoses most commonly linked with panic symptoms are endocrinopathies (e.g., hyper- and hypothyroidism; hypoglycemia), adrenal gland tumors (pheochromocytomas), mitral valve prolapse, and temporal lobe epilepsy. These disorders may produce various combinations of the physical concomitants of panic attacks: sweating, tremors, palpitations, flushes, light-headedness, abdominal distress, and short-ness of breath, as well as associated surges of subjective anxiety. Fur-ther, research has revealed elevated rates of these disorders in panic patients. For instance, patients with comorbid panic disorder with agora-phobia and major depression have been found to have an 11 to 13 percent rate of hyperthyroidism, compared to 1.9 to 2.7 percent in the general population (Lesser, Rubin, & Lydiard, 1987; Orenstein, Peskind, & Raskind, 1988). Likewise, the reported prevalence of mitral valve pro-lapse in panic patients averages 18 percent, compared with 1 percent of normal controls (Margraf, Ehlers, & Roth, 1986), although research suggests the mitral valve prolapse in panic patients tends to be mild and typically clinically insignificant (Gorman et al., 1988). A broad range of medical conditions inducing panic symptoms is presented in Table 1–2. When such disturbances are identified as initiating or maintaining prominent, recurrent, panic attacks, the appropriate diagnosis is anxiety disorder due to a general medical condition.

Psychoactive Substances

Psychoactive substances (e.g., amphetamines, cocaine, or caffeine) may cause intoxication symptoms or withdrawal symptoms (e.g., from alco-hol or barbituates) that may include panic symptoms; these would not be considered part of a panic disorder. A substantial portion of alcohol and substance users manifest panic-related anxiety syndromes (Cox, Nor-ton, Swinson, & Endler, 1990), which should be diagnosed as substance-induced anxiety disorder. It is well known that substances such as marijuana and cocaine can bring about not only symptoms of panic but also full-blown attacks (e.g., Aronson & Craig, 1986). Substances caus-ing panic symptoms include anticholinergic drugs, hallucinogens, steroids, sympathomimetics, alcohol, narcotics, sedative hypnotics, and caffeine. (See Table 1–2.)

Caffeine is of particular interest because of its near-universal inges-tion. Both caffeine intoxication and withdrawal can mimic panic and generalized anxiety disorders, and panic patients have lower thresholds for caffeine-induced panic attacks (cf. Uhde, 1988, 1990). Several case report studies describe individuals with clinically significant anxiety states who were found to be consuming from several hundred to over 1,000 milligrams of caffeine per day, whose symptoms dissipated with tapering of the caffeine. (See Uhde, 1990, for discussion.) Interest-ingly, based on his review of the case findings, Uhde (1990), proposes a caffeine-anxiety link in which chronic caffeine overingestion leads to a generalized anxiety disorder presentation, whereas acute caffeine overingestion mimics panic disorder.

In addition, many panic patients self-regulate their caffeine ingestion because of the extreme sensitivity to caffeine-provoked arousal symptoms (Uhde, 1990). Still, some may unwittingly provoke frightening and seemingly uncued panic attacks with caffeine ingestion, and thus caffeine consumption should be assessed routinely. Patients should be asked to report on their patterns of caffeine ingestion in the form of coffee, tea, chocolate, or colas.

Substance-induced anxiety disorder requires evidence of substance intoxication or withdrawal, with anxiety symptoms developing within one month of significant intoxication or withdrawal, and evidence that the symptoms are not better accounted for by a non-substance abuse anxiety disorder. Comorbid presentation of anxiety and substance abuse symptoms would yield an independent DSM-IV anxiety disorder diagnosis if the anxious syndrome predates the onset of the substance abuse, persists for at least a month following the cessation of intoxication or withdrawal periods, is excessive compared to what would be expected from the nature of the substance use, or there is other evidence supporting a non-substance-induced anxiety disorder (e.g., history of non-substance-related panic attacks). The diagnosis of substance-induced anxiety disorder requires specification of the type of substance used, if known; the time of onset of anxiety symptoms (i.e., during intoxication or withdrawal); and the nature of the anxiety symptoms (i.e., panic attacks, generalized anxiety, obsessions, or compulsions).

ATYPICAL PRESENTATIONS OF PANIC DISORDER: NONFEARFUL PANIC, NOCTURNAL PANIC, IRRITABLE PANIC

Several atypical presentations of panic disorder have been reported, including cases of panic without fear, sleep-related panic attacks, and irritable/explosive attacks resembling panic episodes. In each case, it is important to rule out other conditions that may account for the symptoms.

Nonfearful Panic

Nonfearful panic cases involve the sudden onset of significant and uncomfortable autonomic symptoms without the cognitive component of fear. DSM-IV allows for the diagnosis of panic disorder without the fearful aspects of panic, although theorists have debated whether one can truly label a symptom cluster an anxiety condition in the absence of subjective anxiety (c.f. Kushner & Beitman, 1990). In a review of this topic, Kushner and Beitman (1990) report that medical populations, rather than those in the mental health system, account for most of the occurrence of this presentation, with 20 to 40 percent of the panic disorder in such populations presenting without fear. Research suggests that apart from the cognitive variable of fear, fearful and nonfearful panickers have similar clinical profiles (Beitman, Kushner, Lamerti, & Mukerji, 1990) and show similar responses to antipanic pharmacologic treatments (Rosenbaum, 1987). Nonfearful panic disorder should be differentiated from a disorder concerning preoccupation with physical health or somatic symptoms. In fearless panic, the patient experiences the sudden onset of intense physiologic symptoms and discomfort associated with the symptoms themselves, rather than an ongoing belief in being medically ill (hypochondriasis) or persistent multiple somatic complaints for which no physical disorder has been found (somatization disorder).

Nocturnal Panic
Because the DSM includes no discussion of nocturnal panic as part of the panic disorder phenomenology, panic attacks occurring during sleep have received relatively little attention. However, recent research suggests that nocturnal panic attacks are not uncommon. Barlow (1988) states that 25 percent of all panickers presenting at his anxiety disorders clinic report a history of at least one episode of sleep panic. Mellman and Uhde (1990) report that in a sample of 45 panic disorder patients receiving treatment at anxiety disorders specialty clinics, 69 percent reported at least one prior sleep panic attack, with 33 percent indicating these were "common" events, compared with 92 percent of normal control sample reporting no history of sleep panic attacks. Taylor and associates (1986) monitored panic patients for heart rate changes for six days, 24 hours per day. They found that spontaneous panic attacks occur most frequently during the early hours, or slow-wave periods, of sleep, when subjects are presumably most relaxed. Mellman and Uhde (1990) also found that nocturnal panics occur primarily during non-REM sleep and have fewer but similar symptoms to daytime panics. Barlow and Craske (1988), on the other hand, found that 54 percent of sleep panickers

reported that their nocturnal panics were more severe than their day-time ones. Barlow (1988) suggests that nocturnal panics are triggered by patients' perceptions of subtle physiological changes (such as reduced heart rate and breathing changes) occurring with deeper relaxation, pointing out that panic patients are hypersensitive to bodily cues and that people are capable of remaining aware of personally relevant cues even when asleep.

Because nocturnal panics tend to involve brief awakenings before the onset of the panic attack and often involve shortness of breath (Barlow, 1988), clinicians may mistake these episodes for sleep apnea, a condition involving spontaneous pauses in breathing during sleep. Patients with sleep apnea, in fact, commonly report awakening in a state of intense fear, with choking or smothering sensations, heart palpitations, and other symptoms leading to the sense that they are ill or dying. The differential diagnosis of sleep apnea from nocturnal panic has important intervention implications; for example, while minor tranquilizers often are given for panic, they are contraindicated for sleep apnea. Sleep apnea may be differentiated by its frequently associated obesity and by a pattern of repeated awakenings throughout the night, rather than concentrations within the first few hours of sleep like nocturnal panic (Barlow, 1988).

Irritable Panic

Several case reports have described patients with angry outbursts resembling or co-occurring with panic attacks. One report detailing six case studies described patients whose panic attacks involved angry or violent outbursts and severe depersonalization in addition to unusually severe autonomic symptoms (Edlund, Swann, & Clothier, 1987). While there was no phobic avoidance, extreme social withdrawal developed in the hours or days following the attacks. The patients were found to have neurologic disturbances or temporal lobe electroencephalogram abnormalities. Additional case reports of patients free of neurologic abnormalities have concerned patients with fearful panic attacks with temporally associated rage outbursts (George, Anderson, & Nutt, 1989; Korn et al., 1992), as well as those with surging autonomic symptoms who have violent outbursts without associated terror or panic (Fava, Anderson, & Rosenbaum, 1990; McGrath, Robinson, & Stewart, 1985). The clinician may thus consider a panic condition with an explosive rage presentation, but should also rule out other possible explanations. The limited data on cases presenting with an irritable panic suggests that this atypical presentation should be viewed with caution and may reflect a phenomenon other than panic disorder, or reflect a comorbid explosive disorder.

CONCLUSION

Since panic disorder is the most common presenting problem among people seeking mental health services, and causes significant distress and impairment in those who suffer from it, it is essential that clinicians recognize the symptoms of the disorder. Appropriate recognition of the disorder is especially important because many treatments are available that have demonstrated effectiveness. Panic disorder may be difficult to discern from other psychiatric and organic conditions, because of its broad symptom array, which substantially overlaps with many psychiatric disorders and mimics various medical illnesses and substance-induced conditions. This chapter presents the phenomenology of panic disorder with and without agoraphobia, outlines detailed criteria of the many conditions that may obfuscate detection of the disorder, and provides assessment guidelines for clarifying diagnoses. The purpose has been to guide the clinician in detecting panic disorder, to aid in difficult diagnostic decisions, to alert the clinician to various presentations of the disorder, and to highlight relevant changes from DSM-III-R to DSM-IV criteria.

The descriptions and guidelines covered in this chapter are intended to provide the clinician with a solid grasp of the phenomenology of panic disorder.

REFERENCES

American Psychiatric Association (1987). *Diagnostic and statistical manual of mental disorders* (3rd ed., revised). Washington, DC: Author.

American Psychiatric Association (1994). *Diagnostic and statistical manual of mental disorders* (4th ed.). Washington, DC: Author.

Aronson, T. A., & Craig, T. J. (1986). Cocaine precipitation of panic disorder. *American Journal of Psychiatry, 143,* 643–645.

Ballenger, J. C., Burrows, G., Dupont, R., Noyes, R., Pecknold, J. C., Rifkin, A., Rubin, R., Swinson, R. P. (1988). Alprazolam in panic disorder and agoraphobia: Results from a multicenter trial. 1. Efficacy. *Archives of General Psychiatry, 45,* 413–422.

Ballenger, J. C., & Fyer, A. J. (1993). Examining criteria for panic disorder. *Hospital and Community Psychiatry, 44,* 226–228.

Barlow, D. H. (1988). *Anxiety and its disorders.* New York: Guilford Press.

Barlow, D. H., & Craske, M. G. (1988). The phenomenology of panic. In S. Rachman & D. Maser (Eds.), *Panic: Psychological perspectives* (pp. 11–35). Hillsdale, NJ: Lawrence Erlbaum Associates.

Barlow, D. H., Craske, M. G., Cerny, J. A., & Klosko, J. S. (1989). Behavioral treatment of panic disorder. *Behavior Therapy, 20,* 261–282.

Barlow, D. H., Vermilyea, J., Blanchard, E. B., Vermilyea, B., DiNardo, P. A., & Cerny, J. A. (1985). The phenomenon of panic. *Journal of Abnormal Psychology, 94,* 320–328.

Beitman, B. D., Basha, I., & Flaker, G. (1987). Atypical or nonanginal chest pain: Panic disorder or coronary artery disease? *Archives of Internal Medicine, 147,* 1550–1552.

Beitman, B. D., Kushner, M. G., Lamerti, J. W., & Mukerji, V. (1990). Panic disorder without fear in patients with angiographically normal coronary arteries. *Journal of Nervous and Mental Diseases, 178,* 307–312.

Boyd, J. H. (1986). Use of mental health services for the treatment of panic disorder. *American Journal of Psychiatry, 143,* 1569–1574.

Breier, A., Charney, D. S., & Heninger, G. R. (1986). Agoraphobia with panic attacks. *Archives of General Psychiatry, 43,* 1029–1036.

Burns, L. E., & Thorpe, G. L. (1977). The epidemiology of fears and phobias with particular reference to the national survey of agoraphobics. *Journal of Internal Medicine Research, 5,* 1–7.

Cox, B. J., Norton, G. R., Swinson, R. P., & Endler, N. S. (1990). Substance abuse and panic-related anxiety: A critical review. *Behavior Research and Therapy, 28,* 385–393.

Craske, M. G., & Barlow, D. H. (1988). A review of the relationship between panic and avoidance. *Clinical Psychology Review, 8,* 667–685.

Craske, M. G., Miller, P. P., Rotunda, R., & Barlow, D. H. (1990). A descriptive report of features of initial unexpected panic attacks in minimal and extensive avoiders. *Behaviour Research and Therapy, 28,* 395–400.

Craske, M. G., Rapee, R. M., & Barlow, D. H. (1988). The significance of panic expectancy for individual patterns of avoidance. *Behavior Therapy, 19,* 577–592.

Craske, M. G., Sanderson, W. C., & Barlow, D. H. (1987). The relationships among panic, fear, and avoidance. *Journal of Anxiety Disorders, 1,* 153–160.

Darwin, C. R. (1965). *The expressions of emotions in man and animals.* London: John Murray. (Original work published 1872)

Depeu, R. A., & Monroe, S. M. (1986). Conceptualization and measurement of human disorder in life stress research: The problem of chronic disturbance. *Psychological Bulletin, 99,* 36–51.

Doctor, R. M. (1982). Major results of a large-scale pretreatment survey of agoraphobics. In R. L. DuPont (Ed.), *Phobia: A comprehensive summary of modern treatments* (pp. 203–214). New York: Brunner/Mazel.

Edlund, M. J., Swann, A. C., & Clothier, J. (1987). Patients with panic attacks and abnormal EEG results. *American Journal of Psychiatry, 144,* 508–509.

Faravelli, C. (1985). Life events preceding the onset of panic disorder. *Journal of Affective Disorders, 9,* 103–105.

Faravelli, C., & Pallanti, S. (1989). Recent life events and panic disorder. *American Journal of Psychiatry, 146,* 622–627.

Fava, M., Anderson, K., & Rosenbaum, J. (1990). "Anger attacks": Possible variants of panic and major depressive disorders. *American Journal of Psychiatry, 147,* 867–870.

Finlay-Jones, R., & Brown, G. W. (1981). Types of stressful life events and the onset of anxiety and depressive disorders. *Psychological Medicine, 11,* 803–815.

Flor, H., Turk, D. C., & Birbaumer, N. (1985). Assessment of stress-related psychophysiological reactions in chronic back pain patients. *Journal of Consulting and Clinical Psychology, 53,* 354–364.

Frances, A., Pincus, H. A., Widiger, T. A., Davis, W. W., & First, M. B. (1990). DSM-IV: Work in progress. *American Journal of Psychiatry, 147,* 1439–1448.

Fyer, A. J., Mannuzza, S. M., Klein, D. F., & Endicott, J. (1985). *Schedule for Affective Disorders and Schizophrenia-Lifetime Version Modified for the Study of Anxiety Disorders (SADS-LA).* New York: New York State Psychiatric Institute.

George, D. T., Anderson, P., & Nutt, D. J. (1989). Aggressive thoughts and behavior: Another symptom of panic disorder? *Acta Psychiatrica Scandinavia, 79,* 500–502.

Gittelman, R., & Klein, D. F. (1985). Childhood separation anxiety and adult agoraphobia. In A. Tuma & J. D. Maser (Eds.), *Anxiety and the anxiety disorders.* Hillsdale, NJ: Lawrence Erlbaum Associates.

Gittelman-Klein, R. (1975). Psychiatric characteristics of the relatives of school phobic children. In D. V. Sivà Sanker (Ed.), *Mental health in children* (Vol. 1). Westbury, NY: PPJD Publications.

Goldstein, A. J., & Chambless, D. L. (1978). A reanalysis of agoraphobia. *Behavior Therapy, 9,* 47–59.

Gorman, J. M., Goetz, R. R., Fyer, M., King, D. L., Fyer, A. J., Liebowitz, M. R., & Klein, D. F. (1988). The mitral valve prolapse–panic disorder connection. *Psychosomatic Medicine, 50,* 114–122.

Hammen, C., Mayol, A., de Mayo, R., & Marks, I. (1986). Initial symptom levels and the life-event-depression relationship. *Journal of Abnormal Psychology, 95,* 114–122.

Horwath, E., Lish, J. D., Johnson, J., Hornig, C. D., & Weissman, M. M. (1993). Agoraphobia without panic: Clinical reappraisal of an epidemiologic finding. *American Journal of Psychiatry, 150,* 1496–1501.

Insel, T. R., & Akiskal, H. S. (1986). Obsessive-compulsive disorder with psychotic features: A phenomenologic analysis. *American Journal of Psychiatry, 143,* 1527–1533.

Joyce, P. R., Bushnell, J. A., Oakley-Browne, M. A., Wells, J. E., & Hornblow, A. R. (1989). The epidemiology of panic symptomatology and agoraphobic avoidance. *Comprehensive Psychiatry, 30,* 303–312.

Keller, M. B., & Baker, L. A. (1992). The clinical course of panic disorder and depression. *Journal of Clinical Psychiatry, 53* (Suppl. 3), 5–8.

Klein, D. F. (1964). Delineation of two drug-responsive anxiety syndromes. *Psychopharmacologica, 5,* 397–408.

Klein, D. F. (1981). Anxiety re-conceptualized. In D. F. Klein & J. Rabkin (Eds.), *Anxiety: New research and changing concepts.* New York: Raven Press.

Klein, D. F., & Gorman, J. M. (1987). A model of panic and agoraphobic development. *Acta Psychiatria Scandinavia, 335* (Suppl.), 87–95.

Klein, D. F., & Klein, H. M. (1989). The nosology, genetics, and theory of spontaneous panic attacks and phobia. In P. J. Tyrer (Ed.), *Psychopharmacology of Anxiety* (pp. 163–190). New York: Oxford University Press.

Klerman, G. L., Weissman, M., Ouellette, R., Johnson, J., & Greenwald, S. (1991). Panic attacks in the community: Social morbidity and health care utilization. *Journal of the American Medical Association, 265* (6), 742–746.

Koranyi, E. K. (1979). Morbidity and rate of undiagnosed physical illness in a psychiatric clinic population. *Archives General Psychiatry, 36,* 414–449.

Korn, M., Kotler, M., Molcho, A., Botsis, A. J., Grosz, D., Chen, C., Plutchik, R., Brown, S., & van Praag, H. M. (1992). Suicide and violence associated with panic attacks. *Biological Psychiatry, 31,* 607–612.

Kushner, M. G., & Beitman, B. D. (1990). Panic attacks without fear: An overview. *Behaviour Research & Therapy, 28,* 469–479.

Last, C. G., Barlow, D. H., & O'Brien, G. T. (1984). Precipitants of agoraphobia: Role of stressful life events. *Psychological Reports, 54,* 567–570.

Leckman, J. F., Clubb, M. M., & Pauls, D. L. (1990). Comorbidity of panic disorder and major depression: A review of epidemiological and genetic data. In J. C. Ballenger (Ed.), *Clinical aspects of panic disorder* (pp. 141–150). New York: Alan Liss.

Lelliot, P., Marks, I., McNamee, G., & Tobena, A. (1989). Onset of panic disorder with agoraphobia: Toward an integrated model. *Archives of General Psychiatry, 46,* 1000–1004.

Lesser, I. M., Rubin, R. T., & Lydiard, R. B. (1987). Past and current thyroid function in subjects with panic disorder. *Journal of Clinical Psychiatry, 48,* 473–476.

Liebowitz, M. R. (1992). Diagnostic issues in anxiety disorders. In A. Tasman & B. Michealle (Eds.), *American Psychiatric Press Review of Psychiatry,* vol. 11 (pp. 247–259). Washington, DC: APA Press.

Liebowitz, M. R., & Klein, D. F. (1991). Clinical psychiatric conferences: Assessment and treatment of phobic anxiety. *Journal of Clinical Psychology, 40,* 486–492.

Lundy, M. S. (1993). Panic as a traumatic stressor. [Letter]. *American Journal of Psychiatry, 150,* 841–842.

Magraf, J., Ehlers, A., & Roth, W. T. (1986). Biological models of panic disorder and agorophobia: A review. *Behavior Research and Therapy, 24,* 553–567.

Markowitz, J., Weissman, M. M., Ouellette, R., & Lieb, J. (1989). Quality of life in panic disorder. *Archives of General Psychiatry, 46,* 984–992.

Marks, J. M. (1987). *Fears, phobias, and rituals.* New York: Oxford University Press.

Marks, I., & Lader, M. (1973). Anxiety states (anxiety neurosis): A review. *Journal of Nervous and Mental Disease, 156,* 3–18.

Maser, J. D., & Cloninger, R. (1990). *Comorbidity of mood and anxiety disorders.* Washington, DC: American Psychiatric Press.

McGrath, P. J., Robinson, D., & Stewart, J. W. (1985). Atypical panic attacks in major depression. *American Journal of Psychiatry, 142,* 1224.

McNally, R. J., & Lukach, B. M. (1992). Are panic attacks traumatic stressors? *American Journal of Psychiatry, 149,* 824–826.

Mellman, T. A., & Uhde, T. W. (1990). Sleep in panic and generalized anxiety disorders. In J. C. Ballenger (Ed.), *Neurobiology of Panic Disorder* (pp. 365–376). New York: Alan Liss.

Mendel, J. G. C., & Klein, D. F. (1969). Anxiety attacks with subsequent conditioned agoraphobia. *Comprehensive Psychiatry, 10,* 190–195.

Newman, S. C., & Bland, R. C. (1994). Life events and the 1-year prevalence of major depressive episode, generalized anxiety disorder, and panic disorder in a community sample. *Comprehensive Psychiatry, 35,* 76–82.

Nagy, L. M., Krystal, J. H., Woods, S. W., & Chang, D. S. (1989). Clinical and medication outcome after short-term alprazolam and behavioral group treatment of panic disorder. *Archives of General Psychiatry, 46,* 996–999.

Noyes, R., Garvey, M. J., & Cook, B. L. (1989). Problems with tricyclic antidepressant use in patients with panic disorder or agoraphobia: Results of a naturalistic follow-up study. *Journal of Clinical Psychiatry, 50,* 163–169.

Noyes, R., Reich, J., Christiansen, J., Suelzer, M., Pfohl, B., & Coyrell, W. A. (1990). Outcome of panic disorder: Relationship to diagnostic subtypes and comorbidity. *Archives of General Psychiatry, 47,* 809–818.

Orenstein, H., Peskind, A., & Raskind, M. A. (1988). Thyroid disorders in female psychiatric patients with panic disorder or agoraphobia. *American Journal of Psychiatry, 145,* 1428–1430.

Pollack, M. H., Otto, M. W., Rosenbaum, J. F., Sachs, G. S., O'Neil, C., Asher, R., & Meltzer-Brody, S. (1990). Longitudinal course of panic disorder: Findings from the Massachusetts General Hospital Naturalistic Study. *Journal of Clinical Psychiatry, 51*(Suppl. 12A), 12–16.

Rachman, S., & Lopatka, C. (1986). Match and mismatch in the prediction of fear—I. *Behavior Research and Therapy, 24,* 387–393.

Raj, A., & Sheehan, D. V. (1987). Medical evaluation of panic attacks. *Journal of Clinical Psychiatry, 48,* 309–313.

Robins, L. N., Helzer, J. E., Croughan, J., & Ratcliff, K. S. (1981). The National Institute of Mental Health Diagnostic Interview Schedule: Its history, characteristics, and validity. *Archives of General Psychiatry, 38,* 381–389.

Rosenbaum, J. F. (1987). Limited-symptom panic attacks. *Psychosomatics, 28,* 407–412.

Roth, M. (1959). The phobic-anxiety-depersonalization syndrome. *Proceedings of the Royal Society of Medicine, 52,* 587–596.

Sanderson, W. C., Rapee, R. M., & Barlow, D. H. (1987, November). *The DSM-III-Revised anxiety disorder categories: Description and patterns of comorbidity.* Paper presented at the annual meeting of the Association for the Advancement of Behavior Therapy, Boston.

Shalomskas, D. E., Wickamaratne, P. J., Dogloo, L., O'Brien, D. W., Leaf, P. J., & Woods, S. W. (1993). Postpartum onset of panic disorder: A coincidental event? *Journal of Clinical Psychiatry, 54,* 476–480.

Sheehan, D. V., Ballenger, J., & Jacobsen, G. (1980). Treatment of endogenous anxiety with phobic, hysterical, and hypochondriacal symptoms. *Archives of General Psychiatry, 37,* 51–59.

Starcevic, V., Uhlenhuth, E. H., Kellner, R., & Pathak, D. (1992). Patterns of comorbidity in panic disorder and agoraphobia. *Psychiatry Research, 42,* 171–183.

Taylor, C. B., Sheikh, J., Agras, W. S., Roth, W. T., Margraf, J., Ehlers, A., Maddock, R. J., & Gossard, D. (1986). Self-report of panic attacks: Agreement with heart rate changes. *American Journal of Psychiatry, 143,* 478–482.

Tearnan, B. H., Telch, M. J., & Keefe, P. (1984). Etiology and onset of agoraphobia: A critical review. *Comprehensive Psychiatry, 25,* 51–62.

Telch, M. J., Brouillard, M., Telch, C., Agras, W. S., & Taylor, C. B. (1989). Role of cognitive appraisal in panic-related avoidance. *Behavior Research and Therapy, 27,* 373–383.

Telch, M. J., Lucas, J. A., & Nelson, P. (1989). Nonclinical panic in college students: An investigation of prevalence and symptomatology. *Journal of Abnormal Psychology, 98,* 300–306.

Thyer, B. A., Nesse, R. M., Cameron, O. G., & Curtis, G. C. (1985). Agoraphobia: A test of the separation anxiety hypothesis. *Behaviour Research and Therapy, 23,* 75–78.

Thyer, B. A., Nesse, R. M., Curtis, G. C., & Cameron, O. G. (1986). Panic disorder: A test of the separation anxiety hypothesis. *Behaviour Research and Therapy, 24,* 209–211.

Uhde, T. W. (1988). Caffeine: Practical facts for the psychiatrist. In P. Roy-Byrne (Ed.), *Anxiety: New research findings for the Clinician.* Washington, DC: American Psychiatric Press.

Uhde, T. W. (1990). Caffeine provocation of panic: A focus on biological mechanisms. In J. C. Ballenger (Ed.), *Neurobiology of Panic Disorder,* (pp. 219–242). New York: Alan Liss.

Van Der Molen, G. M., Van Den Hout, M. A., Van Dieren, A. C., & Griez, E. (1989). Childhood separation anxiety and adult-onset panic disorders. *Journal of Anxiety Disorders, 3,* 97–106.

Von Korff, M., Eaton, W., & Keyl, P. (1985). The epidemiology of panic attacks and disorder: Results from three community surveys. *American Journal of Epidemiology, 122,* 970–981.

Weissman, M. M. (1988). The epidemiology of panic disorder and agoraphobia. In R. E. Hales & A. Frances (Eds.), *Review of Psychiatry,* vol. 7 (pp. 54–66). Washington, DC: American Psychiatric Press.

Weissman, M. M., Klerman, G. L., Markowitz, J. S., & Ouellette, S. (1989). Suicidal ideation and suicide attempts in panic disorder and attacks. *New England Journal of Medicine, 321,* 1209–1218.

Wilson, K. G., Sandler, L. S., Asmundson, G. J. G., Ediger, J. M., Larsen, D. K., & Walker, J. R. (1992). Panic attacks in the nonclinical population: An empirical approach to case identification. *Journal of Abnormal Psychology, 101,* 460–468.

Wing, J. K., Nixon, J. M., Mann, S. A., & Leff, J. P. (1977). Reliability of the PSE (9th edition), used in a population study. *Psychological Medicine, 7,* 505–516.

Wittchen, H. U. (1986). Epidemiology of panic attacks and panic disorders. In I. Hand & H. U. Wittchen (Eds.), *Panic and phobias: Empirical evidence of theoretical models and long-term effects of psychological treatments* (pp. 18–27). New York: Springer-Verlag.

World Health Organization (1992). *Manual for the international statistical classification of diseases, injuries, and causes of death* (10th rev.). Geneva: Author.

2

The Epidemiology of Panic

WILLIAM W. EATON AND
PENELOPE M. KEYL

Although the distinct quality of panic anxiety was noticed at least as early as Freud, the epidemiology of panic and panic disorder was not studied separately from other anxiety disorders prior to the publication, in 1980, of the third edition of the American Psychiatric Association (APA) *Diagnostic and Statistical Manual* (DSM-III; APA, 1980). In the DSM-III, panic was elevated from the status of one among many varied symptoms of anxiety to a distinct nosologic entity. The change was consistent with, and even prescient of, new information about the biologic and phenomenologic uniqueness of panic attacks. But the fact remains that the epidemiologic literature on panic and panic disorder is very limited. In a review of the literature on panic and phobia in 1987, Marks cited only one study (Weissman, Myers, & Harding, 1978) wherein the prevalence of panic disorder, according to the Research Diagnostic Criteria, was estimated. Since that time, there has been a voluminous amount of research on panic disorder, and one series of good epidemiologic studies, the National Institute of Mental Health (NIMH) Epidemiologic Catchment Area (ECA) Program, begun at the time of the publication of the DSM-III (Eaton, Regier, Locke, & Taube, 1981). Most of the evidence on the epidemiology and course of panic to be summarized is from that collaborative study.

In this chapter we present a summary of what is known about the epidemiology and course of panic and panic disorder. In the remainder of this section we present a brief description of the main source of our data, the ECA Program. In the section entitled "Descriptive Epidemiology," we present basic descriptive data on the epidemiology of panic, including a brief presentation and discussion of recent data from the National Comorbidity Survey (NCS). Estimates of the lifetime prevalence of panic and panic disorder in the population are presented, including data on simple panic attacks, on the symptoms that accompany the attacks, and on the diagnosis of panic disorder. Then we present the point prevalence of panic disorder by sex and ethnicity, and display symptom profiles for those suffering panic attacks in different ethnic groups. In "Incidence and Risk Factors," we present analyses of the incidence of panic and panic disorder, including risk factors for onset. In "Course and Sequelae," we present information on the course of panic, including important sequelae.

The ECA Program consists of collaborative community surveys carried out by five university-based research teams in different locations in the United States. In addition to a prevalence survey of each site's sample, there was also a one-year follow-up interview. The methods of the ECA surveys are more fully described elsewhere (Eaton & Kessler, 1985). Area probability samples of households were drawn and household members selected at random for interview from among people 18 years of age or older. Response rates of 68 to 80 percent were achieved. Institutionalized persons were sampled as well, but they are not included in the analyses that follow.

The National Comorbidity Survey (NCS) was a nationwide survey designed to produce data on the prevalence of psychiatric morbidity (Kessler et al., 1994). It was based on a probability sample of the continental population of the United States, in contrast to the ECA sample, which is an amalgamation of five metropolitan areas. The NCS sample includes age ranges from 15 (as compared to lower range of 18 for ECA) through 54 (as compared to no upper limit for ECA). Fieldwork for the NCS was carried out from 1990 to 1992.

Persons agreeing to be interviewed in the ECA surveys participated in a 90-minute interview that included the Diagnostic Interview Schedule (DIS; Robins et al., 1985). The DIS portion of the interview consisted of prespecified questions directly pertinent to *Diagnostic and Statistical Manual of Mental Disorders,* third edition (DSM-III) diagnostic criteria for a series of mental disorders. For panic disorder, the initial question was: Have you ever had a spell or attack when all of a sudden you felt frightened, anxious or very uneasy in a situation when most people wouldn't be afraid? If the answer to that question was positive, a series of probe questions followed to distinguish trivial occurrences from those designated as "severe": occurrences that led to seeking professional help, taking medication at least twice, or disruption of the individual's life. Follow-up probes also sought to eliminate panic attacks caused by medication, drugs, alcohol, physical illness, or injury (i.e., of organic origin). Severe attacks not explained by these nonpsychiatric causes are considered plausible psychiatric symptoms in the DIS terminology and are designated as "severe, unexplained" attacks in the text.

The field procedures for the NCS differed slightly. A descendant of the DIS called the Composite International Diagnostic Interview (CIDI) was used (Wittchen et al., 1991). The CIDI makes DSM-III-R (third edition, revised) diagnoses, as opposed to the DSM-III diagnoses made by the DIS. In the CIDI, the initial question about panic was included in the beginning of the interview, instead of midway through as in the DIS.

DESCRIPTIVE EPIDEMIOLOGY

The ECA survey found that panic disorder occurs in about 2 percent of the general population over the course of their lives (lifetime prevalence), but about 10 percent report the occurrence of a panic attack. In Table 2–1, the reader can follow a DSM-III algorithm explicitly, examining prevalences at each step. DSM-III requires a panic attack to have four or more concomitant psychophysiological symptoms. These "intense" attacks occurred in 5.9 percent (3.8 percent "severe" and 2.1 percent "nonsevere") of the sample. Intense attacks usually are severe and not explained by drugs, medication, alcohol, physical illness, or injury. In only 1.7 percent of the population, or less than half of those with intense and severe attacks, have the attacks occurred at least three times in three weeks, that is, often enough to meet the DSM-III criteria for recurrence. Persons with intense, recurrent attacks are diagnosed as having panic disorder if the attacks have occurred at least once with no obvious phobic stimulus. It is rare for severe, intense, and recurrent panic attacks to have occurred solely in the presence of a phobic stimulus: 0.1 percent occurred only when confronted by a social or simple

TABLE 2–1
Prevalence of Panic Symptoms and Disorder in Two Surveys

Type of Panic Attack	Simple Prevalence of This Type of Attack (%)		
	ECA		NCS
	Severe[a]	Nonsevere	
Any attack	5.5	4.2	15.6
Intense attack	3.8	2.1	11.0
Intense recurrent	1.7	0.5	
Solely in phobic situations:			
Social/simple only	0.1	0.0	
Agoraphobic	0.2	0.0	
In phobic situations and spontaneous:			
Social/simple only	0.2	0.0	
Agoraphobic	0.5	0.0	
No phobia	0.7	0.2	
Panic Disorder	1.4	0.3	3.5

Source: Adapted from Eaton, Dryman, and Weissman, 1991, Table 7–5.

[a]Severe symptoms are those meeting one of three criteria: a professional was told about it, medication was taken for it more than once, or it interfered with life activities a lot. In addition, for panic attacks to be severe, at least one attack was not explained by alcohol, drugs, physical illness, exertion, or a situation that would be expected to be frightening.

phobic situation and 0.2 percent in an agoraphobic situation (and perhaps in other phobic situations as well), but not spontaneously. Thus 17 percent of all persons experiencing severe recurrent panic attacks had them only in phobic situations (.3 percent/1.7 percent). The remainder (1.7 − 0.3 = 1.4 percent) had severe, intense, recurrent panic attacks at least once in the absence of a phobic stimulus. This group is comprised of individuals who had attacks sometimes accompanied by phobic stimuli (row titled "In phobic situation and spontaneous") as well as individuals who had never had a phobic stimulus present during an attack (row titled "No phobia").

The rightmost column in Table 2–1 presents data from the NCS (Eaton, Kessler, Wittchen, & Magee, 1994). Due to differences in questions included and differences in wording, direct comparisons can be made only for three rows in the table. The column shows lifetime prevalence of "fearful spell" (equivalent to ECA definition of panic attack) to be 15.6 percent in the NCS. The comparable "limited symptom attack" of Katerndahl and Realini's San Antonio survey (1993) had a lifetime prevalence of 11.6 percent. While both estimates are higher than the ECA figure of 9.7 percent, the San Antonio figure is only marginally higher. The prevalence of "intense attack" (equivalent to "intense fearful spell" in the NCS data reported by Eaton et al. in 1994) is more than twice as high in the NCS as the ECA (11.0 percent versus 5.9 percent). The lifetime prevalence of DSM-III-R panic disorder, as measured by the CIDI in the NCS, is 3.5 percent, more than twice as high as the ECA estimate.

Differences between the ECA and NCS are probably not the result of sampling error, since both have very large samples. While it is difficult to state with certainty, it seems probable that the differences are not the result of different target population areas being sampled, since there is a broad range of sociodemographic characteristics, not markedly different in the two surveyed populations. Eaton and coworkers (1994) show data suggesting that the differences in prevalence are not totally the result of age differences in the populations sampled. It seems unlikely that the passage of time between the ECA (1978–1983) and the NCS (1990–1992) would have produced an upsurge in rate of panic. The DSM-III and DSM-III-R are not very different in how panic is operationally defined, and analyses by Eaton and coworkers (1994) suggest that differences in diagnostic convention and algorithm would be unlikely to cause such a large difference. What remains is the difference in methods in conducting the surveys. In particular, when the initial question on panic occurs midway through the interview (as in the ECA), the subject may be tiring of the process and be more reluctant to answer positively than when the initial question is asked at the very beginning (as in the NCS). In both surveys, if the initial question on panic is answered negatively, the entire section is skipped; therefore, this difference might produce differences in all categories of paniclike experiences shown in Table 2–1. The upshot of this discussion is that the epidemiologic data on panic, and probably in emotional disorders generally, are highly dependent on the precise placement and phrasing of questions. This intuition has led many researchers in the area to concentrate on verbatim-style interviews, such as the DIS and CIDI.

Most panic attacks occur with psychophysiological symptoms. Figure 2–1 shows, for those reporting an attack sometime during their lifetime, the percentages reporting the occurrence of these symptoms during one of their worst attacks. We discuss three profiles presented in the figure: one for those meeting the criteria for DIS/DSM-III panic

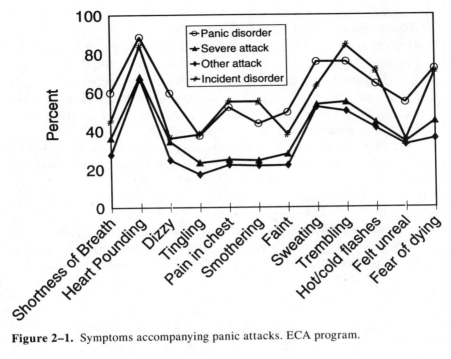

Figure 2–1. Symptoms accompanying panic attacks. ECA program.

disorder ("prevalent disorder"); a second for individuals who had an attack judged to be severe, and not explained by reasons of medical illness or substance abuse, but not meeting criteria for disorder, either because the attacks were not recurrent or because they were never spontaneous; and a third for attacks not meeting criteria of severity. Figure 2–1 includes a fourth line labeled "incident disorder," which is discussed later. The three types of prevalent attacks differ in the degree to which they entail psychophysiological symptoms. In particular, more symptoms occur for those meeting criteria for disorder than for others, and the corresponding line is higher on the figure. But what seems more striking to us is the parallel quality of the profiles (noticed earlier in analyses from three ECA sites by Von Korff, Eaton, & Keyl, 1985). For this reason, it seems premature to present epidemiologic data solely on panic disorder without including information on panic attacks not meeting criteria for disorder as well.

The proportion of the population with panic disorder at any given time is about one-third the lifetime prevalence (labeled "one-month prevalence" in Table 2–2), with about one-half of 1 percent reporting symptoms meeting criteria for DSM-III panic disorder in the month prior to the interview. The table shows that females have about twice the prevalence of panic disorder as males throughout all the ethnic groups. This difference is consistent with the literature on anxiety in general. There are no differences in prevalence of panic disorder by race/ethnic groups across the two types of prevalence rate. But blacks and Hispanics have lower lifetime prevalence rates than whites.

Panic attacks are experienced differently by distinct cultures. For example, in a study in South Florida (Eaton & Garrison, 1992), about 10 percent of both Haitian and Cuban entrant samples reported the occurrence of a panic attack, similar to data presented in Table 2–1. But fully 67 percent of the Cubans reported that they were frightened "very much," or "almost unbearably" by the attack. The analogous figure for the Haitians was 35 percent—about half. Figure 2–2 shows symptom profiles for five separate cultural groups: whites, blacks, and Mexican-Americans

TABLE 2–2
Population Prevalence of Panic Disorder by Sex and Ethnicity

| | | Prevalence (%) (SE) | | | |
	Sample Size	One-Month		Lifetime	
Total	19,498[a]	0.53	(0.7)	1.57	(.13)
Both Sexes					
White	12,968	0.50	(.08)	1.62	(.14)
Black	4,668	0.64	(.26)	1.31	(.37)
Hispanic	1,604	0.51	(.32)	0.87	(.41)
Men					
All groups	8,375	0.35	(.09)	0.99	(.15)
White	5,573	0.33	(.09)	1.02	(.16)
Black	1,855	0.27	(.25)	0.57	(.36)
Hispanic	818	0.31	(.36)	0.41	(.41)
Women					
All groups	11,123	0.69	(.12)	2.10	(.21)
White	7,395	0.65	(.13)	2.17	(.23)
Black	2,813	0.94	(.42)	1.93	(.60)
Hispanic	786	0.69	(.52)	1.31	(.71)

Source: Adapted from Eaton, Dryman, and Weissman, 1991, Table 7–2.

[a]For lifetime prevalence, the total sample size is 19,501. These three additional cases also are included when calculating lifetime prevalence for the subgroups.

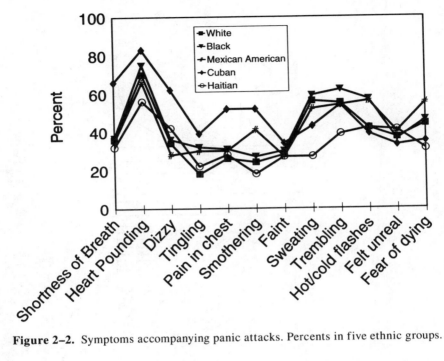

Figure 2-2. Symptoms accompanying panic attacks. Percents in five ethnic groups.

from the ECA project, and Cubans and Haitians from the South Florida project. "Heart pounding" is the most common symptom accompanying panic attacks in all five groups. But apart from this similarity, the profiles are not comparable. Cubans have the highest rate of accompanying symptoms; for the other groups, the prevalence depends on the particular symptom. It seems clear that the cultural background of the individual influences the way in which panic attacks occur.

INCIDENCE AND RISK FACTORS

Incidence is the rate at which new cases develop in the population. In estimating a rate of incidence, the population at risk includes only those who have not met criteria for case definition already. Incidence is better than prevalence for understanding the force of morbidity in the population, because comparisons between different risk groups are not contaminated by different mortality or chronicity of the disorder in the different groups.

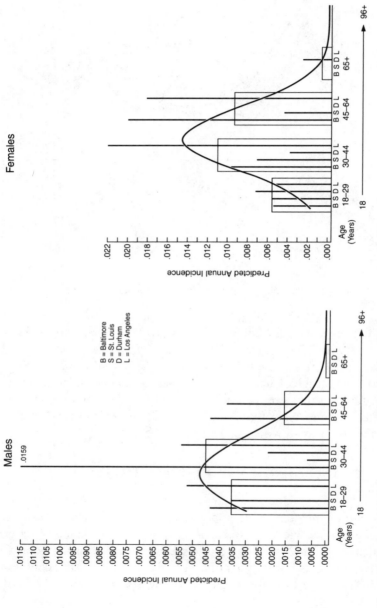

Figure 2–3. Annual incidence of DIS/DSM-III panic disorder.

How does the incidence of panic disorder change over the course of life? Figure 2–3 presents rates of incidence by age for each gender separately. The figures are drawn to allow comparisons of the age curves, and the scales are different. Out of over 10,000 person-years of risk for onset, there are 61 new cases of panic disorder. Females have higher rates of incidence than males, and the overall difference is statistically significant. Onset of panic disorder was rarely observed among the elderly. The highest rates tend to be in the two middle-age groups. For females, the curve is similar to that for major depressive disorder, but it has a much narrower peak in middle age. The peak onset for panic disorder appears to be earlier for males than females.

Sociodemographic and psychopathologic risk factors for onset of a severe panic attack, not explained by injury, illness, or ingestion of drugs or alcohol, are shown in Table 2–3. In this table we are forced to

TABLE 2–3
Relative Odds of Incident Panic Attacks
According to Sociodemographic and Psychopathologic Characteristics
Epidemiologic Catchment Area Program 1980–83

	Relative Odds (95% Confidence Interval)
	Severe, Unexplained Panic Attacks
Age[a] (years)	
18–29	0.87 (0.49–1.56)
45–64	0.94 (0.53–1.67)
65+	0.48 (0.27–0.87)
Female	1.46 (0.93–2.29)
Black	0.68 (0.38–1.21)
Other nonwhite	0.32 (0.14–0.73)
Not married	1.17 (0.76–1.80)
Occupational prestige[b]	0.95 (0.87–1.04)
Cardiac symptoms	2.16 (1.27–3.68)
Shortness of breath	3.79 (2.10–6.82)
Depression or major grief episode	4.24 (2.24–8.02)
Drug abuse or dependence	3.45 (1.56–7.62)
Alcohol abuse or dependence	2.34 (1.28–4.28)
Seizures	2.15 (0.56–8.27)

Source: Adapted from Keyl and Eaton, 1990, Tables 2 and 3.

[a]Compared with 30- to 44-year-olds.
[b]For an increase of 10 percentiles within the distribution for the occupational prestige scale (see text).

focus on panic attacks, instead of panic disorder, because there were not enough new cases of panic disorder to analyze this number of antecedent variables. The dependent variable in the table is the panic attack meeting DIS criteria of severity, as explained earlier and included in Figure 2–1. The risk factors for panic disorder are similar to those for panic attack, as suggested by the comparisons of symptomatology presented in Figure 2–1 and by our own examination of the limited data on panic disorder (Keyl & Eaton, 1990). The top half of the table shows relative odds for developing panic attacks for each sociodemographic group as compared to a reference category (which has relative odds of 1.00), adjusted for all other sociodemographic variables. Relative odds are highest for the group aged 30 to 44, and for females, as suggested in Figure 2–3. Whites have the highest rates, as suggested by the comparisons of lifetime prevalence in Table 2–2. Higher occupational prestige appears to be protective.

The bottom half of Table 2–3 shows relative odds for developing a severe panic attack, for those with and without certain types of somatic and psychopathologic symptomatology at the first interview. Here the relative odds are adjusted for sociodemographic variables in the top half of the table but not for other indicators of psychopathology. A history of cardiac symptoms was examined because of the possible relation between such cardiovascular conditions as mitral valve prolapse and panic disorder (Crowe, Pauls, & Kerber, 1981; Liberthson, Sheehan, King, & Weyman, 1986); and because of the cardiovascular nature of some of the symptoms that accompany a panic attack. A history of cardiac symptoms was considered to be present at the first interview if a history of chest pain, palpitations, or shortness of breath was reported during questions concerned with somatization disorder. A history of shortness of breath also was examined alone, because there is a growing interest in the role of carbon dioxide in provoking panic attacks. (See Chapter this volume.) The DIS/DSM-III diagnosis of major depressive disorder was examined as a risk factor because of the controversy concerning the distinction between anxiety and depression (Eaton & Ritter, 1988). People who met the criteria for diagnosis of depression but for whom the episode was triggered by grief were included since the depressive reaction itself, regardless of cause, might trigger the onset of panic attacks. The DIS/DSM-III diagnosis of drug abuse or dependence was included because of findings suggesting that drugs, especially marijuana and cocaine, have strong stimulant effects on the heart (Anthony, Tien, &

Petronis, 1989). The DIS/DSM-III diagnosis of alcohol abuse or dependence was included because alcohol has such a pervasive effect on health in general. The occurrence of a seizure or convulsion since 12 years of age was included because of the possible relation of panic attacks and epilepsy (Harper & Roth, 1962). The wording of the question about seizures included the definition "where you were unconscious but your body jerked."

These six factors all had strong associations with the onset of severe, unexplained panic attacks. A lifetime history of depression or a major grief episode was the strongest of the risk factors, with adjusted relative odds of 4.24. The 95 percent confidence intervals exclude the value of 1.00 for five of the six variables, with the exception of seizures. Elsewhere (Keyl & Eaton, 1990) we have shown that a history of seizures does have a strong and statistically significant predictive relationship to panic attacks, but only those accompanied by a specific subset of psychological symptoms, such as feelings of unreality and fear of acting crazy. The predictive power of cardiac symptoms, shortness of breath, depression, and drug abuse are all consistent with an etiology of panic involving the locus coeruleus (e.g., Gorman, Liebowitz, Fyer, & Stein, 1989), but the predictive power of a history of seizures is more difficult to relate to this possible etiology.

COURSE AND SEQUELAE

The natural history of panic attacks has not been described in the literature with appropriate data from population-based samples. The ECA period of follow-up was only one year long—not long enough to obtain a very clear picture of natural history. The comparison of symptom profiles of incident with prevalent cases of panic disorder gives some insight into the course, however. The line in Figure 2–1 labeled "incident disorder" shows the percentages experiencing the symptoms, among those who met criteria for disorder for the first time in their lives during the year between waves of interviews. The profile is very similar to that for prevalent cases of panic disorder. This indirect evidence suggests that, at a population level, the course is relatively stable, once criteria for disorder are met.

Several sequelae of panic attacks have been studied (Anthony & Petronis, 1991; Eaton & Keyl, 1990; Weissman et al., 1989). In Table 2–4 the annual rates of agoraphobia, suicide attempts, suicide ideation,

TABLE 2–4
Annual Rates Per 100 of Sequelae for Individuals with Anxiety Symptoms
Five ECA Sites

	Agoraphobia	Suicide Attempt	Suicide Ideation	Depression or Grief Episode	Drug Abuse or Dependence	Alcohol Abuse or Dependence
Panic disorder	21.4	6.8	13.8	22.9	5.5	7.3
Severe, unexplained panic attacks	9.6	3.4	12.2	16.5	2.3	5.2
Other panic attacks	4.2	2.7	6.1	13.6	3.5	6.0
Nervous person	3.7	1.0	7.7	9.9	2.2	3.6
None of the above	1.5	0.5	3.1	3.8	1.3	3.6

depression or grief episode, drug abuse or dependence, and alcohol abuse or dependence are presented for five separate groups. The groups are defined by responses to DIS questions at wave 1 of the ECA survey in the following manner: (1) those meeting criteria for panic disorder; (2) those having severe, unexplained panic attacks, as described earlier, but not meeting criteria for panic disorder; (3) those having panic attacks not meeting DIS criteria of severity, as described earlier, and also not fitting into groups 1 or 2; (4) those who have never had a panic attack but who report they are a "nervous person"; and (5) those who have never had a panic attack and who do not report they are nervous people. The question on "nervous person" was affirmed by over 25 percent of the respondents and is the most sensitive measure of general anxiety in the DIS (Eaton et al., 1991). The group definitions thus span a continuum of severity of anxiety from panic disorder to few or no symptoms of anxiety.

For each of the sequelae examined, annual rates are highest for individuals with panic disorder and lowest for individuals who had neither experienced a panic attack nor described themselves as nervous people. (See Table 2–4.) Except for drug abuse or dependence and alcohol abuse or dependence, rates for sequelae were lower for individuals with severe, unexplained panic attacks than for those with panic disorder, and lower for those with other panic attacks than for those with severe, unexplained panic attacks. For drug or alcohol abuse or dependence, rates were higher for those with other panic disorder than for those with severe, unexplained panic attacks, but both rates were lower than the rate for those with panic disorder.

Depression is the most frequently experienced of the sequelae examined, and agoraphobia and suicide ideation are the next most frequently sequelae experienced. (See Chapter 5.) For individuals with panic disorder, the annual rates for depression are 22.9 per 100 individuals; rates of agoraphobia are 21.4 per 100 individuals; and rates of suicide ideation are 13.8 per 100 individuals. Thus individuals with panic disorder have a fairly high probability of requiring care for additional health problems. The relative risk for a specific sequelae can be calculated from the data in Table 2–4 for any two categories. For example, the relative risk for depression in the next 12 months for individuals with panic disorder, compared to individuals with neither panic nor a history of nervousness, is the ratio of the rates for the categories (i.e., 22.9/3.8, or 6.03 percent). For individuals with panic disorder, compared to those who had neither experienced a panic attack nor described themselves as nervous people, the sequelae with the largest relative risk are agoraphobia (relative risk of 14.3 percent) and suicide attempt (relative risk of 13.6 percent). Thus, although depression is the most frequently observed consequence of panic, it is more frequent in the general population, and the power of panic in predicting other, rarer sequelae is greater.

The antecedents and consequences of panic, as displayed in Tables 2–3 and 2–4, reveal considerable comorbidity with other types of psychopathology. Although the occurrence of panic is a relatively time-limited event, the other types of psychopathology wax and wane much more slowly, over months and years; and panic disorder, even if due only to operational criteria established in the DSM-III, had duration of at least three weeks. The limitation of the ECA follow-up period to only one year compromises our ability to distinguish cause and effect, when the psychopathologies under study have such elongated ebb and flow.

CONCLUSION

Panic attacks are widely distributed in the population, and the epidemiologic pattern of higher morbidity in females and in young adults is established. The comorbidity of panic with other types of psychopathology, along with the accelerated understanding of its biological aspects, suggests research in panic may yield widely beneficial results. Epidemiologic research on panic lacks information about natural course. Improved knowledge of the course of panic will be synergistic with improved knowledge of biology and comorbidity, with the potential for prevention of panic and other disorders.

REFERENCES

American Psychiatric Association. (1980). *Diagnostic and statistical manual of mental disorders* (3rd ed.). Washington, DC: Author.

Anthony, J. C., & Petronis, K. R. (1991). *Archives of General Psychiatry, 48,* 1114.

Anthony, J. C., Tien, A. Y., & Petronis, K. R. (1989). Epidemiologic evidence on cocaine use and panic attacks. *American Journal of Epidemiology, 129,* 543–549.

Crowe, R. R., Pauls, D. L., & Kerber, R. E. (1981). Panic disorder and mitral valve prolapse. In D. F. Klein & J. G. Rabkin (Eds.), *Anxiety: New research and changing concepts* (pp. 103–114). New York: Raven Press.

Eaton, W. W., Dryman, A., & Weissman, M. M. (1991). Panic and phobia. In L. Robins & D. A. Regier (Eds.), *Psychiatric disorders in America* (pp. 155–179). New York: Free Press.

Eaton, W. W., & Garrison, R. (1992). Mental health in Mariel Cubans and Haitian boat people. *International Migration Review, 26,* 1395–1415.

Eaton, W. W., & Keyl, P. (1990). Risk factors for the onset of Diagnostic Interview Schedule/DSM-III Agoraphobia in a prospective, population-based study. *Archives of General Psychiatry, 47,* 819–824.

Eaton, W. W., & Kessler, L. G. (Eds.). (1985). *Epidemiologic field methods in psychiatry: The NIMH Epidemiologic Catchment Area Program.* New York: Academic Press.

Eaton, W. W., Kessler, R. C., Wittchen, H. U., & Magee, W. J. (1994). Panic and panic disorder in the United States. *American Journal of Psychiatry, 151,* 413–420.

Eaton, W. W., Kramer, M., Anthony, J. C., Dryman, A., Shapiro, S., & Locke, B. Z. (1989). The incidence of specific DIS/DSM-III mental disorders: Data from the NIMH Epidemiologic Catchment Area Program. *Acta Psychiatrica Scandinavica, 79,* 163–178.

Eaton, W. W., Regier, D. A., Locke, B. Z., & Taube, C. A. (1981). The Epidemiologic Catchment Area Program of the National Institute of Mental Health. *Public Health Reports, 96,* 319–325.

Eaton, W. W., & Ritter, C. (1988). Distinguishing anxiety and depression with field survey data. *Psychological Medicine, 18,* 155–166.

Gorman, J. M., Liebowitz, M. R., Fyer, A. J., & Stein, J. (1989). A neuroanatomical hypothesis for panic disorder. *American Journal of Psychiatry, 146,* 148–161.

Harper, M., & Roth, M. (1962). Temporal lobe epilepsy and the phobic anxiety-depersonalization syndrome. Part I: A comparative study. *Comprehensive Psychiatry, 3,* 129–151.

Katerndahl, D. A., & Realini, J. P. (1993). Lifetime prevalence of panic states. *American Journal of Psychiatry, 150,* 246–249.

Kessler, R. C., McGonagle, K. A., Zhao, S., Nelson, C. B., Hughes, M., Eshleman, S., Wittchen, H-U., & Kendler, K. S. (1994). Lifetime and 12-month prevalence of DSM-III-R psychiatric disorders in the United States: Results from the National Comorbidity Survey. *Archives of General Psychiatry, 51,* 8–19.

Keyl, P. M., & Eaton, W. W. (1990). Risk factors for the onset of panic disorder and other panic attacks in a prospective, population-based study. *American Journal of Epidemiology, 131,* 301–311.

Liberthson, R. R., Sheehan, D. V., King, M. E., & Weyman, A. E. (1986). The prevalence of mitral valve prolapse in patients with panic disorders. *American Journal of Psychiatry, 143,* 511–515.

Marks, I. M. (1987). *Fears, phobias, and rituals: Panic, anxiety, and their disorders.* New York: Oxford University Press.

Robins, L. N., Helzer, J. E., Orvaschel, H., Anthony, J. C., Blazer, D. G., Burnam, A., & Burke, J. D. (1985). The Diagnostic Interview Schedule. In W. W. Eaton & L. G. Kessler (Eds.), *Epidemiologic field methods in psychiatry: The NIMH Epidemiologic Catchment Area Program* (pp. 143–170). New York: Academic Press.

Von Korff, M. R., Eaton, W. W., & Keyl, P. M. (1985). The epidemiology of panic attacks and panic disorder: Results of three community surveys. *American Journal of Epidemiology, 122,* 970–981.

Weissman, M. M., Klerman, G. L., Markowitz, J. S., Ouellette, R., & Phil, M. (1989). Suicidal ideation and suicide attempts in panic disorder and attacks. *New England Journal of Medicine, 321,* 1209–1214.

Weissman, M. M., Myers, J. K., & Harding, P. S. (1978). Psychiatric disorders in a US urban community. *American Journal of Psychiatry, 135,* 459–462.

Wittchen, H-U, Robins, L. N., Cottler, L. B., Sartorius, N., Burke, J. D., Regier, D. A., and participants in the Multicentre WHO/ADAMHA Field Trials. (1991). Cross-cultural feasibility, reliability and sources of variance of the Composite International Diagnostic Interview (CIDI). *British Journal of Psychiatry, 159,* 645–653.

3

The Genetics of Panic Disorder

CATHERINE L. WOODMAN AND
RAYMOND R. CROWE

The role of heredity in panic disorder has been recognized for over a century. Since Da Costa's description of "irritable heart" in 1871, various authors have commented on the familial clustering of neurasthenia, neurocirculatory asthenia, effort syndrome, and anxiety neurosis, each of which significantly overlaps with panic disorder. Genetics research in psychiatry traditionally has taken an epidemiological approach because disease mechanisms at a molecular level have been poorly understood and few biological markers have been available. Family studies have reported data on the rates of anxiety disorders in family members as well as on the patterns of transmission of illness. Twin studies have helped determine the extent to which the familial clustering is genetic. Transmission models have been employed to investigate the mechanisms underlying the familial transmission of panic disorder. Recently, with the rapid evolution in molecular genetics, linkage studies have been used as well. This chapter reviews the relevant strategies in genetic research as they have been applied to panic disorder.

EPIDEMIOLOGY

Panic disorder is characterized by recurrent, spontaneous panic attacks that last from minutes to hours. The frequency of attacks varies widely and ranges from several attacks daily to a few attacks per year. The lifetime prevalence of panic disorder is estimated from 1 to 5 percent, with twice as many women as men affected. The attacks typically begin in the third decade. Studies have found an average age of onset of 25 years, with a standard deviation of about 10 years (Noyes, 1988; Weissman, Merikangas, Wickrematne, Prussoff, & Kidd, 1986). In addition to uncomplicated panic disorder, agoraphobia is now considered to be a form of panic disorder in which the panic attacks have produced phobic avoidance and the phobias have become the predominant feature of the illness. Also, evidence from some family studies suggest that persons who suffer from panic attacks that do not meet criteria from the third revised edition of the *Diagnostic and Statistical Manual of Mental Disorders* (DSM-III-R) for panic disorder because of limited symptoms or infrequent attacks should be classified as panic disorder. (See Chapter 2 for an extended review.)

FAMILY STUDIES

Family studies can provide evidence of familial aggregation of a particular condition although they cannot establish that an illness is hereditary. If a disorder is familial, the prevalence of the condition is higher among relatives of the index case than among those of controls. Ideally, the distribution of a disorder within the family would be consistent with a known genetic condition, but this has not been the case with psychiatric illness.

The results of nine family history studies and four family studies of patients with panic disorder are presented in Tables 3–1 and 3–2 (Brown, 1942; Cloninger, Martin, Clayton, & Guze, 1981; Cohen, Badal, Kilpatrick, Reed, & White, 1951; Crowe, Noyes, Pauls, & Slymen, 1983; Hopper, Judd, Derrick, & Burrows, 1987; McInnes, 1937; Mendlewicz, Papadimitriou, & Wilmotte, 1993; Moran & Andrews, 1985; Noyes, Clancy, Crowe, Hoenk, & Slymen, 1978; Noyes et al., 1986; Oppenheimer & Rothchild, 1918; Wheeler, White, Reed, & Cohen, 1948; Wood, 1941). Early studies were done with anxiety neurosis patients, and family history data was collected by interviewing the proband rather than by interviewing family members individually. The percentage of families of patients with panic disorder with an affected relative ranged from 28 to 67 percent (mean = 50 percent) compared to 10 to 38 percent (mean = 20 percent) for control families. In the family studies,

TABLE 3–1
Data from Family History Studies of Panic Disorder

Author	Probands	% Families Affected		% Relatives Affected	
		Anxiety	Control	Anxiety	Control
Oppenheimer & Rothchild (1918)[b]	Anxiety neurosis	56	38	—	—
McInnes (1937)[a]	Anxiety neurosis	28	18	14	12
Wood (1941)[a]	Anxiety neurosis	25–42	—	—	—
Brown (1942)[a]	Anxiety neurosis	—	—	15	5
Cohen et al. (1951)[a]	Anxiety neurosis	67	12	35	1
Noyes et al. (1978)[a]	Anxiety neurosis	—	—	18	3
Cloninger et al. (1981)[a]	Anxiety neurosis	—	—	6	2
Moran & Andrews (1985)[a]	Agoraphobia	—	—	13	—
Hopper et al. (1987)[a]	Panic disorder	—	—	12	—

[a]Degree of Relationship = First.
[b]Degree of Relationship = Second.

first-degree relatives were contacted directly to obtain diagnoses. The percentage of relatives affected ranged from 13 to 49 percent (mean = 24 percent) as compared to 1 to 7 percent (mean = 4.6 percent) for families of control probands. Several studies adjusted for age, which may explain the higher percentage of affected relatives found in these studies. However, in all studies the rate of panic disorder is substantially higher than in the general population. Pauls, Noyes, and Crowe (1979) reported that the rate of panic disorder in second degree relatives is 9.8 percent, which is roughly half the rate among first-degree relatives and twice the rate seen in the general population. Studies that have reported on the transmission of panic disorder from one generation to the next have found that the risk to first-degree relatives is greatest when both parents have anxiety neurosis and least when neither have it.

TABLE 3–2
Data from Family Studies of Panic Disorder

Study	Probands	% Relatives Affected	
		Anxiety	Control
Wheeler et al. (1948)	Anxiety neurosis	49	6
Crowe et al. (1983)	Panic disorder	25	2
Noyes et al. (1986)	Panic disorder	16	7
	Agoraphobia	17	7
Mendlewicz et al. (1993)	Panic disorder	13	1

TABLE 3–3
Sex-Specific Rates of Panic Disorder in Family Studies

	Prevalence in Relatives (%)	
Study	Males	Females
Cohen et al. (1951)	12	20
Pauls et al. (1979)	5	14
Cloninger et al. (1981)	2	13
Crowe et al. (1983)	17	33
Noyes et al. (1986)	13	24

Panic disorder occurs twice as frequently in women as in men. Table 3–3 presents the results of five family studies that look at the sex-specific rates (Cloninger et al., 1981; Cohen et al., 1951; Crowe et al., 1983; Noyes et al., 1978; Pauls et al., 1979). The percentage of affected female relatives of panic disorder probands ranged from 13 to 33 percent (mean = 17 percent) compared to the percentage of affected male relatives, which ranged from 2 to 17 percent (mean = 9 percent).

Since agoraphobia is considered to be a form of panic disorder, Noyes and associates (1986) conducted a family study of agoraphobia and panic disorder. In families of agoraphobics, 7 percent of relatives were affected with panic disorder and 9.4 percent with agoraphobia. In families of panic disorder patients, 14.9 percent of relatives were affected with panic disorder and 1.7 percent affected with agoraphobia. The figures for control families were 3.5 percent for each diagnosis. In families of panic disorder probands, 17 percent were affected with a form of panic disorder; in families of agoraphobic probands, 16 percent of relatives were affected. The rates of illness were almost identical, but the agoraphobic form of the illness was limited almost entirely to the families of agoraphobics.

The family studies of panic disorder probands demonstrate a substantial familial predisposition to panic disorder, but this information cannot establish that the illness is hereditary because familial aggregation also may reflect a shared environment. However, family studies do suggest that panic disorder is likely to have a genetic basis.

TWIN STUDIES

Monozygotic (MZ) twins share 100 percent of their genes, while dizygotic (DZ) twins share an average of 50 percent and, therefore, are genetically equivalent to their siblings. This difference makes twins a particularly powerful natural experiment with which to separate genetic and environmental contributions to disease liability. MZ concordance rates that exceed DZ rates implicate genetic risk factors, and MZ concordance rates less than 100 percent implicate environmental factors as well. More quantitatively, the total variance in disease risk can be partitioned into genetic and environmental components, and the latter can be further partitioned into shared and special environment. Shared environment is common to both members of the twin pair, such as the family environment in which they were reared. Special environment represents the unique experiences of each member of the pair. A depressed parent would be a shared environment; a depressed college roommate would be a special environment. By partitioning the disease liability into its respective components, the relative magnitude of each component can be estimated.

Slater and Shields (1969) studied 17 MZ and 28 DZ twins with anxiety neurosis, a diagnosis that overlaps with the modern concept of panic disorder. They reported a MZ concordance rate of 41 percent compared to a DZ concordance rate of 4 percent. Torgersen (1983) identified 13 MZ and 16 DZ twins with panic disorder from a nationwide survey of adult same-sex twins, at least one of whom had been treated for psychiatric illness, in Norway. He reported a MZ concordance rate of 31 percent and a DZ concordance rate of 0 percent. The MZ concordance rate for all anxiety disorders was 46 percent, and the DZ rate was 25 percent. Kendler, Neale, Kessler, Heath, and Eaves (1993) interviewed both members of a population sample of 1,033 female-female twin pairs in Virginia and have published the results of the panic disorder diagnoses. They diagnosed the twins using clinician ratings as well as computer algorithms, and used a broad and a narrow concept of panic disorder with each method. The narrow diagnoses all met DSM-III-R criteria for panic disorder. Only the narrow, clinician-rated diagnoses are considered here, to make the results more comparable to the other twin studies. The concordance rates were 23.9 percent for MZ and 10.9 percent for DZ pairs. Although the MZ/DZ ratio of 2.2 was small, the difference was statistically significant and supported a genetic predisposition to panic disorder.

All three twin studies are in agreement that genes make a modest contribution to the liability to panic disorder, and since the MZ concordance rates are considerably less than 100 percent, the environment makes a substantial contribution as well. Kendler and associates (1993) looked at the relative contributions and found that a model composed of genes and special environment accounted for the results best. Each component accounted for approximately 50 percent of the variance. It is interesting to note that no evidence for the influence of shared environment was found. These results argue against learning theories based on shared environment, such as modeling, and suggest that whatever the environmental risk factors are, they are extrafamilial experiences.

The twin data were further analyzed with a multiple threshold model that assumed that panic disorder with agoraphobia is a more severe variant of panic disorder and requires a greater load of genetic and/or environmental risk factors to develop. The results were compatible with the hypothesis and estimated a heritability of 34 percent. This is consistent with a genetic explanation for panic disorder but suggests that the genetic contribution is modest.

Taken as a whole, the twin studies speak for a modest genetic predisposition to panic disorder, accounting for approximately half of the variance. How do these results compare with the results of family studies, which indicate a substantial familial recurrence risk? One possible explanation is that the family studies were selected from more severely affected populations of patients. Since these studies all have been drawn from patient populations, this is a reasonable hypothesis. However, the Slater and Shields and Torgersen twins also were drawn from patient populations, and if severity correlated with heritability, they should have greater concordance rates and MZ/DZ ratios than the Kendler sample, which is a population sample. While the trends are in that direction, the similarities in the results of the three studies are greater than their differences.

MODE OF INHERITANCE

For the sake of simplicity, modes of inheritance are usually thought of as monogenic and polygenic. Monogenic inheritance is characterized by Medelian transmission, although incomplete penetrance and variable expression of the disease gene can cause considerable variation in the classical patterns. Polygenic inheritance is typically quantitative, being caused by multiple genes, each of small, equal, and additive effect. However, polygenic inheritance can cause discrete traits, such as disease, if a dosage effect is required for the trait to appear. Thus, the genes contribute to a liability that is dichotomized by a threshold effect into affected and unaffected phenotypes.

In pure form, Mendelian inheritance is easy to recognize and distinguish from polygenic transmission. However, variations in the expression of the disease gene can make this distinction difficult in many cases. To address this problem, computer programs have been developed to determine mathematically which genetic model best fits the observed data. Thus, one can model a mechanism (e.g., single vs. multiple genes) and complicating parameters, such as incomplete penetrance. Each model generates expected probabilities of being affected, which can then be compared with the observed data and tested with a statistic for goodness of fit. Models can be tested against each other, and the best-fitting model can be identified in this way.

One of the first models proposed that with polygenic inheritance the ancestral pairs of affected relatives would be unilateral (both members of the pair would be on either the maternal or the paternal side of the family) twice as frequently as bilateral (one on each paternal side), and that the appearance of unilateral pairs in excess of the predicted ratio would be evidence for single-gene transmission. Pauls and associates (1979) used this model to evaluate 14 panic disorder pedigrees. They found 37 of the 41 ancestral pairs to be unilateral (90 percent), which represented a significant excess of unilateral pairs over the expected 2:1 ratio. They interpreted their results as suggesting monogenic transmission of panic disorder.

Segregation analysis is a more rigorous way of determining the mode of inheritance because it uses the entire distribution of affected individuals within the pedigree. Pauls, Bucher, Crowe, and Noyes (1980) also performed a segregation analysis on 19 pedigrees, from which the 14 used in the ancestral pairs analysis were drawn. This analysis was limited to single-locus models, and therefore, the polygenic model was not tested. The results (Table 3–4) predicted a disease gene frequency of 0.014 with a penetrance of 0.75 (75 percent of persons who are either homozygous or heterozygous for the gene will express it) and an average age of onset of 22 years. The model predicted that 2.8 percent of the population would carry the gene, with a maximum, age-dependent penetrance of 75 percent, approximately 2 percent would be affected. This last prediction is close to the 3.5 percent rate found in the National Comorbidity Survey and suggests that the pedigrees analyzed were representative of panic disorder in the population (Eaton, Kessler, Wittchen, & Magee, 1994).

TABLE 3–4
Genetic Models of Panic Disorder

Study	Model	Gene Frequency	Penetrance	Populations Prevelance
Pauls et al. (1980)	Dominant	.014	.70	2.1
Crowe et al. (1983)	Dominant	.05	.36	3.5
Vieland et al. (1993)	Dominant	.01	.50	2.0
Vieland et al. (1993)	Recessive	.20	.70	4.0

A characteristic feature of panic disorder is a sex distribution with twice as many women affected as men (Eaton et al., 1994). This feature was modeled in a multiple threshold analysis of family study data (Crowe et al., 1983). The analysis models women as having a lower threshold for symptoms regardless of whether the inheritance is single-locus or polygenic. The results of the single-locus analysis predicted a relatively common gene with a frequency of 5 percent, accounting for a female disease prevalence of 4.5 percent and a male prevalence of 2.5 percent. A polygenic model with sex thresholds also fit the data, but it predicted an unacceptably high population prevalence of 17 percent in women and 9 percent in men.

Vieland, Hodge, Lish, Adams, and Weissman (1993) performed a segregation analysis of 30 two- and three-generation pedigrees. They found that either a dominant gene or a recessive model could explain the transmission. The dominant model predicted a disease gene frequency of 1 percent with a penetrance of 50 percent, resulting in a 2 percent population prevalence. The recessive model predicted a disease frequency of 20 percent with a penetrance of 70 percent, resulting in a 4 percent population prevalence.

One of the uses of genetic modeling is to determine which mechanisms of inheritance might explain the familial transmission of a disease. This information is useful in planning further genetic studies, such as searches for a disease gene. A limitation of modeling is that, while it can identify the most likely genetic hypothesis, it cannot prove that the hypothesis is correct. Thus, modeling is by nature exploratory and not confirmatory. Confirmation of genetic hypotheses requires proof at the genetic level. If disease vulnerability genes can be found and the DNA sequence responsible for the vulnerability clarified, the mechanisms responsible for the disease can be worked out.

LINKAGE STUDIES OF PANIC DISORDER

Genes are found with linkage by searching for transmission of disease in conjunction with one of the alleles at a marker locus within families. While joint transmission of the two could be a chance event, a statistically significant excess over the null hypothesis of random assortment is evidence that the two are physically linked on the chromosome. Dense marker maps of the humane genome permit systematic searches for linkage to disease genes. Once linkage is found, candidate genes in the linked region of the genome can be searched for disease mutations. If the search is successful, it would hold the promise of uncovering the causes of the disease through studying the gene, improved diagnosis based on DNA testing, and the possibility of better treatment.

Several efforts to search the genome in panic disorder are under way, and the interim results of one have been published (Crowe, 1994). Fourteen panic disorder pedigrees were studied with approximately 150 restriction fragment-length polymorphisms (RFLPS). Definite or probable DSM-III panic disorder or agoraphobia with panic attacks was considered to be the affected state (APA, 1980). Probable cases were individuals with spontaneous panic attacks that failed to meet the DSM-III criteria of attack frequency or symptom number. Linkage was tested assuming a dominant gene as predicted by the analysis of Pauls and coworkers (1980). No evidence of linkage was found in the 29 percent of the genome that was tested by this set of markers. The rapid development of highly informative human linkage maps will make it possible in a few years to determine whether a gene accounts for the majority of cases of familial panic disorder.

If linkage cannot be found through a systematic genome search, an alternative approach would be to study selected genes that are candidates for the etiology of panic disorder. Examples of candidate genes include those involved in the norepinephrine and gamma-aminobutyric acid (GABA) pathways, since both systems are capable of modulating the symptoms of panic attacks. This strategy is exemplified by a study of the norepinephrine system of panic disorder.

A large family of adrenergic receptors has been characterized; two major subtypes are alpha- and beta-adrenoceptors, with each major subtype having a number of additional subtypes. In addition, tyrosine hydroxylase is the rate-limiting enzyme in the biosynthesis of norepinephrine. Tyrosine hydroxylase and the alpha-1, alpha-2, beta-1, and beta-2 adrenergic receptor loci were examined in panic disorder and found to not be linked to the disease in 14 pedigrees (Mutchler, Crowe, Noyes, & Wesner, 1990; Wang, Crowe, & Noyes, 1992). Although these findings argue against gene mutations in the system causing panic disorder, they do not exclude a different neurotransmitter system as the etiological basis for panic disorder, dysfunctions in gene expression, or defects in second messenger systems.

PANIC DISORDER COMORBIDITY

Epidemiological and clinical studies have shown that individuals with panic disorder have an increased risk for other psychiatric illnesses over their lifetime. Patients with panic disorder have a fourfold increased risk of alcohol abuse as compared to the general population. Several family studies have found an increased risk for alcoholism among the relatives of panic disorder probands, with the greatest risk among male relatives (Cohen et al., 1951; Crowe et al., 1983; Noyes et al., 1986). It is not known whether alcoholism is secondary to the anxiety disorder, masking an anxiety disorder, or independent of the anxiety disorder.

Patients with a history of major depression have an 18-fold increased risk of panic disorder when compared to the general population. The frequent coexistence of panic disorder and major depression has raised questions about the diagnostic homogeneity of the two disorders. If panic disorder and depression are unrelated disorders occurring in the same individual, then relatives of probands with both disorders should exhibit panic disorder at a rate comparable to relatives of probands with panic disorder alone. If the two disorders are different manifestations of the same illness, and patients who have panic disorder and depression are more severely ill, then they should have an increased number of affected relatives as compared to relatives of either depressed or panic disorder probands. If a mixture of panic disorder and depressive symptoms represents a third illness, then relatives of these patients should exhibit the mixed illness rather than depression or panic disorder alone. If depression is secondary to panic disorder, then relatives of patients with panic disorder and depression will have an increase in panic disorder but not depression.

Five family studies have looked at the coexistence of panic disorder and depression (Coryell et al., 1988; Leckman, Weissman, Merikangas, Pauls, & Prusoff, 1983; Mendlewicz et al., 1993; Noyes et al., 1986;

Weissman et al., 1993). All studies have found that when depression complicates panic disorder, an increased number of relatives have panic disorder. Leckman and associates (1983) and Coryell and coworkers (1988) found that the relatives of patients with depression complicated by panic attacks had a greater number of relatives with depression than did relatives of patients with uncomplicated depression, but Weissman and associates (1993) and Mendlewicz and coworkers (1993) failed to find this. Family studies of panic disorder probands have not found an increased rate of primary affective disorder in first-degree relatives, but Noyes and associates (1986) did find an increased rate of secondary depression in family members.

Weissman, Leckman, Merikangas, Gammon, and Prusoff (1984) studied the children of depressed patients with and without anxiety disorders. They found that depression in a parent increased the child's risk of both anxiety disorders and depression. Panic disorder in the parent conferred a more than threefold risk of separation anxiety in the child.

Kendler, Heath, Martin, and Eaves (1986, 1987) analyzed twin data from Australia and found that there was an association between symptoms of anxiety and symptoms of depression that was not accounted for by environmental factors alone. They concluded, therefore, that genetic factors must play a role. Unfortunately, data for this study were collected via self-report instruments that the subjects mailed to the investigators, and psychiatric diagnoses of the subjects were not known.

These studies suggest a relationship between panic disorder and depression that may be familial. Family studies support a distinction between panic disorder and depression, and when depression co-occurs in patients with panic disorder, it may be secondary to the panic disorder. The genetic nature of the relationship is not known. (See Chapter 4 for an extended review.)

CLINICAL IMPLICATIONS

A working knowledge of the current issues and advances in genetics can be useful to the clinician. Psychiatrists need to be aware of the familial recurrence risks and likely modes of transmission of the disorder. This information can be useful in arriving at a working diagnosis in patients who do not meet criteria for a definitive DSM-IV (fourth edition) diagnosis as well as in those cases where the difference between panic disorder and another illness is difficult. While few patients will be interested in genetic counseling in the usual sense of that term, many do wonder how likely their children are to develop the disorder and whether anything can be done to prevent it. A candid discussion of the familial nature of the illness as well as the wide range in age of onset, types of symptoms, and severity can be helpful to these individuals. With this knowledge they can recognize symptoms early in their children, and by recognizing that panic disorder and agoraphobia are treatable illnesses, arrange for appropriate evaluation and treatment.

REFERENCES

American Psychiatric Association (1980). *Diagnostic and statistical manual of mental disorders* (3rd ed.). Washington, DC: Author.

Brown, F. W. (1942). Heredity in psychoneurosis. *Proceedings of the Royal Society of Medicine, 35,* 785–790.

Cloninger, R. L., Martin, R. N., Clayton, P., & Guze, S. B. (1981). A blind follow-up study and family study of anxiety neurosis: Preliminary analysis of the St. Louis 500. In D. F. Klein & J. Rabkin (Eds.), *Anxiety: New Research and Changing Concepts* (pp. 137–148). New York: Raven Press.

Cohen, E. W., Badal, D. W., Kilpatrick, A., Reed, E. W., & White, P. D. (1951). The high familial prevalence of neurocirculatory asthenia (anxiety neurosis, effort syndrome). *American Journal of Human Genetics, 3,* 126–158.

Coryell, W., Endicott, J., Andreason, N. C., Keller, M. B., Clayton, P. J., & Hirshfeld, R. M. A. (1988). Depression and panic attacks: The significance of overlap as reflected in follow-up and family study data. *American Journal of Psychiatry, 145,* 293–300.

Crowe, R. R. (1994). The Iowa Linkage study of panic disorder. In *Genetic approaches to mental disorders* (pp. 291–309). Washington, DC: American Psychiatric Press.

Crowe, R., Noyes, R., Jr., Pauls, D. L., & Sylmen, D. (1983). A family study of panic disorder. *Archives of General Psychiatry, 40,* 1065–1069.

Eaton, W. W., Kessler, R. C., Wittchen, H. U., & Magee, W. J. (1994). Panic and panic disorder in the United States. *American Journal of Psychiatry, 151,* 413–420.

Hopper, J. L., Judd, F. K., Derrick, P. L., & Burrows, G. D. (1987). A family study of panic disorder. *Genetic Epidemiology, 4,* 33–41.

Kendler, K. S., Heath, A., Martin, N. G., & Eaves, L. J. (1986). Symptoms of anxiety and depression in a volunteer twin population—the etiologic role of genetic and environmental factors. *Archives of General Psychiatry, 43,* 213–221.

Kendler, K. S., Heath, A., Martin, N. G., & Eaves, L. J. (1987). Symptoms of anxiety and symptoms of depression—same genes, different environment? *Archives of General Psychiatry, 44,* 451–457.

Kendler, K. S., Neale, M., Kessler, R., Heath, A., & Eaves, L. J. (1993). A population-based twin study of panic disorder in women. *Psychological Medicine, 23,* 397–406.

Leckman, J. F., Weissman, M. M., Merikangas, K. R., Pauls, D. L., & Prusoff, B. A. (1983). Panic disorder and major depression: Increased risk of depression, alcoholism, panic, and phobic disorder in families with depressed probands with panic disorder. *Archives of General Psychiatry, 40,* 1055–1060.

McInnes, R. (1937). Observations on heredity in neurosis. *Proceedings of the Royal Society of Medicine, 30,* 895–904.

Mendlewicz, J., Papadimitriou, G., & Wilmotte, J. (1993). Family study of panic disorder: Comparison with generalized anxiety disorder, major depression, and normal subjects. *Psychiatric Genetics, 3,* 73–78.

Moran, C., & Andrews, G. (1985). The familial occurrence of agoraphobia. *British Journal of Psychiatry, 146,* 262–267.

Mutchler, K., Crowe, R. R., Noyes, R., Jr., & Wesner, R. W. (1990). Exclusion of the tyrosine hydroxylase gene in 14 panic disorder pedigree. *American Journal of Psychiatry, 147,* 1367–1369.

Noyes, R., Jr. (1988). The natural history of anxiety disorders. In R. Noyes, M. Roth, R. Noyes, Jr. (Eds.), *Handbook of Anxiety* (pp. 115–133). Amsterdam: Elsevier.

Noyes, R., Jr., Clancy, J., Crowe, R., Hoenk, P. R., & Slymen, D. J. (1978). The familial prevalence of anxiety neurosis. *Archives of General Psychiatry, 35,* 1057–1059.

Noyes, R., Jr., Crowe, R. R., Harris, E. L., Hampa, B. J., McChesney, C. M., & Chaudhry, D. R. (1986). Relationship between panic disorder and agoraphobia: A family study. *Archives of General Psychiatry, 43,* 227–232.

Oppenheimer, B. J., & Rothchild, M. A. (1918). The psychoneurotic factor in the irritable heart of soldiers. *Journal of the American Medical Association, 70,* 1919–1922.

Pauls, D. L., Bucher, K. D., Crowe, R. R., & Noyes, R., Jr. (1980). A genetic study of panic disorder pedigrees. *American Journal of Human Genetics, 32,* 639–644.

Pauls, D. L., Noyes, R., Jr., & Crowe, R. R. (1979). The prevalence in second degree relatives of patients with anxiety neurosis (panic disorder). *Journal of Affective Disorders, 1,* 279–285.

Slater, E., & Shields, J. (1969). Genetical aspects of anxiety. *British Journal of Psychiatry, 3,* 62–71.

Torgersen, S. (1983). Genetic factors in anxiety disorders. *Archives of General Psychiatry, 40,* 1085–1089.

Vieland, J. E., Hodge, S. E., Lish, J. D., Adams, P., & Weissman, M. M. (1993). Segregation analysis of panic disorder. *Psychiatric Genetics, 3,* 63–71.

Wang, Z., Crowe, R. R., & Noyes, R., Jr. (1992). Adrenergic receptor genes as candidate genes for panic disorder: a linkage study. *American Journal of Psychiatry, 149,* 470–474.

Weissman, M., Leckman, J. F., Merikangas, K. R., Gammon, G. D., & Prusoff, B. A. (1984). Depression and anxiety disorders in parents and children: Results from the Yale Family Study. *Archives of General Psychiatry, 41,* 845–852.

Weissman, M. J., Merikangas, K. R., Wickramaratne, P. N., Prusoff, B. A., & Kidd, K. K. (1986). Family-genetic studies of psychiatric disorders. *Archives of General Psychiatry, 43,* 1104–1116.

Weissman, M. M., Wickramaratne, P., Adams, P. B., Lish, J. D., Horwarth, E., Charney, D., Woods, S. W., Leeman, E., & Frosch, E. (1993). The relationship between panic disorder and major depression: A new family study. *Archives of General Psychiatry, 50,* 767–780.

Wheeler, E. D., White, P. D., Reed, E., & Cohen, M. E. (1948). Familial incidence of neurocirculatory asthenia. *Journal of Clinical Investigation, 27,* 562.

Wood, P. (1941). Aetiology of Da Costa's syndrome. *British Medical Journal, 1,* 835–841.

4

Comorbidity of Panic Disorder

SCOTT WETZLER AND
WILLIAM C. SANDERSON

Comorbidity, an underappreciated issue in psychiatry, refers to the presence of independent psychiatric disorders. In instances of comorbidity, the patient meets diagnostic criteria for more than one syndrome and is therefore assigned multiple diagnoses. These multiple diagnoses, taken together, account for the patient's entire clinical presentation, symptomatology, and course of illness.

Past classification systems, such as the third edition of the *Diagnostic and Statistical Manual of Mental Disorders* (DSM-III) (APA, 1980), impeded the identification of comorbid syndromes because they contained hierarchical exclusionary rules that, for the most part, prohibited the assignment of more than one Axis I diagnosis to a patient. In the DSM-III hierarchical system, certain diagnoses took precedence, and other diagnoses were subsumed under disorders that occupied a higher diagnostic status. When a patient presented with a heterogeneous clinical picture, all symptomatology was considered a manifestation of the principal disorder, and the patient was therefore assigned only one diagnosis. For example, since affective disorders occupied a higher position than anxiety disorders in the DSM-III, the presence of panic attacks did not require the diagnosis of panic disorder if the clinician judged that the panic attacks were "due to" major depression. Another important exclusion was the comorbid diagnosis of generalized anxiety disorder in the presence of panic disorder, because recurrent panic attacks typically are associated with intercurrent anxiety.

The hierarchical exclusion rules used in DSM-III artificially obscured the independence of anxiety disorders, including panic disorder. Since there was, in fact, no empirical evidence that anxiety disorders were secondary to depressive disorders (e.g., Sanderson, Beck, & Beck, 1990), these exclusion rules were, for the most part, dropped in the revised edition of the DSM-III (DSM-III-R), allowing clinicians to give "multiple diagnoses when different syndromes occur together in one episode of illness" (APA, 1987, page xxiv). This change in diagnostic practice was perpetuated in the fourth edition (DSM-IV). Based on the relative severity and interference with the patient's functioning, one of the multiple diagnoses is identified as the patient's "principal" disorder, although the other disorders also are accorded clinical significance. Thus, DSM-III-R and DSM-IV recognize the importance of comorbidity more fully than any prior diagnostic systems.

With the elimination of exclusion rules in DSM-III-R, panic disorder could be diagnosed in patients with other comorbid psychiatric disorders, especially patients with major depression or other anxiety disorders. Thus, comorbid panic states were for the first time fully appreciated and were no longer artifically obscured. This is noteworthy since, as will be seen, panic disorder typically is associated with other psychiatric syndromes. The one exclusion rule that remains in DSM-IV concerns panic attacks occurring in the presence of a phobic stimulus (which are more appropriately diagnosed as specific or social phobias).

In order to avoid confusion, we have suggested that an important distinction be made between the terms "principal diagnosis" and "primary diagnosis" (Sanderson, Beck, & Beck, 1990). In DSM-IV, the term "principal diagnosis" is reserved for that disorder among inpatients which is "chiefly responsible for occasioning the admission." For outpatients with multiple diagnoses, the term "reason for visit" refers to "the condition that is chiefly responsible for . . . services received during the visit. In most cases, the principal diagnosis or the reason for visit is also the main focus of attention or treatment" (APA, 1994, p. 3). We have recommended that the term "primary diagnosis" should be used for the diagnosis that chronologically preceded all other diagnoses (Sanderson et al., 1990; e.g., Cloninger, Martin, Guze, & Clayton, 1990; Starcevic, Uhlenhuth, Kellner, & Pathak, 1993). However, others use the term "primary" to refer to the relative severity of comorbid disorders (e.g., Barlow, DiNardo, Vermilyea, Vermilyea, & Blanchard, 1986; DeRuiter, Ruken, Garssen, van Schaik, & Kraaimaat, 1989).

The issues of chronology and temporal primacy are crucial for understanding patterns of comorbidity. If past psychiatric disorders (i.e., those conditions that are fully in remission now) are considered comorbid conditions, then the frequency of comorbidity would be expected to be greatly increased. Since it is difficult to obtain accurate lifetime diagnoses of psychiatric disorders, this chapter considers only those comorbid disorders that are simultaneously present. Psychiatric disorders that are primary must, therefore, continue to exhibit symptoms to be considered as a comorbid syndrome. Furthermore, a current comorbid disorder would be expected to have greater clinical significance than a past comorbid disorder.

Interestingly, when panic disorder is a comorbid disorder, the issue of temporal primacy is also quite relevant. One recent study has found that panic disorder typically appears sequentially as the secondary disorder (Starcevic et al., 1993). Further, patients with primary panic disorder have less psychopathology and phobic avoidance than do patients with secondary panic disorder (Starcevic et al., 1993).

SIGNIFICANCE OF COMORBIDITY

Patterns of comorbidity have important clinical and scientific implications, and thus it is unfortunate that prior to DSM-III-R comorbid psychiatric diagnoses were, relatively speaking, ignored. In fact, comorbid diagnoses are very common (Boyd et al., 1984). Recent studies using DSM-III (without exclusion rules) and DSM-III-R criteria have shown that a majority of outpatients seeking treatment may be diagnosed with multiple Axis I disorders (Barlow et al., 1986; DeRuiter et al., 1989; DiNardo & Barlow, 1990; Sanderson et al., 1990; Sanderson, DiNardo, Rapee, & Barlow, 1990; Wolf et al., 1988). These data are consistent with Boyd and associates (1984) initial finding that the presence of any psychiatric disorder increased the likelihood of having another disorder. It appears that when clinicians carefully evaluate patients using structured interviews, they usually uncover multiple disorders. These studies support the changes made in DSM-III-R (and continued in DSM-IV) that allow clinicians to diagnose multiple disorders to account for the full range of presenting symptomatology.

The practice of assigning a single diagnosis is, in many cases, inadequate to convey the overall level of psychopathology. By recognizing the presence of more than one disorder, clinicians are in a position to offer better, more comprehensive treatment. Conversely, by ignoring comorbid diagnoses, clinicians will offer less than optimal treatment.

The course, prognosis, and treatment response for patients with multiple psychiatric disorders have been shown to differ from that of patients with a single disorder (c.f. Fyer, Liebowitz, & Klein, 1990). Indeed, having two disorders would be expected to be worse than suffering from just one.

Patterns of comorbidity have important scientific implications as well. For example, when two disorders typically co-occur, a common etiology or a shared vulnerability that predisposes the individual to both disorders may be considered. Alternatively, the etiology of comorbid disorders may be different from the etiology of any single disorder when it presents in isolation. That is, a patient with panic disorder and major depression may have a different underlying pathology than a patient with either panic disorder or major depression alone. In particular, patterns of comorbidity might provide information concerning the genetic transmission of psychiatric illnesses.

In summary, close attention should be paid to diagnosing multiple disorders. There are good clinical and scientific reasons to do so. Once a clinician or researcher identifies one psychiatric disorder, he or she should continue the assessment to ascertain the presence of other disorders. All current evidence suggests that comorbid mental disorders are quite frequent.

FREQUENCY OF COMORBIDITY

The best estimate of the comorbidity of panic disorder may be derived from epidemiological studies. Comorbidity data from the recent Epidemiological Catchment Area study are available concerning panic disorder. In the general population, 67 percent (114 out of 171) of people with panic disorder have co-occurring major psychiatric disorders (Johnson, Weissman, & Klerman, 1990). A more skewed estimate may be obtained by examining patients who present for treatment, although this population is self-selected and may be more severe (Sanderson & Barlow, 1990).

There are two ways to calculate the frequency of comorbidity of panic disorder: by asking what the frequency of other psychological disorders is when panic disorder is the principal diagnosis and by asking what the frequency of panic disorder is when another psychological disorder is the principal diagnosis. Here "comorbidity" refers to the concurrent presence of each disorder, and past history of psychiatric disorders is disregarded.

Table 4–1 summarizes the findings for the frequency of comorbid diagnoses for patients with a principal diagnosis of panic disorder, and Table 4–2 summarizes the findings for the frequency of panic disorder as an additional diagnosis for patients with other psychological conditions. The most striking overall finding is that 59 percent (range: 46 to 83 percent) of patients with panic disorder had an additional disorder. The magnitude of this comorbidity may be appreciated by comparing it to rates of comorbidity of other anxiety and depressive disorders. For example, in the same studies, 68 percent (range: 45 to 91 percent) of generalized anxiety disorder patients (c.f. Sanderson & Wetzler, 1991), 41 percent (range: 0 to 57 percent) of simple phobic patients, and 68 percent (range: 65 to 100 percent) of major depression patients had an additional disorder. (See Table 4–2 for the rates of comorbidity for each disorder.)

The frequency of panic disorder for patients with other syndromes is presented in Table 4–2. Overall, the frequency of panic disorder as a co-morbid diagnosis was 13 percent (range: 7 to 35 percent). Although nearly all patients with anxiety disorders experience "panic attacks" (Rapee, Sanderson, McCauley, & DiNardo, 1992), panic disorder is di-agnosed as a comorbid disorder in only a minority of cases. This is be-cause the so-called panic attacks usually are cued and therefore judged to be due to the principal disorder (e.g., panic attacks cued by public speaking for a social phobic patient, panic attacks cued by an obsessive thought in an obsessive-compulsive disorder patient, or panic attacks cued by a snake in a simple phobic patient). Similarly, "panic attacks" commonly occur in the context of major depression (Coryell et al., 1988), but panic disorder is rarely diagnosed because the occurrence of these attacks does not meet the diagnostic criteria (e.g., does not meet frequency criteria of DSM-III, associated worry criteria of DSM-III-R, or persistent concern, worry about implications, or change in behavior criteria of DSM-IV).

TABLE 4-1

Comorbidity of DSM-III and DSM-III-R Disorders in Patients with a Principal Diagnosis of Panic Disorder

Study / Diagnostic Criteria	N	% with Comorbidity	% with Comorbid (Additional) Diagnoses	Comment
Barlow et al. (1986) DSM-III	58[a]	62 (36/58)	24 Dysthymia (14/58) 22 Social Phobia (13/58) 21 Simple Phobia (12/58) 14 Major Depression (8/58) 7 Obsessive Compulsive (4/58) 2 Generalized Anxiety Disorder	Modified DSM-III hierarchical exclusion rules. Structured Interview: Anxiety Disorders Interview Schedule.
DeRuiter et al. (1989) DSM-III-R	73[b]	60 (44/73)	47 Simple Phobia (34/73) 10 Social Phobia (7/73) 7 Dysthymia (5/73) 5 Obsessive Compulsive (4/73) 3 Post-Traumatic Stress Disorder (2/73)	Structured Interview: Anxiety Disorders Interview Schedule-Revised.
DiNardo & Barlow (1990) DSM-III	153[a]	46 (70/153)	20 Simple Phobia (30/153) 12 Social Phobia (19/153) 11 Generalized Anxiety Disorder (17/153) 10 Dysthymia (16/153) 5 Major Depression (8/153) 3 Obsessive Compulsive (4/153)	Same as Barlow et al. (1986). Used a severity threshold—counted only those diagnoses that reached "clinical severity" (i.e., required treatment).
Sanderson, DiNardo et al. (1990) DSM-III-R	55[b]	69 (38/55)	40 Simple Phobia (22/55) 22 Social Phobia (12/55) 18 Dysthymia (10/55) 13 Generalized Anxiety Disorder (7/55) 11 Major Depression (6/55) 2 Obsessive Compulsive (1/55)	Structured Interview: Anxiety Disorders Interview Schedule-Revised.
Stein et al. (1990) DSM-III-R	63[b]	not reported	30 Social Phobia (19/63) 14 Dysthymia (9/63) 5 Obsessive Compulsive (3/63)	Structured Interview: Schedule for Affective Disorders and Schizophrenia-Lifetime (SADS-LA) version modified

TABLE 4-1 (Continued)

Study Diagnostic Criteria	N	% with Comorbidity	% with Comorbid (Additional) Diagnoses	Comment
Starcevic et al. (1993) DSM-III-R	54[b]	83 (45/54)	52 Generalized Anxiety Disorder (28/54) 48 Major Depression (26/54) 44 Simple Phobia (24/54) 41 Social Phobia (22/54) 37 Alcohol Abuse (20/54) 31 Drug Abuse (17/54) 13 Dysthymia (7/54) 11 Obsessive Compulsive (6/54)	for the study of anxiety disorders. Subjects were excluded from DSM-III-R if they met criteria for Major Depression. Structured Interview: Structured Clinical Interview for DSM-III-R (SCID)-Upjohn version.

Note: Patients were eligible to receive more than one comorbid diagnosis.

[a]Includes patients with panic disorder and agoraphobia with panic attacks (DSM-III categories).
[b]Includes patients with panic disorder and panic disorder with agoraphobia (DSM-III-R categories).

TABLE 4-2

Percentage of Patients Receiving Panic Disorder as a Comorbid Diagnosis

Study	Principal Diagnosis	% Receiving Any Comorbid Diagnosis	% Receiving Panic Disorder as Comorbid Diagnosis
Barlow et al. (1986)[a]	Social Phobia	47 (9/19)	0 (0/19)
	Generalized Anxiety Disorder	83 (10/12)	17 (2/12)
	Simple Phobia	57 (4/7)	29 (2/7)
	Obsessive Compulsive	100 (6/6)	33 (2/6)
	Major Depression	100 (6/6)	50 (3/6)
	OVERALL	70 (35/50)	18 (9/50)
Ross et al. (1988)[a]	Alcohol and Drug Problems	68 (349/511)	16 (79/511)
DeRuiter et al. (1989)[b]	Generalized Anxiety Disorder	67 (6/9)	0 (0/9)
	Major Depression	100 (8/8)	100 (8/8)
	Dysthymic Disorder	88 (7/8)	38 (3/8)
	Simple Phobia	0 (0/3)	0 (0/3)
	Social Phobia	67 (2/3)	33 (1/3)
	Obsessive Compulsive	33 (1/3)	33 (1/3)
	Agoraphobia without panic	100 (3/3)	0 (0/3)
	OVERALL	73 (27/37)	35 (13/37)
DiNardo & Barlow (1990)[a]	Social Phobia	42 (20/48)	4 (2/48)
	Generalized Anxiety Disorder	45 (14/31)	3 (1/31)
	Simple Phobia	33 (8/24)	4 (1/24)
	Obsessive Compulsive	47 (7/15)	7 (1/15)
	Major Depression	73 (8/11)	27 (3/11)
	Dysthymia	78 (7/9)	11 (1/9)
	OVERALL	46 (64/138)	7 (9/138)
Sanderson, DiNardo, et al. (1990)[b]	Social Phobia	58 (14/24)	17 (4/24)
	Generalized Anxiety Disorder	91 (20/22)	27 (6/22)
	Simple Phobia	53 (9/17)	0 (0/17)
	Obsessive Compulsive	83 (10/12)	8 (1/12)
	OVERALL	71 (53/75)	15 (11/75)
Sanderson, Beck, & Beck (1990)[b]	Major Depression	65 (128/197)	10 (19/197)
	Dysthymia	67 (42/63)	6 (4/63)
	OVERALL	65 (170/260)	9 (23/260)

[a]DSM-III criteria were used but exclusion rules were suspended. [b]DSM-III-R criteria.

In conclusion, the majority of patients with panic disorder receive co-morbid diagnoses. Thus, when the clinician treats a patient with panic disorder, he or she should make certain to evaluate for other conditions as well. Interestingly, the frequency of panic disorder as a comorbid syndrome is relatively rare.

COMORBIDITY OF PANIC DISORDER AND DEPRESSIVE DISORDERS

As Table 4–1 indicates, 24 percent (range: 7 to 61 percent) of panic disorder patients have a comorbid depressive disorder, with dysthymia more common than major depression. However, a much higher percentage of panic disorder patients suffer from depressive symptoms without meeting diagnostic criteria for a depressive disorder. (The mean Beck Depression Inventory score among panic disorder patients equals 15.3 [Sanderson et al., 1990]). This occasionally has been referred to as a "demoralization reaction" to the social and occupational impairments caused by panic disorder (Breier, Charney, & Heninger, 1984). As Table 4–2 indicates, 14 percent (range: 9 to 69 percent) of patients with primary depressive disorders have a comorbid panic disorder, and only 18 percent of major depression patients experience panic attacks (Coryell et al., 1988).

When lifetime history of major depression is considered, then the percentage of panic disorder patients with comorbid major depression increases substantially, to 63 to 68 percent (Breier et al., 1984; Stein, Tancer, & Uhde, 1990[*]). Although Lesser and associates (1988) and Noyes and coworkers (1990) found that only 36 to 45 percent of panic disorder patients had a lifetime history of depressive disorders, these large studies systematically excluded panic disorder patients with primary major depression. In instances of lifetime comorbidity, an equal percentage of patients have temporally primary panic disorder as major depression (Breier et al., 1984; Stein et al., 1990). These findings suggest that when panic disorder first occurs, past episodes of major depression may have already remitted (although they may reoccur at a later date) and that the occurrence of panic attacks are relatively infrequent during a depressive episode.

---

*Stein and associates (1990) may have underestimated the comorbidity of panic disorder and lifetime major depression since they excluded panic disorder patients with a current major depression.

All studies to date confirm that panic disorder patients with a current or past history of major depression have a worse course and symptomatology (Breier et al., 1984; Clayton et al., 1991; Coryell et al., 1988; Noyes et al., 1990; Weissman, Leckman, Merikangas, Gammon, & Prusoff, 1984; cf. Grunhaus, 1988). These patients with comorbid panic disorder and major depression were ill longer; had more severe symptoms, more frequent panic attacks, more extensive phobic avoidance; and were more likely to have associated personality disorders than panic disorder patients without a comorbid major depression (Breier et al., 1984; Lesser et al., 1988; Noyes et al., 1990; Stein et al., 1990). Based on a two-year follow-up, relapse was much higher in the comorbid group (Coryell et al., 1988; Coryell, Endicott, & Winokur, 1992).

What is not clear, however, is whether comorbidity of major depression and panic disorder adversely affects response to pharmacological treatment. Lesser and coworkers (1988) found that panic disorder patients with major depression had an equally favorable response to treatment with alprazolam (Xanax) as did panic disorder patients without major depression, whereas Noyes and associates (1990) found that a comorbid major depression interfered with effective treatment of panic disorder with benzodiazepines. Although there are no data to support such a speculation, it is conceivable that among panic disorder patients the presence of a comorbid major depression would predict a favorable response to antidepressant treatment. However, Grunhaus (1988) concluded that patients with concurrent panic disorder and major depression had an unfavorable response to conventional antidepressant treatment, and recommended use of monoamine oxidase inhibitors.

These findings regarding the comorbidity of panic disorder and major depression might suggest that this comorbid syndrome is a different condition from either panic disorder alone or major depression alone. However, we believe that it is more parsimonious to continue to utilize multiple diagnoses rather than to introduce a new diagnostic category.

The interrelationship between panic disorder and major depression and the high rate of comorbidity between panic disorder and major depression, especially lifetime comorbidity, also have led to speculation that these syndromes represent different facets of a unitary condition. Were family studies to demonstrate increased risk for panic disorder among family members of probands with major depression, or vice versa, this might lend credence to the hypothesis of a shared genetic vulnerability. To the contrary, studies examining this question did *not* find an increased risk, and indicate that panic disorder and major depression are distinct disorders that, despite the high degree of comorbidity, are independently transmitted (c.f. Weissman et al., 1993).

Of interest, a provocative recent study has suggested an association between panic disorder and "soft" bipolar conditions (e.g., hypomania, cyclothymia, hyperthymia) (Savino et al., 1993). Since there is little confirmatory data, this line of investigation clearly requires further study.

Finally, patients with panic disorder plus major depression present with complications that require modifications of psychotherapeutic treatment as compared with patients with panic disorder alone. Specifically, it is imperative that clinicians address the patients' hopelessness and pessimistic attitudes, which pose significant obstacles to their participation in therapy, especially the various components of cognitive behavior therapy. (See Chapter 13.)

COMORBIDITY OF PANIC DISORDER AND OTHER ANXIETY DISORDERS

As Tables 4–1 and 4–2 indicate, a diagnosis of panic disorder does not preclude the diagnosis of other anxiety disorders as well. For example, 24 percent (range: 0 to 47 percent) of panic disorder patients have simple phobia, and 17 percent (range: 10 to 30 percent) have social phobia. In contrast, obsessive compulsive disorder and post-traumatic stress disorder among panic disorder patients are extremely rare.

In cases of comorbidity, panic disorder usually is assigned principal status due to the acute and distressing nature of panic attacks, which are of great concern to patients and their main reason for seeking treatment. It would be a mistake, however, for the clinician to subsume all anxiety symptoms under the diagnostic rubric of panic disorder. Simple (specific) and social phobias are occasionally present, although they are not the principal reason for seeking treatment. Furthermore, in our experience successful treatment of panic disorder does not ameliorate the symptoms of other anxiety disorders. Once the more severe condition of panic disorder has been eliminated, the comorbid anxiety condition assumes greater prominence, requiring treatment.

COMORBIDITY OF PANIC DISORDER AND SUBSTANCE ABUSE DISORDERS

Recent conceptualizations of substance abuse have focused on the possible underlying role of anxiety disorders and panic disorder in particular

(Kushner, Sher, & Beitman, 1990). One survey found that 22 percent of patients with alcohol or other drug problems had a lifetime history of panic disorder (Ross, Glaser, & Germanson, 1988), and in general, the panic symptoms preceded the alcoholism (Cox, Ron Norton, Swinson, & Endler, 1990). Over 83 percent of panic disorder patients report using alcohol to self-medicate their panic attacks; 72 percent believe that this strategy is effective (Cox, Ron Norton, Dorward, & Fergusson, 1989).

Although panic disorder appears to be the primary disorder when associated with substance abuse, problems secondary to substance abuse—the significant impairment caused by its side effects and the emerging tolerance and dependence—eventually become the principal syndrome. If the focus of substance abuse treatment is solely on abstinence, then its underlying cause will be ignored. Optimal treatment of substance abuse must deal with the panic disorder as well, even when the panic attacks, anticipatory anxiety, and avoidance behavior are masked.

COMORBIDITY OF PANIC DISORDER AND PERSONALITY DISORDERS

In our discussion, we have thus far ignored the issue of the comorbidity of panic disorder and the various personality disorders. Over the past several years, there has been an increasing interest in the prevalence and significance of personality disorders in patients with anxiety disorders. Much of the renewed interest in comorbid personality disorders is due to research demonstrating that a personality disorder diagnosis may predict a poor response to psychological and pharmacological treatment (Green & Curtis, 1988; Noyes et al., 1990; Reich, 1988).

As can be seen in Table 4–3, several recent studies have found high rates of personality disorder diagnoses among panic disorder patients. Since the assessment of personality disorders is less reliable than the assessment of other psychiatric conditions (in part due to the commingling of state and trait), methodological factors account for the wide range of reported prevalence rates. Structured interview-based assessment is, in our opinion, the most reliable method and thus provides the best estimate of the comorbidity of panic disorder and personality disorders. Based on the six interview studies, the comorbidity of panic disorder and any personality disorder is 39 percent (range: 26 to 58 percent). This prevalence estimate of comorbid personality disorders, although substantial, is lower than for most other anxiety disorders

TABLE 4–3
Comorbidity of Personality Disorders in Patients with a
Principal Diagnosis of Panic Disorder

Study	Any Personality Disorder %	Any Cluster A %	Paranoid %	Schizoid %	Schizotypal %	Any Cluster B %	Antisocial %
INTERVIEW BASED:							
Sanderson et al. (1994)							
SCID-II (*N*=145)	26	0	—	—	—	6	—
Noyes et al. (1990)							
SIDP (*N*=89)	45	NR	NR	NR	NR	NR	NR
Green & Curtis (1988)							
SCID-II (*N*=25)	52	12	4	—	8	8	4
Reich (1988)							
SCID-II (*N*=52)	40	8	NR	NR	NR	15	NR
Reich & Troughton (1988)							
SIDP (*N*=88)	43	6	6	—	—	15	1
Friedman et al. (1987)							
SCID-II (*N*=26)	58	0	—	—	—	19	—
SELF-REPORT:							
Wetzler et al. (1989)							
MCMI (*N*=15)	73	13	—	13	—	20	—
Mavissakalian & Hamann (1988)							
PDQ (*N*=187)	40	11	5	—	16	8	NR
Reich & Troughton (1988)							
PDQ (*N*=88)	54	34	5	1	34	27	1
MCMI (*N*=88)	63	12	1	11	1	28	5
Reich (1988)							
MCMI (*N*=52)	37	23	NR	NR	NR	27	NR
CHART REVIEW:							
Koenigsberg et al (1985)							
(*N*=32)	50	0	—	—	—	25	—

(Sanderson, Wetzler, Beck, & Betz, 1994), major depression (Reich & Noyes, 1987; Sanderson, Wetzler, Beck, & Betz, 1992; Wetzler, Kahn, Cahn, van Praag, & Asnis, 1989), and dysthymia (Sanderson et al., 1992). That there is substantial comorbidity of panic, depression and certain personality disorders is not surprising, although they are never listed as differential diagnostic alternatives in DSM-III-R or DSM-IV.

Cluster C (anxious/fearful) personality disorders were most commonly associated with panic disorder, and Cluster A (odd/eccentric) personality disorders were quite rare. The relationship between anxious/fearful personality disorders and panic disorder may be artifactual—that is, due to the difficulty of distinguishing between Axis I symptomatology and Axis

TABLE 4–3
(Continued)

Borderline %	Histrionic %	Narcissist %	Any Cluster C %	Avoidant %	Dependent %	Obsessive-Compulsive %	Passive-Aggressive %	Not Otherwise Specified %
1	3	1	19	8	7	8	3	3
NR	NR	NR	NR	NR	NR	NR	NR	NR
—	4	—	40	20	8	12	—	8
NR	NR	NR	35	NR	NR	NR	NR	NR
7	10	—	35	21	18	8	2	NR
4	8	8	19	4	4	8	4	19
7	20	7	53	13	27	7	33	—
3	13	—	22	21	19	—	1	NR
16	17	1	38	13	27	12	1	NR
11	12	6	54	16	31	24	11	NR
NR	NR	NR	33	19	25	NR	NR	NR
13	13	—	13	—	9	3	—	13

II behavioral traits. On the other hand, the consistency of these findings suggests that there is a genuine linkage. If so, this might reflect that: the presence of a preexisting anxious/fearful personality disorder increases vulnerability for panic disorder; the functional and interpersonal impairments caused by chronic panic disorder (which may exist for many years) have sequelae in terms of personality dysfunction; or anxious/fearful personality disorders and panic disorder share a common underlying risk factor (e.g., temperament). However, the linkage between Cluster C personality disorders and panic disorder is not specific, since other anxiety and depressive disorders also exhibit a preponderance of Cluster C personality disorders (Sanderson et al., 1992, 1994). Thus, there may be a nonspecific association between Cluster C personality disorders and affective disorders in general.

Because the core symptoms of panic disorder—panic attacks—are episodic and short-lived, many clinicians believe that the disorder does not pervade the patient's entire personality and functioning. In contrast, the core symptoms of major depression (prolonged depressed mood, pessimistic outlook), generalized anxiety disorder (chronic apprehensiveness, catastrophic thinking), and social phobia (social discomfort) have a pervasive influence, which may explain why these disorders are associated with higher rates of personality disorders.

As is true for all Axis I/Axis II interactions, the presence of a comorbid personality disorder associated with panic disorder will influence its clinical presentation and psychotherapeutic treatment. It is not sufficient to restrict psychological or pharmacological treatment to symptom relief. The entire comorbid configuration must be the focus of treatment.

For example, in our clinical experience, a panic disorder patient with dependent personality disorder is strikingly different from a panic disorder patient with borderline personality disorder. The dependent patient is clingy, submissive, and constantly seeking reassurance. This patient's panic often is triggered by dependency conflicts, such as separation or a threat to security. In contrast, the borderline patient is more chaotic, with tumultuous interpersonal relationships. The borderline patient's panic attacks often are triggered by his or her identity disturbance, which then leads to hostility within relationships. Thus, psychotherapeutic tactics must take into account the characterological profile of the panic disorder patient.

CONCLUSION

Based on this review of the literature, we may reach three conclusions: Panic disorder patients have a high rate of comorbidity, including depressive disorders, other anxiety disorders, and associated personality disorders; patients with other principal diagnoses are relatively unlikely to have a comorbid panic disorder; and panic disorder patients with a comorbid disorder have worse symptomatology, course, prognosis, and treatment response. The high rate of comorbidity of panic disorder and other psychiatric disorders supports the revisions in diagnostic criteria made in DSM-III-R and DSM-IV that allow for diagnosis of multiple syndromes.

Considering the clinical and treatment implications of a comorbid diagnosis, it is important that clinicians conduct a thorough assessment of all Axis I and Axis II syndromes even after they have reached a diagnosis of panic disorder. All too often, clinicians make a single diagnosis of panic disorder and neglect the information provided by additional diagnoses. This is especially true for associated personality disorders, which typically are overlooked.

Although in the majority of instances panic disorder is not made as an additional diagnosis, the prevalence of panic disorder in depression and substance abuse is not negligible. To provide adequate treatment for these disorders, recognition of the panic syndrome is essential.

REFERENCES

American Psychiatric Association. (1980). *Diagnostic and Statistical Manual* (3rd ed.). Washington, DC: Author.

American Psychiatric Association. (1987). *Diagnostic and Statistical Manual* (3rd ed., revised). Washington, DC: Author.

American Psychiatric Association. (1994). *Diagnostic and Statistical Manual* (4th ed.). Washington, DC: American Psychiatric Press.

Barlow, D. H., DiNardo, P. A., Vermilyea, B. B., Vermilyea, J., & Blanchard, E. B. (1986). Co-morbidity and depression among the anxiety disorders. *Journal of Nervous and Mental Disease, 174,* 63–72.

Boyd, J. H., Burke, J. D., Gruenberg, E., Hoszer, C. E., Rae, D. S., George, L. K., Karno, M., Stoltzman, R., McEvoy, L., & Nestadt, G. (1984). Exclusion criteria of DSM-III. *Archives of General Psychiatry, 41,* 983–989.

Breier, A., Charney, D. S., & Heninger, G. R. (1984). Major depression in patients with agoraphobia and panic disorder. *Archives of General Psychiatry, 41,* 1129–1135.

Clayton, P. J., Grove, W. M., Coryell, W., Keller, M., Hirschfeld, R., & Fawcett, J. (1991). Follow-up and family study of anxious depression. *American Journal of Psychiatry, 148,* 1512–1517.

Cloninger, C. R., Martin, R. L., Guze, S. B., & Clayton, P. J. (1990). The empirical structure of psychiatric comorbidity and its theoretical significance. In J. D. Maser & C. R. Cloninger (Eds.), *Comorbidity of anxiety and mood disorders* (pp. 439–462). Washington, DC: American Psychiatric Press.

Coryell, W., Endicott, J., Andreasen, N. C., Keller, M. B., Clayton, P. J., Hirschfeld, R. M. A., Scheftner, W. A., & Winokur, G. (1988). Depression and panic attacks: The significance of overlap as reflected in follow-up and family study data. *American Journal of Psychiatry, 145,* 293–300.

Coryell, W., Endicott, J., & Winokur, G. (1992). Anxiety syndromes as epiphenomena of primary major depression: Outcome and family psychopathology. *American Journal of Psychiatry, 149,* 100–107.

Cox, B. J., Ron Norton, G., Dorward, J., & Fergusson, P. A. (1989). The relationship between panic attacks and chemical dependencies. *Addictive Behaviors, 14,* 53–60.

Cox, B. J., Ron Norton, G., Swinson, R. P., & Endler, N. S. (1990). Substance abuse and panic-related anxiety: A critical review. *Behaviour Research and Therapy, 28,* 385–393.

DeRuiter, C., Ruken, H., Garssen, B., van Schaik, A., & Kraaimaat, F. (1989). Comorbidity among the anxiety disorders. *Journal of Anxiety Disorders, 3,* 57–68.

DiNardo, P. A., & Barlow, D. H. (1990). Syndrome and symptom comorbidity in the anxiety disorders. In J. D. Maser & C. R. Cloninger (Eds.), *Comorbidity in anxiety and mood disorders* (pp. 205–230). Washington, DC: American Psychiatric Press.

Friedman, C. J., Shear, M. K., & Frances, A. (1987). DSM-III personality disorders in panic patients. *Journal of Personality Disorders, 1,* 132–135.

Fyer, A. J., Liebowitz, M. R., & Klein, D. F. (1990). Treatment trials, comorbidity, and syndromal complexity. In J. D. Maser & C. R. Cloninger (Eds.), *Comorbidity in anxiety and mood disorders* (pp. 669–680). Washington, DC: American Psychiatric Press.

Green, M. A., & Curtis, G. C. (1988). Personality disorders in panic patients: Response to termination of antipanic medication. *Journal of Personality Disorders, 2*(4), 303–314.

Grunhaus, L. (1988). Clinical and psychobiological characteristics of simultaneous panic disorder and major depression. *American Journal of Psychiatry, 145,* 1214–1221.

Johnson, J., Weissman, M. M., & Klerman, G. L. (1990). Panic disorder, comorbidity, and suicide attempts. *Archives of General Psychiatry, 47,* 805–808.

Koenigsberg, H. W., Kaplan, R. D., Gilmore, M. M., & Cooper, A. M. (1985). The relationship between syndrome and personality disorder in DSM-III: Experience with 2,462 patients. *American Journal of Psychiatry, 142,* 207–212.

Kushner, M. G., Sher, K. J., & Beitman, B. D. (1990). The relation between alcohol problems and the anxiety disorders. *American Journal of Psychiatry, 147,* 685–695.

Lesser, I. M., Rubin, R. T., Pecknold, J. C., Rifkin, A., Swinson, R. P., Lydiard, R. B., Burrows, G. D., Noyes, R., Jr., & DuPont, R. L., Jr. (1988). Secondary depression in panic disorder and agoraphobia. *Archives of General Psychiatry, 45,* 437–443.

Mavissakalian, M., & Hamann, M. S. (1988). Correlates of DSM-III personality disorder in panic disorder and agoraphobia. *Comprehensive Psychiatry, 29,* 535–544.

Noyes, R., Jr., Reich, J., Christiansen, J., Suelzer, M., Pfohl, B., & Coryell, W. A. (1990). Outcome of panic disorder. *Archives of General Psychiatry, 47,* 809–818.

Rapee, R. M., Sanderson, W. C., McCauley, P. A., & DiNardo, P. A. (1992). Differences in reported symptom profile between panic disorder and other DSM-III-R anxiety disorders. *Behaviour Research and Therapy, 30,* 45–52.

Reich, J. H. (1988). DSM-III personality disorders and the outcome of treated panic disorder. *American Journal of Psychiatry, 145,* 1149–1152.

Reich, J. H., & Noyes, R., Jr. (1987). A comparison of DSM-III personality disorders in acutely ill panic and depressed patients. *Journal of Anxiety Disorders, 1,* 123–131.

Reich, J., Noyes, R., Jr., Coryell, W., & O'Gorman, T. W. (1986). The effect of state anxiety on personality measurement. *American Journal of Psychiatry, 143,* 760–763.

Reich, J., & Troughton, E. (1987). Frequency of DSM-III personality disorders in patients with panic disorder: Comparison with psychiatric and normal control subjects. *Psychiatry Research, 26,* 89–100.

Reich, J., & Troughton, E. (1988). Comparison of DSM-III personality disorders in recovered depressed and panic disorder patients. *Journal of Nervous and Mental Disease, 176,* 300–304.

Ross, H. E., Glaser, F. B., & Germanson, T. (1988). The prevalence of psychiatric disorders in patients with alcohol and other drug problems. *Archives of General Psychiatry, 45,* 1023–1031.

Sanderson, W. C., & Barlow, D. H. (1990). A description of patients diagnosed with DSM-III-R generalized anxiety disorder. *Journal of Nervous and Mental Disease, 178,* 588–591.

Sanderson, W. C., Beck, A. T., & Beck, J. (1990). Syndrome comorbidity in patients with major depression or dysthymia: Prevalence and temporal relationships. *American Journal of Psychiatry, 147,* 1025–1028.

Sanderson, W. C., DiNardo, P. A., Rapee, R. M., & Barlow, D. H. (1990). Syndrome comorbidity in patients diagnosed with a DSM-III-R anxiety disorder. *Journal of Abnormal Psychology, 99,* 308–312.

Sanderson, W. C., & Wetzler, S. (1991). Chronic anxiety and generalized anxiety disorder: Issues in comorbidity. In R. M. Rapee & D. H. Barlow (Eds.), *Chronic anxiety, generalized anxiety disorder and mixed anxiety-depression* (pp. 119–135). New York: Guilford Press.

Sanderson, W. C., Wetzler, S., Beck, A. T., & Betz, F. (1992). Prevalence of personality disorders in patients with major depression and dysthymia. *Psychiatry Research, 42,* 93–99.

Sanderson, W. C., Wetzler, S., Beck, A. T., & Betz, F. (1994). Prevalence of personality disorders among patients with anxiety disorders. *Psychiatry Research, 51,* 167–174.

Savino, M., Perugi, G., Simonini, E., Soriani, A., Cassano, G. B., & Akiskal, H. S. (1993). Affective comorbidity in panic disorder: Is there a bipolar connection? *Journal of Affective Disorders, 28,* 155–163.

Starcevic, V., Uhlenhuth, E. H., Kellner, R., & Pathak, D. (1993). Comorbidity in panic disorder: II. Chronology of appearance and pathogenic comorbidity. *Psychiatry Research, 46,* 285–293.

Stein, M. B., Tancer, M. E., & Uhde, T. W. (1990). Major depression in patients with panic disorder: Factors associated with course and recurrence. *Journal of Affective Disorders, 19,* 287–296.

Weissman, M. M., Leckman, J. F., Merikangas, K. R., Gammon, G. D., & Prusoff, B. A. (1984). Depression and anxiety disorders in parents and children: Results from the Yale Family Study. *Archives of General Psychiatry, 41,* 845–852.

Weissman, M. M., Wickramaratne, P., Adams, P. B., Lish, J. D., Horwath, E., Charney, D., Woods, S. W., Leeman, E., & Frosch, E. (1993). The relationship between panic disorder and major depression. *Archives of General Psychiatry, 50,* 767–780.

Wetzler, S., Kahn, R. S., Cahn, W., van Praag, H. M., & Asnis, G. M. (1989). Psychological test characteristics of depressed and panic patients. *Psychiatry Research, 31,* 179–192.

Wolf, A. W., Schubert, D. S. P., Patterson, M. B., Grande, T. P., Brocco, K. J., & Pendleton, L. (1988). Associations among major psychiatric diagnoses. *Journal of Consulting and Clinical, 56,* 292–294.

5

Panic Disorder and Suicidal Behavior

DAVID H. ARNOLD,
WILLIAM C. SANDERSON, AND
AARON T. BECK

Prior to 1989, the topic of panic disorder and suicidal behavior received little attention, in part because traditional clinical wisdom held that patients with panic disorder were not likely to attempt suicide. However, Weissman, Klerman, Markowitz, and Ouellette (1989) reported a surprising finding: Persons with panic disorder have a much higher risk of suicidal behaviors than those with no disorder and a rate equal to that of persons with depression. Since their report, studies examining the relationship between panic disorder and suicide attempts have reported widely discrepant results. For example, in contrast to the aforementioned findings, Beck, Steer, Sanderson, and Skeie (1991) found no relationship between panic disorder and suicidal behavior. Our review of studies examining the prevalence of suicide attempts in patients with panic disorder revealed a large discrepancy, ranging from 0 percent to 57 percent. (See Table 5–1.) This disparity has even been noted in the popular press, with, for example, the *New York Times* and *Science News* commenting on the inconclusive findings (Bower, 1992; Goleman, 1992).

TABLE 5–1

Summary of Studies Evaluating Suicidal Behaviors in Patients with Panic Disorder

Study	Subjects	Assessment of Panic	Results
Andrews & Lewinsohn (1992)	Community sample of 1710 older adolescents; 14 with panic disorder	Structured interviews to determine lifetime prevalence	No association between panic and suicide attempts
Anthony & Petronis (1991)	40 ECA respondents with panic who recently attempted vs. 160 matched controls, followed 1 year later	Structured Clinical Interview for DSM-III-R (SCID)	Panic and suicide associated only if control for 6 other variables in a regression equation
Asnis et al. (1993)	47 outpatients with panic disorder, 614 other outpatients	Semistructured interview to determine principal diagnosis	9% attempts in panic, 35% in major depression
Beck et al. (1991)	Outpatients: (1) 73 panic disorder without agoraphobia, (2) 78 panic disorder with agoraphobia, (3) 485 with mood disorders, (4) 264 with other disorders	SCID	Attempts: (1) 0%, (2) 1.3%, (3) 7%, (4) 1.5%
Coryell et al. (1982)	113 former inpatients with panic disorder, 35 years after admission	Retrospective chart review	Mortality rate from unexpected causes 4.5 times higher than expected
Coryell et al. (1986)	12-year follow-up of 155 outpatients with anxiety neurosis	Chart screening	Mortality rate from suicide no higher than expected
Cox et al. (1994)	106 outpatients with panic disorder	SCID	18% had history of attempt; most had history of depression, substance abuse, or previous psychiatric hospitalization
Friedman et al. (1992)	Outpatients: 59 with panic disorder and borderline, 234 with panic disorder, and 0 borderline	Retrospective review of intakes and charts	Attempts: panic: 2%, panic + borderline: 25%
Henriksson et al. (1993)	229 suicide victims	Consensus diagnoses based on structured interviews with family members	11% of the victims had an anxiety disorder, compared to 31% diagnosed with major depression; however, when principal diagnoses were considered, only 1% were given the principal diagnosis of an anxiety disorder, compared with 30% with major depression

Study	Sample	Method	Findings
Johnson et al. (1990)	ECA community data: 57 with panic disorder and no other Axis I disorder, 13,672 with no Axis I disorder	Lifetime diagnoses by structured interview by lay interviewers; Diagnostic Interview Schedule (DIS)	Lifetime attempts: panic 7%, no Axis I: 1%
Lepine et al. (1993)	100 outpatients with panic disorder	Clinical interview + Schedule for Affective Disorders and Schizophrenia (SADS)-Lifetime Version	42% had history of attempt, 17% of those without major depression or substance abuse
Mannuzza et al. (1992)	44 with panic disorder, who were relatives and acquaintances of anxiety clinic patients	SADS	High rates of suicide attempts among a group with panic disorder (11%), but suicide attempts preceded the onset of panic disorder in 71% of the cases, in all cases attempts were made in the contexts of other mental illness
Massion et al. (1993)	294 patients with panic disorder from 11 sites; 8% had a history of a suicide attempt, however, the rate was less than 3% among those without a history of major depression	Various structured interviews	8% had a history of a suicide attempt, however, the rate was less than 3% among those without a history of major depression
Norton et al. (1993)	51 Canadian drug abusers vs. 21 drug abusers with panic	Self-report Panic Attack Questionnaire	Attempts: 57% of those with panic disorder and substance abuse, 21% of those with substance abuse alone
Noyes et al. (1991)	70 patients (almost all outpatients with panic disorder from the University of Iowa Anxiety Clinic, recontacted 7 years later	Structured interview by a trained research assistant	3 completed suicides, 5 serious attempts, 7 of these 8 patients had personality disorders, all had major depression
Rudd et al. (1993)	209 outpatients with a history of suicide attempts or who were considered to be at high risk for eventual suicide	DIS	None of these patients were diagnosed with uncomplicated panic disorder, while less than 4% had panic disorder along with another comorbid diagnosis, in contrast, 88% of the sample was diagnosed with a depressive disorder

TABLE 5-1 *(Continued)*

Study	Subjects	Assessment of Panic	Results
Sanderson et al. (1992)	15 panic disorder outpatients, 7 of those with personality disorders	Structured interviews: Structured Clinical Interview for DSM-III-Patient Edition (SCID-P), Structured Clinical Interview for DSM-III-Personality Disorders (SCID-II)	Attempts: 4 of 7 among those with personality disorders, 0 of 8 among others
Weissman et al. (1989)	ECA community data; (1) 254 with panic disorder, (2) 667 with panic attacks, (3) 4,857 with other disorders, (4) 12,233 with no disorder	Lifetime diagnoses by structured interview by lay interviewers (DIS)	Suicide attempts by (1) 20%, (2) 12%, (3) 6%, (4) 1%

This chapter provides an overview of studies that have examined the association of panic disorder and suicide, attempts to account for the divergent findings, and provides suggestions for future studies aimed at clarifying this association.

As stated, Weissman and her colleagues were the first to report a positive relationship between panic disorder and suicide attempts, using data collected as part of the Epidemiological Catchment Area (ECA) Study (Johnson, Weissman, & Klerman, 1990; Markowitz, Weissman, Ouellette, Lish, & Klerman, 1989; Weissman et al., 1989). This project evaluated a random sample of over 18,000 adults from five cities, assessing all patients with the Diagnostic Interview Schedule (DIS) and a structured interview designed for lay interviewers (Robins, Helzer, Croughan, & Ratcliff, 1981). Subjects were categorized in terms of lifetime diagnoses of Axis I disorders. Results indicated that nearly 20 percent of patients with panic disorder had made a suicide attempt (Weissman et al., 1989). However, most patients with panic disorder also had a history of major depression, leaving the cause of the attempt unclear. A further analysis (Johnson et al., 1990) addressed this issue by examining the group of patients diagnosed with panic disorder only (i.e., "uncomplicated"); 7 percent of this group had made a suicide attempt. This was comparable to the suicide attempt rate in patients diagnosed with major depression (7.5 percent) and was substantially higher than the rate for those with no psychiatric disorder (1 percent). The authors concluded that even uncomplicated panic disorder is a major risk factor for suicide attempts.

Other researchers' data have supported these findings. Cox, Doremfeld, Swinson, and Norton (1994) evaluated a sample of 106 outpatients who had been diagnosed with panic disorder by interview questions based on the Structured Clinical Interview for DSM-III-R (SCID-R; Spitzer & Williams, 1987). They found that 18 percent had attempted suicide at some point during their lives.

Consistent with these results, Lepine, Chignon, and Teherani (1993) found high rates of suicide attempts in their sample of 100 patients who were referred for treatment of panic disorder to an outpatient clinic in Paris. The diagnosis of panic disorder in these patients was based on the administration of the Schedule for Affective Disorders and Schizophrenia (SADS)—Lifetime Version structured interview (Fyer, Endicott, Mannuzza, & Klein, 1985). Seventeen percent of patients with no history of major depression or substance abuse had attempted suicide at some point in their lives. The presence of major depression and substance abuse substantially elevated the rate of suicide attempts. Fifty percent of panic disorder patients with a lifetime history of major depression but no history of substance abuse made a suicide attempt. Forty-six percent of those with a lifetime history of substance abuse but no history of major depression had made a suicide attempt. Among panic disorder patients with a history of both major depression and substance abuse, 72 percent had a history of an attempt.

However, conclusions about the relation between panic disorder and suicide attempts are complicated by other studies that have found a much weaker association. Beck and associates (1991) administered the SCID-R to 900 outpatients from the Center for Cognitive Therapy in Philadelphia. Of the 151 patients with a principal diagnosis of panic disorder, only one reported a history of suicide attempts, a rate far lower than that reported in the ECA data. In contrast, the rate of suicide attempts found in patients with mood disorders (7 percent) was consistent with rates observed in the ECA data. The authors concluded that panic disorder alone does not constitute a suicide risk factor.

Similarly, Rudd, Dahm, and Rajab (1993) failed to validate panic disorder as an independent risk factor for suicide attempts. They examined 209 outpatients who had a history of suicide attempts or who were considered to be at high risk for eventual suicide. None of these patients was diagnosed with uncomplicated panic disorder using the DIS, while less than 4 percent had panic disorder along with another comorbid diagnosis. In contrast, 88 percent of the sample was diagnosed with a depressive disorder.

Asnis and coworkers (1993) studied 651 patients who were treated at a hospital outpatient clinic in the Bronx, New York. These patients were assigned principal diagnoses based on a semistructured clinical interview. Forty-seven patients received a principal diagnosis of panic disorder; four (9 percent) of those reported at least one previous suicide attempt. In contrast, 35 percent of patients with a principal diagnosis of major depression made a suicide attempt.

Finally, Andrews and Lewinsohn (1992) evaluated a community sample of high school students ($N = 1,710$) using the SADS for School-Age Children (Puig-Antich & Chambers, 1983). One hundred twenty-one (7.1 percent) had attempted suicide some time in their life. Fifty-seven percent of adolescents who attempted suicide were diagnosed with major depression. None of the 14 adolescents diagnosed with panic disorder made a suicide attempt. Of course, since this study evaluated adolescents, the findings cannot be directly compared to the studies reviewed earlier.

FACTORS CONTRIBUTING TO
THESE DIVERGENT FINDINGS

Assessment Methods

Lifetime Assessment

Studies that used lifetime diagnoses of panic disorder found the highest rates of suicidal behavior. It could be that this method inflates results. For example, for a panic disorder patient, history of a suicide attempt is counted, even if it is unclear if the suicide attempt occurred within the duration of the illness (i.e., the suicide attempt may have occurred prior to the development of panic disorder). Therefore, the temporal relationship between panic and suicide needs to be considered, which is very difficult to do using a lifetime assessment paradigm. Two studies that have attempted to examine the temporal relationship directly have found contrasting results. Lepine and associates (1993) asked their patients whether their panic attacks or suicide attempts came first, and found that 74 percent attempted suicide after their panic attacks began. In contrast, Mannuzza, Aronowitz, Chapman, Klein, and Fyer (1992) found high rates of suicide attempts among a group with panic disorder (11 percent), but reported that the suicide attempt preceded the onset of panic disorder in 71 percent of the cases.

Anthony and Petronis (1991) took another approach to avoid the problems of the lifetime diagnosis by examining 40 of the ECA respondents who had recently attempted suicide and 160 matched controls. They found that panic disorder did not directly predict suicide attempts. However, when they evaluated this relationship in a regression model controlling for depression, educational achievement, marital status, alcohol abuse, cocaine use, and the interaction between depression and suicide, the relationship between panic disorder and suicide attempts became significant. One must consider this result with caution, as this regression model assumes that each of these variables contributes to risk in a linear, noninteractive fashion—a tentative assumption at best. Prospective studies are needed in order to examine this question more accurately, as to date the temporal relationship of these problems remains poorly understood.

Diagnosis of Panic Disorder

Most of the studies that reported a weak association between panic and suicide utilized structured interviews by experienced clinicians to assess panic disorder. Use of these structured interviews is supported by fairly good reliability and validity data (e.g., Riskind, Beck, Berchick, Brown, & Steer, 1987; Spitzer, Williams, Gibbon, & First, 1992). The ECA data relied on lay interviewers using the DIS. This structured interview is one of the most extensively validated in psychology, with reports of acceptable levels of reliability and generally close agreement with clinician diagnoses (e.g., Anthony et al., 1985; Helzer et al., 1985; Robins et al., 1981; Robins, Helzer, Ratcliff, & Seyfried, 1982). However, DIS diagnoses of panic disorder agree less well with clinician ratings than most other disorders, with a stricter threshold for the diagnosis of panic disorders than clinicians. Specifically, those diagnosed with panic disorder on the DIS also are diagnosed by clinicians 90 percent of the time or more, but the DIS may diagnose only half as many with panic disorder as do clinicians (Helzer et al., 1985). Since the ECA data relied on the DIS, it is likely that those diagnosed with panic in this study are a more severe group, which probably accounts for a portion of the higher incidence of suicide attempts. On the other hand, these differences cannot entirely account for the hugh discrepancy between the ECA and other rates.

Assessment of Suicide

In contrast to the large amount of research on various methods used for assessing psychological disorders, little is known about the effects of various methods of assessing suicidal behaviors. Most studies reviewed here simply asked patients whether they had ever attempted suicide. Rudd and coworkers (1993) assessed suicidal risk with the Modified Scale for Suicide Ideation (Miller, Norman, Bishop, & Dow, 1986) and the Suicide Probability Scale (Cull & Gill, 1990), while Asnis and associates (1993) gave patients a self-report inventory that assessed suicidal behaviors (Harkavy-Friedman & Asnis, 1989). Unfortunately, little is known about how different methods of assessing suicide also might affect risk estimates, though it is plausible that they might give different results, particularly given social stigmas associated with suicide. For example, people may be more willing to admit suicide attempts to an anonymous interviewer than to a therapist with whom they are building a relationship. In this case the ECA data would reflect truer rates of suicide attempts than the studies that relied on clinician assessment.

Treatment Seekers

Questions about the relationship of treatment seeking and suicide are not addressed by current data; it is unknown if those who seek treatment for panic disorder are at higher or lower risk than those with untreated panic disorder. Treatment seeking might serve as a marker of high suicide risk, since those who seek treatment for psychiatric problems are generally more severely disordered than those who do not. If this were the case, then examining the temporal relationship of panic and suicide would become quite important, and global lifetime assessment of suicide attempts would be insufficient. For example, high risk of suicide in treatment seekers might reflect despair at their severe panic disorder, or might reflect an artifactual association because of high general dysfunction that has little to do with panic directly.

On the other hand, treatment seeking, particularly with panic as their principal diagnosis, might actually indicate low risk for suicide attempts. We expect that those who are seeking treatment for panic disorder are a more "hopeful" group than those who do not and that hopefulness serves as a buffer against suicide. Further, the capacity to seek treatment may indicate effective coping skills and higher functioning.

We expect that those experiencing failed treatment would be at especially high risk and that the recent advances in the treatment of panic actually may have influenced the risk of suicide. The ECA data were collected approximately 10 years earlier than the Beck, Asnis, and Rudd data sets. Information about the treatment of panic disorder has become more available to the general public during this time. Such information may have decreased hopelessness and risk of suicide in those with panic. Thus, increased treatment information may account for a portion of the lower rates in these later studies. Unfortunately, the ECA studies provided no information about treatment seeking in their groups, and the other studies of panic patients provided no information about response to treatment. For those who were previously in treatment, the success of treatment should be examined, but none of the studies reviewed have provided such information.

Completed Versus Attempted Suicides

On one hand, any suicide attempt is a matter of concern, especially since those who attempt and fail are more likely to try again success-fully. Nonetheless, one must be careful in assuming that risk of suicide attempts reflects the risk of completed suicide, particularly in the case of panic. Panic patients tend to be young females, the demographic group that is at the highest risk of suicide attempts but not of suicide completion. Lepine and coworkers (1993) reported that only 14 percent of the suicide attempts among his sample resulted in hospitalization in an intensive care unit and that only 57 percent required even 24 hours of hospitalization. Thus, while studies of suicide attempts are important, studies of suicide completers must be considered as well. Henriksson and associates (1993) studied 229 suicide victims. Eleven percent of the victims had an anxiety disorder, compared to 31 percent diagnosed with major depression. However, only 1 percent were given the principal di-agnosis of an anxiety disorder, compared with 30 percent with the prin-cipal diagnosis of major depression. These results suggest that very few, if any, suicide completers had an anxiety disorder alone. Coryell and colleagues (Coryell, Noyes, & Clancy, 1982; Coryell, Noyes, & House, 1986) conducted two studies that examined panic patients across time. In their first study, (Coryell et al., 1982) they located 113 inpatients 35 years after they had been hospitalized. The mortality rate from unnat-ural causes was 4.5 times higher than would be expected in a community sample. However, while chart review indicated that all had met criteria for panic disorder at the time of hospitalization, this diagnostic category did not exist at the time they were hospitalized, so the diagnoses had to be derived post hoc. Further, the authors speculate that much of the mortality in this study might have been due to depression or substance abuse, but this hypothesis was not evaluated. In their second study (Coryell et al., 1986), 155 outpatients were followed 12 years after they were first evaluated. Only one of these patients completed suicide dur-ing this time, not a significant difference from rates in community sam-ples. Because these samples may have differed on a number of dimensions including severity of disorder and comorbid diagnoses, these discrepant findings are difficult to interpret.

FACTORS ASSOCIATED WITH
SUICIDAL BEHAVIORS IN
PANIC DISORDER PATIENTS

While much remains to be understood about the relationship between panic and suicide, several factors have been identified that appear to increase the risk of suicide behavior in patients with panic disorder.

Comorbid Diagnoses

Axis I Disorders

Studies that have reported information on other Axis I disorders consistently found high rates of suicide attempts among those with panic and comorbid disorders. For example, the ECA data found that the combination of depression and panic was associated with very high risk of suicide attempts. Mannuzza and associates (1992) reported that in the cases of six of their seven attempters, the attempt was made during an episode of depression, dysthymia, and/or alcohol abuse. The seventh attempt was preceded by a long history of dysthymia. Cox and coworkers (1994) reported that those who had attempted suicide were likely to have experienced previous episodes of major depression, psychiatric hospitalizations, or substance abuse. Massion, Warshaw, and Keller (1993) conducted a study of 294 patients with panic disorder and found that 8 percent had a history of a suicide attempt. The rate was less than 3 percent among those without a history of major depression.

However, these studies do not provide comprehensive information on Axis I diagnoses. While each of these studies suggest the importance of comorbid disorders, none of the studies summarized presents information on all comorbid Axis I disorders, and all provide insufficient information to evaluate the specific effects of panic. For example, in the ECA data, 77 percent of those with both panic and depression also had at least one additional disorder whose effects on suicide were not reported. Further, none of these studies presented patients' principal diagnoses. Due to this omission, it is unknown whether a patient with panic disorder and secondary major depression is at the same risk as a patient with principal major depression and comorbid panic disorder. On the other hand, the Beck and Asnis samples are described in terms of principal diagnoses, but no information is provided on additional disorders.

One particularly important area for further research is the effect of comorbid alcohol or substance abuse. Given the high rate of substance abuse among panic patients (Kushner, Sher, & Beitman, 1990; Noyes, 1990) and the high rate of suicide among substance abusers (Guze & Robins, 1976; Murphy & Wetzel, 1990), one would expect this to be an important factor. The Lepine data discussed earlier are consistent with this hypothesis; comorbid substance abuse increased panic patients' risk of attempt from 21 percent to 46 percent. However, this study did not examine a group of drug abusers without panic disorder, making it difficult to determine whether panic increases risk among abusers. Norton, Rockman, Luy, and Marion's (1993) data suggest that it may. They evaluated a group of 72 drug abusers, 21 of whom were diagnosed with panic disorder based on a self-report index of panic. Two-thirds of the panic patients had attempted suicide, in contrast to 21 percent of the drug abusers without panic disorder. Patients were not evaluated in terms of other psychiatric disorders. Similarly, Noyes and coworkers (1991) followed 74 panic patients from the University of Iowa Anxiety Clinic for seven years after their initial visit to the clinic. Of this sample, 57 percent of drug abusers with panic disorder had attempted suicide, compared to 22 percent of their drug abusers without panic disorder. The ECA (Markowitz et al., 1989) and other (e.g., Friedman, Jones, Chernan, & Barlow, 1992) studies also have found disproportionate rates of alcohol and drug abuse among the panic patients who had attempted suicide. Unfortunately, these studies do not present information on other Axis I disorders, while the ECA studies do not present detailed information on substance abuse.

Axis II Disorders

Similarly, we hypothesize that comorbid Axis II diagnoses account for much of the suicide risk in patients with panic disorder. Specifically, it may be that those who attended the outpatient clinics of Beck or Asnis had low rates of personality disorders or that those with untreated panic disorders identified in the ECA studies had a high incidence of personality disorders. Unfortunately, none of the studies discussed earlier assessed for the presence of Axis II disorders, but several other studies suggest that personality disorders have dramatic effects on rates of suicide attempts. For example, Friedman and associates (1992) conducted chart reviews of 293 patients with panic disorder; they found that suicide attempts were reported by 25 percent of those diagnosed with borderline personality disorder but only by 2 percent of the patients without this disorder. However, no standard protocol was used for assessing suicide attempts in the nonborderline group, which may have resulted in an underestimate of the number of attempts. Noyes and coworkers (1991) found that three of their sample of 70 patients completed suicide and five others made serious attempts; this study has been cited as evidence of elevated suicide risk in panic. However, seven of these eight patients were diagnosed as having personality disorders. In fact, 34 percent of those with personality disorders attempted suicide, compared to only 2 percent of those without personality disorders. Similarly, Sanderson, Friedman, Wetzler, Kaplan, and Asnis (1992) reported that four of seven (57 percent) outpatients diagnosed with both panic disorder and a personality disorder had attempted suicide, compared with none of the eight without a personality disorder.

These studies indicate the importance of assessing for personality disorders in studies of panic and suicide. On the other hand, they do not include comparison groups of those with personality disorders alone, making it impossible to evaluate the extent to which panic disorder increases the risk of suicide in those with a personality disorder. Further, these studies do not provide information on comorbid depression, substance abuse, or other Axis I disorders, leaving it impossible to evaluate the specific effect of panic disorder.

In sum, there is a great need for comprehensive information about comorbid diagnoses and information on patients' principal diagnosis. To date, no study has even included information on both comorbid Axis I and Axis II disorders in looking at the suicide attempts of panic disorder patients. No study has examined truly uncomplicated panic, and it is premature to conclude that panic disorder alone increases the risk of suicide attempt.

Severity of Disorder

Differences in results also may reflect sample differences in terms of severity of dysfunction, but this variable has been poorly studied. At the very least it would be simple for studies to present data on panic patients with and without agoraphobia, since agoraphobia might be expected to increase suicide risk through increased social isolation, hopelessness, depression, and difficulty in seeking treatment, but this hypothesis has not been addressed adequately. The one study that presents relevant data seems to support this hypothesis. Markowitz and coworkers (1989) examined the ECA data and found elevated rates of suicide attempts in those with agoraphobia compared to those without, suggesting that this is an important outcome factor. In the only suicide risk study that directly examined the severity of panic disorder, Noyes and associates (1991) found that attempters in their sample had more severe symptoms than those who did not attempt. Weissman, Klerman, and Johnson (1992) have argued that the outpatient samples of the Beck study may be unusually mild cases of panic disorder. Unfortunately, none of the studies reviewed provided any information about the severity of the disorder, though information about assessment methods may provide some indirect clues about differences in sample severity.

CONCLUSIONS

Ultimately, a theoretical model of the processes involved in suicidal behavior is needed, including the mechanisms by which panic may contribute to the risk of making a suicide attempt. For example, if panic does increase risk, does this association reflect desperation to escape panic, social isolation, hopelessness, and demoralization, or simply the comorbidity between panic and other disorders? Similarly, what is the temporal relation between these variables, and do interventions modify the risk of suicide? Unfortunately, at present these questions are premature and the field is many steps removed from a theoretical model, lacking even clear descriptive conclusions about the risk accompanying panic. The relationship between panic disorder and suicide is poorly understood because studies have provided incomplete information about sample differences, comorbid diagnoses, and temporal relationships, and because of important variations in assessment procedures.

One consistent finding that emerged from this literature is that those who exhibit panic disorder along with depression, substance abuse, and personality disorders are at increased risk for suicide attempts. However, the mechanisms and specifics of even these relationships remain unclear, as does the extent to which panic contributes to this risk.

Ideally, large-scale prospective studies will be conducted that will provide (1) information about all comorbid Axis I and Axis II disorders, (2) diagnostic information from multiple sources including carefully structured interviews, (3) detailed sample information, (4) information about the severity of disorders and suicide attempts as well as treatment status and outcome, and (5) careful documentation of the temporal unfolding of these problems. Once such descriptive data are amassed, it may be possible to begin to identify key psychological and clinical variables toward a theoretical understanding of suicidal processes and useful clinical information for identifying those patients at increased risk.

REFERENCES

Andrews, J.A., & Lewinsohn, P.M. (1992). Suicidal attempts among older adolescents: Prevalence and co-occurrence with psychiatric disorders. *Journal of the American Academy of Child and Adolescent Psychiatry, 31,* 655–662.

Anthony, J.C., Folstein, M., Romanoski, A.J., Von Korff, M.R., Nestadt, G.R., Chahal, R., Merchant, A., Brown, H., Shapiro, S., Kramer, M., & Gruenberg, E.M. (1985). Comparison of the lay diagnostic interview schedule and a standardized psychiatric diagnosis. *Archives of General Psychiatry, 42,* 667–675.

Anthony, J.C., & Petronis, K.R. (1991). Panic attacks and suicide attempts. *Archives of General Psychiatry, 48,* 1114.

Asnis, G.M., Friedman, T.A., Sanderson, W.C., Kaplan, M.L., van Praag, H.M., & Harkavy-Friedman, J.M. (1993). Suicidal behaviors in adult psychiatric outpatients, I: Description and prevalence. *American Journal of Psychiatry, 150,* 108–112.

Beck, A.T., Steer, R.A., Sanderson, W.C., & Skeie, T.M. (1991). Panic disorder and suicidal ideation and behavior: Discrepant findings in psychiatric outpatients. *American Journal of Psychiatry, 148,* 1195–1199.

Bower, B. (1992). New data question panic, suicide relation. *Science News, 141,* 358.

Coryell, W., Noyes, R., & Clancy, J. (1982). Excess mortality in panic disorder: A comparison with primary unipolar depression. *Archives of General Psychiatry, 39,* 701–703.

Coryell, W., Noyes, R., & House, J.D. (1986). Mortality among outpatients with anxiety disorders. *American Journal of Psychiatry, 143,* 508–510.

Cox, B.J., Doremfeld, D.M., Swinson, R.P., & Norton, G. R. (1994). Suicidal ideation and suicidal attempts in panic disorder and social phobia. *American Journal of Psychiatry, 151,* 882–887.

Cull, J.G., & Gill, W.S. (1990). *Manual for the Suicide Probability Scale.* Los Angeles: Western Psychological Services.

Friedman, S., Jones, J.C., Chernan, L., & Barlow, D.H. (1992). Suicidal ideation and suicide attempts among patients with panic disorder: A survey of two outpatient clinics. *American Journal of Psychiatry, 149,* 680–685.

Fyer, A.J., Endicott, J., Mannuzza, S., & Klein, D.F. (1985). *Schedule for Affective Disorders and Schizophrenia—Lifetime Version (modified for the study of affective disorders)*. New York: Anxiety Disorders Clinic, New York State Psychiatric Institute.

Goleman, D. (1992, January 8). Heart seizure or panic attack? Disorder is a terrifying mimic. *New York Times,* p. C1.

Guze, S.B., & Robins, E. (1976). Suicide and primary affective disorder. *British Journal of Psychiatry, 117,* 437–438.

Harkavy-Friedman, J.M., & Asnis, G.M. (1989). Assessment of suicidal behavior: A new instrument. *Psychiatric Annals 19,* 382–387; correction *19,* 438.

Helzer, J.E., Robins, L.N., McEvoy, L.T., Spitznagel, E.L., Stoltzman, R.K., Farmer, A., & Brockington, I.F. (1985). A comparison of clinical and Diagnostic Interview Schedule diagnoses. *Archives of General Psychiatry, 42,* 657–666.

Henriksson, M.M., Aro, H.M., Marttunen, M.J., Heikkinen, M.E., Isometsa, E.T., Kuoppasalmi, K.I., & Lonnqvist, J.K. (1993). Mental disorders and comorbidity in suicide. *American Journal of Psychiatry, 150,* 935–940.

Johnson, J., Weissman, M.M., & Klerman, G.L. (1990). Panic disorder, comorbidity, and suicide attempts. *Archives of General Psychiatry, 47,* 805–808.

Kushner, M.G., Sher, K.J., & Beitman, B.D. (1990). The relationship between alcohol problems and the anxiety disorders. *American Journal of Psychiatry, 147,* 685–695.

Lepine, J.P., Chignon, J.M., & Teherani, M. (1993). Suicide attempts in patients with panic disorder. *Archives of General Psychiatry, 50,* 144–149.

Mannuzza, S., Aronowitz, B., Chapman, T., Klein, D.F., & Fyer, A.J. (1992). Panic disorder and suicide attempts. *Journal of Anxiety Disorders, 6,* 261–274.

Markowitz, J.S., Weissman, M.M., Ouellette, R., Lish, J.D., & Klerman, G.L. (1989). Quality of life in panic disorder. *Archives of General Psychiatry, 46,* 984–992.

Massion, A.O., Warshaw, M.G., & Keller, M.B. (1993). Quality of life and psychiatric morbidity in panic disorder and generalized anxiety disorder. *American Journal of Psychiatry, 150,* 600–607.

Miller, I.W., Norman, W.H., Bishop, S.B., & Dow, M.G. (1986). The Modified Scale for Suicidal Ideation: Reliability and validity. *Journal of Consulting and Clinical Psychology, 54,* 724–725.

Murphy, G.E., & Wetzel, R.D. (1990). The lifetime risk of suicide in alcoholism. *Archives of General Psychiatry, 47,* 383–392.

Norton, G.R., Rockman, G.E., Luy, B., & Marion, T. (1993). Suicide, chemical abuse, and panic attacks: A preliminary report. *Behavior Research and Therapy, 31,* 37–40.

Noyes, R. (1990). The psychiatric consequence of anxiety. *Psychiatric Medicine, 8,* 41–66.

Noyes, R., Christianson, J., Clancy, J., Garvey, M.J., Suelzer, M., & Anderson, D.J. (1991). Predictors of serious suicide attempts among patients with panic disorder. *Comprehensive Psychiatry, 32,* 261–267.

Puig-Antioch, J., & Chambers, W.J. (1983). *Schedule for Affective Disorders and Schizophrenia for School-Age Children (6–18).* Pittsburgh, PA: Western Psychiatric Institute and Clinic.

Riskind, J.H., Beck, A.T., Berchick, R.J., Brown, G., & Steer, R. A. (1987). Reliability of DSM-III diagnoses for major depression and generalized anxiety disorder using the Structured Clinical Interview for DSM-III. *Archives of General Psychiatry, 44,* 817–820.

Robins, L.N., Helzer, J.E., Croughan, J., & Ratcliff, K.S. (1981). National Institute of Mental Health Diagnostic Interview Schedule. *Archives of General Psychiatry, 38,* 381–389.

Robins, L.N., Helzer, J.E., Ratcliff, K.S., & Seyfried, W. (1982). Validity of the Diagnostic Interview Schedule, Version II: DSM-III diagnoses. *Psychological Medicine, 12,* 855–870.

Rudd, D.M., Dahm, F.P., & Rajab, H.M. (1993). Diagnostic comorbidity in persons with suicidal ideation and behavior. *American Journal of Psychiatry, 150,* 928–934.

Sanderson, W.C., Friedman, T., Wetzler, S., Kaplan, M., & Asnis, G.M. (1992, November). *Personality disorders in patients with major depression, panic disorder, and generalized anxiety disorder.* Paper presented at the annual conference of the Association for the Advancement of Behavior Therapy, Boston.

Spitzer, R.L., & Williams, J.B. (1987). *The Structured Clinical Interview for DSM-III-R (SCID-R):* New York: Biometrics Research, New York State Psychiatric Institute.

Spitzer, R.L., Williams, J.B., Gibbon, M., & First, M.B. (1992). The Structured Clinical Interview for DSM-III-R (SCID): I. History, rationale, and description. *Archives of General Psychiatry, 49,* 624–629.

Weissman, M.M., Klerman, G.L., & Johnson, J. (1992). Panic disorder and suicidal ideation. *American Journal of Psychiatry, 149,* 1411–1412.

Weissman, M.M., Klerman, G.L., Markowitz, J.S., & Ouellette, R. (1989). Suicidal ideation and suicide attempts in panic disorder and attacks. *New England Journal of Medicine, 321,* 1209–1214.

PART II
Biological Underpinnings of Panic Disorder

6

The Norepinephrine System in Panic Disorder

GREGORY M. ASNIS AND
HERMAN M. van PRAAG

The norepinephrine (NE) system has been hypothesized by many investigators to be central to the emotion of anxiety. In particular, noradrenergic hyperactivity, specifically in the locus coeruleus (LC), has been hypothesized to underline the central biochemical dysfunction of panic disorder (Redmond, 1977; Redmond, 1979; Redmond & Huang, 1979).

Redmond and his colleagues have elegantly probed the LC in stumptail monkeys to study the relationship of the LC and NE to anxiety. Increased activity in the LC was recorded when monkeys were exposed to threatening situations. Electrical stimulation of the LC produced an alerting response, consisting of yawning, hair pulling, hand wringing, teeth grinding, struggling to escape, opening and closing of the mouth, and other behaviors, all phenomena similar to that seen when these animals were confronted by humans. Their work also demonstrated that a similar anxiety state was produced by drugs that increased LC activity, such as yohimbine or piperoxan, both alpha-2-antagonists. Accompanying the anxiety-induced states was an increased secretion of NE and its major metabolite, 3-methoxy-4-hydroxyphenylethylene glycol (MHPG). Conversely, procedures that reduced LC firing (surgical

119

ablation of the LC or LC-inhibiting drugs such as benzodiazepines, clonidine, morphine, tricyclic antidepressants [TCAs]) decreased the anxiety induced by threatening stimuli.

According to Redmond's work, the LC is a critical center in fear and anxiety responses. The LC is anatomically located in the dorsolateral tegmentum of the pons, and contains over 70 percent of the brain's noradrenergic cell bodies. This site receives extensive sensory input (reticular formation, spinal cord, and brain stem) and sends out a significant number of efferent pathways to diverse areas of the brain (hippocampus, hypothalamus, limbic area, spinal cord, and cerebellum) (Grant & Redmond, 1981). Thus, the LC may have a central position in modulating and processing information that could directly affect an organism's anxiogenic response to threatening stimuli.

Redmond's pioneer work in the stumptail monkey, suggesting an interrelationship between increased LC activity, noradrenergic hyperactivity, and anxiety, has been supported in humans. Drugs that increase LC activity in the animal model (e.g., yohimbine, caffeine, lactate) also increase anxiety in humans, whereas drugs that decrease LC activity in the animal model (e.g., imipramine and benzodiazepines) decrease anxiety in humans (Nutt, Glue, & Lawson, 1990).

A number of other studies in humans have found a positive relationship between anxiety and NE. Normal volunteers subjected to psychological stress have increases in plasma MHPG and epinephrine (Rose, 1980). Furthermore, a positive correlation has been shown between anxiety and cerebrospinal fluid (CSF) levels of NE and MHPG in depressed patients (Post et al., 1978). Patients with panic disorder and comorbid major depression were found to have a significantly higher urinary MHPG output than patients with major depression alone (Garvey, Tollefson, & Orsulak, 1987). Neese and colleagues (1985a) also demonstrated that when simple phobics are confronted with their feared object in in vivo exposure therapy, they have marked increases in plasma NE and epinephrine. Opiate abstinance and abrupt TCA discontinuation, which both can result in withdrawal states with prominent anxiety, are accompanied by increases in plasma MHPG (Charney, Heninger, Sternberg, & Landis, 1982; Glazer, Charney, & Heninger, 1987). There is clearly a strong association between anxiety and noradrenergic hyperactivity in humans.

Although support for the LC hypothesis of anxiety and panic disorder is a strong one, a few inconsistencies do exist. A number of drugs that increase LC activity fail to elicit significant anxiety in humans. For example, efaroxan, a highly selective alpha-2-adrenoceptor antagonist, even more specific than yohimbine, induces minimal anxiety (Clifford, Hoare, Jennings, & Nichols, 1989). In addition, buspirone, which also increases LC activity, fails to be anxiogenic (Sanghera, McMillen, & German, 1983); in fact, it is effective in generalized anxiety disorder but ineffective in panic disorder (Sheehan, Raj, Sheehan, & Soto, 1990). (See also Chapter 12.) Lactate and carbon dioxide which provoke panic attacks in patients with panic disorder are not associated with elevation of NE secretion (Charney, Heninger, & Jatlow, 1985; Liebowitz et al., 1986). (See Chapters 9 and 11.) Thus, when taken all together, the data supporting the LC hypothesis of anxiety are nonetheless convincing. It was anticipated that patients with panic disorder would demonstrate hyperactivity of the NE system.

This chapter reviews evidence for a NE hypothesis in panic disorder. It carefully examines the noradrenergic functioning of patients with panic disorder under various paradigms. It reviews NE functioning: (1) at rest to assess basal levels of NE output; (2) during exposure to behaviorally sensitized phobic stimuli; (3) by using selective noradrenergic challenge tests; and (4) by using peripheral adrenoceptor evaluations.

Most studies assessing NE secretion in panic disorder have utilized plasma MHPG and, to a lesser extent, plasma NE. (The latter is much less stable, with a very short half-life in comparison to MHPG.) Also, plasma MHPG has been shown to be highly correlated with brain and CSF levels of MHPG (Elsworth, Redmond, & Roth, 1982). Although most of the plasma MHPG is derived from the peripheral nervous system, 25 percent is believed to be of central nervous system origin. MHPG appears to diffuse freely across the blood/brain barrier (Kopin, Gordon, Jimerson, & Polinsky, 1983). Others have suggested that central and peripheral NE functioning may act in harmony. Changes in one most frequently parallel changes in the other (Crawley, Hattox, Maas, & Roth, 1978). Thus, plasma MHPG may be a good indicator of central as well as peripheral noradrenergic functioning. A small number of studies have assessed CSF NE and MHPG in patients with panic disorder with the understanding that CSF sampling reflects brain neurotransmitter turnover more accurately than plasma and urinary MHPG. Unfortunately, CSF NE is subject to many peripheral inputs, including active secretion and resorption of NE from the spinal cord (Nutt et al., 1988).

BASELINE NOREPINEPHRINE
FUNCTIONING AT REST

As can be seen in Table 6–1, a large number of investigators have evaluated baseline NE functioning in panic disorder patients. The overwhelming majority of the studies failed to support the hypothesis that baseline NE functioning was increased in panic disorder. Only three of 12 studies suggested increased NE output; one of these three studies was clearly significant (Nutt, 1989); another showed a significant trend (Neese, Cameron, Curtis, McCann, & Huber-Smith, 1984); and the third found that panic disorder patients were significantly different only during nighttime assessments—12-hour urinary NE—demonstrating a trend during daytime assessments (Neese et al., 1985a). Half of the studies found that NE levels were similar to normal controls (Abelson et al., 1992; Cameron et al., 1990; Charney & Heninger, 1986; Eriksson, Westberg, Alling, Thuresson, & Modigh, 1991; Uhde, Joffe, Jimerson, & Post, 1988; Woods, Charney, McPherson, Gradman, & Heninger, 1987). Interestingly, three of the studies reviewed suggested that baseline NE levels were actually lower in panic disorder than in normal controls. (Cameron, Lee, Curtis, & McCann, 1987; Edlund, Swann, & Davis, 1987; Hamlin et al., 1983).

This inconsistent picture may be due to a number of methodological problems in many of the studies. About half of the studies had small sample sizes, with most groups having less than 10 subjects. False negative findings are a risk in such investigations. Another potential problem is that many of the studies did not control dietary intake; in particular, most studies did not use a vanillylmandelic acid exclusion diet or low monoamine diet (Cameron et al., 1990; Edlund et al., 1987; Eriksson et al., 1991; Neese et al., 1984, 1985; Nutt, 1989). The latter eliminates foods that can contribute to catecholamine formation such as chocolate and coffee. In most studies normal controls were chosen who were not specifically age-matched to patients with panic disorder, although ages between the groups approximated each other. Age is an important variable since plasma NE increases 4 picograms per milliliter per year of life (Pfeifer et al., 1983). In addition, only two studies specifically sex-matched the samples (Eriksson et al., 1991; Nutt, 1989), although gender does not appear to be an important factor in NE secretion (Stene et al., 1980).

Another methological issue is that a few of the studies evaluated baseline NE as part of an ongoing challenge test (Charney & Heninger,

TABLE 6–1
Baseline Norepinephrine Output in Panic Disorder

Investigator	Subjects		Methods	Results
Hamlin et al., 1983	12 PD	6F (20–40 yrs)	+ diet, − challenge	Urinary MHPG;
	11 NC	6F (23–43 yrs)	drug free ≥ 2 wks	PD < NC
Neese et al., 1984	14 PD	11F 34 yrs	− diet, + challenge	Plasma MHPG;
	6 NC	2F 29 yrs	drug free? − PA	PD > NC (p < .06)
Neese et al., 1985a	23 PD	18F 32 yrs	− diet, − challenge	Urinary NE;
	9 NC	2F 26 yrs	drug free > 2 wks	PD > NC daytime (p < .09)
				PD > NC nighttime (p < .04)
Charney & Heninger, 1986	26 PD	24F 36 yrs	+ diet, + challenge	Plasma MHPG;
	21 NC	18F 32 yrs	drug free > 3 wks	PD = NC
Edlund et al., 1987	28 PD	18F 37 yrs	− diet, − challenge	Plasma MHPG;
	21 NC	11F 37 yrs	drug free > 1 mo	PD < NC
Cameron et al., 1987	8 PD	6F 33 yrs	+ diet, − challenge	Plasma MHPG & NE;
	4 NC	2F 29 yrs	drug free > 1 wk	PD = NC
			+ PA	urinary NE;
				PD < NC (p < .06)
				PD + PA = PD − PA
Woods et al., 1987	18 PD	14F 40 yrs	− diet, + challenge	Plasma MHPG;
	13 NC	10F 38 yrs	drug free > 1 mo	PD = NC
Uhde et al., 1988	12 PD	8F 32 yrs	+ diet, − challenge	Plasma MHPG;
	12 NC	5F 31 yrs	drug free > 2 wks	PD = NC
			+ PA	PD + PA = PD − PA
Nutt, 1989	16 PD	12F 37 yrs	− diet, + challenge	Plasma MHPG;
	16 NC	12F 37 yrs	drug free, duration?	PD > NC
			4 pts on benzos	
Cameron et al, 1990	24 PD	14F 33 yrs	− diet, − challenge	Plasma MHPG;
	8 GAD	5F 32 yrs	drug free > 10 days	PD & GAD = NC
	32 NC	12F 32 yrs		
Eriksson et al., 1991	17 PD	11F 33 yrs	− diet, − challenge	CSF MHPG;
	17 NC	11F 35 yrs	most drug free > 3 mos	PD = NC
			11 pts occasional benzos	
Abelson et al., 1992	10 PD	5F 36 yrs	− diet, + challenge	Plasma MHPG;
	14 NC	7F 33 yrs	drug free > 2 wks	PD = NC

NC	= Normal controls
PD	= Panic disorder
GAD	= Generalized anxiety disorder
F	= Females
diet	= VMA-free diet
challenge	= Part of procedure
PA	= Some panic attacks within 24 hours or during procedure
benzos	= benzodiazepines

1986; Neese et al., 1984; Nutt, 1989). The latter would occur for one to three hours with an instructional set that the challenging agent might be placebo or drug, and that the challenge might actually have accompanying side effects and possibly induce a panic attack. Thus, the experimental set was not conducive to accurate baseline assessments and was potentially axiogenic in its own right. One would anticipate that potential hyperarousal would be more pronounced in patients with panic disorder versus normal controls since the anticipated physiological experience is a more fearful stimulus for these patients (Roth et al., 1992). Interestingly, most of the studies reporting that patients with panic disorder had elevated baseline NE were part of a challenge paradigm. The two studies that reported significantly decreased NE were not attached to a challenge test (Edlund et al., 1987; Hamlin et al., 1983).

Since antidepressants and benzodiazepines decrease the firing of the LC with an associated decrease in NE secretion (Redmond, 1977, 1979; Redmond & Huang, 1979), the presence of a drug-free state for NE output studies is imperative. Although most studies clearly state that patients were drug free from one week to three months prior to investigations, a few studies were unclear as to the duration patients were drug free or even whether patients actually were drug free (Neese et al., 1984; Nutt, 1989). In addition, the recent use of benzodiazepine was allowed in some patients (Eriksson et al., 1991; Nutt, 1989). Future studies should attempt to require that patients be drug free of all psychotropics for at least one month. Recently, Asnis and coworkers (1990) demonstrated that an acute dose of desipramine (DMI) lingered in the plasma in a small subgroup of subjects for as long as three weeks. It is possible that the presence of psychotropics in patients with panic disorder either due to lack of a significant duration of a drug-free state or allowance of continued administration contributed to the lack of positive findings; that is, increased NE output in panic disorder may have been muted by recent/current treatments.

One of the potential methodological problems contributing to these diverse findings is that increased NE output may be related to the actual panic attack and not to accompanying anxiety, anticipatory anxiety, phobias, avoidant behavior, and/or dysfunction relating to this disorder. In fact, the panic attack, with its accompanying autonomic discharge (palpitations, dizziness, etc.), is what is most stressful to the patient. Usually panic attacks are infrequent. The third revised edition of the *Diagnostic and Statistical Manual of Mental Disorders* (DSM-III-R) allows the diagnosis for patients who have had only one panic attack if it followed by at least a month of fear of another attack. The fourth edition (DSM-IV) does require that uncued panic attacks be recurrent but not necessarily frequent. (See Chapter 1 for a review of DSM-III-R and DSM-IV.) The studies cited in Table 6–1 all required at least one panic attack occurring in the last three weeks. Since panic attacks usually are brief in duration, lasting five to ten minutes and rarely one hour or more, it is conceivable that unless a panic attack occurs during the procedure, NE increases may have been overlooked. Only two studies (Cameron et al., 1987; Uhde et al., 1988) noted that some of their patients (10 patients, or approximately 50 percent of their panic disorder sample) had (recent) panic attacks during or within 24 hours of the NE assessment. NE levels were found to be no higher in those patients. One study noted that none of its panic patients had recent panic attacks (Neese et al., 1984); most other studies failed to state whether attacks were recent or not (Abelson et al., 1992; Cameron et al., 1990; Charney & Heninger, 1986; Edlund et al., 1987; Eriksson et al., 1991; Hamlin et al., 1983; Neese et al., 1985a; Nutt, 1989; Woods et al., 1987). Due to the small number of subjects studied with recent panic attacks, this issue needs to be investigated further.

In summary, baseline assessments of the NE system in panic disorder have been controversial with no consistent findings. Further studies are necessary to answer more fully the questions of whether NE secretion is abnormal in panic disorders. The studies should take into account factors such as dietary restriction, duration of drug-free state, the age and sex of matched normal controls, and other cited criteria. One proposal is to conduct 24-hour cannula studies (not attached to a challenge paradigm) with sampling every 20 to 30 minutes for plasma MHPG in a subgroup of patients with panic disorder who have frequent spontaneous panic attacks (many attacks per day), so that any potential interrelationship between naturally occurring panic attacks and the NE system could be clarified. This model could answer the key questions without a large sample size.

NOREPINEPHRINE FUNCTIONING DURING SITUATIONALLY PROVOKED PANIC ATTACK

Another approach to evaluate the status of NE functioning in panic disorder is to evaluate NE output during behaviorally provoked panic attacks. Two studies have evaluated NE output in patients with panic disorder and agoraphobia prior to and during situationally provoked panic attacks. Ko and coworkers (1983) studied extensively a small number of patients ($N = 6$) with panic disorder and agoraphobia. Patients had a plasma MHPG assessment (single blood specimen) on a day without a panic attack, on a day immediately after a panic attack that was precipitated in a behavioral session, and finally again on another day without a panic attack. All specimens were taken at approximately the same time of the day, during placebo and active treatments (clonidine and imipramine). MHPG increased significantly from baseline immediately after a panic attack. In addition, MHPG was significantly correlated to the severity of anxiety. Active treatment suppressed the MHPG rise seen after an attack, supporting the belief that antipanic medication works at least partially through decreasing NE output.

Woods and associates (1987) similarly studied situationally induced panic attacks. In contrast to the Ko study (1983), Woods studied not only patients with panic disorder but also normal controls, exposing the latter to the patients' phobic stimuli (bridges, malls, etc.). In the normal controls, they noted a significant rise in plasma MHPG over baseline despite the fact that the normals did not experience a panic attack. Furthermore, there were no significant differences in plasma MHPG between groups. The authors suggest that the rise in MHPG during the experiment was secondary to exercise. Thus, although MHPG increases during situationally induced panic attacks in the studies of Ko et al. (1983) and Woods et al. (1987), the latter clearly suggests that this rise in MHPG is not specific to panic attacks. Unfortunately, these two studies do not shed direct light on the relationship of spontaneous panic attacks to NE output.

NORADRENERGIC CHALLENGES

One way to study a neurotransmitter system of a given psychiatric disorder is through the use of relatively selective neurotransmitter agonist and/or antagonist probes. By stimulating and monitoring changes in particular hormones/peptides, behaviors, and the like that are known to be at least partially regulated by that neurotransmitter, one can infer the status of that neurotransmitter system in the illness under investigation. If a response to a neurotransmitter challenge is greater or lesser than that for normal controls, the system is either hypofunctioning or hyperfunctioning respectively. The following sections review a number of noradrenergic probes in panic disorder.

Yohimbine
Yohimbine is a highly selective alpha-2-adrenoceptor antagonist that readily penetrates the blood brain barrier and increases the firing of the

LC. The latter phenomenon is believed to be due to increased discharge of noradrenergic neurons secondary to blockade of presynaptic alpha-2-adrenoceptors (antoceptors). Yohimbine previously has been shown to be anxiogenic and to induce a rise in MHPG, blood pressure, pulse, and cortisol (Charney, Heninger, & Sternberg, 1982; Holmberg & Gershon, 1961). A number of investigators have utilized this noradrenergic probe to explore for differential neuroendocrine and behavioral responses in patients with panic disorder in comparison to other control groups. A differential response in panic disorder would suggest an alpha-2-adrenoceptor dysregulation.

Charney, Heninger, and Breier (1984) gave a challenge with 20 mg yohimbine orally to 39 drug-free patients with panic disorder with or without agoraphobia and 20 normal controls. This study was placebo-controlled, single-blind in a fixed order with placebo being the first test. Both psychological and physiological responses were assessed. They found that as a group, patients with panic disorder had a similar release of plasma MHPG as normal controls. Nonetheless, certain clinical dimensions of panic disorder appeared to be related to yohimbine-stimulated MHPG responses. The plasma MHPG rise significantly correlated with the frequency of panic attacks per week for patients. The patients who had greater than or equal to 2.5 panic attacks per week had a greater MHPG response to yohimbine than normal controls. Interestingly, baseline plasma MHPG did not differ between patients with more frequent and less frequent panic attacks and normal controls.

Regarding the anxiogenic response to yohimbine, patients with panic disorder had a greater increase in "nervousness," anxiety, and various somatic symptoms (hot and cold flashes, etc.) than normal controls. Patients with higher frequency of panic attacks (≥ 2.5 per week) had more anxiety and somatic symptoms than those with less frequent panic attacks. In this study, clear criteria to define whether a panic attack was induced were not used; nonetheless, patients described their anxiety symptoms secondary to yohimbine as similar to those naturally occurring during panic attacks. In addition, yohimbine induced greater increases in both sitting and standing systolic and diastolic blood pressure in patients than in normal controls; there were no differences between patients with higher frequency and lower frequency of panic attacks.

In a replication study of their prior work with a similar methodology, Charney, Woods, Goodman, and Heninger (1987) evaluated 68 patients with agoraphobia with panic attacks or panic disorder and 20 normal controls with 20 mg oral yohimbine; they found that yohimbine induced panic attacks in 54 percent of patients with panic disorder in comparison to 5 percent of normal controls ($p < 0.04$). Patients who had panic attacks had a greater increase in plasma MHPG, plasma cortisol, systolic/diastolic blood pressures, and heart rate than normal controls. The group of patients who had yohimbine-induced panic attacks had higher baseline MHPG levels. This data supported the hypothesis that a subgroup of patients with panic disorder had alpha-2-adrenoceptor dysregulation.

Gurgius and Uhde (1990) evaluated the yohimbine challenge (20 mg orally) in 11 patients with panic disorder and seven normal controls in a double-blind, placebo-controlled design. Similar to Charney and coworkers (1987), Gurgius and associates (1990) found that yohimbine induced a significantly greater prevalence of panic attacks in panic disorder patients in comparison to normal controls (55 vs. 0 percent). Panic patients had greater increases of anxiety and "panicky emotions" than normal controls. Interestingly, yohimbine-induced MHPG secretion showed only a trend to be higher in panic disorder than in normal controls. This may represent a false negative finding due to the small sample sizes assessed. Nonetheless, yohimbine-induced MHPG rises did correlate significantly with yohimbine-induced anxiety.

Regarding other psychiatric diagnoses, Heninger, Charney, and Price (1988) studied the yohimbine challenge in a large group of patients with major depression ($N = 45$) and normal controls ($N = 20$). In comparison to prior studies with panic disorder, they found that patients with major depression demonstrated relatively normal alpha-2-adrenoceptor sensitivity. The depressed patients and normal controls had similar MHPG and anxiogenic responses. Charney, Woods, and Heninger (1989) also investigated yohimbine in generalized anxiety disorder. They studied 20 patients with generalized anxiety disorder in comparison to 20 normal controls previously studied. The behavioral, cortisol, and cardiovascular responses did not differ between patients and normal controls. Thus, in contrast to panic disorder, generalized anxiety disorder, another type of anxiety disorder, does not exhibit altered alpha-2-adrenoceptor regulation. Yohimbine also has been studied in obsessive compulsive disorder and schizophrenia; these groups also had similar responses to normal controls (Glazer et al., 1987; Rasmussen, Goodman, Woods, Heninger, & Charney, 1987). Thus, alpha-2-adrenoceptor dysregulation appears to be central to panic disorder and distinguishes it from other anxiety and psychiatric disorders (mood disorders and schizophrenia).

If the yohimbine model for panic disorders has a strong relationship to naturally occurring panic attacks, one would expect that effective antipanic treatment should have a significant effect on yohimbine-induced responses. Treatment with diazepam and alprazolam significantly decreases the anxiety response to yohimbine, although only alprazolam blocks the yohimbine-induced MHPG response (Charney & Heninger, 1985a; Charney, Heninger, & Redmond, 1983). Bendzodiazepine receptors on noradrenergic neurons clearly can regulate LC discharge. Interestingly, chronic imipramine treatment, also an effective antipanic treatment, failed to alter the anxiety and MHPG response to yohimbine. This finding presents a problem to the yohimbine model in panic disorder. Charney and Heninger (1985b) suggest that this inconsistency may be explained by various interactions. Yohimbine, which blocks presynaptic alpha-2-adrenoceptors, prevents further NE (which is built up from the NE reuptake blockade secondary to imipramine) from working at the presynaptic neuron. In addition, imipramine may affect the metabolism and/or absorption of yohimbine, which has not yet been studied.

In summary, the yohimbine studies (the yohimbine model) of panic disorder appear to demonstrate consistently an alpha-2-adrenoceptor dysregulation. The MHPG data suggest alpha-2-adrenoceptor hyposensitivity. The altered behavioral, neuroendocrine, and cardiovascular responses suggest a combination of presynaptic and postsynaptic alpha-2-adrenoceptor dysregulation. These altered responses to yohimbine are highly specific for panic disorder; responses are normal in other anxiety disorders, major depression, and schizophrenia. Successful treatments appear to normalize these abnormalities, although imipramine is an exception. Despite these unambiguous findings, a relatively small number of investigators have utilized yohimbine to study panic disorder. Further studies are indeed important.

Clonidine Challenge

Clonidine is an alpha-2-adrenoceptor agonist that induces a number of neuroendocrine, cardiovascular, and behavioral responses. In contrast to the findings with yohimbine—an alpha-2-adrenoceptor antagonist—the neuroendocrine, cardiovascular, and behavioral findings with clonidine have been inconsistent for panic disorder.

The Growth Hormone Response

Clonidine is a reliable releaser of growth hormone. The latter release is believed to be predominantly under postsynaptic alpha-2-adrenoceptor regulation at the level of the hypothalamus. Five studies have assessed the human growth hormone (HGH) response to clonidine in panic disorder. Four of these studies consistently demonstrated that the HGH response was significantly blunted in comparison to normal controls (Abelson et al., 1992; Charney & Heninger, 1986; Nutt, 1989; Uhde, Vittone, Siever, Kaye, & Post, 1986); the study by Uhde and associates (1986) also compared patients with panic disorder to patients with major depression as well as normal controls; the two patient groups had a similar HGH response, and both had a significantly lower HGH response in comparison to normal controls. Only one study (Schittecatte, Charles, Depauw, Mesters, & Wilmotte, 1988) failed to replicate the blunted HGH response to clonidine in panic disorder. This study had the smallest sample size— seven subjects in each group—and therefore was subject to type II error. In addition, the clonidine challenge was not placebo controlled.

In summary, of the total five studies assessing the HGH response to clonidine, 56 panic patients and 57 control subjects were studied. (A few subjects were removed from the analysis due to elevated baseline HGH levels, which may affect HGH release to a challenge.) If a blunted HGH response is defined as a failure of clonidine to induce a release of HGH 5 nanograms per milliliter above baseline levels, 66 percent of patients with panic disorder and 32 percent of normal controls ($x^2 = 13.5$, $p < 0.001$) were blunters. In regard to diagnostic specificity, the clonidine HGH response has been most well studied in major depression, where the HGH response has been consistently blunted in comparison to normal controls (Amsterdam, Maisling, Skolnick, Bervish, & Winokur, 1989; Uhde et al., 1986). A blunted HGH response also may occur in other anxiety disorders—generalized anxiety disorder (Abelson et al., 1991) and obsessive compulsive disorder (Siever, Insel, & Jimerson, 1983). Thus, a postsynaptic alpha-2-adrenoceptor insensitivity apparent in panic disorder is not specific for this condition; it occurs in other anxiety disorders as well as major depression.

The Cortisol Response

The cortisol response to clonidine has been minimally studied in humans. It appears to be mediated via both presynaptic and postsynaptic alpha-2-adrenoceptors, resulting in a minimal lowering of baseline cortisol. Only two studies have evaluated the cortisol response to clonidine in panic disorder. Stein and Uhde (1988) evaluated 10 patients with panic disorder in comparison to 10 normal controls and 10 patients with major depression. There was a trend for the three groups to differ (p < 0.10), with the depressive group having a greater fall than patients with panic disorder (p < 0.06). When the investigators evaluated the percent of drop of cortisol below baseline, the groups failed to reveal any differences, suggesting that higher baseline cortisol levels in major depression might have been responsible for the findings. Charney and Heninger (1986) studied the cortisol response to clonidine in 26 patients with panic disorder in comparison to 21 normal controls. In this study, patients with panic disorder had a significantly greater placebo-corrected drop in cortisol than the normal control group; nonetheless, there were no diagnosis by drug by time interactions. These inconsistent findings suggest that the clonidine cortisol assessment is an unreliable measure of alpha-2-adrenoceptor functioning.

The MHPG Response

Clonidine is known to lower plasma MHPG via a direct presynaptic alpha-2-adrenoceptor effect. The MHPG response to clonidine in panic disorder has been studied by a small number of investigators. Charney and Heninger (1986) evaluated a large group of panic disorder patients ($N = 26$) and normal controls ($N = 21$); they found that clonidine-placebo differences were significantly different between the groups; the panic disorder patients had a greater drop in plasma MHPG than the normal controls. This was replicated by Nutt (1989), but this study did not use a placebo control (saline) infusion. Recently, Abelson and associates (1992) failed to replicate the Charney & Heninger (1986) findings using a placebo-controlled challenge in panic disorder ($N = 14$) and normal controls ($N = 14$). They found that both normal controls and panic disorder patients had a similar MHPG decrease secondary to clonidine.

Blood Pressure and Pulse Response

Clonidine lowers blood pressure and pulse in humans via a combination of presynaptic and postsynaptic alpha-2-receptor effects at both peripheral and CNS sites. A number of investigators have attempted to assess whether the fall in any of these vital signs was significantly different for panic disorder patients versus normal controls, which would suggest a dysregulation of the alpha-2-adrenoceptor. Charney and Heninger (1986), in comparing 26 panic disorder patients to 21 normal controls, demonstrated that patients had a significantly greater placebo-corrected fall in diastolic blood pressure (sitting and standing) and a trend for a greater fall in systolic blood pressure than the controls. Heart rate increases were similar between the groups. Interestingly, patients had significantly higher baseline systolic and diastolic blood pressure as well as heart rate. This study had a single-blind, placebo-controlled design.

Nutt (1989) replicated these findings, also demonstrating an exaggerated fall in diastolic and systolic blood pressure; heart rate had a similar fall between groups. Panic disorder patients had nonsignificant differences in baseline blood pressure but did have a significantly higher baseline heart rate (71 $\pm$ 2.2 beats per minute vs. 64 $\pm$ 2.2 beats per minute). Unfortunately, this study was not placebo controlled.

Uhde and coworkers (1989) evaluated clonidine in the only double-blind, placebo-controlled assessment of a clonidine challenge in panic disorder ($N = 14$) and normal controls ($N = 10$). Blood pressure and heart rate significantly decreased to clonidine in both groups with no significant differences in their responses. The investigators also found that baseline blood pressure and heart rate were all minimally but significantly higher in the panic disorder group versus the normal controls.

Abelson and associates (1992) recently attempted to replicate the clonidine cardiovascular findings in panic disorder reported by Charney and Heninger (1986). The investigators also used a single-blind, placebo-controlled challenge. They found that both patients with panic disorder ($N = 14$) and normal controls ($N = 14$) had a similar decline in blood pressure and heart rate.

The Behavioral Response

Clonidine has been shown to affect certain behaviors in humans. In particular, a sedative and anxiolytic response is seen in patients with major depression and opiate withdrawal (Gold, Redmond, & Kleber, 1978; Siever & Uhde, 1984). These behaviors are believed to be under pre- and postsynaptic alpha-2-adrenoceptor regulation. Thus, it was of great interest to evaluate the effect of clonidine on these behaviors in panic disorder. Charney and Heninger (1986) evaluated the sedative and anxiolytic response (via visual analog scales) of clonidine in panic disorder ($N = 26$) and normal controls ($N = 21$). Both groups experienced sedation to clonidine; the panic disorder patients experienced significantly less sedation than the normal controls. The anxiolytic response was not significantly different between the groups.

Nutt (1989) demonstrated that panic disorder patients ($N = 16$) experience a significantly greater anxiolytic response than normal controls

($N = 16$) (not placebo controlled). Similar to the findings of Charney and Heninger (1986), panic disorder patients had a significantly reduced sedation response than normal controls.

Uhde and coworkers (1989) demonstrated that clonidine significantly reduced anxiety. Panic disorder patients ($N = 14$) had a significantly greater reduction of anxiety than the normal controls ($N = 10$). In addition, clonidine induced a significant sedative effect, but it was experienced similarly among the groups. In contrast, Abelson and others (1992) found that panic disorder patients ($N = 14$) and normal controls ($N = 14$) had a similar anxiolytic and sedative responses to clonidine.

In summary, the use of clonidine in panic disorder has revealed one consistent finding: Patients with panic disorder have a blunted HGH response, suggesting postsynaptic alpha-2-adrenoceptor insensitivity. Nonetheless, the blunted HGH response is not specific for panic disorder; it occurs in other psychiatric disorders as well. Clonidine-induced changes in cortisol, MHPG, blood pressure, pulse, and various behaviors (anxiety and sedation) are inconsistent and may not be reliable measures to discriminate alpha-2 functioning in panic disorder from other patient groups or normal controls. Possibly contributing to these inconsistent findings are a few methological differences among the seven clonidine studies in panic disorder. For example, specific doses and methods of clonidine administration varied; some studies used 2 micrograms per kilogram intravenously (μg/kg IV) given over five minutes (Abelson et al., 1992; Uhde et al., 1986, 1989; Stein & Uhde, 1988); 1.5 μg/kg IV over five minutes (Charney & Heninger, 1986); 1.5 μg/kg IV given over 10 minutes (Nutt, 1989); and a fixed dose of 150 μg administered over 10 minutes (Schittecatte et al., 1988). In addition, of the seven studies, three were not placebo controlled (Nutt, 1989; Schittecatte et al., 1988; Uhde et al., 1986); two studies were placebo controlled but single blind (Abelson et al., 1992; Charney & Heninger, 1986); and only two studies were double-blind, placebo-controlled (Stein & Uhde, 1988; Uhde et al., 1989).

Desipramine Challenge

Desipramine (DMI) in low doses is a relatively selective reuptake inhibitor of NE (Randrup & Braestrup, 1977). When administered acutely, either intramuscularly (75 mg) or intravenously (12.5–50 mg), it reliably releases cortisol (Asnis et al., 1985; Asnis, Sanderson, & van Praag, 1993; Laakman, Schoen, Blaschke, & Witmann, 1985). Laakman and associates (1986) have demonstrated that this cortisol response to

DMI is predominately under alpha-1-adrenoceptor regulation; pretreatment with prazosin, an alpha-1-adrenoceptor antagonist, blocks the cortisol rise to DMI in contrast to neglible effects from pretreatment with propranolol, a beta-adrenoceptor antagonist, and methysergide, a serotonergic antagonist. Thus, the cortisol response to DMI appears to be an index of noradrenergic functioning and probably alpha-1-adrenoceptor regulation.

We have previously demonstrated that patients with major depression have a blunted cortisol response to DMI in comparison to normal controls, suggesting alpha-1-adrenoceptor insensitivity (Asnis et al., 1985, 1993). Here we present preliminary findings of an ongoing study investigating the cortisol response to DMI in a large group of patients with panic disorder and major depression as well as normal controls. The main question was whether panic disorder had a dysfunction of alpha-1-adrenoceptor regulation similar to that for major depression.

The cortisol response to 75 milligrams (mg) intramuscularly (IM) DMI was studied in a group of 32 patients with panic disorder, 63 patients with major depression, and 53 normal controls. All subjects were evaluated with the schedule for Affective Disorders and Schizophrenia (Endicott & Spitzer, 1978) and given appropriate psychiatric diagnoses according to Research Diagnostic Criteria (Spitzer, Endicott, & Robins, 1978). All subjects had discontinued prior psychotropic medications for a minimum of three weeks. Prior to receiving the DMI challenge, all patients had normal physical and laboratory examinations including an electrocardiogram, complete blood count, and differential and admission chemistry screen with thyroid function tests. Subsequently, the patients fasted from midnight, the night before the study, and awakened at 7A.M. the following morning. By 9A.M. the subjects arrived at our neuroendocrine laboratory, where a catheter was inserted in a forearm vein and kept patent with heparined saline. After one hour of adaptation, with monitoring of cortisol every 15 minutes, 75 mg DMI was administered intramuscularly into the gluteal muscle. Cortisol was monitored every 15 minutes for the next two hours.

Figure 6–1 demonstrates the cortisol response to DMI over 120 minutes for patients with panic disorder, major depression, and normal controls. The three groups differed significantly (group by time) from each other ($F = 2.8$, $p < 0.0001$); panic disorder and major depression had similar responses (group by time, $F = 0.45$, $p = NS$). In addition, panic disorder and major depression had significantly (group by time) blunted

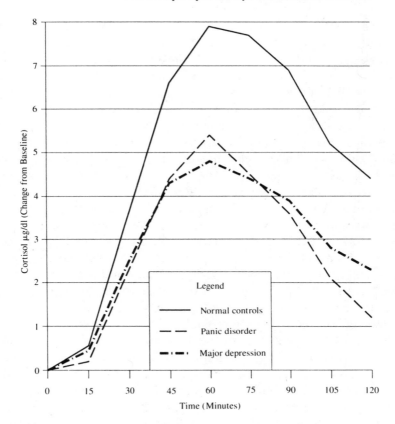

Figure 6–1. Cortisol response to 75 mg IM DMI.

cortisol responses in comparison to the normal controls ($F = 3.8$, $p < 0.003$ and $F = 4.2$, $p < 0.0001$ respectively).

Thus, the DMI cortisol response suggests that panic disorder patients have an alpha-1-adrenoceptor insensitivity similar to that for major depression. Whether this abnormality normalizes with treatment is currently under investigation. Furthermore, a blunted cortisol response to DMI in panic disorder must be replicated in other studies.

Isoproterenol Infusions/A Beta-Adrenergic Agonist

The role of the adrenergic system in panic disorder has long been suspected by many investigators. Lindemann (1935) and Lindemann and

Finesinger (1938) demonstrated that epinephrine induced significant anxiety attacks in patients with anxiety disorder in contrast to nonanxiety psychiatric disorders. In addition, Pyke and Greenberg (1986) found that NE infusions induced panic attacks in patients with panic disorder. As the fact that epinephrine and NE stimulate both alpha- and beta-adrenoceptors and the main symptomatology of panic disorder—palpitations, shortness of breath, tremulousness—has suggested involvement of the beta-adrenergic system; a logical focus would be directed to the beta-adrenergic system in panic disorder. Furthermore, interest in the role of the beta-adrenergic system in panic disorder has developed from the basic noradrenergic model of anxiety developed by Redmond. The NE-containing neurons of the LC stimulate beta-adrenoceptors throughout the brain (Grant & Redmond, 1981). The importance of beta-adrenoceptors to LC-mediated anxiety was demonstrated by Huang, Maas, & Redmond (1977); monkeys pretreated with a beta-adrenoceptor antagonist, propranolol, did not experience behavioral activation subsequent to LC stimulation. A number of investigators have pursued evaluations of the beta-adrenergic system in panic disorder with a selective beta-adrenoceptor agonist, isoproterenol.

Frohlich, Tarazi, and Dustan (1969) studied 14 patients formally called "hyderdynamic beta-adrenergic circulatory state," which had many of the autonomic features of panic disorder patients, in comparison to 13 patients with essential hypertension and 25 nornotensive controls. Isoproterenol was infused at increasing rates of 1 to 3 µg per minute. Nine of the 14 patients with this "panic disorder–like syndrome" had uncontrollable "hysterical outbursts," which were terminated by 10 mg IV propranolol but not by placebo. These outbursts were not well described but probably were panic attacks. Easton and Sherman (1976) similarly found that isoproterenol induced anxiety states in four patients who had a history of panic attacks; the latter were blocked by 2.5 to 5 mg IV propranolol.

Neese and coworkers (1984) gave an isoproterenol infusion (increasing the dose from 0.06 to 4.0 µg every 10 minutes with each new dose double the prior one) to eight patients with panic disorder and six normal controls in a complex design. The procedure lasted four hours including multiple challenges (e.g., an exercise assessment). Nonetheless, the investigators found that the isoproterenol-induced increases in heart rate were significantly lower in patients with panic disorder than in normal controls. Their data did not support an increased beta-adrenoceptor sensitivity for panic disorder where the latter patients should have had a greater rise in heart rate than the control group. Indeed, Neese and coworkers (1984) suggested that their data supported a beta-adrenoceptor hyposensitivity syndrome. They hypothesized that the latter may be due to down-regulation of beta-adrenoceptors secondary to an increased NE output state in panic disorder. The latter was supported in their project by a significantly increased baseline heart rate in patients with panic disorder in comparison to normal controls (84 vs. 58 beats per minute, $p < 0.001$). The rejection of beta-adrenergic hypersensitivity theory was further supported by the finding that none of the panic disorder patients panicked during the isoproterenol infusions.

The most comprehensive assessment utilizing the isoproterenol challenge in panic disorder have been conducted by Pohl and associates (1988). Three challenges—isoproterenol, lactate (1 molar solution), and dextrose (placebo)—were administered double blind and in random order to 86 patients with panic disorder and 45 normal controls; 66 percent of the panic disorder group panicked to isoproterenol in comparison to only 9 percent of the normal controls ($x^2 = 36.8$, $p < 0.001$). Patients rated their attacks as similar to their naturally occurring attacks but somewhat less intense.

Successful treatment of panic disorder with TCAs appears to also block isoproterenol-induced panic attacks. Pohl and associates (1985) restudied 10 patients with panic disorder, seven of whom had panicked to isoproterenol after responding to a course of a TCA. The isoproterenol challenge was part of a placebo-controlled, double-blind paradigm. Only one of the 10 patients experienced a panic attack. The specificity of isoproterenol-induced panic attacks for panic disorder has been minimally studied in comparison to normal controls and even less well studied in other psychiatric diagnoses. Pohl and coworkers (1986) found that nine of 13 patients with bulimia panicked after an isoproterenol infusion. Rainey and associates (1987) found that two of seven patients with post-traumatic disorders experienced panic attacks. These studies with small sample sizes suggest that other diagnostic categories that tend to have anxiety symptoms also may have a beta-adrenergic dysfunction similar to panic disorder. Further studies to assess the specificity of isoproterenol-induced panic attacks are necessary.

A number of questions and inconsistencies are of particular concern regarding the finding of beta-adrenergic hyperactivity in panic disorder. First, it has been suggested that isoproterenol, like catecholamines, does not penetrate the blood brain barrier very well (Weil-Malherke, Axelrod, & Tomchick, 1959). Nonetheless, intravenous doses of isoproterenol produce significant electroencepholographic changes in curarized animals, suggesting CNS activation (Goldstein & Munoz, 1961). Whether anxiety and arousal secondary to beta-adrenergic stimulation is due to direct CNS effects or indirect stimulation of the peripheral nervous system is not clear. Second, if the beta-adrenergic system was hyperactive in panic disorder, one would hypothesize that a beta-adrenergic blockers would be therapeutic. The overall results of a number of studies are that propranolol is not a highly effective treatment for panic disorder. Therapeutic effects may occur for somatic symptoms (e.g., palpitations and tremors) but not for the core psychological symptoms such as fear (Noyes, 1982). It has been suggested that higher doses of propranolol may ameliorate psychological symptoms of anxiety (Kathol et al., 1980). A complicating aspect of beta-receptors is that their blockade results in up-regulation (Lima & Turner, 1983). This may partially explain why Noyes and associates (1984) found that propranolol apparently was effective in week 1 of treatment but lost efficacy by week 2. Thus, propranolol blocks attacks acutely, either spontaneous ones (early in treatment) or those induced by isoproterenol, but fails to be therapeutic with long-term use.

PERIPHERAL NORADRENERGIC RECEPTORS

Circulating lymphocytes and platelets have been found to possess beta-adrenoceptors and alpha-2-adrenoceptors respectively. Therefore, these peripheral blood cells, which are easily accessible, have provided a non-invasive methodology to study neurotransmitter receptor function.

Lymphocyte Beta-Adrenoceptor

The kinetics of the lymphocyte beta-adrenoceptor have been evaluated in four studies. Three studies have found a reduced B_{max}/binding in panic disorder (Aronson, Carasiti, McBane, & Whitaker-Azmitia, 1989; Brown, Charney, Woods, Heninger, & Tallman, 1988; Maddock, Carter, Magliozzi, & Gietzen, 1993); one study has found an increased B_{max} in panic disorder versus normal controls (Albus, Bondy, & Ackenheil, 1986). The latter study, the only one finding increased beta-adrenoceptor density, was rather small and did not clearly state its methodology nor the nature or number of its controls. In summary, although there are only a limited number of studies, the majority do suggest a decrease in lymphocyte B-adrenoceptor number for panic disorder. Interestingly, this decrease of peripheral noradrenergic function is supported by a number of studies finding reduced lymphocyte cyclic adenosine monophosphate (AMP) responses to isoproterenol in patients with "incapacitating anxiety" (Lima & Turner, 1983) and panic disorder (Charney, Innis, Duman, Woods, & Heninger, 1989; Maddock, Carter, Magliozzi, & Gietzen, 1993). In addition, reduced beta-adrenoceptor functioning is supported by Neese and coworkers (1984), finding a reduced heart rate response in panic disorder patients to an isoproterenol infusion in comparison to normal controls.

Decreased peripheral beta-receptor function is not unique for panic disorder and can be seen in a number of physical illnesses, such as hypertension (Feldman, 1987), as well as another psychiatric illness, major depressive disorder (Extein, Tallman, Smith, & Goodwin, 1979; Magliozzi et al., 1989). Since major depression also is associated with lowered beta-adrenoceptor functioning, an important question to answer is whether the panic disorder studies demonstrating decreased beta-adrenoceptor functioning ($N = 3$) might be related to a concurrent major depression, a past history of major depression, or perhaps depressive symptoms per se. Of the four studies reviewed here, two studies failed to state whether patients had a history of depression, (Albus et al., 1986; Aronson et al., 1989). Two of these studies had a subgroup of patients with current and/or past history of major depression. Brown and associates (1988) studied 12 patients with panic disorder and found that panic patients with concurrent major depression ($N = 4$) or with a history of major depression ($N = 7$) did not differ in their lymphocyte beta-adrenoceptor functioning from the panic group who never had major depression. In contrast, Maddock, Gietzen, and Goodman (1993), in a study of 12 patients with panic disorder, found that panic patients with concurrent major depression or a past history of major depression ($N = 3$) had significantly lower lymphocyte beta-adrenoceptor functioning than panic patients without depression. Furthermore, they found that lymphocyte beta-adrenoceptor functioning was correlated negatively with severity of depressive symptoms (Beck Inventory Score) in the total sample. Thus, the contribution of depression is unclear on these panic disorder findings.

Interestingly, beta-adrenoceptor down-regulation appears to be adaptive in animals undergoing stress; stressed animals develop decreased beta-adrenoceptor functioning and have less stress-related organic pathology (Stone & Platt, 1982). Maddock, Gietzen, and Goodman (1993) also have suggested that down-regulation of beta-adrenoceptors may be adaptive for patients with panic disorder. They found that patients with decreased lymphocyte beta-adrenoceptor number had less severe panic disorder and a more favorable treatment response.

In summary, lymphocyte beta-adrenoceptor functioning in patients with panic disorder appears to be decreased or down-regulated in comparison to normal controls. Unfortunately, only a few studies have assessed this model of noradrenergic functioning in panic disorder adequately. Decreased lymphocyte beta-adrenoceptor functioning appears to be nonspecific for panic disorder, occurring also in major depression. The role of depression must be evaluated further in panic disorder patients to ensure the validity of these findings for panic disorder. Since the lymphocyte is so readily accessible, further studies should investigate these issues.

Platelet Alpha-2-Adrenoceptor

As described earlier, a number of investigations have suggested a dysregulation of the alpha-2-adrenoceptor in panic disorder, as evidenced by altered biochemical, neuroendocrine, behavioral, and cardiovascular responses to the alpha-2-adrenoceptor agonist clonidine and to the alpha-2-adrenoceptor antagonist yohimbine. A small number of studies also have examined the alpha-2-adrenoceptor of the platelet in panic disorder. Of six studies that evaluated the platelet alpha-2-adrenoreceptor kinetics, three found no differences in alpha-2-adrenoceptor receptor density in panic disorder in comparison to normal controls (Charney, Innis, Duman, Woods, & Heninger, 1989; Norman, Kimber, Judd, Burrow, & McIntyre, 1987; Nutt & Fraser, 1987), and three studies found a decrease in the number of alpha-2-receptors (Albus et al., 1986; Cameron, Smith, Hollingsworth, Neese, & Curtis, 1984; Cameron et al., 1990). As discussed earlier, the Albus study must be viewed with caution due to a number of methodological problems. Thus, there are only two methodologically acceptable studies, both by Cameron and coworkers (1984, 1990), suggesting decreased alpha-2-adrenoceptor binding sites. Even here, with the same investigator group, the data are somewhat contradictory; although the earlier study (1984) found that the number of binding sites assessed with tritiated clonidine in panic disorder ($N = 11$) was similar to normal controls ($N = 13$), the latter study

(1990) found the clonidine B_{max} was significantly lower in panic patients ($N = 22$) in comparison to normal controls ($N = 31$). When tritiated yohimbine, an alpha-2-agonist, was the ligand used, the number of binding sites in both studies (Cameron et al., 1984, 1990) was lower in panic patients in comparison to normal controls.

In summary, the data for platelet alpha-2-adrenoceptor kinetics in panic disorder is inconsistent and the studies are minimal in number. Only one investigator group has satisfactorily demonstrated decreased platelet alpha-2-adrenoceptor number in panic disorder. Furthermore, if there is a positive finding here for panic disorder, there is a suggestion that it is nonspecific, being found also in major depression and generalized anxiety disorder (Cameron et al., 1984, 1990). The platelet may not be the best model to study noradrenergic receptors. In contrast to beta-adrenoceptors on lymphocytes, which are responsive to circulating catecholamines, alpha-2-adrenoceptors on platelets appears to adapt minimally to changes in concentration of catecholomines (Egan, Neubig, & Julius, 1985) and therefore do not behave like the alpha-adrenoceptor in the central nervous system. Nonetheless, since platelet alpha-2-adrenoceptor assessments are so readily accessible, as are lymphocyte beta-adrenoceptors, further studies should evaluate their potential usefulness.

SUMMARY AND CONCLUSIONS

The role of the NE system in panic disorder was investigated with the working hypothesis that hyperactivity of the NE system was associated with panic disorder (the LC hypothesis of panic disorder). A number of paradigms of NE functioning were intensively reviewed. The baseline NE output studies at rest were found to be inconsistent (predominantly not supporting the NE hypothesis), but a number of methodological problems were enumerated. Two studies examining NE output to behaviorally induced panic attacks found increased NE secretion, although exercise appears to have been the major factor and not panic attacks per se (Ko et al., 1983; Woods et al., 1987). The analysis of the peripheral noradrenergic receptors on circulating blood cells—alpha-2-adrenoceptors on platelets and beta-adrenoceptors on lymphocytes—has suggested decreased beta-adrenoceptor functioning with inconsistent alpha-2-adrenoceptor findings. These findings must be viewed tentatively due to an extremely small number of adequate studies.

The most consistent and well-replicated studies of NE functioning in panic disorder have been the neuroendocrine and behavioral challenge studies using relatively selective noradrenergic probes. The yohimbine studies have consistently demonstrated a marked exaggerated response in anxiety, cortisol, blood pressure, pulse, and MHPG, suggesting alpha-1-adrenoceptor dysregulation. These findings were specific for panic disorder in that other anxiety disorders (generalized anxiety disorder and obsessive compulsive disorder), major depressive disorder, and schizophrenia had normal responses. In addition, the yohimbine response normalizes with antipanic treatments. Thus, the yohimbine model should be utilized further to understand the pathophysiology of panic disorder. The clonidine challenge consistently found a blunted HGH response in most studies in panic disorder with inconsistent behavioral findings. The blunted HGH response believed to represent postsynaptic alpha-2-insensitivity is not specific for panic disorder, occurring in other diagnostic categories. The cortisol response to a DMI challenge was blunted in panic patients, consistent with alpha-1-insensitivity; this was nonspecific for panic disorder, occurring also in patients with major depression. The beta-adrenergic system has been studied predominately by isoproterenol challenges. These studies have suggested a down-regulation of peripheral beta-adrenoceptors (decreased isoproteronol responses of heart rate and lymptocyte cyclic AMP) as well as an up-regulation of CNS beta-adrenoceptors (e.g., an increased anxiogenic response to isoproteronol). Furthermore, disturbances in the beta-adrenergic system in panic disorder are nonspecific and appear to normalize with treatment.

The fact that the most consistent noradrenergic abnormalities were demonstrated by challenge studies assessing receptor function and not by baseline and peripheral neurotransmitter assessments is not totally surprising. A biological system may be dysfunctional but at baseline may be in a state of equilibrium. Only through perturbations of the system by stressors—challenge tests—may dysregulation visibly appear. This has been observed in corticosteroid regulation in major depression, where basal cortisol secretion may be normal but still the corticosteroid sensitivity (brought out with challenge tests) can be altered (Asnis et al., 1987).

This review of NE functioning in panic disorder clearly supports a significant role of NE in the pathophysiology of panic disorder. It would be myopic to suggest that only NE may have a potentially important role in this disorder. It is clear that NE can affect and/or be affected by other neurotransmitters and peptides that are also associated with anxiety and panic disorder. (See Chapters 7 to 11.) Asnis, Wetzler, Sanderson, Kahn, and van Praag, (1992) recently found that subjects who had a blunted DMI cortisol response (evidence of a noradrenergic dysfunction) also had an exaggerated cortisol response to mChlorophenylpiperazine (mCPP) (evidence of a serotonergic dysfunction).

In summary, evidence is presented that supports a noradrenergic dysfunction in panic disorder. Some studies support hyperactivity of the NE system (e.g., isoproteronol and yohimbine exaggerated anxiety responses), while other studies have suggested hypofunctioning of the NE system (e.g., decreased MHPG response to yohimbine and a blunted HGH response to clonidine). These complicated findings are not inconsistent with the diverse nature of the noradrenergic receptor system. For example, Heninger and Charney (1987) have reviewed that tricyclic antidepressants can induce a number of potential changes on beta-adrenoceptors, depending on what area of the brain is examined; for example, up-regulation occurs in the pineal gland, down-regulation occurs in the cerebral cortex, and no changes occur in the hippocampus. Since NE has an important role in panic disorder, further NE studies to better understand the pathophysiology of this illness are required. Using sophisticated neuroimaging techniques, one may well learn specific adrenoceptor subtypes and brain areas that are dysfunctional in panic disorder, which will lead to benefits in treatment.

REFERENCES

Abelson, J. L., Glitz, D., Cameron, O. G., Lee, M. A., Bronzo, M., & Curtis, G. C. (1991). Blunted growth hormone response to clonidine in patients with generalized anxiety. *Archives of General Psychiatry, 48,* 157–162.

Abelson, J. L., Glitz, D., Cameron, O. G., Lee, M. A., Bronzo, M., & Curtis, G. C. (1992). Endocrine, cardiovascular, and behavioral response to clonidine in patients with panic disorder. *Biological Psychiatry, 32,* 18–25.

Albus, M., Bondy, B., & Ackenheil, M. (1986). Adrenergic receptors on blood cells: Relation to the pathophysiology of anxiety. *Clinical Neuropharmacology, 9,* 359–361.

Amsterdam, D., Maisling, G., Skolnick, B., Bervish, N., & Winokur, A. (1989). Multiple hormone responses to clonidine administration in depressed patients and healthy volunteers. *Biological Psychiatry, 26,* 265–278.

Aronson, T. A., Carasiti, I., McBane, D., & Whitaker-Azmitia, P. (1989). Biological correlates of lactate sensitivity in panic disorder. *Biological Psychiatry, 26,* 463–477.

Asnis, G. M., Halbreich, U., Rabinovich, H., Ryan, N. D., Sachar, E. J., Nelson, B., Puig-Antich, J., & Novacenko, H. (1985). The cortisol response to desipramine in endogenous depressive and normal controls: Preliminary findings. *Psychiatric Research, 14,* 225–233.

Asnis, G. M., Halbreich, U., Ryan, N., Rabinovich, H., Puig-Antich, J., Nelson, B., Novacenko, H., & Harkavy-Friedman, J. (1987). The relationship of the dexamethasone suppression test (1 mg and 2 mg) to basal plasma cortisol levels in endogenous depression. *Psychoneuroendocrinology, 42,* 295–301.

Asnis, G. M., Harkavy-Friedman, J. M., Iqbal, N., Bajwa, W. K., Kalus, O., Rubinson, E., van Praag, H. M., & Cooper, T. B. (1990). The drug free period: A methodological issue. *Biological Psychiatry, 27,* 657–660.

Asnis, G. M., Sanderson, W. C., & van Praag, H. M. (1993). The cortisol response to intramuscular desipramine in patients with major depression and normal control subjects: A replication study. *Psychiatry Research, 44,* 237–250.

Asnis, G. M., Wetzler, S., Sanderson, W. C., Kahn, R. S., & van Praag, H. M. (1992). The functional interrelationship of serotonin and norepinephrine: Cortisol response to MCPP and DMI in panic, depression and normals. *Psychiatry Research, 43,* 65–76.

Brown, S. L., Charney, D. S., Woods, S. W., Heninger, G. R., & Tallman, J. (1988). Lymphocyte beta-adrenergic receptor binding in panic disorder. *Psychopharmacology, 94,* 24–28.

Cameron, O. G., Lee, M. A., Curtis, G. C., & McCann, D. S. (1987). Endocrine and physiological changes during "spontaneous" panic attacks. *Psychoneuroendocrinology, 12,* 321–331.

Cameron, O. G., Smith, C. B., Hollingsworth, P. J., Neese, R. M., & Curtis, G. C. (1984). Platelet alpha$_2$-adrenergic receptor binding and plasma catecholamines: Before and during imipramine treatment in patients with panic anxiety. *Archives of General Psychiatry, 41,* 1144–1148.

Cameron, O. G., Smith, C. B., Lee, M. A., Hollingsworth, P. J., Hill, E. M., & Curtis, G. C. (1990). Adrenergic status in anxiety disorders: Platelet alpha-2-adrenergic receptor binding, blood pressure, pulse, and plasma catecholamines in panic and generalized anxiety disorder patients and in normal subjects. *Biological Psychiatry, 28,* 3–20.

Charney, D. S., & Heninger, G. R. (1985a). Noradrenergic function and the mechanism of action of antianxiety treatment I. The effect of long-term alprazolam treatment. *Archives of General Psychiatry, 42,* 458–467.

Charney, D. S., & Heninger, G. R. (1985b). Noradrenergic function and the mechanism of action of antianxiety treatment II. The effect of long-term imipramine treatment. *Archives of General Psychiatry, 42,* 473–481.

Charney, D. S., & Heninger, G. R. (1986). Abnormal regulation of noradrenergic function in panic disorder. *Archives of General Psychiatry, 43,* 1042–1054.

Charney, D. S., Heninger, G. R., & Breier, A. (1984). Noradrenergic function in panic anxiety: Effects of yohimbine in healthy subjects and patients with agoraphobia and panic disorder. *Archives of General Psychiatry, 41,* 751–763.

Charney, D. S., Heninger, G. R., & Jatlow, P. I. (1985). Increase anxiogenic effects of caffeine in panic disorder. *Archives of General Psychiatry, 42,* 233–243.

Charney, D. S., Heninger, G. R., & Redmond, D. E., Jr. (1983). Yohimbine-induced anxiety and increased noradrenergic function in humans: Effects of diazepam and clonidine. *Life Sciences, 33,* 19.

Charney, D. S., Heninger, G. R., & Sternberg, D. E. (1982). Assessment of x-adrenergic autoreceptor function in humans: Effects of oral yohimbine. *Life Sciences, 30,* 2033–2041.

Charney, D. S., Heninger, G. R., Sternberg, D. E., & Landis, D. H. (1982). Abrupt discontinuation of tricyclic antidepressant drugs: Evidence for noradrenergic hyperactivity. *British Journal of Psychiatry, 141,* 377–386.

Charney, D. S., Innis, R. B., Duman, R. S., Woods, S. W., & Heninger, G. R. (1989). Platelet alpha-2-receptor binding and adenylate cyclase activity in panic disorder. *Psychopharmacology, 98,* 102–107.

Charney, D. S., Redmond, D. E., Jr., Gallaway, M. P., Kleber, H. D., Heninger, F. R., Murberg, M., & Roth, R. H. (1988). Nultrexone precipitated opiate withdrawal in methdone-addicted human subjects: Evidence for noradrenergic hyperactivity. *Life Sciences, 35,* 1263–1272.

Charney, D. S., Woods, S. W., & Heninger, G. R. (1989). Noradrenergic function in generalized anxiety disorder: Effects of yohimbine in healthy subjects and patients with generalized anxiety disorder. *Psychiatry Research, 27,* 173–182.

Charney, D. S., Woods, S. W., Goodman, W. K., & Heninger, G. R. (1987). Neurobiological mechanisms of panic anxiety: Biochemical and behavioral correlates of yohimbine-induced panic attacks. *American Journal of Psychiatry, 144,* 1030–1036.

Clifford, J. N., Hoare, R. C., Jennings, M., & Nichols, J. D. (1989). Safety, tolerance and disposition of efaroxan in healthy nonpatient volunteers. *British Journal of Clinical Pharmacology, 28,* 217P–218P.

Crawley, J. N., Hattox, S. E., Maas, J. W., & Roth, R. H. (1978). 3-Methoxy-4-hydroxy-phenethylene glycol increase in plasma after stimulation of the nucleus locus coeruleus. *Brain Research, 141,* 380–384.

Easton, J. D., & Sherman, D. G. (1976). Somatic anxiety attacks and propranolol. *Archives of Neurology, 33,* 689–691.

Edlund, M. J., Swann, A. C., & Davis, C. M. (1987). Plasma MHPG in untreated panic disorder. *Biological Psychiatry, 22,* 1488–1491.

Egan, G., Neubig, R., & Julius, S. (1985). Pharmacologic reduction of sympathetic drive increases platelet alpha-2-receptor number. *Clinical Pharmacological, 38,* 519–524.

Elsworth, J., Redmond, D. E., & Roth, R. (1982). Plasma and cerebrospinal fluid 3-methoxy-4-hydroxyphenylethylene glycol (MHPG) as indices of brain norepinephrine metabolism in primates. *Brain Research, 235,* 155–174.

Endicott, J., & Spitzer, R. L. (1978). A diagnostic interview: The Schedule for Affective Disorders and Schizophrenia. *Archives of General Psychiatry, 35,* 837–844.

Eriksson, E., Westberg, P., Alling, C., Thuresson, K., & Modigh, K. (1991). Cerebrospinal fluid levels of monoamine metabolites in panic disorder. *Psychiatry Research, 36,* 243–251.

Extein, J., Tallman, J., Smith, C. C., & Goodwin, F. K. (1979). Changes in lymphocyte beta-adrenergic receptors in depression receptors in depression and mania, *Psychiatry Research, 1,* 191–197.

Feldman, R. D. (1987). Beta-adrenergic receptor alterations in hypertension: Physiological and molecular correlates. *Canadian Journal of Physiology and Pharmacology, 65,* 1666–1672.

Frohlich, E. D., Tarazi, R. C., & Dustan, H. P. (1969). Hyperdynamic beta-adrenergic circulatory state. *Archives of Internal Medicine, 123,* 1–7.

Garvey, M. J., Tolleson, G. D., & Orsulak, P. J. (1987). Elevations of urinary MHPG in depressed patients with panic attacks. *Psychiatry Research, 20,* 183–187.

Glazer, W. M., Charney, D. S., & Heninger, G. R. (1987). Noradrenergic function in schizophrenia. *Archives of General Psychiatry, 44,* 898–904.

Gold, M. S., Redmond, D. E., Jr., & Kleber, H. D. (1978). Clonidine in opiate withdrawal. *Lancet 1,* 929–930.

Goldstein, L., & Munoz, C. (1961). Influence of adrenergic stimulant and blocking drugs on cerebral and electrical activity in curarized animals. *Journal of Pharmacology and Experimental Therapy, 132,* 345–353.

Grant, S. J., & Redmond, D. E., Jr. (1981). The neuroanatomy and pharmacology of the nucleus locus ceruleus. In H. Lal & S. Fielding (Eds.), *Pharmacology of clonidine* (pp. 5–27) New York: Alan R. Liss.

Gurguis, G. N. M., & Uhde, T. W. (1990). Plasma 3-methoxy-4-hydroxyphenylethylene glycol (MHPG) and growth hormone response to yohimbine in panic disorder patients and normal control. *Psychoneuroendocrinology, 15,* 217–224.

Hamlin, C. L., Lydiard, R. B., Martin, D., Dackis, C. A., Pottash, A. C., Sweeney, D., & Gold, M. S. (1983). Urinary excretion of noradrenaline metabolite decreased in panic disorder. *Lancet 2,* 740–741.

Heninger, G. R., & Charney, D. S. (1987). Mechanisms of action of antidepressant treatments: Implications for the etiology and treatment of depressive disorders in psychopharmacology. In H. Y. Meltzer (Ed.), *The third generation of progress* (pp. 535–552). New York: Raven Press.

Heninger, G. R., Charney, D. S., & Price, L. H. (1988). Alpha$_2$-adrenergic receptor sensitivity in depression. The plasma MHPG, behavioral and cardiovascular responses to yohimbine. *Archives of General Psychiatry, 45,* 718–726.

Holmberg, J., & Gershon, S. (1961). Autonomic and psychiatric effects of yohimbine hydrochloride. *Psychopharmacology, 2,* 93–106.

Huang, Y. H., Maas, J. W., & Redmond, D. E., Jr. (1977). Evidence for noradergic specificity of behavioral effect of electrical stimulation of the nucleus locus ceruleus. *Society of Neuroscience, Abstracts, 3,* 251.

Kathol, R. G., Noyes, R., Jr., Slymen, D. J., Crowe, R. R., Clancy, J., & Kerber, R. E. (1980). Propranolol in chronic anxiety disorders: A controlled study. *Archives of General Psychiatry, 37,* 1361–1365.

Ko, G. N., Elsworth, J. D., Roth, R. H., Rifkin, B. G., Leigh, H., & Redmond, E., Jr. (1983). Panic-induced elevation of plasma MHPG levels in phobic-anxious patients. *Archives of General Psychiatry, 40,* 425–430.

Kopin, I. J., Gordon, E. K., Jimerson, D. C., & Polinsky, R. J. (1983). Relation between plasma and cerebrospinal fluid levels of 3-methoxy-4-hydroxyphenylglycol. *Science, 219,* 73–75.

Laakman, G., Schoen, H. W., Blaschke, D., & Wittman, M. (1985). Dose-dependent growth hormone, prolactin and cortisol stimulation after I.V. administration of desipramine in human subjects. *Psychoneuroendocrinology, 10,* 83–93.

Laakman, G., Schön, H. W., Zygan, K., Weiss, A., Meissner, R., Miller, O. A., & Stalla, G. K. (1986). Effects of receptor blockers (methysergide, propranolol, phentolamine, yohimbine and prazosin) on desipramine-induced pituitary hormone stimulation in humans: III. Hypothalamo-pituitary-adreno-cortisol axis. *Psychoneuroendocrinology, 11,* 475–489.

Liebowitz, M. R., Gorman, J. M., Fyer, A., Dillon, D., Levitt, M., & Klein, D. F. (1986). Possible mechanisms for lactate's induction of panic. *American Journal of Psychiatry, 143,* 495.

Lima, D. R., & Turner, P. (1983). Propranolol increases reduced beta-receptor function in severely anxious patients. *Lancet, 2,* 1505.

Lindemann, E. (1935). The psychopathological effect of drugs affecting the vegetative system. *American Journal of Psychiatry, 91,* 983–1008.

Lindemann, E., & Finesinger, J. (1938). The effect of adrenaline and mecholyl in states of anxiety in psychoneurotic patients. *American Journal of Psychiatry, 95,* 353–370.

Maddock, R. J., Carter, C. S., Magliozzi, J. R., & Gietzen, D. W. (1993). Evidence that decreased function of lymphocyte B adrenoreceptors reflects regulatory and adaptive processes in panic disorder with agoraphobia. *American Journal of Psychiatry, 150,* 1219–1224.

Maddock, R. J., Gietzen, D. W., & Goodman, T. A. (1993). Decreased lymphocyte beta-adrenoreceptor function correlates with less agoraphobia and better outcome in panic disorder. *Journal of Affective Disorders, 29,* 27–32.

Magliozzi, J. R., Gietzen, D., Maddock, R. J., Haack, D., Doran, A. R., Goodman, T., & Weiler, P. G. (1989). Lymphocyte beta-adrenoreceptor density in patients with unipolar depression and normal controls. *Biological Psychiatry, 26,* 15–25.

Mason, S. T., & Fubizer, H. C. (1979). Current concepts. I. Anxiety: The locus ceruleus disconnection. *Life Sciences, 25,* 2141–2147.

Neese, R. M., Cameron, O. G., Curtis, G. C., McCann, D. S., & Huber-Smith, M. J. (1984). Adrenergic function in patients with panic anxiety. *Archives of General Psychiatry, 41,* 771–776.

Neese, R. M., Cameron, O. G., Buda, A. J., McCann, D. S., Curtis, G. C., & Huber-Smith, M. J. (1985a). Urinary catecholamines and mitral valve prolapse in panic-anxiety patients. *Psychiatry Research, 14,* 67–74.

Neese, R. M., Curtis, G. C., Thyer, B. A., McCann, D., Huber-Smith, J., & Knoff, R. F. (1985b). Endocrine and cardiovascular responses during phobic anxiety. *Psychosomatic Medicine, 47*(1), 320–332.

Norman, T. R., Kimber, N. M., Judd, F. K., Burrows, G. D., & McIntyre, L. M. (1987). Platelet ^{3}H-rauwolscine binding in patients with panic attacks. *Psychiatry Research, 22,* 43–48.

Noyes, R., Jr. (1982). Beta-blocking drugs and anxiety. *Psychosomatics, 23,* 155–170.

Noyes, R., Jr., Anderson, D. J., Clancy, J., Crowe, R. R., Slymen, D. J., Ghoneim, M. M., & Hinricks, J. V. (1984). Diazepam and propranolol in panic disorder and agoraphobia. *Archives of General Psychiatry, 41,* 287–292.

Nutt, D. J. (1989). Altered central alpha-2-adrenoceptor sensitivity in panic disorder. *Archives of General Psychiatry, 46,* 165–169.

Nutt, D. J., Adinoff, B., Ravitz, B., George, T., Flowers, D., Eckardt, M., Bone, G., Martin, P., & Linnoila, M. (1988). CSF studies in alcoholics and violent offenders. *Australia Alcohol and Drug Review, 7,* 105–108.

Nutt, D. J., & Fraser, S. (1987). Platelet binding studies in panic disorder. *Journal of Affective Disorders, 12,* 7–11.

Nutt, D. J., Glue, P., & Lawson, C. (1990). The neurochemistry of anxiety: An update. *Progress in Neuro-Psychopharmacology and Biological Psychiatry, 14,* 737–752.

Pfeifer, P. N., Weinberg, C. R., Cook, D., Best, J. D., Reenan, A., & Halter, J. (1983). Differential changes of autonomic nervous system functioning with age in man. *American Journal of Medicine, 75,* 249–258.

Pohl, R., Rainey, J., Ortiz, A., Balon, R., Singh, H., & Berchou, R. (1985). Isoproterenol anxiety states. *Psychopharmacology Bulletin, 21,* 424–427.

Pohl, R., Yeragani, V. K., Balon, R., Rainey, J. M., Lycaki, H., Ortiz, A., Berchou, R., & Weinberg, P. (1988). Isoproterenol-induced panic attacks. *Biological Psychiatry, 24,* 891–902.

Pohl, R., Yeragani, V., Rainey, J., Balon, R., Ortiz, A., Berchou, R., Lycaki, H., & Weinberg, P. (1986, December 14–17). *Isoproterenol and lactate infusions in bulimics with and without panic anxiety.* Abstracts of the 15th Collegium Internationale Neuro-Psychopharmacologicum Congress, p. 187. San Juan, Puerto Rico.

Post, R. M., Lake, C. R., Jimerson, D. C., Bunney, W. E., Wood, J. H., Zeigler, M. G., & Goodwin, F. K. (1978). CSF norepinephrine in affective illness. *American Journal of Psychiatry, 135,* 907–912.

Pyke, R. E., & Greenberg, H. S. (1986). Norepinephrine challenges in panic patients. *Journal of Clinical Psychopharmacology, 6,* 279–285.

Rainey, J. M., Jr., Aleem, A., Ortiz, A., Yeragani, V., Pohl, R., & Berchou, R. (1987). A laboratory procedure for the induction of flashbacks. *America Journal of Psychiatry, 144,* 1317–1319.

Randrup, A., & Braestrup, C. (1977). Uptake inhibitor of biogenic amines by newer antidepressant drugs: Relevance to the dopamine hypothesis. *Psychopharmacology, 53,* 309.

Rasmussen, S. A., Goodman, W. K., Woods, S. W., Heninger, G. R., & Charney, D. S. (1987). Effects of yohimbine in obsessive-compulsive disorder. *Psychopharmacology, 93,* 308–313.

Redmond, D. E. (1977). Alterations in the function of the nucleus locus coeruleus: A possible model for studies in anxiety. In I. Hanin, & H. Usdin (Eds.). *Animal Models in Psychiatry and Neurology* (pp. 293–305). Oxford: Pergamon Press.

Redmond, D. E. (1979). New and old evidence for the involvement of a brain norepinephrine system in anxiety. In W. E. Fann, I. Karacan, A. D. Pokorny, & R. L. William (Eds.), *Phenomenology and Treatment of Anxiety* (pp. 153–203). New York: SP Medical and Scientific Books.

Redmond, D. E., Jr., & Huang, Y. H. (1979). New evidence for a locus coeruleus–norepinephrine connection with anxiety. *Life Sciences, 25,* 2149–2162.

Rose, R. M. (1980). Endocrine responses to stressful psychological events. In E. J. Sachar (Ed.), *Psychiatric Clinics of North America. Advances in Psychoneuroendocrinology, 3*(2), 251–276.

Roth, W. T., Margraf, J., Ehlers, A., Taylor, B., Maddock, R. J., Davies, S., & Agras, S. (1992). Stress test reactivity in panic disorder. *Archives of General Psychiatry, 49,* 301–310.

Sanghera, M. K., McMillen, B. A., & German, D. C. (1983). Buspirone, a non-benzodiazepine anxiolytic, increases locus coeruleus noradrenergic neuronal activity. *European Journal of Pharmacology, 86,* 107–110.

Schittecatte, M., Charles, G., Depauw, Y., Mesters, P., & Wilmotte, J. (1988). Growth hormone response to clonidine in panic disorder patients. *Psychiatry Research, 23,* 147–151.

Sheehan, D. V., Raj, B. A., Sheehan, K. H., & Soto, S. (1990). Is busipone effective for panic disorder? *Journal of Clinical Psychopharmacology, 10*(1), 3–11.

Siever, L. J., Insel, T. R., & Jimerson, D. C. (1983). Growth hormone response to clonidine in obsessive-compulsive patients. *British Journal of Psychiatry, 142,* 184–187.

Siever, L. J., & Uhde, T. W. (1984). New studies and perspectives on the noradrenergic receptor system in depression: Effects of the alpha-2-adrenergic agonist clonidine. *Biological Psychiatry, 19,* 131–156.

Spitzer, R. L., Endicott, J., & Robins, E. (1978). Research Diagnostic Criteria: Rationale and reliability. *Archives of General Psychiatry, 35,* 773–782.

Stein, M. D., & Uhde, T. W. (1988). Cortisol response to clonidine in panic disorder and normal controls. *Biological Psychiatry, 24,* 322–330.

Stene, M., Panagiotis, N., Tuck, M. L., Sowers, J. R., Mayes, D., & Berg, J. (1980). Plasma norepinephrine levels are influenced by sodium lactate, glucocorticoid administration and circadian changes in normal man. *Journal of Clinical Endocrinology and Metabolism, 51,* 1340–1345.

Stone, E. A., & Platt, J. E. (1982). Brain adrenergic receptors and resistance to stress. *Brain Research, 237,* 405–414.

Uhde, T. W., Joffe, R. T., Jimerson, D. C., & Post, R. M. (1988). Normal urinary free cortisol and plasma MHPG in panic disorder: Clinical and theoretical implications. *Biological Psychiatry, 23,* 575–585.

Uhde, T. W., Stein, M. B., Vittone, B. J., Siever, L. J., Boulenger, J.-P., Klein, E., & Mellman, T. A. (1989). Behavioral and physiologic effects of short-term and long-term administration of clonidine in panic disorder. *Archives of General Psychiatry, 46,* 170–177.

Uhde, T. W., Vittone, B. J., Siever, L. J., Kaye, W. H., & Post, R. M. (1986). Blunted growth hormone response to clonidine in panic disorder patients. *Biological Psychiatry, 21,* 1077–1081.

Weil-Malherbe, N., Axelrod, J., & Tomchick, R. (1959). Blood-brain barrier for adrenaline. *Science, 129,* 1226–1227.

Woods, S. W., Charney, D. S., McPherson, C. A., Gradman, A. H., & Heninger, G. R. (1987). Situational panic attacks. *Archives of General Psychiatry, 44,* 365–375.

7

Increased Serotonin Function and Panic Disorder

RENÉ S. KAHN,
HERMAN G. M. WESTENBERG, AND
CLARE MOORE

Recent years have witnessed an explosive growth of studies examining a possible role of serotonin (5-hydroxytryptamine [5HT]) dysfunction in the pathogenesis of various psychiatric disorders. Initially, 5HT dysfunction was hypothesized to be a pathogenetic abnormality in depression (van Praag & Korf, 1971). More recently, however, it has been suggested that abnormal 5HT function is involved in the pathogenesis of some anxiety disorders, such as obsessive compulsive disorder (Zohar & Insel, 1987) and panic disorder (Kahn & van Praag, 1988) as well as aggression regulation (Coccaro, 1989; van Praag, 1986). This chapter focuses on the serotonin hypothesis of panic disorder as formulated earlier (Kahn & van Praag, 1988).

Although a role for 5HT in anxiety and panic anxiety has become the focus of study in human subjects only recently, there have been a substantial number of animal investigations since 1974 indicating that 5HT and anxiety are related. Before examining a role for 5HT in panic anxiety in human subjects, we briefly review the compelling evidence from animal studies suggesting a role for 5HT in anxiety.

ANIMAL EXPERIMENTS

Animal Anxiety Models

A major methodological problem in animal laboratory studies of anxiety (as well as affect) is that the emotion must be inferred exclusively from external behavior. Generally, two main categories of animal models can be distinguished: models based on conditioned behavior and models that involve unconditioned behavior. In the former models, responses are controlled by operant conditioning procedures; the latter models rely on natural behavioral reactions and do not require specific training. Examples of animal models based on conditioned behavior are introduction of a conflict situation, the fear-potentiated startle response, the periaqueductal gray stimulation (PAG), the conditioned taste aversion, the conditioned defense burying, and the conditioned adult ultrasonic vocalization. Examples of unconditioned models are light-dark exploration test, elevated plus maze, social interaction test, and separation-induced ultrasonic vocalization in pups. Some of the more frequently used procedures are summarized here.

In the social interaction test, animals are placed in pairs in an open arena, which may be either familiar or unfamiliar to the animal and may be brightly or dimly lit. The most aversive situation is obviously a brightly lit unfamiliar environment. Under these circumstances, animals tend to show decreased exploratory behavior (Crawley & Goodwin, 1980) and decreased social interaction (File, 1985), both of which are considered to be indicators of anxiety.

In conflict paradigms, ongoing behavior is suppressed by aversive stimulation. Suppressed behavior is either lever pressing for food in hungry animals or water licking in thirsty animals. Lever pressing following a distinct stimulus (e.g., light) results in the presentation of food or water and a punishment (e.g., electric shock) (Geller & Seifter, 1960). The animal faced with a conflict situation (between reward and punishment) decreases its bar pressing. The suppression of bar pressing is interpreted to be a behavioral manifestation of anxiety.

A more recently developed test is the fear-potentiated startle paradigm (Davis, 1988). The startle reflex to a signal is potentiated in the presence of a neutral stimulus (e.g., light), previously coupled with an electric shock (unconditioned stimulus). Several recently developed novel anxiolytics, such as the 5HT1a agonists, seem to work in this model.

Focal stimulation of the dorsal part of the PAG produces aversive behavioral responses in animals, reflected by fear and flight reactions. Anxiolytic drugs raise the threshold for these reactions. This model has strong face validity for panic disorder because electrical stimulation in the dorsal midbrain in humans also has been reported to result in panic-like reaction (Nashold, William, & Slaughter, 1969).

The elevated plus maze is an exploratory behavioral model in which rats are placed in an elevated maze consisting of two (opposite) open and two closed alleys. The open arms are more aversive to rats than the closed ones, and anxiolytics will overcome the fear-induced inhibition of open alley exploration (Montgomery, 1955). In this model, benzodiazepines show up as anxiolytics, but more novel compounds, such as the 5HT1a agonists, do not produce consistent results.

To assess a possible relationship between 5HT function and anxiety in animals, studies have measured animal anxiety equivalents and manipulated 5HT function, by decreasing and increasing it. A general difficulty with most animal models of anxiety is that their face and construct validity is poor. Most models use the induction of "fear" as an analogy to human anxiety, and the validation is usually based on responses to benzodiazepines. The latter are considered the treatment of choice in generalized anxiety disorders, but their efficacy in panic disorder is less consistent. Moreover, drugs that have shown to be efficacious in panic disorder do not seem to be effective in most of the above-cited animal models of anxiety. This caveat should be kept in mind when results from animal studies are interpreted as evidence for the role of 5HT in panic disorder.

Decreasing 5HT Function

5HT function can be decreased at different levels of the 5HT neuron. The postsynaptic 5HT receptor can be blocked (i.e., using 5HT antagonists), synthesis of 5HT can be inhibited (i.e., using the 5HT synthesis inhibitor, parachlorophenylalinine [PCPA]); or 5HT neurons can be destroyed using a toxin for 5HT neurons (i.e., 5,7-dihydroxytryptamine [DHT]). These different paradigms have all been applied in animal anxiety studies.

Nonspecific 5HT2 antagonists such as methysergide, cinanserin, cyproheptadine, and metergoline and the mixed 5HT2a/5HT2c antagonist ritanserin all show inconsistent results in several tests of anxiety. Generally, their anxiolytic activity is rather weak as compared to benzodiazepines. The effects of the selective 5HT2 antagonist ritanserin are controversial (Brocco, Koek, Degryse, & Colpaert, 1990; Jenck, Broekkamp, & Van Delft, 1990; Ketelaars & Bruinvels, 1989; Pellow, Johnston, & File, 1987; Stefanski, Palejko, Bidzinski, Kostowski, & Plaznik, 1993). Stutzmann and associates (1991), who studied the selective 5HT2a antagonist RP 62203 and ritanserin in the elevated plus maze, found that RP 62203 dose-dependently increased the number of entries into the open arms, while ritanserin was without effect in this model. The PAG model also yields conflicting results. Cyproheptadine and ritanserin are found to be anxiogenic whereas ketanserin, a selective 5HT2a blocker, is anxiolytic in this model. Information on the anxiolytic activity of 5HT3 antagonists is limited, but ondansetron, zacopride, and ICS 205-930 exhibit anxiolytic activity in several models of anxiety (Costall & Naylor, 1992; Kilfoil, Michel, Montgomery, & Whiting, 1989). In contrast, Mos, Heyden, and Olivier (1989) failed to find anxiolytic effects of ondansetron in the pup ultrasonic vocalization test. Moreover, the social interaction test has yielded also inconsistent results (Costall, Domeney, & Gerrard, 1989; File & Johnston, 1989; Jones, Oakley, & Tyers, 1987).

Studies inhibiting 5HT synthesis using PCPA consistently find that it decreases anxiety. This effect is countered by the administration of 5-hydroxytryptophan (5HTP, the precursor of 5HT) (Engel, Hjorth, Svensson, Carlsson, & Liljequist, 1984; Geller & Blum, 1970; Stein, Wise, & Berger, 1973; Tye, Iversen, & Green, 1979) as well as by the $5HT_{1a}$ agonists 5-methoxy dimethyl tryptamine (5MeODMT) (Shepard, Buxton, & Broadhurst, 1982) and 8-hydroxy-depropylamino-tetralin (8OHDPAT) (Engel et al., 1984). Augmentation of dopamine (DA) and norepinephrine (NE) function through administration of dehydroxy-phenylalanine (DOPA), the precursor of both DA and NE, does not reverse the PCPA effect (Tye et al., 1979), suggesting that catecholamines are not involved in PCPA's anxiolytic effects.

Localized destruction of 5HT-containing regions also has consistently resulted in diminished anxiety responses when the effects were measured about 10 to 14 days after the administration of the toxins (Briley, Chopin, & Moret, 1990; Lippa, Nash, & Greenblatt, 1979; Tye et al., 1977). 5, 7-Dehydroxytryptamine lesioning of the dorsal raphe (in a novel environment model) resulted in anxiety reduction 12 days later, in contrast to median raphe lesionings, which did not (File, Hyde, & Macleod, 1979). The latter findings suggest functional specificity for different 5HT anatomic regions and possibly a greater involvement of the dorsal raphe systems in anxiety mechanisms. Anxiolytic effects also were observed 14 days after lateral septum lesioning. In contrast, no anxiety reduction was found after destruction of catecholamine (CA) neurons with 6-hydroxydopamine (6OHDA), suggesting catecholamine (CA) systems were not involved (Clarke & File, 1982).

Increasing 5HT Function

Since diminishing 5HT function results in anxiety reduction, one may predict that increasing 5HT availability would cause the opposite effect. When the 5HT agonist alpha-methyl-tryptamine was used, a nonspecific effect (i.e., motor inhibition) was observed (Graeff & Schoenfeld, 1970; Stein et al., 1973; Winter, 1972). Similar nonspecific effects were observed when other 5HT agonists were used, such as m-chlorophenylpiperazine (MCPP), fenfluramine (Kilts, Commissaris, Cordon, & Rech, 1982), and 5MeODMT (Shepard et al., 1982). A problem of differentiating the cause of the behavioral inhibition arises, though, because increased 5HT function also is associated with generalized motor inhibition. Consequently, in these models, 5HT-induced anxiogenic effects cannot be differentiated from the general effects of 5HT on motor behavior. The nonselective 5HT2c agonist MCPP has shown anxiolytic effects in the conflict model and social interaction test (Kennedy, Gibson, O'Connell, & Curzon, 1993; Kennett, Whitton, Shah, & Curzon, 1989; Kilts, Commissaris, Cordon, & Rech, 1982) but was without effect in other models, such as the potentiated startle paradigm (Mansbach & Geyer, 1988), or had anxiogenic effects, as in the PAG model (Jenck, Broekkamper, & Van Delft, 1989; Jenck et al., 1990). Local application of MCPP into the hippocampus was anxiogenic, but injections into the amygdala had no effect in the social interaction model. The effect of MCPP in the social interaction test could be blocked by nonselective 5HT2 antagonists such as cyproheptadine and metergoline and the 5HT3 antagonist ICS 205 930, but not by ketanserin, a selective 5HT2a antagonist. B-adrenergic antagonists, which also display 5HT1a/1b antagonists properties as do cyanopindolol and propranolol, also were unable to block the effects of MCPP. These findings suggest that the anxiogenic effects of MCPP in animals is mediated through 5HT2c or 5HT3 receptors.

Behavioral Effects of 5HT1a Agonists

Studies with (partial) 5HT1a agonists are complicated by the fact that this class of receptors is located both presynaptically (where it exerts a release-controlling inhibitory effect on 5HT neurotransmission) and postsynaptically. For buspirone, a partial agonist of the 5HT1a receptors, the results are on the whole consistent in the conflict test when animals were deprived of water, while results in other models were more variable. Other 5HT1a partial agonists, such as ipsapirone and gepirone, have been found to be active in several models of anxiety, including the conflict test, social interaction test, the elevated plus maze, the startle paradigm, and the ultrasonic "distress" vocalization test. (For review see Westenberg & Den Boer, 1994.) Flesinoxan, a novel 5HT1a agonist, surpassing buspirone and the other azapirones in selectivity and affinity for that receptor, was reported to be anxiolytic in the ultrasonic vocalization test in pups but ineffective in the two-compartment model (Mos & Olivier, 1990).

The mechanism through which these drugs exert their behavioral profiles reminiscent of anxiolysis is still unclear. One possibility is stimulation of the 5HT-release–inhibiting autoreceptors, resulting in a reduced firing rate of the 5HT neurons, particularly those arising from the dorsal raphe. It is also possible that the anxiolysis is produced through the postsynaptic 5HT1a receptors. Consistent with the last idea, Schreiber and De Vry (1993) found that lesioning of the dorsal raphe by 5, 7-DHT did not attenuate the anxiolytic effects of ipsapirone. In addition, local injection into the hippocampus and amygdala led to anxiolytic responses, suggesting that postsynaptic receptors are involved. Since it is generally agreed that a decrease in 5HT functioning has anxiolytic effects in animals, it has been hypothesized that 5HT1a agonists may achieve this effect either through their agonistic effects at the somatodendritic autoreceptors (where they are full agonists) or through their antagonistic effects at the postsynaptic receptors (where they are assumed to have partial agonistic properties). When the latter assumption is true, one would expect 5HT1a antagonists to be anxiolytic as well. Consistent with this idea, Fletcher, Cliffe, and Dourish, (1993) found WAY 100135, a 5HT1a antagonist, to display anxiolytic activity in the light-dark box test.

Conclusion

Animal models of anxiety suggest, for the most part, that anxiety correlates with an increase in 5HT function. An important problem with most animal models of anxiety is, however, that they rely on the suppression of ongoing behavior by a conditioned fear of a specific aversive stimulus, which by itself is known to be regulated by 5HT systems. Moreover, validation of animal models is usually based on responses to benzodiazepines, which are considered the treatment of choice in gener-alized anxiety disorder. To infer that humans may respond to 5HT ma-nipulation in the same manner as do animals may require a leap of faith. For one, panic anxiety may be different from the anxiety operational-ized in the animal anxiety paradigms just reviewed. However, there are very interesting parallels between the results of animal anxiety studies and human studies examining the role of 5HT in panic disorder.

PANIC DISORDER

Assessment of 5HT Function

Many methods have been used to assess different aspects of 5HT func-tion in humans. These have included challenge studies with 5HT agonists and treatment studies with agents altering 5HT availability.

Measurement of the 5HT metabolite 5-hydroxyindole acetic acid (5HIAA) in cerebrospinal fluid (CSF) is perhaps the most informative method for assessing central 5HT metabolism. There is currently one report on CSF 5HIAA levels in panic disorder patients (Eriksson, West-berg, Alling, Thuresson, & Modigh, 1991). In this study panic disorder patients did not differ from age- and sex-matched normal controls.

The so-called challenge paradigm is particularly well suited to assess-ment of central 5HT receptor sensitivity. It is valid only, however, if the challenge agents have high selectivity for the 5HT receptor (van Praag, Lemus, & Kahn, 1986). Several 5HT agonists have been used to assess 5HT function in panic disorder: the 5HT precursors tryptophan and 5-hydroxytryptophan; the 5HT releasing agent fenfluramine; and the nonelective 5HT agonist MCPP. Measurement of hormonal and behav-ioral responses following the administration of a 5HT agonist permits an assessment of the state of the central 5HT receptor system. Several studies of this nature have been conducted on panic disorder patients.

Last, treatment studies of panic disorder using drugs selective for 5HT systems also have been useful in exploring the relationship between 5HT and panic anxiety in humans.

Treatment Studies

A number of investigations using 5HT agents to study the treatment of panic disorder suggest that indirect 5HT agonists are effective antipanic agents. Table 7–1 summarizes the results of these studies. One study compared the effects of l-5HTP (150 milligrams [mg] per day with 150

TABLE 7–1
Serotonergic Treatment Studies in Panic Disorder

Author	Diagnosis (N)	Drugs Used	Dose (max) (mg/day)	Time (weeks)	Therapeutic Effect
Charney et al. (1986)	PD(74)	TRZ IMI ALP	250 141 3.1	8	IMI = ALP > TRZ
Evans et al. (1986)	PD (25)	ZIM IMI PLA	150 150	6	ZIM > IMI = PLA
Kahn et al. (1987)	PD (35) GAD (7)	5HTP CMI PLA	150 150	8	CMI = 5HTP > PLA
Den Boer et al. (1987)	PD (50)	CMI FLU	150 100	8	CMI = FLU
Den Boer & Westenberg (1988)	PD (44)	FLU MAP	150 150	6	FLU > MAP
Cassano et al. (1988)	PD (59)	CMI IMI	128 144	10	CMI = IMI*
Johnston et al. (1988)	A (108)	CMI PLA	83	8	CMI > PLA
Sheehan et al. (1988)	PD (52)	BUSP IMI PLA	57 292	8	IMI > BUSP = PLA
Pohl et al. (1989)	PD (60)	BUSP IMI PLA	60 300	8	IMI = BUSP = PLA
Den Boer & Westenberg (1990b)	PD (60)	FLU RIT PLA	150 20	8	FLU > RIT = PLA
Hoehn-Saric et al. (1994)	PD (116)	FLU PLA	300	8	FLU > PLA
Woods et al. (1994)	PD (121)	FLU PLA	300	8	FLU > PLA
Gorman & Wolkow (1994)	PD (320)	SER PLA	50, 100, 200	12	SER 50, 100, 200 > PLA

*Clomipramine earlier effect than imipramine.

5HTP = 5hydroxytryptophan		ZIM = zimeldine
IMI = imipramine		MAP = maprotiline
TRA = trazodone		BUSP = buspirone
FLX = fluoxetine		RIT = ritanserin
CMI = clomipramine		SER = sertraline
FLU = fluvoxamine		

All studies are parallel.

mg/day of the peripheral decarboxylase inhibitor carbidopa) and clomipramine (150 mg/day) in an eight-week placebo-controlled design ($N = 57$). Both compounds displayed antianxiety and antipanic effects (Kahn, Westenberg, Verhoeven, Gispen-de-Wied, & Kamerbeek, 1987). Two other studies examined the efficacy of clomipramine in panic disorder and agoraphobic patients (Cassano et al., 1988; Johnston, Troyer, & Whitsett, 1988). In the latter study, clomipramine was found to be significantly superior to placebo in reducing both agoraphobic symptoms and panic attacks in 108 female patients suffering from agoraphobia with panic attacks (Johnston et al., 1988). The former study compared the effects of imipramine to those of clomipramine in reducing panic attacks in 59 patients with panic disorder. Although both drugs were equally efficacious, clomipramine had a faster onset of action (Cassano et al., 1988). Attributing the effectiveness of clomipramine solely to 5HT mechanisms is problematic since its main metabolite, desmethylclomipramine, possesses NE reuptake blocking properties. Thus, its therapeutic effects might be mediated through NE systems. Since the antipanic effects of clomipramine were equivalent to those of fluvoxamine, a selective 5HT reuptake inhibitor, in a six-week double-blind study comprised of 50 patients (Den Boer, Westenberg, Kamerbeek, Verhoeven, & Kahn, 1987), it is likely that clomipramine's effects also are mediated through the 5HT system. Moreover, in a six-week study of 44 panic disorder patients comparing fluvoxamine to the selective NE reuptake inhibitor maprotiline, Den Boer and Westenberg (1988) found fluvoxamine to be effective in reducing panic attacks, in contrast to maprotiline. Finally, fluvoxamine was found to be superior to placebo in reducing panic attacks in 60 panic disorder patients (Den Boer & Westenberg, 1990b), a finding that recently has been confirmed by two large multicenter trials (Hoehn-Saric, Fawcett, Munjack, & Roy-Byrne, 1994; Woods, Black, & Brown, 1994). Evans, Kenardy, Schneider, and Hory (1986), comparing zimeldine (also a selective 5HT reuptake inhibitor) and imipramine in a placebo-controlled study, found zimeldine but not imipramine to have anitpanic effects. The inefficacy of imipramine in this study is somewhat surprising (see Liebowitz, 1985, for a review) and might be related to the small number of patients in the placebo group ($N = 4$). Sertraline, a potent and highly selective 5HT reuptake inhibitor, which is currently approved for the treatment of depression, also has been shown to reduce the frequency of panic attacks and symptoms of anxiety in patients with panic disorder (Gorman & Wolkow, 1994). Open pilot studies using other indirect 5HT agonists such as 5HTP (Kahn & Westenberg, 1985), zimeldine (Evans & Moore, 1981; Kokzacks, Holmberg, & Wedin, 1981), trazodone (Mavissakalian, 1986), and fluoxetine (Gorman et al., 1987) lend further support to the efficacy of these agents in panic disorder. Though the question remains whether blockade of the 5HT uptake site is the only pharmacological target of these compounds, there is convincing evidence that 5HT reuptake inhibitors are effective in diminishing both the frequency and severity of panic attacks as well as in reducing anticipatory anxiety and agoraphobic avoidance (presumably as a result of decreased panic frequency).

In treatment studies involving indirect 5HT agonists, an initial period of symptom exacerbation has been observed by most investigators. This "biphasic response," in which improvement in symptoms follows an initial period of symptom exacerbation, was first observed in a 12-week, open pilot study of panic disorder patients ($N = 10$) treated with 150 to 300 mg l-5HTP in combination with 150 mg carbidopa. Fifty percent of the patients reported initial increased anxiety. They reported increased severity and frequency of panic attacks, as well as aggravation or induction of depressed mood during the initial 10 to 14 days of treatment (Kahn & Westenberg, 1985). This initial deterioration, however, appeared to be transient: Continuation of treatment for two to four weeks eventually resulted in clinical improvement (compared to pretreatment status) in terms of both generalized anxiety and severity and frequency of the panic attacks. These preliminary findings were confirmed in a larger 5HTP/clomipramine study ($N = 57$) in which the initial worsening of anxiety symptoms occurred in about 50 percent of patients receiving 5HTP and in about 30 percent of patients receiving clomipramine. In fact, four out of five dropouts in the 5HTP group and three out of four in the clomipramine group did so within the first two weeks because of increased anxiety, panic, and depression (Kahn et al., 1987). It is unlikely that this effect involves NA systems since it also has been reported using the selective 5HT reuptake inhibitors fluvoxamine (Den Boer & Westenberg, 1990b; Den Boer et al., 1987) and fluoxetine (Gorman et al., 1987), but not with the NA reuptake inhibitor maprotiline (Den Boer & Westenberg, 1988).

This biphasic effect appears to be unique to panic disorder since it has not been reported in the multitude of studies using indirect 5HT agonists in depressed patients, obsessive compulsive patients, and in some studies with patients suffering from social phobia. We have hypothesized that it is due to a hypersensitive 5HT receptor function in panic disorder patients (to be discussed more fully later in this chapter).

Although suggestive of a role for 5HT in the treatment of panic anxiety, the use of 5HT reuptake inhibitors does not provide information on which 5HT system may be abnormal in panic disorder. Recent availability of agents selective for a particular subset of 5HT receptors—such as the 5HT1a partial agonists buspirone, gepirone, and ipsapirone and the full 5HT1a agonist flesinoxan; the 5HT2a/5HT2c antagonist ritanserin; and the 5HT3 antagonists ondansetron and zacopride—may enable us to examine their efficacy in panic disorder and thus elucidate a possible role for these 5HT receptors in its pathogenesis. Only very few studies with such agents have been conducted to date. One study comparing the antipanic effects of fluvoxamine to those of ritanserin (and to placebo) found that ritanserin was not effective in reducing panic symptoms (Den Boer & Westenberg, 1990b). This finding suggests that 5HT2 receptors are not hypersensitive in panic disorder patients, but it does not exclude that the antipanic effects of 5HT reuptake inhibitors may be mediated through this receptor subtype. In a more recent study, Pols and associates (1993) studied the effects of the addition of ritanserin to fluvoxamine in the treatment of panic disorder. The combination of ritanserin and fluvoxamine was not different from placebo and fluvoxamine, suggesting that 5HT reuptake inhibitors do not exert their effect through 5HT2 receptors. The caveat here is that ritanserin, in dosages that can be used safely (20 mg P.O.), is not a very potent 5HT2 antagonist. Studies with more potent 5HT2 antagonist are warranted to fully include or exclude the involvement of 5HT2 receptors. A study comparing the 5HT1a partial agonist buspirone (60 mg P.O.) with imipramine and placebo provided somewhat ambiguous data on the efficacy or lack of efficacy of buspirone. While imipramine was superior to placebo in reducing panic attacks and generalized anxiety symptoms, buspirone was neither more effective than placebo nor less effective than imipramine in reducing panic attacks (Raj, Sheehan, & Soto, 1988). Another study found buspirone to be ineffective (Pohl, Balon, Yeragani, & Gershon, 1989). This study's findings are difficult to interpret as well, since imipramine which has antipanic properties, was found to be equally effective or ineffective as buspirone and placebo. Preliminary data suggest that gepirone might be effective in panic disorder, but so far only one open trial has been published (Pecknold, Luthe, Scott-Fleurie, & Jenkins, 1993). Flesinoxan, a 5HT1a agonist that surpasses buspirone and gepirone in affinity for the 5HT1a receptor subtype, recently has also been investigated in panic disorder patients. In this small study with a placebo run-in phase and a double-blind cross-over design with 2.4 mg flesinoxan and placebo, panic disorder patients experienced a significant aggravation of their anxiety symptoms (Westenberg & Den Boer, 1993). This anxiogenic effect was dose dependent, in that lowering the dose of flesinoxan resulted in a profile indistinguishable from placebo. To date no studies have been published with other selective 5HT agonists and antagonists in panic disorder.

In conclusion, the efficacy of 5HT reuptake inhibitors in the treatment of panic attacks is well documented and replicated by large multi-center clinical trials. Unfortunately, the two studies using partial 5HT1a agonists provide less convincing results, but the results from the flesinoxan trial suggests that full 5HT1a agonists are anxiogenic rather than anxiolytic. The latter finding contrasts with results in patients suffering from generalized anxiety disorders and suggests a differential role for 5HT1a receptors in these disorders. Clinical trials are awaited to determine whether 5HT3 antagonist have anxiolytic or antipanic properties. Similarly, more potent and selective 5HT2 antagonists are required to draw firm conclusions with regard to the role of this receptor subtype in the pathogenesis of panic disorder.

Challenge Studies

The use of 5HT agonists in panic disorder has provided additional information regarding the pathogenesis of this disorder. Several, for the most part, nonselective agents have been used although most studies remain unreplicated. 5HT precursors, such as tryptophan, 5HTP, the 5HT releasing agent fenfluramine, and the nonselective 5HT receptor agonist MCPP have been investigated (See Table 7–2).

Challenge studies using 5HT agonists may bear some similarity to the exacerbation seen with 5HT reuptake inhibitors during the first week of treatment. Thus, challenges using oral MCPP, a nonselective 5HT agonist, which displays a particularly high affinity for the 5HT2c and 5HT3 receptor subtypes, produce increased rates of anxiety, especially in panic disorder patients (Kahn, Wetzler, van Praag, Asnis, & Strauman, 1988b; Klein, Zohar, Geraci, Murphy, & Uhde, 1991). Of note, differential responses to MCPP relative to controls are not observed in intravenous studies (Charney, Woods, Goodman, & Heninger, 1987a). MCPP given intravenously (0.1 mg/kilogram [kg]) induced anxiety in panic disorder patients and in normal controls to the same extent. In contrast, MCPP

TABLE 7–2
Serotonin Challenge Studies in Panic Disorder

Study	Challenge Agent	Dx (N)	Panic Attacks Drug (%)	PLA (%)	Hormonal Effect
Charney & Heninger	TRY	PD (23)			P↑
(1986)	(7 gr IV)	NC (21)			P↑
Charney et al.	MCPP/PLA	PD (23)	52	0	C↑, P↑
(1987a)	(0.1 mg/kg IV)	NC (19)	32	5	C↑, P↑
Kahn et al.	MCPP/PLA	PD (13)	45	0	C↑↑
(1988a, 1988b)	(0.25 mg/kg P.O.)	NC (15)	5	0	C =
		MD (17)	10	0	C =
Targum & Marshall	FEN/PLA	PD (9)	66	0	C↑↑, P↑↑
(1989)	(60 mg P.O.)	MD (9)	0	0	C =, P↑
		NC (9)	22	0	C =, P↑
Den Boer & Westenberg	5HTP/PLA	PD (20)	0	0	C↑↑
(1990b)	(60 mg IV)	NC (20)	0	0	C↑↑
Targum	FEN/PLA	PD (26)	65	0	
(1991)	(60 mg P.O.)	NC (12)	17	0	

TRY = tryptophan
MCPP = m-chlorophenylpiperazine
PLA = placebo
FEN = fenfluramine
5HTP = 5-hydroxytryptophan
PD = panic disorder
NC = normal controls
MD = major depression
C = cortisol
P = prolactin
↑ increase as compared to baseline or placebo
↑↑ augmented increase as compared to baseline or placebo
= no change as compared to baseline or placebo
*70% panic attacks on MCPP and 70% panic attacks on caffeine

given orally in a dose up to 0.5 mg/kg did not induce anxiety in normal subjects (Kahn, Wetzler, Asnis, & van Praag, 1990), while even lower oral dosages (0.25 mg/kg) of MCPP were found to increase anxiety in panic disorder patients (Kahn et al., 1988b). Anxiogenic effects, but not panic responses, of MCPP (0.5 mg/kg P.O.) in panic disorder patients were also seen by Klein and associates (1991).

These findings suggest that panic disorder patients are hypersensitive to the anxiogenic effects of MCPP, probably due to increased sensitivity of some postsynaptic 5HT receptors (Kahn & van Praag, 1988).

Hormonal responses to MCPP appear to corroborate this hypothesis. While a low oral dose of MCPP (0.25 mg/kg) induced augmented cortisol release in panic disorder patients only (Kahn, van Praag, Wetzler, Asnis, & Barr, 1988a), higher doses (e.g., 0.1 mg/kg MCPP IV) resulted in increased cortisol levels in both patients and controls (Charney et al., 1987a). Oral administration of 60 mg fenfluramine (a 5HT-releasing agent) appears to further support the 5HT receptor hypersensitivity hypothesis. Fenfluramine induced both anxiety and an augmented cortisol and prolactin release in (female) panic disorder patients in contrast to normal controls and patients with major depression (Targum & Marshall, 1990). Such exaggerated responses to 5HT agonists may be interpreted to reflect deafferation 5HT hypersensitivity in patients with panic disorder. An absence of anxiogenic response to 5-HTP (Den Boer & Westenberg, (1990a) has complicated this view. In evaluating the cortisol and B-endorphin response to a challenge with 5HTP, the authors found similar cortisol and B-endorphin releases in panic disorder patients and normal controls. Despite the severe gastrointestinal side effects (the majority of the normal subjects and nine out of the 20 patients vomited during the test), most patients became less anxious by the end of the test. It cannot be excluded, though, that stress-related effects may have obscured any differential response on the cortisol and B-endorphin release. Another study, using the 5HT precursor tryptophan to challenge 5HT receptors, found similar increases in prolactin response in panic disorder patients and controls (Charney & Heninger, 1986). One could explain these discrepant findings by assuming a presynaptic impairment in panic disorder patients (Kahn & van Praag, 1990). However, in a test of the effect of acute reduction of 5HT neurotransmission on the occurrence of panic attacks, Goddard, Goodman, and Woods (1992) report no effects following administration of tryptophan-depleting solution, which reduces central 5HT levels, suggesting that presynaptic 5HT functioning is not abnormal. This is corroborated by the data of Erikssen and associates (1991), who found no evidence for a disturbed 5HT metabolism. In view of the paucity of information on clinical effects of selective 5HT agonists and antagonists, it is impossible to draw firm conclusions about the roles of specific 5HT subtypes. The 5HT system in the brain shows a large diversity and complexity in terms of receptor heterogeneity and neurochemical coupling to intracellular processes. Moreover, there are indications that the 5HT system is composed of two parallel systems, originating from the dorsal raphe and median raphe nuclei; these systems are morphologically and functionally different and could innervate overlapping projection fields, for example, the cortex, but also specific areas, such as the hippocampus (median raphe) and thalamus (dorsal raphe). Finally, disturbances in the balance between opposing effects of 5HT receptors should be taken into account.

5HT and Panic or 5HT and Anxiety

Is the abnormality in 5HT function—increased postsynaptic 5HT receptor sensitivity—specific to panic disorder, or is it related to anxiety in general? There are some data to suggest that the impairment revealed by the MCPP test is not specific to panic disorder. We examined cortisol responses to 0.25 mg/kg MCPP in 20 panic disorder patients and 22 patients with major depression without a history of panic attacks. All subjects were given a standardized interview, the Schedule for Affective Disorders and Schizophrenia (SADS) (Endicott & Spitzer, 1978) and received diagnoses according to Research Diagnostic Criteria (RDC) (Spitzer, Endicott, & Robins, 1978). All subjects had normal laboratory and physical exams (including thyroid indices), were drug free for at least two weeks, and had no evidence of drug or alcohol abuse in the preceding six months. In the week prior to the challenge test, patients were rated once on two psychopathological dimensions: anxiety (Clinical Anxiety Scale [CAS]) (Snaith, Baugh, & Clayden, 1982) and depression (Montgomery Asberg Depression Rating Scale [MADRS]) (Montgomery & Asberg, 1979). The subjects fasted (except for water intake) from midnight on the day of the procedure. At 9:00 A.M., an in-dwelling intravenous catheter was inserted. After a one-hour adaptation period, all subjects received orally either placebo or 0.25 mg/kg MCPP. Tablets were administered in a randomized double-blind design. The phlebotomists were blind to the patients' diagnoses. Blood samples were taken at 30-minute intervals from 9:00 A.M. until 1:30 P.M. Cortisol was assessed by a radioimmunoassay kit (Diagnostic Products, California) in all samples. MCPP (obtained from Aldrich Chemical Company) was measured by High Performance Liquid Chromatography in samples taken between 10:00 A.M. and 1:30 P.M. (Suckow, Cooper, & Kahn, 1990). Pearson product moment correlations were conducted using maximal change (peak minus baseline) in cortisol and prolactin response and CAS and MADRS as variables.

As Figure 7–1 indicates, a significant correlation ($r = 0.53$; $N = 42$, $p < 0.0001$) was found between the maximal increase in cortisol response

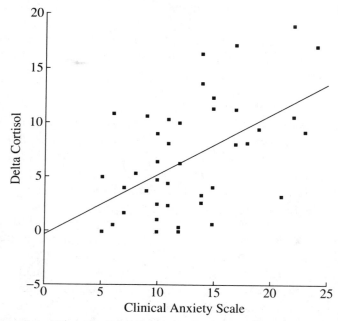

Figure 7–1. Correlation between anxiety and cortisol response to MCPP.

to MCPP and anxiety as measured by the CAS across all subjects. Interestingly, this relationship was not found for CAS and maximal prolactin response ($r = 0.22$, $N = 41$, $p = 0.17$). Correlations between depressive symptoms (MADRS) and maximal cortisol and prolactin responses were not significant ($r = 0.11$ and $r = 0.14$, respectively).

Thus, our data suggest that augmented cortisol responses provoked by MCPP may be related to anxiety, irrespective of diagnosis, and not to the nosological entity of panic disorder.

A relationship between 5HT and anxiety in major depression is suggested by the twin findings that anxiety is often a prominent component of affective disorders and that 5HT has been implicated in the pathogenesis of depression. Only a few studies, however, have investigated this directly. Both Banki (1977) and Rydin, Schalling, and Asberg (1982) found an inverse correlation between CSF 5HIAA and anxiety in depressed patients. Redmond and associates (1986) also found such a correlation though it was less pronounced than the relationship between anxiety and 3-methoxy-4-hydroxyphenylethylene glycol (MHPG), the main metabolite of NE.

Other data, however, suggest a differential role for 5HT in anxiety disorders. Thus, the 5HT1a partial agonist buspirone, the 5HT2 antagonist ritanserin, and the 5HT1a full agonist flesinoxan are effective anxiolytics in patients with generalized anxiety disorder (Ceulemans, Hoppenbrouwers, Gelders, & Reyntgens, 1985a; Leysen, Gommeren, & van Gompel, 1985; Rickels, Weisman, & Norstad, 1982; Westenberg & Den Boer, 1993), but ineffective or even anxiogenic (flesinoxan) in panic disorder (Pohl et al., 1989; Westenberg & Den Boer, 1993).

Whether 5HT dysfunction is more related to panic disorder or to anxiety as a symptom is one of the important questions that recent research into the role of 5HT in panic disorder has raised.

5HT AND OTHER FORMS OF PSYCHOPATHOLOGY

Other than anxiety, 5HT dysfunction has been linked to depressive disorders (van Praag & Korf, 1971), suicidal behavior (review: van Praag, 1986), and outwardly directed aggression (review: Valzelli, 1984). The implication of 5HT in these disturbances may, however, further illuminate the function of 5HT in anxiety. Clinically, affective, anxiety, and aggression disorders tend to cluster. That anxiety and depression are associated clinically is a well-documented phenomenon. For example, major depression is often concomitant with panic disorder and obsessive compulsive disorder (Breier, Charney, & Heninger, 1984; Gittleson, 1966a), and depressed patients have an augmented occurrence of panic attacks (Breier, Charney, & Heninger, 1985), generalized anxiety (Roth, Gurney, Garside, & Kerr, 1972), and obsessive-compulsive symptoms (Gittleson, 1966b). Correspondingly, depression, suicide, and outwardly directed aggression are correlated insofar as depression is a frequent precursor to suicidal behavior and depressed patients demonstrate more outwardly directed aggression (Weissman, Fox, & Klerman, 1973). The finding that there is an accretion in suicide rates among patients with histories of violent behavior suggests that suicidal and aggressive behaviors are interrelated.

The connection between these psychopathological entities and 5HT disturbances (including anxiety) can be considered only at a theoretical level at present. Is each disorder independently linked to specific disturbances of the central 5HT system, or is a unique 5HT disturbance associated with a particular psychopathological characteristic that prevails in all the disorders? These are just two of many questions that need be addressed. At the very least, preparation and use of behavioral measurement instruments with high resolving power is crucial to the clarification of these issues. In this respect, assessment methodology is lacking at present and technical improvements are urgently needed (Wetzler, 1986).

5HT AND OTHER THEORIES OF ANXIETY

5HT, NA, and Anxiety

Increased NA function is an alternative pathogenic factor in panic attacks has been proposed (Charney & Redmond, 1983; Redmond & Huang, 1987) since a single dose of yohimbine (an alpha-2 antagonist) elicits more anxiety and panic and a greater MHPG increase in panic disorder patients than in normal controls (Charney, Woods, Goodman, & Heninger, 1987b). Additionally, many different antipanic medications (e.g., imipramine and alprazolam) (Carr et al, 1986; Charney & Heninger, 1985a) have been shown to reduce plasma MHPG levels during a successful treatment program.

How can the role of 5HT in the pathogenesis of anxiety be reconciled with the evidence of noradrenergic involvement? At this point, a number of hypotheses must be considered. For example, might not certain anxiety states be related to a predominant abnormality in one neurotransmitter system while other anxiety states are related to disturbances in the other neurotransmitter system? Alternatively, since 5HT and NE systems have extensive connecting pathways, a disturbance in one may cause secondary or complementary effects in the other. 5HT neurons, for example, project from the dorsal raphe to the locus coeruleus (LC, the main nucleus of NE-containing neurons) as shown by autoradiographic (Descarries & Leger, 1978), immunocytochemical (Pickel, Tong, & Reis, 1978), and histochemical methods (Leger, Wiklund, Descarries, & Persson, 1979). Destruction of the mesencephalic part of the raphe system reportedly caused an increase in NA turnover within the LC (Pujol, Keane, McRae, Lewis, & Renaud, 1978). Furthermore, stimulation of dorsal raphe nuclei blocked the increase in LC firing typically observed after administration of noxious stimuli. Moreover, this inhibitory effect of dorsal raphe stimulation on the LC is abolished or diminished by pretreatment with PCPA, 5,7-DHT, and methysergide (Segal, 1979). Also, direct application of 5HT on the LC suppressed its firing (Segal, 1979). Conversely, increase NE function caused increased 5HT activity in the raphe nuclei (Baraban & Aghajanian, 1980; Marwaha & Aghajanian, 1982). Based on these 5HT/NA interactions, one possible conclusion is that NA's anxiogenic effects are mediated through 5HT function. This view is corroborated by a recent paper reporting on the effects of fluvoxamine, a 5HT reuptake inhibitor, on yohimbine-induced anxiety (Goddard, Woods, Sholomskas, Charney, & Heninger, 1993). The main finding of this study was blunting of the anxiogenic response to yohimbine in the fluvoxamine-treated but not in the placebo-treated panic disorder patients.

The aforementioned examples imply that no simple dysfunction in any one neurotransmitter system can account for anxiety production and that complex interactions between multiple neurotransmitters are likely to be involved. This becomes further apparent in examining the role of another neurochemical system, gama-aminobutyric acid (GABA), which is also implicated in anxiety mechanisms.

5HT, GABA, AND ANXIETY

Some investigators have postulated a benzodiazepine-GABA hypothesis of anxiety production (Paul, Marangos, & Skolnick, 1981) based on the discovery of benzodiazepine (BZ) receptors and the augmented understanding of the role and of the clinical efficacy of BZs. The basic premise of this hypothesis is that BZs decrease anxiety by facilitating GABA function. According to the hypothesis, BZs exert their anxiolytic effect by stimulating GABA's inhibitory effects on neuronal excitability (through the facilitation of cellular influx of chloride (Cl⁻) ions resulting in increased neuronal polarity) (Costa, Guidotti, & Mao, 1975). Evidence substantiating this hypothesis is derived from studies wherein administration of BZ receptor antagonists induces anxietylike behavior in monkeys (Ninan et al., 1982) and in humans (Dorow, Horowski, Paschelke, & Amin, 1983).

Since benzodiazepines are effective in panic disorder, it may be postulated that panic disorder is characterized by an abnormality in the BZ-GABA complex. Several studies have examined this issue by challenging panic disorder patients with a benzodiazepine or with a benzodiazepine-antagonist. One study examined the effect of 15 mg diazepam po in eight healthy subjects and seven panic disorder patients. The patients appeared less sensitive to the effect of diazepam on cognitive function than the normal subjects (Woods, Charney, Silver, Krystal, & Heninger, 1991). However, the study was small and its results should be regarded as preliminary. Another study examined the effects of the benzodiazepine-receptor antagonist flumazenil in 11 panic disorder patients and five healthy controls (Roy-Byrne, Lewis, Villacres, 1989). Flumazenil induced panic attacks in four out of 10 patients when a low oral dose (200 mg) was administered, but no patient-control comparisons could be made due to the small number of controls in the study (Roy et al., 1989). In another study comparing 10 panic disorder patients with 10 healthy controls, flumazenil in a dose of 2 mg iv induced panic attacks in eight out of 10 patients but in none of the controls (Nutt, Glue, Lawson, & Wilson, 1990). Anxiety and physiological responses were also higher in the patients. These findings suggest that panic disorder patients may have an abnormal benzodiazepine receptor sensitivity.

GABA's role in anxiety also should be considered in the context of its interaction with other neurotransmitters. For example, recent evidence shows that the GABA and 5HT systems are both anatomically and functionally intertwined. We have already reviewed evidence relating the anxiolytic action of BZs to 5HT function. Other findings include: (1) certain neurons of the raphe nuclei contain both 5HT and GABA (Belin et al., 1983, Nanopoulos, Belin, Maitre, Vincendon, & Pujol, 1982); (2) systemic administration of GABA agonists decreases 5HT synthesis and 5HT transmission (probably by inhibition of raphe neuronal activity) (Nishikawa & Scatton, 1983, 1985); (3) local infusion of GABA in the raphe nuclei caused decreased 5HT activity in their projection area (Nishikawa & Scatton, 1985); (4) GABA agonists and antagonists injected in the median raphe respectively caused decreased and increased 5HT turnover (Forchetti & Meek, 1981); and (5) in-vivo voltammetry showed that GABA inhibited striatal 5HT transmission (Scatton, Serrano, Rivot, & Nishikawa, 1984). In summary, evidence suggests that BZs may exert their anxiolytic effects by indirectly diminishing 5HT function (through their facilitation of GABA). Confirmation of the suggested association between GABA and 5HT requires further investigation but is a distinct and intriguing possibility.

Conclusion

This chapter reviewed the animal and human findings concerning the relationship between 5HT function and panic anxiety. Generally, the results from animal studies suggest that increasing 5HT function is anxiogenic, but this overly broad generalization does not take into account the differences in results between animal models and clinical research, nor does it account for the differential effects of various compounds in different forms of anxiety. Animal models of anxiety suggest, for the most part, that anxiety correlates with increased 5HT function, but clinical data is more inconsistent. Challenge studies are by and large in keeping with animal data, but treatment studies sometimes hint at the reverse. Thus, electrophysiological and microdialysis data suggest that selective 5HT reuptake inhibitors increase 5HT release after long-term treatment, while clinical trials consistently reveal their efficacy in panic disorder. One could argue that sustained increased availability of 5HT at the postsynaptic receptors has down-regulated the supersensitive receptors, but evidence to support this idea is still lacking. Evidence from challenge studies suggest that postsynaptic 5HT2a/2c (or 5HT3) function may be increased, but clinical trials with ritanserin (a 5HT2a/2c antagonist) were negative. The limited potency of this compound may account for these negative findings. Studies with more potent and selective 5HT antagonists are warranted to further dissect the role of 5HT in the pathogenesis of panic disorder. One of the main questions to be resolved is whether the postulated 5HT abnormality is related to panic disorder or to anxiety in general, irrespective of diagnosis.

REFERENCES

Banki, C. M. (1977). Correlation of anxiety and related symptoms with cerebrospinal fluid 5-hydroxyindoleacetic acid in depressed women. *Journal of Neural Transmission, 41*, 135–143.

Baraban, F. M., & Aghajanian, G. K. (1980). Suppression of firing activity of 5HT neurons in the dorsal raphe by alpha-adrenoceptor antagonist. *Neuropharmacology, 19*, 355–363.

Belin, M. F., Nanopoulos, D., Didier, M. I., Aguera, M., Steinbusch, H., Verhofstad, A., Maite, M., & Pujol, J. F. (1983). Immunohistochemical evidence for the presence of gamma-aminobutyric acid and serotonin in one nerve cell. A study on the raphe nuclei of the rat using antibodies to glutamate decarboxylase and serotonin. *Brain Research, 275*, 329–339.

Breier, A., Charney, D. S., & Heninger, G. R. (1984). Major depression in patients with agoraphobia and panic disorder. *Archives of General Psychiatry, 41*, 1129–1135.

Breier, A., Charney, D. S., & Heninger, G. R. (1985). The diagnostic validity of anxiety disorders and their relationship to depressive illness. *American Journal of Psychiatry, 142,* 787–797.

Briley, M., Chopin, P., & Moret, C. (1990). Effect of serotonergic lesion on "anxious" behavior measured in the elevated plus-maze test in the rat. *Psychopharmacology, 101,* 187–189.

Brocco, M. J., Koek, W., Degryse, A. D., & Colpaert, F. C. (1990). Comparative studies on the anti-punishment effects of chlordiazepoxide, buspirone and ritanserin in the pigeon, Geller-Seifter and Vogel conflict procedures. *Behavioural Pharmacology, 1,* 403–418.

Carr, D. B., Sheehan, D. V., Surman, O. S., Coleman, J., Greenblatt, D., Heninger, G., Jones, K., Levine, P., & Watkins, W. (1986). Neuroendocrine correlates of lactate-induced anxiety and their response to chronic alprazolam therapy. *American Journal of Psychiatry, 143,* 483–494.

Cassano, G. B., Petracca, A., Perugi, G., Nisita, C., Mussetti, L., Mengali, F., & McNair, D. M. (1988). Clomipramine for panic disorder: I. The first 10 weeks of a long-term comparison with imipramine. *Journal of Affective Disorders, 14,* 123–127.

Ceulemans, D. L. S., Hoppenbrouwers, M. L., Gelders, Y. G., & Reyntgens, A. J. (1985a). The influence of ritanserin, a serotonin antagonist, in anxiety disorders: A double-blind placebo-controlled study versus lorazepam. *Pharmacopsychiatry, 18,* 303–305.

Ceulemans, D. L. S., Hoppenbrouwers, M. L., Gelders, Y. G., & Reyntgens, A. J. (1985b, August). *The effect of benzodiazepine withdrawal on the therapeutic efficacy of a serotonin antagonist in anxiety disorders.* Paper presented at the IVth World Congress of Biological Psychiatry. Philadelphia: PA.

Charney, D. S., & Heninger, G. R. (1985a). Noradrenergic function and the mechanism of action of antianxiety treatment I. The effect of long-term alprazolam treatment. *Archives of General Psychiatry, 42,* 458–467.

Charney, D. S., & Heninger, G. R. (1985b). Noradrenergic function and the mechanism of action of antianxiety treatment II. The effect of long-term imipramine treatment. *Archives of General Psychiatry, 42,* 473–481.

Charney, D. S., & Heninger, G. R. (1986). Serotonergic function in panic disorders. *Archives of General Psychiatry, 43,* 1059–1065.

Charney, D. S., & Redmond, D. E., Jr. (1983). Neurobiological mechanisms in human anxiety. Evidence supporting central noradrenergic hyperactivity. *Neuropharmacology, 22,* 1531–1536.

Charney, D. S., Woods, S. W., Goodman, W. K., & Heninger, G. R. (1987a). Serotonin function in anxiety: II. Effects of the serotonin agonist mCPP in panic disorder patients and healthy subjects. *Psychopharmacology, 92,* 14–24.

Charney, D. S., Woods, S. W., Goodman, W. K., & Heninger, G. R. (1987b). Neurobiological mechanisms of panic anxiety: Biochemical and behavioral correlates of yohimbine-induced panic attacks. *American Journal of Psychiatry, 144,* 1030–1036.

Charney, D. S., Woods, S. W., Goodman, W. K., Rifkin, B., Kinch, M., Aiken, B., Quadrino, L. M., & Heninger, G. R. (1986). Drug treatment of panic disorder: The comparative efficacy of imipramine, alprazolam, and trazodone. *Journal of Clinical Psychiatry, 47,* 580–586.

Clarke, A., & File, S. E. (1982). Selective neurotoxin lesions of the lateral septum: Changes in social and aggressive behaviours. *Pharmacology of Biochemistry Behavior, 17,* 623–628.

Coccaro, E. F. (1989). Central serotonin and impulsive aggression. *British Journal of Psychiatry, 155,* 52–62.

Costa, E., Guidotti, A., & Mao, C. C. (1975). New concepts on the mechanism of action of benzodiazepines. *Life Science, 17,* 167–186.

Costall, B., Domeney, A. M., & Gerrard, P. A., (1989). The anxiolytic activities of the 5-HT3 receptor antagonists GR 38032F, ICS-930 and BRL 43694. In P. Bevan, A. R. Cools, & T. Archer (Eds.), *Behavioural Pharmacology of 5-HT,* 35th ed. (pp. 383–387). Hillsdale, NJ: Lawrence Erlbaum Associates.

Costall, B., & Naylor, R. J. (1992). Anxiolytic potential of 5-HT3 receptor antagonists. *Pharmacology Toxicology, 70,* 157.

Crawley, J., & Goodwin, F. K. (1980). Preliminary report of a simple animal behavior model for the anxiolytic effects of benzodiazepines. *Pharmacology of Biochemistry Behavior, 13,* 167–170.

Davis, M. (1988). The potentiated startle response as a measure of conditioned fear and its relevance to the neurobiology of anxiety. *Animal Models of Psychiatry Disorder, 1,* 61.

Den Boer, J. A., & Westenberg, H. G. (1988). Effect of a serotonin and noradrenaline uptake inhibitor in panic disorder: A double-blind comparative study with fluvoxamine and maprotiline. *International of Clinical Psychopharmacology, 3,* 59–74.

Den Boer, J. A., & Westenberg, H. G. M. (1990a). Behavioral, neuroendocrine and biochemical effects of 5-hydroxytryptophan administration in panic disorder. *Psychiatry Research, 31,* 267–278.

Den Boer, J. A., & Westenberg, H. G. M. (1990b). Serotonin function in panic disorder: A double blind placebo controlled study with fluvoxamine and ritanserin. *Psychopharmacology, 102,* 85–94.

Den Boer, J. A., Westenberg, H. G. M., Kamerbeek, W. D. J., Verhoeven, V. M., & Kahn, R. S. (1987). Effect of serotonin uptake inhibitors in anxiety disorders: A double-blind comparison of clomipramine and fluvoxamine. *International of Clinical Psychopharmacology, 2,* 21–32.

Descarries, L., & Leger, L. (1978). Serotonin nerve terminals in the locus coeruleus of the adult rat. In S. Garattini, J. F. Pujol, & R. Samanin (Eds.) *Interaction between putative neurotransmitters in the brain* (pp. 355–367). New York: Raven Press.

Dorow, R., Horowski, R., Paschelke, G., & Amin, M. (1983). Severe anxiety induced by FG 7142, a beta-carboline ligand for benzodiazepine receptors. *Lancet, 92,* 98–99.

Endicott, F., & Spitzer, R. L. (1978). A diagnostic interview: The Schedule for Affective Disorders and Schizophrenia. *Archives of General Psychiatry, 35,* 837–844.

Engel, J. A., Hjorth, S., Svensson, K., Carlsson, A., & Liljequist, S. (1984). Anticonflict effect of the putative serotonin receptor agonist 8-hydroxy-2-(DI-n-Propylamino) tetralin (8-OH-DPAT). *European Journal of Pharmacology, 105,* 365–368.

Erikssen, E., Westberg, P., Alling, C., Thuresson, K., & Modigh, K. (1991). Cerebrospinal fluid levels of monoamine metabolites in panic disorder. *Psychiatry Research, 36,* 243.

Evans, L., Kenardy, J., Schneider, P., & Hory, H. (1986). Effect of a selective serotonin uptake inhibitor in agoraphobia with panic attacks. *Acta Psychiatrica Scandinavica, 73,* 49–53.

Evans, L., & Moore, G. (1981). The treatment of phobic anxiety by zimeldine. *Acta Psychiatrica Scandinavica, 63* (Suppl. 290), 342–345.

File, S. E. (1985). Animal models for predicting clinical efficacy of anxiolytic drugs: Social behaviour. *Neuropsychobiology, 13,* 55–62.

File, S. E., Hyde, J. R. G., & Macleod, N. K. (1979). 5, 7-Dihydroxytryptamine lesions of dorsal and median raphe nuclei and performance in the social interaction test of anxiety and in a home-cage aggression test. *Journal of Affective Disorders, 1,* 115–122.

File, S. E., & Johnston, A. L. (1989). Lack of effects of 5HT3 receptor antagonists in the social interaction and elevated plus-maze tests of anxiety in the rat. *Psychopharmacology, 99,* 248–251.

Fletcher, A., Cliffe, I. A., & Dourish, C. T. (1993). Silent 5-HT1A receptor antagonists: Utility as research tools and therapeutic agents. *Trends in Pharmacological Science, 14,* 441–448.

Forchetti, C. M., & Meek, J. L. (1981). Evidence for a tonic GABAergic control of serotonin neurons in the median raphe nucleus. *Brain Research, 206,* 208–212.

Geller, I., & Blum, K. (1970). The effects of 5-HTP on para-chlorophenylalanine (p-CPA) attenuation of "conflict" behavior. *European Journal of Pharmacology, 9,* 319–324.

Geller, I., & Seifter, J. (1960). The effects of meprobamate, barbiturates, d-amphetamine and promazine on experimentally induced conflict in the rat. *Psychopharmacology, 1,* 482.

Gittleson, N. (1966a). The depressive psychosis in the obsessional neurotic. *British Journal of Psychiatry, 112,* 883–887.

Gittleson, N. (1966b). The fate of obsessions in depressive psychosis. *British Journal of Psychiatry, 112,* 705–708.

Goddard, A. W., Goodman, W. K., & Woods, S. W. (1992, December). *Effects of tryptophan depletion on panic disorder.* Paper presented at the annual meeting of the American College of Neuropsychopharmacology.

Goddard, A. W., Woods, S. W., Sholomskas, D. E., Charney, D. S., & Heninger, G. R. (1993). Effects of the serotonin reuptake inhibitor fluvoxamine on yohimbine-induced anxiety in panic disorder. *Psychiatry Research, 48,* 119–133.

Gorman, J. M., Liebowitz, M. R., Fyer, A. J., Goetz, D., Campeas, R. B., Fyer, M. R., Davies, S. W., & Klein, D. F. (1987). An open trial of fluoxetine in the treatment of panic attacks. *Journal of Clinical Psychopharmacology, 7,* 329–332.

Gorman, J., & Wolkow, R. (1994). Sertraline: A treatment for panic disorder. *Neuropsychopharmacology, 10* (3, pt. 2), 197S.

Graeff, F. G., & Schoenfeld, R. I. (1970). Tryptaminergic mechanisms in punished and nonpunished behavior. *Journal of Pharmacology and Experimental Therapeutics, 173*(2), 277–283.

Hoehn-Saric, R., Fawcett, J., Munjack, D. J., & Roy-Byrne, P. P. (1994). A multicentre, double-blind, placebo-controlled study of fluvoxamine in the treatment of panic disorder. *Neuropsychopharmacology, 10* (3, pt. 2), 102S.

Jenck, F., Broekkamp, C. L., & Van Delft, A. M. (1989). Opposite control mediated by central 5-HT1A and non-5-HT-1A (5-HT1B or 5-HT1C) receptors on periaqueductal gray aversion. *European Journal of Pharmacology, 161,* 219–221.

Jenck, F., Broekkamp, C. L. E., & Van Delft, A. M. (1990). 5-HT1C receptors in the serotonergtic control of periaqueductal gray induced aversion in rats. *Psychopharmacology, 100*(3), 372–376.

Johnston, D. G., Troyer, I. E., & Whitsett, S. F. (1988). Clomipramine treatment of agoraphobic women. *Archives of General Psychiatry, 45,* 453–459.

Jones, B. J., Oakley, N. R., & Tyers, M. B. (1987). The anxiolytic activity of GR38032F, a 5HT$_3$ antagonist, in the rat and cynomolgus monkey. *British Journal of Pharmacology, 90,* 88p.

Kahn, R. S., & van Praag, H. M. (1988). A serotonin hypothesis of panic disorder. *Human Psychopharmacology, 3,* 285–288.

Kahn, R. S., van Praag, H. M., Wetzler, S., Asnis, G. M., & Barr, G. (1988a). Serotonin and anxiety revisited. *Biological Psychiatry, 23,* 189–208.

Kahn, R. S., & van Praag, H. M. (1990). Panic disorder: A pre-synaptic serotonin defect? *Psychiatry Research, 31,* 209–210.

Kahn, R. S., & Westenberg, H. G. M. (1985). 1-5-Hydroxytryptophan in the treatment of anxiety disorders. *Journal of Affective Disorders, 8,* 197–200.

Kahn, R. S., Westenberg, H. G. M., Verhoeven, W. M. A., Gispen-de-Wied, C. C., & Kamerbeek, W. D. (1987). Effect of a serotonin precursor and uptake inhibitor in anxiety disorders: A double-blind comparison of 5-hydroxytryptophan, clomipramine and placebo. *International of Clinical Psychopharmacology, 2,* 33–45.

Kahn, R. S., Wetzler, S., Asnis, G. M., & van Praag, H. M. (1990). The effects of m-chlorophenylpiperazine in normal subjects: A dose-response study. *Psychopharmacology, 100,* 339–344.

Kahn, R. S., Wetzler, S., van Praag, H. M., Asnis, G. M., & Strauman, T. (1988b). Behavioral indications of serotonergic supersensitivity in patients with panic disorder. *Psychiatry Research, 25,* 101–104.

Kennedy, A. J., Gibson, F. L., O'Connell, M. T., & Curzon, G. (1993). Effects of housing, restraint and chronic treatments with mCPP and sertraline on behavioural responses to mCPP. *Psychopharmacology, 113,* 262–268.

Kennett, G. A., Whitton, P., Shah, K., & Curzon, G. (1989). Anxiogenic-like effects of mCPP and TFMPP in animal models are opposed by 5-HT1c receptor antagonists. *European Journal of Pharmacology, 164,* 445–454.

Ketelaars, C. E., & Bruinvels, J. (1989). The anti-conflict effect of cyproheptadine is not mediated by its 5-hydroxytryptamine antagonistic property. *Life Science, 44,* 1743.

Kilfoil, T., Michel, A., Montgomery, D., & Whiting, R. L. (1989). Effects of anxiolytic and anxiogenic drugs on exploratory activity in a simple model of anxiety in mice. *Neuropharmacology, 28,* 901.

Kilts, C. D., Commissaris, R. L., Cordon, J. J., & Rech, R. H. (1982). Lack of central 5-Hydroxytryptamine influence on the anticonflict activity of diazepam. *Psychopharmacology, 78,* 156–164.

Klein, E., Zohar, J., Geraci, F., Murphy, D. L., & Uhde, T. W. (1991). Anxiogenic effects of mCPP in patients with panic disorder: Comparison to caffeine's anxiogenic effects. *Biological Psychiatry, 23,* 973–984.

Kokzacks, S., Holmberg, G., & Wedin, L. (1981). A pilot study of the effect of the 5-HT-uptake inhibitor, zimelidine, on phobic anxiety. *Acta Psychiatrica Scandinavica, 63* (Suppl. 290), 328–341.

Leger, L., Wiklund, L., Descarries, L., & Persson, M. (1979). Description of an indolaminergic cell component in the cat locus coeruleus: A fluorescence histochemical and radioautographic study. *Brain Research, 168,* 43–56.

Leysen, J. E., Gommeren, W., & van Gompel, P. (1985). Receptor binding properties in vitro and in vivo of ritanserin: A very potent and long acting $5HT_2$ antagonist. *Molecular Pharmacology, 27,* 600–611.

Liebowitz, M. R. (1985). Imipramine in the treatment of panic disorder and its complications. *Psychiatric Clinics of North America, 8,* 37–47.

Lippa, A. S., Nash, P. A., & Greenblatt, E. N. (1979). Preclinical neuropsychopharmacological testing procedures for anxiolytic drugs. In S. Fielding and H. Lal (Eds.), *Anxiolytics, industrial pharmacology,* vol. 3 (p. 41). New York: Futura.

Mansbach, R. S., & Geyer, M. A. (1988). Blockade of potentiated startle responding in rats by 5-hydroxytryptamine A receptor ligands. *European Journal of Pharmacology, 156,* 375–383.

Marwaha, J., & Aghajanian, G. K. (1982). Relative potencies of alpha-1 and alpha-2 antagonists in the locus coeruleus, dorsal raphe and dorsal lateral geniculate nuclei: An electrophysiological study. *Journal of Pharmacology and Experimental Therapeutics, 222,* 287–293.

Mavissakalian, M. (1986). *Trazodone in the treatment of panic agoraphobia.* Washington, DC: American Psychiatric Association.

Montgomery, K. C. (1955). The relation between fear induced by novel stimulation and exploratory behavior. *Journal of Comparative Physiology, 48,* 254–260.

Montgomery, S. A., & Asberg, M. (1979). A new depression scale designed to be sensitive to change. *British Journal of Psychiatry, 134,* 382–389.

Mos, J., Heyden, J., & Olivier, J. (1989). Behavioural effects of 5-HT3 antagonists in animal model for aggression, anxiety and psychosis. In P. Bevan & A. R. Cools (Eds.), *Behavioural Pharmacology of 5-HT* (pp. 389–395). London: Lawrence Erlbaum Associates.

Mos, J., & Olivier, B. (1990). Separation-induced ultrasounds in rat pups as a model for anxiety disorders: Psychopharmacological profile. In H. G. M. Westenberg (Ed.), *Stress, biological rhythms and psychiatric disorders* (pp. 89–97). Houten, The Netherlands: Medidart BV.

Nanapoulos, D., Belin, M. F., Maitre, M., Vincendon, G., & Pujol, J. F. (1982). Immunocytochemical evidence for the existence of GABAergic neurons in the nucleus raphe dorsalis. Possible existence of neurons containing serotonin and GABA. *Brain Research, 232,* 375–389.

Nashold, B. S., Jr., William, P. W., & Slaughter, D. G. (1969). Sensations evoked by stimulation in the midbrain of man. *Journal of Neurosurgery, 30,* 14–24.

Ninan, P. T., Insel, T. M., Cohen, R. M., Cook, J. M., Skolnick, P., & Paul, S. M. (1982). Benzodiazepine receptor-mediated experimental "anxiety" in primates. *Science, 218,* 1332–1334.

Nishikawa, T., & Scatton, B. (1983). Evidence for a GABAergic inhibitory influence on serotonergic neurons originating from the dorsal raphe. *Brain Research, 279,* 325–329.

Nishikawa, T., & Scatton, B. (1985). Inhibitory influence of GABA on central serotonergic transmission. Raphe nuclei as the neuroanatomical site of the GABAergic inhibition of cerebral serotonergic neurons. *Brain Research, 331,* 91–103.

Nutt, D. J., Glue, P., Lawson, C., & Wilson, S. (1990). Flumazenil provocation of panic attacks. *Archives of General Psychiatry, 47,* 917–925.

Paul, S. M., Marangos, P. J., & Skolnick, P. (1981). The benzodiazepine-GABA-chloride ionophore receptor complex: Common site of minor tranquilizer action. *Biological Psychiatry, 16,* 213–229.

Pecknold, J. C., Luthe, L., Scott-Fleurie, M. H., & Jenkins, S. (1993). Gepirone in the treatment of panic disorder: An open study. *Journal of Clinical Psychology, 13,* 145–149.

Pellow, S., Johnston, A. L., & File, S. E. (1987). Selective agonists and antagonists for 5-hydroxytryptamine receptor subtypes, and interactions with yohimbine and FG 7142 using the elevated plus-maze test in the rat. *Journal of Pharmacology, 39,* 917–928.

Pickel, V. M., Tong, H. J., & Reis, D. J. (1978). Immunocytochemical evidence for serotonergic innervation of noradrenergic neurons in nucleus locus ceruleus. In S. Garattini, J. F. Pujol, & R. Samanin (Eds.), *Interactions between putative neurotransmitters in the brain* (pp. 369–382). New York: Raven Press.

Pohl, R., Balon, R., Yeragani, V. K., & Gershon, S. (1989). Serotonergic anxiolytics in the treatment of panic disorder: A controlled study with buspirone. *Psychopathology, 22* (Suppl. 1), 60.

Pols, H. J., Griez, E. J., & Verburg, C. (1993). Fluvoxamine-ritanserin combination in the treatment of panic anxiety with avoidant behavior. *Neuropsychopharmacology S3,* 377.

Pujol, J. F., Keane, P., McRae, A., Lewis, B. D., & Renaud, B. (1978). Biochemical evidence for serotonergic control of the locus ceruleus. In S. Garattini, J. F. Pujol, & R. Samanin (Eds.), *Interactions between putative Neurotransmitters* (pp. 401–410). New York: Raven Press.

Redmond, D. E., Jr., & Huang, Y. H. (1987). Current concepts II. New evidence for a locus coeruleus–norepinephrine connection with anxiety. *Life Science, 25,* 2149–2162.

Redmond, D. E., Jr., Katz, M. M., Maas, J. W., Swann, A., Casper, R., & Davis, J. M. (1986). Cerebrospinal fluid amine metabolites: Relationships with behavioral measurements in depressed, manic and healthy control subjects. *Archives of General Psychiatry, 43,* 938–947.

Rickels, K., Weisman, K., & Norstad, N. (1982). Buspirone and diazepam in anxiety: A controlled study. *Journal of Clinical Psychiatry, 43,* 81.

Roth, M., Gurney, C., Garside, R. F., & Kerr, T. A. (1972). The relationship between anxiety states and depressive illness, part I. *British Journal of Psychiatry, 121,* 147–161.

Roy-Byrne, P. P., Lewis, N., & Villacres, E., (1989). Preliminary evidence of benzodiazepine subsensitivity in panic disorder. *Biological Psychiatry, 26,* 744–748.

Rydin, E., Schalling, D., & Asberg, M. (1982). Rorschach ratings in depressed and suicidal patients with low CSF 5-HIAA. *Psychiatry Research, 7,* 229–243.

Scatton, B., Serrano, A., Rivot, J. P., & Nishikawa, T. (1984). Inhibitory GABAergic influence on striatal serotonergic transmission exerted in the dorsal raphe as revealed by in vivo voltammetry. *Brain Research, 305,* 343–352.

Schreiber, R., & Vry, J. de (1993). Neuronal circuits involved in the anxiolytic effects of the 5-HT1A receptor agonists 8-OH-DPAT, ipsapirone and buspirone in the rat. *European Journal of Pharmacology, 249,* 341–351.

Segal, M. (1979). Serotonergic innervation of the locus coeruleus from the dorsal raphe and its action on responses to noxious stimuli. *Journal of Physiology, 286,* 401–415.

Sheehan, D. V., Raj, A. B., Sheehan, H., & Soto, S. (1988). The relative efficacy of busporin, imipramine and placebo in panic disorder: A preliminary report. *Pharmacology, Biochemistry and Behavior, 29,* 815–817.

Shephard, R. A., Buxton, D. A., & Broadhurst, P. L. (1982). Drug interactions do not support reduction in serotonin turnover as the mechanism of action of benzodiazepines. *Neuropharmacology, 21,* 1027–1032.

Snaith, R. P., Baugh, S. J., & Clayden, A. D. (1982). The clinical Anxiety Scale: An instrument derived from the Hamilton Anxiety Scale. *British Journal of Psychiatry, 141,* 518–524.

Spitzer, R. L., Endicott, J., & Robins, E. (1978). Research Diagnostic Criteria: Rationale and reliability. *Archives of General Psychiatry, 35,* 773–782.

Stefanski, R., Palejko, W., Bidzinski, A., Kostowski, W., & Plaznik, A. (1993). Serotonergic innervation of the hippocampus and nucleus accumbens septi and the anxiolytic-like action of the 5-HT3 receptor antagonist. *Neuropharmacology, 10,* 987–993.

Stein, L., Wise, C. D., & Berger, B. D. (1973). Antianxiety action of benzodiazepines: Decrease in activity of serotonin neurones in the punishment system. In S. Garratini, E. Mussini, & L. O. Randall (Eds.), *The benzodiazepines* (pp. 299–326). New York: Raven Press.

Stutzmann, J. M., Eon, B., Darche, F., Lucas, M., Rataud, J., Piot, O., Blanchard, J. C., & Laduron, P. M. (1991). Are 5HT2 antagonists endowed with anxiolytic properties in rodents? *Neuroscience Letters, 128,* 4–8.

Suckow, R. F., Cooper, Th. B., & Kahn, R. S. (1990). High-performance liquid chromatographic method for analysis of plasma m-chlorophenylpiperazine. *Journal of Chromatography, 528,* 228–234.

Targum, S. D. (1991). Panic attack frequency and vulnerability to anxiogenic challenge studies. *Psychiatry Research, 36,* 75–84.

Targum, S. D., & Marshall, L. E. (1989). Fenfluramine provocation of anxiety in patients with panic disorder. *Psychiatry Research, 28,* 295–306.

Tye, N. C., Everitt, B. J., & Iversen, S. D. (1977). 5-Hydroxytryptamine and punishment. *Nature, 268,* 741–742.

Tye, N. C., Iversen, S. D., & Green, A. R. (1979). The effects of benzo-diazepines and serotonergic manipulations on punished responding. *Neuropharmacology, 18,* 689–695.

Valzelli, L. (1984). Reflections on experimental and human pathology of aggression. *Program of Neuro-Psychopharmacology and Biological Psychiatry, 8,* 311–325.

van Praag, H. M. (1986). Biological suicide research: Outcome and limitations. *Biological Psychiatry, 21,* 1305–1323.

van Praag, H. M., & Korf, J. (1971). Endogenous depressions with and without disturbances in the 5-hydroxytryptamine metabolism: A biochemical classification? *Psychopharmacologia, 19,* 148–152.

van Praag, H. M., Lemus, C. Z., & Kahn, R. S. (1986). Peripheral hormones: A window on the central MA? *Psychopharmacology Bulletin, 22,* 565–570.

Weissman, M., Fox, K., & Klerman, J. L. (1973). Hostility and depression associated with suicide attempts. *American Journal of Psychiatry, 130,* 450–455.

Westenberg, H. G. M., & Den Boer, J. A. (1993). Serotonergic basis of panic disorder. In S. A. Montgomery (Ed.). *Psychopharmacology of panic* (pp. 91–109). Oxford: Oxford University Press.

Westenberg, H. G. M., & Den Boer, J. A. (1994). The neuropharmacology of anxiety; a review on the role of serotonin. In J. A. Boer & J. M. A. Sitsen (Eds.), *Handbook of depression and anxiety: A biological approach* (pp. 405–445). New York: Marcel Dekker.

Wetzler, S. (1986). Methodological issues for the differentiation of anxiety and depression. *Clinical Neuropharmacology, 9,* 248–250.

Winter, J. C. (1972). Comparison of chlordiazepoxide, methysergide and cinanserin as modifiers of punished behavior and as antagonists of N, N-dimethyltryptamine. *Archives Internationales De Pharmacodynamie Et De Thérapie, 197,* 147–159.

Woods, S. W., Black, D., Brown, S., Asnis, G., Potkin, S., Hameede, F., & Goddard, A. (1994). Fluvoxamine in the treatment of panic disorder in outpatients: A double-blind, placebo-controlled study. *Neuropsychopharmacology, 10* (3, pt. 2), 103S.

Woods, S. W., Charney, D. S., Silver, J. M., Krystal, J. H., & Heninger, G. R. (1991). Behavioral, biochemical, and cardiovascular responses to the benzodiazepine receptor agonist flumazenil in panic disorder. *Panic Research, 36,* 115–127.

Zohar, J., & Insel, T. R. (1987). Obsessive compulsive disorder: Psychobiological approaches to diagnosis, treatment and pathophysiology. *Biological Psychiatry, 22,* 667–687.

8

Caffeine-Induced Anxiety
An Ideal Chemical Model
of Panic Disorder?

THOMAS W. UHDE

The chemical induction of anxiety has become an accepted research tool for the investigation of panic disorder. The central notion of this research strategy is that the study of the chemical induction of anxiety will increase our knowledge of the pathophysiology of "natural" anxiety states. Chemical models of anxiety have been most widely utilized in the study of panic disorder.

Current wisdom among behavioral neuroscientists is that panic disorder is a distinct anxiety disorder that can be separated from other anxiety disorders in terms of phenomenology, course of illness, and treatment response variables (Uhde & Nemiah, 1989). To the extent that this represents a valid construct, one would expect an "ideal" chemical model to distinguish panic disorder patients from nonpanic patients on the basis of qualitatively and/or quantitatively different behavioral and biochemical responses to specific anxiogenic probes (i.e., chemical panicogenic agents such as caffeine).

The author recognizes the secretarial assistance of Melanie Dubin and the current and past collaborative efforts of Drs. Linda Bierer, Ehud Klein, Thomas Mellman, Robert Post, Murray Stein, Manuel Tancer, Yosey Zohar, and Barbara Scupi and Marilla Geraci. Parts of this manuscript may have appeared in other publications authored or coauthored by Dr. Uhde.

Two research teams (Gorman, Fyer, Liebowitz, & Klein, 1987; Guttmacher, Murphy, & Insel, 1983) have proposed four separate criteria (see Table 8–1) of an "ideal" chemical model of panic disorder. Although there are theoretical flaws and limitations in the application of the criteria listed in the table (Uhde & Tancer, 1989), the four criteria have been widely embraced by the research community and provide, therefore, a common reference point for evaluating the caffeine model of panic disorder. In this review, we present an update of the caffeine model of anxiety within the context of the four criteria for an ideal chemical model of panic disorder.

SYMPTOM CONVERGENCE

Information regarding the symptomatic similarity between natural (i.e., "spontaneous" or "uncued") and caffeine-induced panic attacks are based on anecdotal case reports or survey data (i.e., indirect evidence) and challenge studies under controlled laboratory conditions (i.e., direct evidence).

TABLE 8–1
Four Criteria of an Ideal Chemical Model of Panic Disorder

1. *Symptom convergence:* The quality, duration, and severity of symptoms of an induced panic attack must closely mimic those of the patient's spontaneous panic attacks; the extreme fear and the physiologic symptoms must be present.

2. *Specificity:* The challenge stimulus should exhibit either "complete" or "threshold" specificity for panic disorder patients; complete specificity implies that only panic disorder patients and no other psychiatric or normal control subjects experience panic attacks in response to the challenge stimulus; threshold specificity, a less stringent criteria, implies that healthy and psychiatric controls as well as panic disorder patients can have panic attacks in response to the challenge, but the controls require a larger stimulus.

3. *Clinical validation:* Clinically effective panic-reducing agents, such as imipramine, phenelzine, and alprazolam, should either reduce the frequency or raise the threshold of chemically induced panic attacks; conversely, the frequency or threshold should not be altered by treatments known to be relatively ineffective in panic disorder, such as propranolol.

4. *Replicability:* A susceptible patient should respond predictably to repeated challenges in the absence of changing clinical status.

Indirect Evidence

Case Reports

Greden (1974) reported three cases of caffeine intoxication in patients whose caffeine consumption was between 1,200 and 1,500 milligrams (mg) daily. Greden noted that these patients' symptoms of caffeinism were "indistinguishable" from anxiety neurosis. Although Greden did not explicitly address the relationship of caffeinism to panic attacks, it is interesting that the one individual who had only recently consumed excessive amounts of caffeine reported palpitations, light-headedness, tremulousness, breathlessness, chest discomfort, and irregular heartbeat on a sporadic basis approximately two or three times per day. In contrast, the two individuals who had consumed large amounts of caffeine for years reported symptoms more reminiscent of generalized anxiety disorder. These data suggest that acute caffeine intoxication may mimic panic disorder whereas *chronic* toxicity may mimic symptoms of generalized anxiety.

We also have reported on four cases (Uhde, 1988; Uhde, 1990) of inadvertent caffeine intoxication that mimic symptoms of panic attacks or generalized anxiety. Here we discuss only the symptomatic character of caffeine-induced anxiety and note briefly the degree of avoidance behaviors, for the reader's information.

Case 1. A college student consumed up to 1.8 grams of caffeine while preparing for final examinations. This student had symptoms of a leaping-pounding heart, sweating in his hands and feet, and paresthesia. Analogous to the help-seeking behavior observed in agoraphobic patients, this individual with caffeine-induced panic attacks also sought medical consultation at a local emergency room. He was fearful that he had a life-threatening problem.

Case 2. A young woman requested a medical evaluation due to recurrent episodes of panic anxiety during the past four weeks. She had never previously experienced panic attacks. She had been a low caffeine consumer for years (< 100 mg daily) until her recent move to the area. Her first lifetime episode of panic awakened her from sleep following an evening when she had consumed eight cups of coffee. After discontinuation of her caffeine intake, she had a total remission of symptoms. She did not develop avoidance behaviors.

Case 3. A 43-year-old man complained of sporadic anxiety problems for the past two years. However, several of his "anxious" symptoms (i.e., insomnia, "hot flashes," abdominal "uneasiness," and restless legs) had increased in severity during the past two months. His average caffeine intake consisted of a remarkable 25 to 28 cups of coffee daily over the past three years. He did not report any history of avoidance behaviors; in fact, he accurately attributed many of his symptoms to a pattern of excessive caffeine consumption.

Case 4. A high school student was referred for evaluation of anxiety and poor school performance. His symptoms of anxiety consisted of nervousness, jitteriness, sweating, insomnia, and periodic hand tremor. The patient denied panic attacks but did report dysphoria of several months' duration. Until recently, he had consumed about seven to eight cola drinks per day. To enhance his homework performance (i.e., to combat fatigue) he had gradually increased his caffeine intake from approximately 45 to 90 mg daily to as much as 500 mg daily over several months during the current school year. He had also begun to take NO-DOZ (100 mg/cap) on some school nights. He did not attribute his symptoms to caffeine and had no avoidance behaviors. After discontinuation of caffeine, there was a noticeable improvement in his school performance and a total resolution of his anxious symptomatology.

Retrospective Surveys

Questionnaires have been designed to assess consumption patterns and relative degree of sensitivity to caffeine (see Boulenger & Uhde, 1982; Lee, Cameron, & Greden, 1985; Scupi, Maser, & Uhde, 1992); however, no survey study has been conducted that specifically addresses the question of symptomatic convergence. Nevertheless, a comparison of the criteria of caffeine intoxication versus panic attacks from the third revised edition of the *Diagnostic and Statistic Manual of Mental Disorders* (DSM-III-R) (Table 8–2) indicates that on a purely symptomatic level, there are many areas of overlap between these two conditions. In fact, four of 12 symptoms listed for caffeinism in the table are similar or identical to the criteria for panic attacks. An additional four DSM-III-R symptoms of caffeine intoxication—nervousness, restlessness, excitement, and insomnia (Mellman & Uhde, 1989)—are also reported quite commonly by panic disorder patients. Overall, 67 percent of the DSM-III-R symptoms of caffeine intoxication also are associated with panic

TABLE 8–2
Comparison of DSM-III-R Criteria of Panic Attacks and Caffeine Intoxication

Panic Attacks	Caffeinism
Tachycardia or palpitations	Tachycardia or cardiac arrhythmia
Nausea or abdominal distress	GI disturbance
Flushes or chills	Flushed face
Trembling or shaking	Psychomotor agitation
Fear of going crazy or of doing something uncontrolled	
Fear of dying	
Depersonalization or derealization	
Dizziness, unsteady feelings, or faintness	
Shortness of breath or smothering sensations	
Chest pain or discomfort	
Chocking	
Sweating	
Paresthesias	
	Nervousness
	Restlessness
	Rambling flow of thoughts, speech
	Excitement
	Periods of inexhaustibility
	Muscle twitching
	Insomnia
	Diuresis

disorder. Of the formal criteria of caffeine intoxication, only diuresis and (widely distributed) motor tics may be found more often in acute caffeine intoxication than panic attacks. The major factor that discriminates between these two conditions, therefore, is the *knowledge* that the person has consumed excessive amounts of caffeine.

Direct Evidence

Caffeine Provocation Studies
Two research teams (NIMH led by Uhde and Yale led by Charney) have employed the caffeine challenge paradigm to investigate the neurobiology

of panic disorder. Both groups used DSM-III-R criteria to identify panic attacks. That is, behavioral responses to caffeine were categorized as to whether they did or did not meet criteria for panic attacks. Other than making these categorical distinctions, the Yale group did not ascertain the "quality" of panic attacks in terms of their resemblance to natural panic attacks.

In our recent studies, we have assessed the quality of panic attacks induced in the laboratory after oral (480 mg) caffeine. In these studies, we asked panic disorder patients to rate the nature of their laboratory-related panic attacks, in relation to past natural (i.e., spontaneous) panic attacks, on the following five-point scale: (1) not at all similar to your natural panic attacks; (2) a few symptoms were similar to your natural panic attacks; (3) most symptoms were the same; (4) almost all symptoms were the same; (5) exactly identical. In our oral challenge studies, the average rating on the Panic Attack Similarity Scale (PASS) for patients after caffeine-induced panic attacks has ranged from 3.4 to 4.5. These observations suggest that most caffeine-induced panic attacks are very similar or almost identical to natural panic attacks.

While caffeine-induced panic attacks appear to have excellent symptom convergence with natural panic attacks, few studies have examined the qualitative or quantitative character of panic attacks across different chemical models. Klein, Zohar, Geraci, Murphy, and Uhde (1991) compared the behavioral effects of metachlorophenylproperazine (mCPP), a serotonergic agonist, to the effects of caffeine. A self-rating scale was used to assess the similarity of both mCPP- and caffeine-induced anxiety states to each patient's own spontaneous panic attacks. (See Chapter 7 for further details of mCPP and panic.) Whereas caffeine-induced panic attacks tended to be more intense on a number of rating scales than mCPP-induced panic attacks (Figure 8–1), the overall quality of both drug-induced anxiety states was similar to each patient's natural panic attacks. These data suggest that different chemical models can induce qualitatively similar panic attacks, presumably via different mechanisms of action.

In addition to investigating areas of symptomatic *overlap* among the chemical models in relation to "spontaneous" panic attacks, it is also important to note areas of symptomatic *divergence*. Following oral caffeine administration, several panic disorder patients have reported recurrent panic attacks (i.e., panic attacks that occurred in waves). This is different from the typical temporal sequence of random "spontaneous"

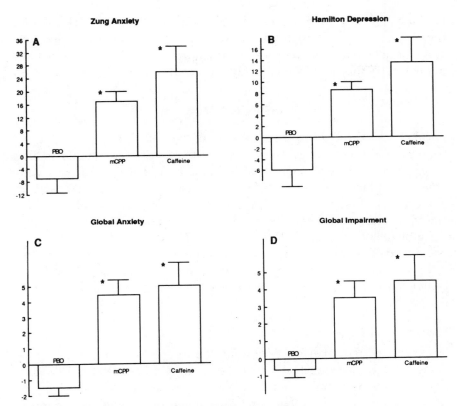

Figure 8–1. Panic disorder patients experienced significantly greater anxiogenic re-sponses to oral mCPP and caffeine compared to placebo. Although the panic disorder patients tended to have more intense symptoms of anxiety after caffeine, caffeine- and mMCPP-induced anxiety states were quite similar in quality (Klein, Zohar, Geraci, Murphy, & Uhde, 1991, p. 978).

panic attacks reported by most panic disorder patients, although some patients do rarely report the occurrence of repeated panic attacks over very short periods of time (e.g., 15 attacks within 20 minutes).

We also have investigated the dose-related effects of intravenous caf-feine (0, 3, 5, 7 mg per kilogram) in 12 normal control subjects (Nick-ell & Uhde, 1991). In this study, all subjects reported caffeine-induced olfactory hallucinations after one or more doses of the caffeine but not after placebo. The olfactory hallucinations appeared to activate vivid images of past experiences. Such olfactory-linked hallucinations and memories in normal control subjects and wavelike episodes of panic in patients appear to be fairly rare in "spontaneous" panic attacks. While there is excellent symptomatic convergence between caffeine-induced panic attacks and "spontaneous" panic attacks, the two phenomena are not perfectly matched in terms of quality or frequency distribution.

SPECIFICITY

For a chemical model to meet criteria of "absolute" specificity, it has been argued that the agent under study (e.g., caffeine) should induce panic attacks in only panic disorder patients and not in patients with other psychiatric syndromes or in normal control subjects. We have argued that no known chemical model meets criteria of absolute specificity. In contrast, several chemical models of panic disorder, including caffeine, meet criteria of "threshold" specificity. Threshold specificity could be called "relative increased sensitivity," denoting that panic disorder patients require a lesser dose to induce panic attacks. What is the evidence for this relative increase in caffeine sensitivity in panic disorder patients?

Indirect Evidence

We evaluated daily caffeine consumption in agoraphobic patients with panic attacks in the early 1980s (Boulenger & Uhde, 1982). This data base was later expanded to include patients with major depression. Patients from each diagnostic group (i.e., panic disorder and major depression) were separately matched for age, gender, and socioeconomic status with normal control subjects.

A significantly lower percentage of patients with panic disorder (67 percent had given up coffee compared to the patients with major depressive disorders (22 percent) or normal controls (13–20 percent) (Boulenger, Uhde, Wolff, & Post, 1984).

The panic disorder patients reported that they had given up coffee consumption because of its psychostimulant or related properties. Unlike the depressed patients, the panic disorder patients also reported that the consumption of one cup of coffee produced significantly greater increases in measures of anxiety ($p < 0.001$), alertness ($p < 0.01$), and insomnia ($p < 0.01$) but not well-being compared to the normal control group. There was also a significant correlation between daily caffeine consumption and measures of trait anxiety ($r = 0.50$, $p = 0.006$), depression (r = 0.56, p = 0.02) and the Symptom Check List-90 (SCL-90) subscales for general symptomatic index (r = 0.44, p = 0.02), positive symptom distress (r = 0.44, p = 0.02), retarded depression (r =0.45, p = 0.01), and agitated depression (r = 0.37, p = 0.04). There were no significant correlations between daily caffeine consumption and any of these measures in either the depressed patients or normal control groups.

Lee and associates (1985) evaluated patterns of daily caffeine consumption and determined subscale scores on the SCL-90-R (Derogatis, 1977) in 124 medical inpatients without a psychiatric illness and 43 outpatients with a primary anxiety disorder (79 percent of whom had panic disorder or agoraphobia with panic attacks by DSM-III diagnostic criteria). The panic disorder patients were found to have a different distribution of daily caffeine consumption compared to the medical comparison group (p < 0.001). Eighty-four percent of the panic disorder patients compared to 41 percent of the medical inpatients were low consumers of caffeine, defined in this study as ≤ 249 mg/day according to the criteria of Victor, Lubetsky, and Greden (1981). In contrast, only 2 percent of the anxiety disorder patients were high consumers (≥ 750 mg/day), whereas 16 percent of the medical comparison group were found to be high consumers.

Using the National Institute of Mental Health-Personality Questionnaire (NIMH-PQ) instrument (Scupi et al., 1992) to assess patterns of caffeine consumption in 1,209 patients with putative panic disorder, our research team has found a similar pattern of caffeine intake: 90.2 percent of the panic disorder patients were "low consumers" (3 or less cups/day [≥ 300 mg]), 8.4 percent were "moderate consumers" (4–6 cups coffee daily [301–700 mg]), and only 1.4 percent were "high consumers" of caffeine (7 or more cups/day [≥ 701 mg]) (Uhde & Scupi, unpublished data). All three of these survey studies (Boulenger et al., 1984; Lee et al., 1985; Uhde & Scupi, unpublished data) provide indirect evidence that panic disorder patients maintain diets low in caffeine content. Panic disorder patients also report greater increases in anxiety after drinking one cup of coffee compared with depressed patients (Boulenger et al., 1984), medical inpatients (Lee et al., 1985) and normal control subjects (Boulenger et al., 1984). In fact, in our initial retrospective survey (Boulenger et al., 1984), we found that 67 percent of a clinical sample of 30 panic disorder patients had totally given up coffee;

this percentage is identical to the proportion of patients (837 of 1,248; 67 percent) in a more recent study (Uhde & Scupi, unpublished data) who stated that caffeine triggered panic attacks.

Direct Evidence

Two research teams (NIMH and Yale) have examined the panicogenic effects of caffeine in panic disorder patients under double-blind, placebo-controlled conditions. In our ongoing series of studies at the National Institute of Mental Health (NIMH) (Uhde, 1990), we have investigated the effects of oral caffeine (480 mg) in 57 patients with panic disorder and in 27 normal control subjects. In our laboratory we used 480 mg caffeine base, equivalent to approximately four to six cups of coffee, because this dose had been shown to produce statistically significant increases in ratings of anxiety (but not panic attacks) in normal control subjects (Uhde, Boulenger, Vittone et al., 1984). The differential rate of caffeine-induced panic attacks and peak changes in ratings of State (Spielberger, Gorsuch, & Lushene, 1970) and Zung anxiety (Zung, 1971) were calculated. To be designated a panic attack, subjects had to experience mental anxiety (i.e., physical distress *without* subjective emotions of anxiety would not be acceptable), meet DSM-III criteria of panic attacks, and report a crescendo rise in anxiety (time to peak anxiety less than five minutes).

None of the patients or normal controls reported panic attacks after placebo (not all subjects received placebo); in contrast, 36.9 percent of the panic disorder patients versus none of the normal control subjects experienced panic attacks after the 480 mg dose of caffeine (Chi-square, $p < 0.05$). Panic disorder patients also had a greater increase in ratings of Spielberger state and Zung anxiety.

The Yale research team (Charney, Heninger, & Jatlow, 1985) also reported that oral caffeine (10 mg/kg) produced a greater rate of panic attacks in panic disorder patients compared to normal control subjects. Fifteen of the 21 patients (71 percent) and none of the controls had panic attacks in response to caffeine. Charney (personal communication) has indicated that none of the patients had panic attacks during the placebo administration.

Of interest, the caffeine doses used in our laboratory (Uhde, Boulenger, Post et al., 1984) are not comparable to those used by Charney and associates (1985), who used caffeine citrate, which is 50 percent caffeine by weight, whereas we used 480 mg caffeine base. Although the explanation for the differences in panic rates is unclear, both studies provided direct evidence that panic disorder patients are significantly more sensitive to the anxiogenic effects of caffeine than normal controls.

In preliminary studies, we also have investigated the anxiogenic effects of caffeine in patients with obsessive compulsive disorder and social phobia. Caffeine fails to increase ratings of anxiety in obsessive convulsive disorder, including the syndromal-specific symptoms of obsessions or compulsions. On the other hand, caffeine does produce anxiety in patients with social phobia. However, the level of anxiety experienced in social phobic patients tends to fall midway between the modest increases in arousal observed in normal control subjects and the severe degrees of panic and anxiety that occur in panic disorder patients.

Critics of chemical models have suggested that the increased rate of panic in panic disorder patients is simply a by-product of interpreting normal physiological cues as "dangerous." Cognitive therapists, therefore, view panic disorder patients as individuals who experience normal changes in interoceptive cues (e.g., changes in heart rate) as potentially dangerous or life-threatening whereas normal individuals perceive identical changes in physiology as a normal variation in bodily function. Margraf, Ehlers, and Roth (1986) theorize that panic disorder patients, relative to normal control subjects, should report greater anxiogenic but identical (or similar) biochemical responses to the chemical induction of panic attacks. To support their contention, Margraf and coworkers (1986) noted that lactate-induced panic attacks in panic disorder patients often are associated with only minor alterations in physiology or biochemistry compared to normal control subjects. Several psychologists have contended that a greater anxiety *plus different* physiological or biochemical responses would support "biological" theories of panic disorder. As reviewed elsewhere (Uhde & Tancer, 1989), there are problems with this viewpoint; nonetheless, given the lack of biological changes associated with some models of panic (Margraf et al., 1986), we were interested in testing for "specificity" of the physiological (blood pressure) or biochemical (cortisol, glucose, lactate) responses to caffeine in panic disorder patients compared to normal controls.

In our aforementioned caffeine study (for review, see Uhde, 1990), 480 mg of caffeine produced a significantly greater main effect increase in cortisol in the panic disorder patients compared to controls ($p < 0.02$). Also, there was a significantly greater glucose ($p < 0.05$) and lactate ($p < 0.04$) rise at 90 minutes following caffeine administration. The "panicking" vs. "nonpanicking" panic disorder patients also had significantly greater increases in lactate ($p < 0.03$).

In terms of the criteria of "specificity," several lines of indirect and/or direct evidence suggest that panic disorder patients have an increased sensitivity (i.e., increased levels of anxiety and higher rates of panic) to caffeine compared with normal control subjects, depressed patients, inpatients with nonspecific medical conditions, social phobic patients, and patients with obsessive compulsive disorder. To counterbalance this increased sensitivity, a majority of panic disorder patients appear to maintain a self-imposed diet low in caffeine content.

CLINICAL VALIDATION

As was suggested by Gorman and associates (1987) and Guttmacher and coworkers (1983), an ideal chemical model of anxiety or panic should have clinical validity. (See Table 8–1.) That is, drugs that are effective in reducing "spontaneous" panic attacks should either reduce the frequency or raise the threshold of chemically induced panic attacks. Little is known about the action of antipanic drugs on caffeine-induced anxiety, and the skimpy available information is mixed.

The effects of two well-known antipanic agents, alprazolam and imipramine, on caffeine-induced anxiety states have been investigated in two separate studies. In the first study we gave single-dose caffeine (480 mg) to 16 panic disorder patients participating in a double-blind, placebo-controlled, alprazolam treatment study. Patients were given caffeine while receiving, in random order, either placebo or alprazolam as a part of a crossover treatment study. Seven of the 16 (43.7 percent) patients had panic attacks during the placebo phase whereas none of the panic disorder patients had panic attacks during the alprazolam phase of the study. Compared to placebo, alprazolam also significantly reduced measures of anxiety on the Zung Anxiety Scale and significantly blunted caffeine-induced peak rises in lactate and cortisol.

Using a similar design, we found that imipramine had complex effects on caffeine-induced anxiety. Imipramine was effective in blocking both "spontaneous" and, later, caffeine-induced panic attacks in some panic disorder patients. However, in most patients, long-term imipramine administration (given at the same therapeutic doses that had been shown to block natural panic attacks effectively) appeared to have only weak action in blocking caffeine-induced anxiety.

Overall, these observations suggest excellent "clinical validation" in relation to alprazolam but only modest, if any, validity of the caffeine model of panic disorder in terms of imipramine pharmacotherapy. It is worth noting that most, if not all, other chemical models also fail to be blocked by all antipanic agents. These findings with the caffeine model, as well as other chemical models of panic disorder, underscore the complex nature of the neurobiology of panic disorder. Rather than discard these chemical models because of their so-called imperfect clinical validation, they may actually provide unique tools for dissecting out the differential roles of different neurotransmitter-receptor systems in the mediation of panic attacks.

REPLICABILITY

The proposed fourth criteria of an ideal chemical model is "replicability." According to Guttmacher and coworkers (1983) and Gorman and associates (1987), the panicogen (e.g., caffeine) should induce panic attacks with each repeated exposure to the chemical probe. Two standard chemical models (e.g., lactate and carbon dioxide inhalation), however, may fail to meet this fourth criteria. (See Chapters 9 and 11.) Repeated lactate (Bonn, Harrison, & Rees, 1973) and carbon dioxide (Griez & van den Hout, 1983) have been associated with desensitization.

Panic disorder patients experience both uncued (i.e., spontaneous) and cued (i.e., situational or context-specific) panic attacks. Various exogenous and neurobiological factors appear to influence the threshold of panic across and within individual patients (Roy-Byrne & Uhde, 1988). Panic disorder patients do not always experience situational panic attacks when exposed to personally relevant phobic stimuli; furthermore, the same patient may report strikingly dissimilar levels of anxiety when exposed to the same phobic stimulus. These observations, combined with the fact that anxiety levels often decrease after repeated exposure to phobic stimuli, lactate, and CO_2 inhalation, have led us to question whether "replicability" is a legitimate criterion for evaluating chemical models. Only the scrutiny of future research will determine the answer to this question.

The study of the mechanisms that underlie "changing" response patterns to chemical models may represent, however, an excellent research tool for investigating the neurobiology of panic disorder. Therefore, rather than reject chemical models that fail to meet the "replicability" criterion, it may be more suitable to investigate mechanisms that mediate changing patterns of sensitivity (i.e., tolerance versus sensitization). Such research strategies may offer insights regarding the neuropathophysiology of panic disorder and/or mechanisms that mediate the therapeutic response to antipanic drugs.

Agents that are initially panicogenic, such as lactate (Carr et al., 1986; Dillon, Gorman, Liebowitz, Fyer, & Klein, 1987; Kelly, Mitchell-Heggs, & Sherman, 1971; Liebowitz et al., 1984; Pitts & McClure, 1967; Rainey et al., 1984, 1987), carbon dioxide (Gorman et al., 1984; Griez, Lousberg, van den Hout, & van den Folen, 1987; Latimer, 1977; Woods et al., 1986), and even imipramine (Aronson & Logue, 1988), have reduced anxiogenic effects or, in fact, may reduce levels of anxiety below baseline levels after repeated administration. We hypothesize that there may be a common mechanism underlying the therapeutic responses to selective drugs (e.g., imipramine) and psychosocial interventions (e.g., exposure). For example, it is possible that both exposure therapy and imipramine treatment increase brain norepinephrine, resulting in the secondary downregulation of pertinent postsynaptic neurotransmitter-receptor (alpha-2 adrenergic) systems.

Given these considerations, we wondered whether repeated caffeine administration would be associated with diminishing, increasing, or stable levels of anxiety. Ten panic disorder patients and eight normal controls were administered oral caffeine (7 mg/kg) on eight consecutive days (Uhde & Mellman, unpublished data). All of the normal controls but only six of 10 (60 percent) patients completed the study. The four patients who dropped out had such intense symptoms of anxiety or panic attacks that they were unable to complete the study. Even with these highly sensitive patients excluded from the data analysis, the remaining patients who completed the study still displayed, in relation to the normal control subjects, greater anxiogenesis. Of interest, the panic disorder patients demonstrated a delayed and incomplete habituation to caffeine's anxiogenic effects compared to the normal control subjects.

Our preliminary findings, therefore, suggest that repeated caffeine administration is associated with greater levels of anxiety in the panic disorder patients compared to normal control subjects. Both groups, however, demonstrated diminishing degrees of anxiety over time with repeated caffeine administration. The fact that the panic disorder patients habituated to repeated caffeine administration has theoretical implications regarding mechanisms mediating positive responses to both psychosocial and drug therapies. Many of the recently developed chemical models have not been tested across diagnostic groups using a multiple-repeat paradigm. It would be valuable to determine whether panic disorder patients have similar patterns of decreased habituation across a range of receptor-specific chemical models (e.g., yohimbine and cholecystokinin [CCK]) of anxiety. Interestingly, one investigator group has suggested that CCK may be the only chemical model that does not demonstrate habituation (Bradwejn, Koszycki, Payeur, Bourin, & Bothwick, 1992). Although these findings are intriguing, replication is necessary. (See Chapters 6 and 10.)

CONCLUSION

Four criteria of an ideal chemical model of anxiety or panic have been proposed by two separate research teams (Gorman et al., 1987; Guttmacher et al., 1983). As reviewed in Table 8–1, the criteria include "symptom convergence," "specificity," "clinical validation," and "replicability." Although these criteria have been partially criticized (Uhde & Tancer, 1989), they provide a framework for evaluating chemical models of panic disorder.

In terms of symptom convergence, caffeine-induced panic attacks are qualitatively similar to "spontaneous" panic attacks. In fact, the symptoms are often almost identical, leading clinicians, at times, to misdiagnose caffeine intoxication as panic disorder. In large quantities (≥ 700 mg), caffeine can trigger panic attacks in normal individuals without a prior history of an anxiety disorder (Uhde, 1990). Therefore, in terms of "specificity," the increased anxiogenic effects of caffeine in panic disorder patients compared with normal control subjects and patients with nonspecific medical conditions, depression, social phobia, and obsessive compulsive disorder would appear to provide strong evidence for "threshold" but not "absolute" specificity.

Alprazolam blocks caffeine-induced panic attacks. Imipramine, however, has mixed effects. Additional studies with clinically effective and ineffective antipanic drugs are required to determine the extent to which the caffeine model of panic disorder meets the "clinical validation" criterion of an ideal chemical model. Almost all chemical models fail to meet this criterion. The reverse, however, is not true. Of the current drug treatments of panic disorder, alprazolam would appear to be the only clinically effective antipanic agent that consistently blocks (or significantly reduces) the panicogenic and anixogenic effects of all the chemical models. Within this context, it would appear that the benzodiazepine-gamma-aminobutyric acid system plays a central role in the neurobiology of panic disorder.

That chemical models should always trigger panic attacks with repeated administration is open to criticism (Uhde & Tancer, 1989). Nonetheless, it is noteworthy that several patients who had panic attacks after the first caffeine challenge refused to participate in subsequent challenges. This pattern of "refusal" in the research setting parallels the secondary avoidance of situations associated with previous "spontaneous" panic attacks in nonresearch (i.e., natural) environments. Compared to normal control subjects, panic disorder had a greater anxiogenic responses to each of eight consecutive daily doses of caffeine. Patients also demonstrated a delayed and incomplete habituation to the anxiogenic effects of repeated caffeine administration. These findings indicate that panic disorder patients have increased sensitivity to the anxiogenic effects of *repeated* caffeine administration. Our findings further suggest that the study of mechanisms that mediate behavioral habituation (i.e., decreased levels of anxiety) to repeated panic attacks (drug-induced or after phobic exposure) will provide new insights into the nature of panic disorder. It will be equally important to investigate neurobiological mechanisms that *prevent or delay* behavioral habituation of anxiety responses.

Chemical induction techniques have been used as tools for the investigation of panic disorder for two major reasons: to study the relevance of *particular neurotransmitter systems* in alarm, arousal, and anxiety; and to investigate the pathophysiology of panic disorder. These areas are intimately related, but, nonetheless have a slightly different focus.

In the first scenario, the site(s) or mechanism(s) of action of the drug or neuropeptide under study (e.g., CCK-4) are thought to be well-known and relatively specific and/or novel. If the drug or neuropeptide (e.g., CCK-4) causes panic attacks, the investigator infers that the site of action (e.g., the cholecystokinin system) may play an important role in the pathophysiology of panic attacks. This application of chemical models is a "forward step" technique and is of potential value in the development of new antipanic agents. In fact, at the present time, several cholecystokinin antagonists are being developed by the pharmaceutical industry as possible antianxiety agents. If the CCK-4 model of panic disorder results in the development of a new class of antianxiety agents, the "forward-step" chemical model strategy will be increasingly valued as a method for drug discovery.

The "reverse-step" chemical model strategy is founded on the notion that we can discover the cause(s) of "spontaneous" panic attacks by understanding the mechanism(s) by which an exogenous chemical agent induces panic attacks. "Symptomatic convergence" and "specificity" would appear to be especially important criteria for selecting a candidate "reverse-step" chemical model as a tool for the investigation of panic disorder. In many respects, caffeine represents an agent with superb "symptomatic convergence" and "specificity"; it could be viewed as an excellent "reverse-step" chemical model of panic disorder. What has the caffeine model of anxiety taught us about the *neurobiology* of panic disorder? Will the caffeine model of panic disorder lead to the development of new antipanic agents?

Several lines of evidence suggest that caffeine's behavioral and biochemical effects are mediated by the antagonism of adenosinergic receptors (Daly, Bruns, & Snyder, 1981; Phillis & Kostopoulos, 1975; Phillis & Wu, 1981; Sattin & Rall, 1970; Snyder, Katims, Annau, Bruns, & Daly, 1981; Stone, 1981). If so, then caffeine might be expected to have neurobiological and behavioral effects opposite those of adenosine. Of interest, adenosine and/or its analogs, N_6 cyclohexyladenosine (CHA), N_6 (R-phenylisopropyl) adenosine (PIA), and 2-chloradenosine (2-Clad), produce sedation (Crawley, Patel, & Marangos, 1981, 1983), decrease blood pressure (Hoffman, Satinover, Miletich, Albrecht, & Gans, 1982; Newberg, Milde, & Michenfelder, 1985), and bradycardia (Berne, Di Marco, & Belardinelli, 1984; Di Marco, Sellers, Berne, West, & Belardinelli, 1983). Adenosine is one of several endogenous agents with natural anticonvulsant properties. (For review, see Dragunow, Goddard, & Laverty, 1985.) As an antagonist, caffeine produces the opposite effects. For example, caffeine and related methyl-xanthine compounds increase blood pressure and heart rate and potentiate seizures (Coffey et al., 1987; Shapira et al., 1987; Vestal, Eriksson, Musser, Ozaki, & Halter, 1983; Yarnell & Chu, 1975). Caffeine also increases verbal and motor output, decreases fatigue, and worsens insomnia in humans (Battig & Buzzi, 1986; Brezinova, 1974; File, Bond, & Lister, 1982; Rapoport et al., 1981; Saletu, Allen, & Itil, 1974). Caffeine, therefore, does appear to have behavioral and physiological effects opposite those of adenosine, thereby implicating the adenosinergic receptor system in the neurobiology of panic disorder.

Stress also seems to influence the adenosinergic system. Although stress and anxiety are not equivalent biological phenomena (Uhde, Joffe, Jimerson, & Post, 1988), the fact that both stress and long-term administration of caffeine up-regulate many central adenosinergic receptors (Boulenger, Patel, Post, Parma, & Marangos, 1983) underscores the important interplay between the biological functions of stress, alarm, and arousal mechanisms in humans. In fact, caffeine is known to either mimic or augment the biological effects of stress in animals and humans (Bennett, Walker, Henry, & Kincaid-Smith, 1983; Cobb, 1974; Doreen, 1977; Henry & Stephens, 1980; Lane, 1983; Muller & Vernikos-Danellis, 1970; Stillner, Popkin, & Pierce, 1978). Taken together, these data suggest that caffeine causes anxiety via antagonism of adenosinergic receptors. Two types of adenosinergic receptors, referred to as A1 and A2, have been identified (Londos, Cooper, & Wolff, 1980). The highest concentrations of A1 and A2 receptors are in the limbic-hippocampal and striatal areas of the brain (Goodman & Synder, 1982). We have recently found that oral caffeine (480 mg) produces greater anxiogenic but *similar* increments in motor activity in panic disorder patients versus normal control subjects. The differential effects of caffeine on behavioral (i.e., experience of anxiety) versus motor activity suggest that A1 receptors located in the limbic-hippocampal area may play a special role in the neurobiology of panic attacks, although other lines of evidence clearly implicate the A2 subtype (Choi, Shamin, Padgett, & Daly, 1988; Coffin & Spealman, 1987).

Many neurotransmitter-neuromodulatory systems have been linked to the important biological functions of fear, alarm, arousal, and anxiety. (See Ballenger, 1990.) Even the anxiogenic effects of caffeine might be mediated, directly or indirectly, by influencing phosphodiesterase (Sutherland & Rall, 1958), nonadrenergic, dopaminergic, or benzodiazepine-gaba-ergic function. (For review, see Uhde, 1990.) The most coherent view of current information, however, would seem to incriminate adenosinergic neuromodulatory systems in the mediation of caffeine-induced panic attacks. Will this presumption, if accurate, lead to the development of new antipanic agents?

Based on the notion that caffeine-induced anxiety states are caused by the blockade of adenosine receptors, one would predict drugs that increased adenosine levels would have antianxiety effects. Dipyridamole is an adenosine reuptake blocker that increases serum levels in humans (Klabunde, 1983; Sollevi, Ostergren, Hjemdahl, Fredholm, & Fagrell, 1984). We hypothesized, therefore, that dipyridamole would have antianxiety effects in panic disorder patients. In a preliminary study (Black, Stein, & Uhde, 1992), we gave dipyridamole (100–300 mg) to 10 patients with panic disorder and two patients with generalized anxiety disorder. Patients were treated for a mean 46 days (range 21–88). Despite the administration of moderate doses given for several weeks, we failed to demonstrate a significant reduction in ratings of anxiety on seven of eight scales. The only evidence of a therapeutic response was based on the percent of time, while awake, that patients spent worrying or feeling anxious. As a group, the patients had a reduction in percent of time feeling anxious from 49 to 35 percent (paired t = 2.39, df = 11, p < 0.04). Nonetheless, the overall response to the dipyridamole trial was negative.

Our results indicate that dipyridamole lacks efficacy in the treatment of panic disorder and, by extrapolation, argue against the adenosinergic hypothesis of panic disorder. However, there are several possible explanations for dipyridamole's ineffectiveness. Higher doses of dipyridamole might be required to sustain increased levels of adenosine at relevant synaptic sites of action. It is also probable that dipyridamole may not readily cross the blood brain barrier. Moreover, increased levels of adenosine in the blood, even if very large, may be rapidly metabolized before they can enter the brain. Any of these conditions would markedly limit the antianxiety action that might be mediated via an adenosine reuptake mechanism. Thus, while our negative findings fail to confirm our hypothesis regarding dipyridamole's antianxiety effects, they do not rule out a possible role for adenosinergic mechanisms in the neurobiology of panic disorder.

In summary, caffeine challenge paradigms represent a valuable research tool for the investigation of panic disorder. As a research tool, caffeine-induced panic attacks, like most chemical models, have limitations. Nonetheless, the caffeine model of panic disorder has stimulated a renewed interest in the possible central role for adenosinergic receptor-neuromodulatory systems in the regulation of anxiety, arousal, alarm, and fear. Compounds with adenosinergic agonist properties should still be investigated as a potential new class of antianxiety agent.

REFERENCES

Aronson, T. A., & Logue, C. M. (1988). Phenomenology of panic attacks: A descriptive study of panic disorder patients' self-reports. *Journal of Clinical Psychiatry, 49,* 8–13.

Ballenger, J. C. (1990). *Neurobiology of Panic Disorder.* New York: Alan R. Liss.

Battig, K., & Buzzi, R. (1986). Effect of coffee on the speed of subject-paced information processing. *Neuropsychobiology, 16,* 126-130.

Bennett, W. M., Walker, R. G., Henry, J. P., & Kincaid-Smith, P. (1983). Chronic interstitial nephropathy in mice induced by psychosocial stress potentiation by caffeine. *Nephron, 34,* 110–113.

Berne, R. M., Di Marco, J. P., & Belardinelli, L. (1984). Dromotropic effects of adenosine and adenosine antagonists in the treatment of cardiac arrhythmias involving the atrioventricular node. *Circulation, 69,* 1195–1197.

Black, B., Stein, M. B., & Uhde, T. W. (1992). Lack of efficacy of the adenosine re-uptake inhibitor dipyridamole in the treatment of anxiety disorders. *Biological Psychiatry, 31*(5A), 35.

Bonn, J. A., Harrison, J., & Rees, L. (1973). Lactate infusion in the treatment of 'free-floating' anxiety. *Journal of the Canadian Psychiatric Association, 18,* 41–46.

Boulenger, J.-P., Patel, J., Post, R. M., Parma, A. M., & Marangos, P. J. (1983). Chronic caffeine consumption increases the number of brain adenosine receptors. *Life Sciences, 32*(1), 135–142.

Boulenger, J.-P., & Uhde, T. W. (1982). Caffeine consumption and anxiety: Preliminary results of a survey comparing patients with anxiety disorders and normal controls. *Psychopharmacology Bulletin, 18,* 53–57.

Boulenger, J.-P., Uhde, T. W., Wolff, E. A., III, & Post, R. M. (1984). Increased sensitivity to caffeine in patients with panic disorder. *Archives of General Psychiatry, 41,* 1067–1071.

Bradwejn, J., Koszycki, D., Payeur, R., Bourin, M., & Bothwick, H. (1992). Study of the replication of action of cholecystokinin in panic disorders. *American Journal of Psychiatry, 149,* 962–964.

Brezinova, V. (1974). Effects of caffeine on sleep. EEG study in late middle age people. *British Journal of Pharmacology, 1,* 203–208.

Carr, D. B., Sheehan, D. V., Surman, O. S., Coleman, J. H., Greenblah, D. J., Heninger, G. R., Jones, K. J., Levine, P. H., & Watkins, W. D. (1986). Neuroendocrine correlates of lactate-induced anxiety and their response to chronic alprazolam therapy. *American Journal of Psychiatry, 143,* 483–494.

Charney, D. S., Heninger, G. R., & Jatlow, P. I. (1985). Increased anxiogenic effects of caffeine in panic disorder. *Archives of General Psychiatry, 42,* 233–243.

Choi, O. H., Shamin, M. T., Padgett, W. L., & Daly, J. W. (1988). Caffeine and theophylline analogues: Correlation of behavioral effects with activity as adenosine receptor antagonists and as phosphodiesterase inhibitors. *Life Sciences, 43,* 387–398.

Cobb, S. (1974). Physiologic changes in men whose jobs were abolished. *Journal of Psychosomatic Research, 18,* 245–258.

Coffey, C. E., Weiner, R. D., Hinkle, P. E., Cress, M., Daughtry, G., & Wilson, W. H. (1987). Augmentation of ECT seizures with caffeine. *Biological Psychiatry, 22,* 637–649.

Coffin, V. L., & Spealman, R. D. (1987). Behavioral and cardiovascular effects of analogs of adenosine in cynomolgus monkeys. *Journal of Pharmacology and Experimental Therapeutics, 241,* 76–83.

Crawley, J. N., Patel, J., & Marangos, P. J. (1981). Behavioral characterization of two long lasting adenosine analogs: Sedative properties and interaction with diazepam. *Life Sciences, 29,* 2623–2630.

Crawley, J. N., Patel, J., & Marangos, P. J. (1983). Adenosine uptake inhibitors potentiate the sedative effects of adenosine. *Neuroscience Letters, 36,* 169–174.

Daly, J. W., Bruns, R. F., & Snyder, S. N. (1981). Adenosine receptors in the central nervous system: Relationship to the central actions of methylxanthines. *Life Sciences, 28,* 2083–2097.

Derogatis, L. R. (1977). *SCL-90-R Manual: I. Scoring and procedure manual for the SCL-90-R.* Baltimore: Clinical Psychometrics Research Unit.

Dillon, D. J., Gorman, J. M., Liebowitz, M. R., Fyer, A. J., & Klein, D. F. (1987). Measurement of lactate-induced panic and anxiety. *Psychiatry Research, 20,* 97–105.

Di Marco, J. P., Sellers, T. D., Berne, R. M., West, G. A., & Belardinelli, L. (1983). Adenosine: Electrophysiologic effects and therapeutic use for terminating paroxysmal supraventricular tachycardia. *Circulation, 68,* 1254–1263.

Doreen, B. (1977). Effects of drugs on rats exposed to cold-restraint stress. *Journal of Pharmacy and Pharmacology, 29,* 748–751.

Dragunow, M., Goddard, G. V., & Laverty, R. (1985). Is adenosine an endogenous anticonvulsant? *Epilepsia, 26,* 480–487.

File, S. E., Bond, A. J., & Lister, R. G. (1982). Interaction between effects of caffeine and lorazepam in performance tests and self-ratings. *Journal of Clinical Psychopharmacology, 2,* 102–106.

Goodman, R. R., & Synder, S. H. (1982). Autoradiographic localization of adenosine receptors in rat brain using [^{3}H]-cyclohexyladenosine. *Journal of Neuroscience, 2*(9), 1230–1241.

Gorman, J. M., Askanazi, J., Liebowitz, M. R., Fyer, A. J., Stein, J., Kinney, J. M., & Klein, D. F. (1984). Response to hyperventilation in a group of patients with panic disorder. *American Journal of Psychiatry, 141,* 857–861.

Gorman, J. M., Fyer, M. R., Liebowitz, M. R., & Klein, D. F. (1987). Pharmacologic provocation of panic attacks. In H. Y. Meltzer (Ed.), *Psychophar-*

macology: A third generation of progress (pp. 985–998). New York: Raven Press.

Greden, J. F. (1974). Anxiety or caffeinism: A diagnostic dilemma. *American Journal of Psychiatry, 131,* 1089–1092.

Griez, E. J. L., Lousberg, H., van den Hout, M. A., & van den Folen, G. M. (1987). CO2 vulnerability in panic disorder. *Psychiatry Research, 20,* 87–95.

Griez, E., & van den Hout, M. A. (1983). Treatment of phonophobia by exposure to CO2-induced anxiety symptoms. *Journal of Nervous and Mental Diseases, 171,* 506–508.

Guttmacher, L. B., Murphy, D. L., & Insel, T. R. (1983). Pharmacologic models of anxiety. *Comprehensive Psychiatry, 24,* 312–326.

Henry, J. P., & Stephens, P. M. (1980). Caffeine as an intensifier of stress-induced hormonal and pathophysiological changes in mice. *Pharmacology, Biochemistry and Behavior, 13,* 719–727.

Hoffman, W. E., Satinover, I., Miletich, D. J., Albrecht, R. F., & Gans, B. J. (1982). Cardiovascular changes during sodium nitroprusside or adenosine triphosphate infusion in the rat. *Anesthesia and Analgesia* (Cleveland), *61,* 99–103.

Kelly, D., Mitchell-Heggs, N., & Sherman, D. (1971). Anxiety and the effects of sodium lactate assessed clinically and physiologically. *British Journal of Psychiatry, 119,* 129–141.

Klabunde, R. E. (1983). Dipyridamole inhibition of adenosine metabolism in human blood. *European Journal of Pharmacology, 93,* 21–26.

Klein, E., Zohar, J., Geraci, M. F., Murphy, D. L., & Uhde, T. W. (1991). Anxiogenic effects of m-CPP in patients with panic disorder: Comparison to caffeine's anxiogenic effects. *Biological Psychiatry, 30,* 973–984.

Lane, J. D. (1983). Caffeine and cardiovascular responses to stress. *Psychosomatic Medicine, 45,* 447–451.

Latimer, P. (1977). Carbon dioxide as a reciprocal inhibitor in the treatment of neurosis. *Journal of Behavior Therapy and Experimental Psychiatry, 8,* 83–85.

Lee, M. A., Cameron, O. G., & Greden, J. F. (1985). Anxiety and caffeine consumption in people with anxiety disorders. *Psychiatry Research, 15,* 211–217.

Liebowitz, M. R., Fyer, A. J., Gorman, J. M., Dillon, D., Appleby, I. L., Levy, G., Anderson, S., Levitt, M., Palij, M., & Davies, S. O. (1984). Lactate provocation of panic attacks: I. Clinical and behavioral findings. *Archives of General Psychiatry, 41,* 764–770.

Londos, C. D., Cooper, M. F., & Wolff, J. (1980). Subclasses of external adenosine receptors. *Proceedings of the National Academy of Sciences of the United States of America, 77,* 2551–2554.

Margraf, J., Ehlers, A., & Roth, W. T. (1986). Sodium lactate infusions and panic attacks: A review and critique. *Psychosomatic Medicine, 48,* 23–51.

Mellman, T. A., & Uhde, T. W. (1989). Electroencephalographic sleep in panic disorder: A focus on sleep-related panic attacks. *Archives of General Psychiatry, 46,* 178–184.

Muller, P. J., & Vernikos-Danellis, J. (1970). Effect of environmental temperature on the toxicity of caffeine and dextroamphetamine in mice. *Journal of Pharmacology and Experimental Therapeutics, 171,* 153–158.

Newberg, L. A., Milde, J. W., & Michenfelder, J. D. (1985). Cerebral and systemic effects of hypotension induced by adenosine or ATP in dogs. *Anesthesiology, 62,* 429–436.

Nickell, P. V., & Uhde, T. W. (1991). Dose-response effects of intravenous caffeine in normal controls. *Biological Psychiatry, 29*(9A), 185.

Phillis, J. W., & Kostopoulos, G. K. (1975). Adenosine as a putative transmitter in the cerebral cortex. Studies with potentiators and antagonists. *Life Sciences, 17,* 1085–1094.

Phillis, J. W., & Wu, P. H. (1981). The role of adenosine and its nucleotides in central synaptic transmission. *Progress in Neurobiology, 16,* 187–239.

Pitts, F. N., Jr., & McClure, J. N. (1967). Lactate metabolism in anxiety neurosis. *New England Journal of Medicine, 277,* 1329–1336.

Rainey, J. M., Aleem, A., Ortiz, A., Yergamio, V., Pohl, R., & Berchou, R. (1987). A laboratory procedure for the induction of flashbacks. *American Journal of Psychiatry, 144,* 1317–1319.

Rainey, J. M., Pohl, R. B., Williams, M., Knitter, E., Freedman, R. R., & Ettedqui, E. (1984). A comparison of lactate and isoproterenol anxiety states. *Psychopathology, 17*(Suppl. 3), 74–82.

Rapoport, J. L., Jensvold, M., Elkins, R., Buchsbaum, M. S., Weingartner, H., Ludlow, C., Zahn, T. P., Berg, C. J., & Neims, A. H. (1981). Behavioral and cognitive effects of caffeine in boys and adult males. *Journal of Nervous and Mental Diseases, 169,* 726–732.

Roy-Byrne, P. P., & Uhde, T. W. (1988). Exogenous factors in panic disorder: Clinical and research implications. *Journal of Clinical Psychiatry, 49,* 56–61.

Saletu, B., Allen, M., & Itil, T. M. (1974). The effect of Coca Cola, caffeine antidepressants, and chlorpromazine on objective and subjective sleep parameters. *Pharmacopsychiatry, Neuropsychopharmacology, 254,* 307–321.

Sattin, A., & Rall, T. W. (1970). The effect of adenosine and adenine nucleotides on the cyclic AMP content of guinea-pig cerebral cortex slices. *Molecular Pharmacology, 6,* 13–23.

Scupi, B. S., Maser, J. D., & Uhde, T. W. (1992). The National Institute of Mental Health Panic Questionnaire (NIMH-PQ): An instrument for assessing clinical characteristics of panic disorder. *Journal of Nervous and Mental Diseases, 180*(9), 566–572.

Shapira, B., Lerer, B., Gilboa, D., Drexler, H., Kugelmass, S., & Calev, A. (1987). Facilitation of ECT by caffeine pretreatment. *American Journal of Psychiatry, 144,* 1199–1202.

Snyder, S. H., Katims, J. J., Annau, Z., Bruns, R. F., & Daly, J. W. (1981). Adenosine receptors and the behavioral actions of methylxanthines. *Proceedings of the National Academy of Sciences of the United States of America, 78,* 3260–3264.

Sollevi, A., Ostergren, J., Hjemdahl, B., Fredholm, B. B., & Fagrell, B. (1984). The effect of dipyridamole on plasma adenosine levels and skin microcirculation in man. *Advances in Experimental Medicine and Biology, 165* (Pt. A), 547.

Spielberger, C. D., Gorsuch, R. L., & Lushene, R. E. (1970). *State-Trait Anxiety Inventory (STAI) manual.* Palo Alto, CA: Consulting Psychologist Press.

Stillner, V. M., Popkin, M. K., & Pierce, C. M. (1978). Caffeine-induced delirium during prolonged competitive stress. *American Journal of Psychiatry, 135,* 855–856.

Stone, T. W. (1981). Physiological roles for adenosine and adenosine-5'-triphosphate in the nervous system. *Neuroscience, 6,* 523–555.

Sutherland, E. W., & Rall, T. W. (1958). Fractionation and characterization of cyclic adenine rebonuleotide formed by tissue particles. *Journal of Biological Chemistry, 232,* 1077–1091.

Uhde, T. W. (1988). Caffeine: Practical facts for the psychiatrist. In P. P. Roy-Byrne (Ed.), *Anxiety: New Research Findings for the Clinician* (pp. 73–98). Washington, DC: American Psychiatric Press.

Uhde, T. W. (1990). Caffeine provocation of panic: A focus on biological mechanisms. In J. C. Ballenger (Ed.), *Neurobiology of panic disorder (Frontiers of clinical neuroscience,* vol. 8) (pp. 219–242). New York: Alan R. Liss.

Uhde, T. W., Boulenger, J.-P., Vittone, B., Jimerson, D. C., & Post, R. M. (1984). Caffeine: Relationship to human anxiety, plasma MHPG and cortisol. *Psychopharmacology Bulletin, 20,* 426–430.

Uhde, T. W., Boulenger, J.-P., Post, R. M., Siever, L. J., Vittone, B. J., Jimerson, D. C., & Roy-Byrne, P. P. (1984). Fear and anxiety: Relationship to nonadrenergic function. *Psychopathology, 17*(3), 8–23.

Uhde, T. W., Joffe, R. T., Jimerson, D. C., & Post, R. M. (1988). Normal urinary free cortisol and plasma MHPG in panic disorder: Clinical and theoretical implications. *Biological Psychiatry, 23,* 575–585.

Uhde, T. W., & Nemiah, J. (1989). Panic and generalized anxiety disorders. In H. I. Kaplan & B. J. Sadock (Eds.), *Comprehensive textbook of psychiatry,* 5th ed. (pp. 952–972). Baltimore, MD: Williams & Wilkins.

Uhde, T. W., & Tancer, M. E. (1989). Chemical models of panic: A review and critique. In P. Tyrer (Ed.), *Psychopharmacology of anxiety* (pp. 110–131). Oxford: Oxford University Press.

Vestal, R. E., Eriksson, C. E., Musser, B., Ozaki, L., & Halter, J. B. (1983). Effect of intravenous aminophylline on plasma levels of catecholamines and related cardiovascular and metabolic responses in man. *Circulation, 67,* 162–171.

Victor, B., Lubetsky, M., & Greden, J. (1981). Somatic manifestation of caffeinism. *Journal of Clinical Psychiatry, 42,* 185–188.

Woods, S. W., Charney, D. S., Loke, J., Goodman, W. K., Redmond, D. E., & Heninger, G. R. (1986). Carbon dioxide sensitivity in panic anxiety: Ventilatory and anxiogenic responses to carbon dioxide in healthy subjects and patients with panic anxiety before and after alprazolam treatment. *Archives of General Psychiatry, 43,* 900–909.

Yarnell, P. R., & Chu, N. J. (1975). Focal seizures and aminophylline. *Neurology, 25,* 819–822.

Zung, W. W. K. (1971). A rating instrument for anxiety disorders. *Psychosomatics, 12,* 371–379.

9

The Lactate Infusion Challenge

DEBORAH S. COWLEY,
STEPHEN R. DAGER, AND
DAVID L. DUNNER

In 1967 Pitts and McClure published their now-classic report of the first lactate infusion study. Noting that patients with anxiety neurosis (which included the current diagnosis of panic disorder) had been found to develop higher lactate levels with exercise than controls (Cohen, Consalazio, & Johnson, 1947; Holmgren & Strom, 1959; Jones & Mellersh, 1946), they hypothesized that elevated lactate levels might be involved in the pathogenesis of anxiety attacks. They infused sodium lactate intravenously in 14 patients with anxiety neurosis and 10 controls. Thirteen of the 14 patients but only one of the 10 controls experienced typical symptoms of anxiety attacks with lactate infusion.

This was an exciting discovery. Now panic attacks, usually unpredictable, fleeting, and thus difficult to capture for study in the laboratory, could be provoked almost at will. Biochemical and physiological measurements could be performed during lactate-induced panic to shed light on the pathophysiology of panic. Furthermore, this study pointed to altered lactate metabolism as a possible culprit in anxiety disorders.

Over the ensuing 25 years, Pitts and McClure's original observations have been confirmed by many independent investigators (Aronson, Carasiti, McBane, & Whitaker-Azmitia, 1989; Bonn, Harrison, & Rees, 1971; Cowley, Hyde, Dager, & Dunner, 1987; Den Boer, Westenberg,

Klompmakers, & van Lint, 1989; Fink, Taylor, & Volavka, 1970; Gaffney, Fenton, Lane, & Lake, 1988; Kelly, Mitchell-Heggs, & Sherman, 1971; Liebowitz et al., 1984; Rainey et al., 1984). The diagnostic specificity, effects of treatment, clinical significance, and physiological correlates of lactate-induced panic have been studied. These investigations have provided a wealth of information about the lactate infusion procedure and several intriguing theories regarding the mechanism of action of lactate. Despite these advances, however, the way in which lactate produces panic symptoms remains a mystery.

In this chapter, we review the lactate infusion literature, summarize what is known about lactate-induced panic, and discuss areas for future study.

LACTATE INFUSION METHODS

In Pitts and McClure's original study (1967), racemic (DL)-sodium lactate was administered intravenously at a dose of 10 cubic centimeters (cc) per kilogram (kg) of a 0.5 molar solution over 20 minutes. This dose was chosen because it was similar to that used "in the initial treatment of acidosis with dehydration" (Pitts & McClure, 1967, p. 1335) and because it seemed effective in producing anxiety in their open pilot trial. Lactate infusion studies since then have used comparable lactate doses. Lactate response is probably dose-related. Pitts (1985), noted that response rates increased with higher lactate doses, while Lapierre, Knott, and Gray (1984) reported lower rates of lactate responses in a study limiting total lactate dose to 500 milliliters (ml) of a 0.5 molar solution.

Most lactate infusion studies have used placebo infusions. At first, these were performed on a different day from the lactate infusion (Fink et al., 1970; Kelly, Mitchell-Heggs, & Sherman, 1971; Pitts & McClure, 1967). Since placebo produced few effects in these studies, more recently the placebo usually has been given immediately before the sodium lactate infusion, primarily to disguise the exact time of administration of lactate. Saline or glucose solutions have been used as placebos. In only two reports (Fink et al., 1970; Pitts & McClure, 1967) were placebo solutions matched with lactate for osmolality and volume, and in neither case did the placebo represent a comparable salt load. Thus, placebo infusions have not controlled for the osmotic salt load delivered during lactate infusion. Of note, a recent pilot study of lactate, normal saline, and hyperosmolar saline infusions demonstrated comparable panic rates with lactate and hyperosmolar saline, suggesting that osmolality may be an important trigger for lactate-induced panic (Jensen et al., 1991).

THE NATURE AND ASSESSMENT OF LACTATE RESPONSES

Assessment of responses to lactate infusions generally has used subjective ratings, by the patient or physician, of anxiety levels and typical panic symptoms. This use of subjective ratings is a result of three factors. First, the diagnosis of naturally occurring panic attacks is subjective and based solely on the patient's history rather than on any pathognomonic laboratory tests or physical signs. Second, no objective measure has reliably distinguished panickers from nonpanickers, although hyperventilation, heart rate acceleration, acid-base changes, electroencephalogram (EEG) findings, and oxygen consumption may show some promise. Last, the actions of lactate in the central nervous system are poorly understood. In using a challenge such as yohimbine, which is known to act on a particular neurotransmitter system, clinical effects can be correlated with biochemical or physiological measures affected by that neurotransmitter system (e.g., 3-methoxy-4-hydroxyphenylethylene glycol (MHPG)). This is not yet possible with lactate, since its actions in the brain or on specific neurotransmitters or receptors are unknown.

The lack of objectively defined response criteria has important implications. Subjective response criteria have included the subject's request to stop the infusion (Ehlers et al., 1986; George, Brewerton, & Jimerson, 1987), the subject's report or indication of experiencing a typical panic attack (Cowley, Hyde et al., 1987; Lapierre et al., 1984; Pitts & McClure, 1967), report by the subject of a feeling ranging from increased anxiety in some studies to terror or a wish to flee in others and accompanied by *Diagnostic and Statistical Manual of Mental Disorders,* 3rd edition (DSM-III) or Research Diagnostic Criteria (RDC) panic symptoms (Aronson et al., 1989; Bonn et al., 1971; Cowley, Hyde et al., 1987; Den Boer et al., 1989; Ehlers et al., 1986; Fink et al., 1970; Gaffney et al., 1988; Kelly et al., 1971; Liebowitz et al., 1984; Pitts & McClure, 1967; Rainey et al., 1984), or investigator observations of the subject during the infusion (Liebowitz et al., 1984). These varying response criteria have resulted in lactate-induced "panic" rates of 40 to 100 percent in patients with panic disorder and 0 to 25 percent in nonpsychiatric control subjects (Cowley & Arana, 1990). The sensitivity of the lactate challenge test clearly increases, but the specificity decreases with the use of less restrictive response criteria (Cowley, Hyde, Dager, & Dunner, 1987; Ehlers et al., 1986).

In addition, Gorman, Dillon, Fyer, Liebowitz, and Klein (1985) have reported higher "panic" rates in patients with panic disorder (73 vs. 51 percent) and lower rates in control subjects (0 versus 11 percent) when investigators using subjective rating methods were aware of the subject's diagnosis as opposed to being "blind." Such possible biases in nonblind studies are exacerbated when no objective measures are available to define a lactate response.

Margraf, Ehlers, and Roth (1986) pointed out the importance of expectancy effects, cognitive variables, and demand characteristics in lactate infusion studies. These variables are likely to affect the results of any study and have been shown to influence reactions to lactate. Van der Molen, van den Hout, Vroemen, Lousberg, and Griez (1986) and Van der Molen and van den Hout (1988) gave lactate to normal volunteers, telling one group that this would cause anxiety and another group that it would produce pleasant excitement. Subjects given the expectation of anxiety reported more distress and showed a greater drop in carbon dioxide pressure and increase in respiratory rate than did subjects told to expect pleasant excitement.

Furthermore, patients with panic disorder may be particularly vulnerable to psychological aspects of the experimental setting. Patients with panic disorder have been shown to be more likely to interpret bodily changes as dangerous and to attend preferentially to stimuli concerning possible harm or threat (Ganellen, Matuzas, Uhlenhuth, Glass, & Easton, 1986; Mathews, 1986). These findings underscore the importance of psychological factors in lactate infusion studies. Such factors are even more likely to affect study results when combined with subjective response criteria and nonblind raters.

Some attempts have been made to develop more standardized assessment measures. Dillon, Gorman, Liebowitz, Fyer, and Klein (1987) have used the Acute Panic Inventory (API) to separate "early panickers" from "late panickers" and control subjects. The API is a 17-item scale that asks patients to rate symptoms of panic on a 0 to 3 (none to severe) scale. The maximum score is 51. A score of 20 or more or an increase of 13 from baseline 10 minutes into the lactate infusion separates patients panicking by this point ("early panickers") from late panickers, nonpanicking patients, or controls with a sensitivity of 84 percent and a specificity of 100 percent. The same API score increases at the end of the infusion separate late panickers from nonpanicking patients and controls with a sensitivity of only 60 percent and a specificity of 82 percent. This is a promising approach, although the API remains a subjective, patient-rated scale and has the disadvantage of not including some DSM-IV panic symptoms such as chest pain, choking, and numbness and tingling.

Gorman and coworkers (1987) have examined heart rate acceleration as a possibly more objective response measure. Their heart rate index, defined as a 10 percent increase in heart rate over the three minutes prior to the point of maximum heart rate, identifies patients with subjectively rated lactate-induced panic with 85 percent sensitivity and 74 percent specificity. Measures such as this may prove very useful in standardizing criteria for a lactate response and allowing more accurate comparisons across sites.

In using lactate infusion as a model for naturally occurring panic attacks, it is important to know how similar lactate-induced and spontaneous panic attacks are. Early reports (Bonn et al., 1971; Kelly et al., 1971; Pitts & McClure, 1967) of patient responses to lactate include reports of typical panic attacks, experiences worse than their usual attacks, and often descriptions of feeling that the subject would be having a panic attack were he or she not reassured by the presence of the physician or the fact that the subject knew the reason for these feelings and that they could be stopped. Thirty-one patients with DSM-III panic disorder or agoraphobia with panic attacks who panicked with lactate infusion in a study by Liebowitz and associates (1984) rated both lactate-induced symptoms and symptoms of their usual panic attacks using the API. Lactate-induced and spontaneous panic attacks were quite similar both in overall API scores and the intensity of individual symptoms. Usual panic attacks tended to involve greater fear of dying, confusion, sense of unreality, trouble concentrating, and sweating, while lactate-induced panic was associated with more twitching and urinary urgency. Ehlers and coworkers (1986) found that lactate effects on anxiety and heart rate were of comparable magnitude to changes during naturally occurring panic attacks studied during ambulatory monitoring, that symptoms reported with lactate were similar to those during usual panic attacks except for more hypocalcemic symptoms with lactate, and that most (seven of 10) of their patients with panic disorder rated lactate effects as being very similar to their usual panic attacks.

Heart rate, respiratory measurements, and API scores were also similar in 17 patients experiencing panic attacks during a placebo infusion versus 19 panicking with lactate (Goetz et al., 1993).

These studies suggest that lactate infusion is a fairly good model for spontaneous panic, producing most of the same symptoms at comparable intensity. Many patients experience an abrupt onset of symptoms with lactate. Some, on the other hand, develop gradually intensifying anxiety that builds to panic levels. This is mirrored by gradually increasing EEG abnormalities during lactate infusions (Knott, 1990) and has been used as a criticism of lactate as a model for panic. However, spontaneous panic attacks often are reported as building over several minutes. Since no comparison of the speed of onset of lactate-induced and usual panic attacks has been performed, it is difficult to know whether a significant discrepancy exists.

A further methodologic problem with the lactate challenge is the lack of established test-retest reliability. Two studies bear indirectly on this issue. Bonn and associates (1971) used six lactate infusions over a three-week period as a successful desensitization treatment for "intractable anxiety," suggesting that retesting may lead to lower panic rates. Yeragani, Balon, and coworkers (1988) found no effects of infusion-related anxiety on the results of subsequent testing in a double-blind, randomized comparison of lactate, isoproterenol, and placebo. However, subjects may have been aware that the three infusions differed and thus would not expect to experience the same anxiety during a later testing day.

Gorman and coworkers (1983), while testing the effects of propranolol on lactate-induced panic, gave six subjects each two lactate infusions two days apart. In each case, the second infusion followed administration of propranolol. All six subjects reported panic attacks with both infusions. Since propranolol would be unlikely to increase lactate effects, this suggests that lactate response is stable over a two-day period.

We examined test-retest reliability of lactate infusion in a small group of seven patients with panic disorder who were treated with placebo as part of a double-blind, controlled trial of alprazolam, and who showed no significant clinical change over the eight-week study (Cowley, Dager, Roy-Byrne, Avery, & Dunner, 1991). As a group, these patients did not differ in API scores, subjective anxiety ratings, or time of peak symptoms with reinfusion with lactate eight weeks after their first, baseline lactate infusion. However, three individual patients reported different responses with reinfusion. Using three response categories of positive (DSM-III symptoms of a panic attack and an increase in anxiety of two points on a 10-point scale to at least moderate levels), panic (a positive response as well as the abrupt onset of symptoms and the report of a typical panic attack), or negative (not meeting criteria for a positive response), one patient was less sensitive with reinfusion, changing from a positive to a negative response. Two others were more sensitive, with one changing from a positive to a panic response and the other from a negative to a positive response. These latter two patients were not clinically worse at week 8 and indeed showed some decrease in panic attack frequency. Further testing of the stability of lactate vulnerability over time is clearly needed.

DIAGNOSTIC SPECIFICITY

Despite the methodological drawbacks just discussed, numerous lactate infusion studies performed in different laboratories using varying methods and response criteria have demonstrated clearly that patients with panic disorder are significantly more sensitive than nonpsychiatric control subjects to lactate. A recent review (Cowley & Arana, 1990) found an overall lactate-induced panic rate of 67 percent in 227 of 338 patients studied by eight independent research groups. The overall response rate for 140 control subjects studied by the same research groups was 13 percent.

Several studies now suggest that lactate vulnerability is specific for individuals with panic attacks, regardless of coexisting diagnosis. Patients with major depression and panic attacks (Cowley et al., 1986; Targum, 1990), RDC minor or intermittent depression with panic attacks (McGrath et al., 1988), and post-traumatic stress disorder with panic attacks (Rainey et al., 1987) respond to lactate at a rate similar to that of patients with panic disorder. Patients with depression, bulimia, obsessive compulsive disorder, social phobia, and alcohol dependence who do not have panic attacks resemble control subjects in their response to lactate (Cowley, Dager, Foster, & Dunner, 1987; Cowley et al., 1989; George et al., 1987; Gorman et al., 1985b; Liebowitz et al., 1985a; Lindy et al., 1988). We also have recently infused five patients with pure dysthymic disorder and no history of major depression or panic attacks (Cowley, Dager, & Dunner, unpublished data), none of whom panicked with lactate, although one developed some slowly increasing anxiety and physical symptoms.

Several diagnostic groups deserve special comment. Patients with panic attacks as infrequent as once a year have been shown to respond to lactate at a rate comparable to that of patients with panic disorder (Cowley, Dager, & Dunner, 1987). However, most of these subjects also experienced significant ongoing anticipatory anxiety at the time of the infusion. This study supports the change in the revised edition of DSM-III (DSM-III-R) to include in the category of panic disorder those patients with infrequent attacks but significant, persisting fears of having another attack. In a study of patients with atypical depression and a history of panic attacks, McGrath and associates (1988) found that lactate response rates dropped to control levels in subjects whose most recent attack was more than one year prior to the infusion, and the likelihood of lactate-induced panic increased with the severity of current panic symptoms, suggesting that lactate vulnerability depends on the presence of current or recent illness and distress.

Patients with prospectively confirmed premenstrual syndrome (PMS) also have been shown to panic with lactate at a greater rate than control subjects (Facchinetti, Romano, Fava, & Genazzani, 1992; Sandberg, Endicott, Harrison, Nee, & Gorman, 1993). Although some of these patients had a history of panic attacks, lactate-induced panic also was observed at a high rate in subjects without a history of panic. This finding suggests a possible relationship between PMS and panic disorder and lends support to the idea that lactate response may be related to current levels of severe anxiety, arousal, or distress.

Patients with post-traumatic stress disorder (PTSD) frequently report paniclike symptoms during flashbacks. Rainey and coworkers (1987) have demonstrated provocation of both flashbacks and subsequent panic symptoms with lactate infusion in patients meeting criteria for both post-traumatic stress disorder and panic disorder. Lactate infusion then may provide an interesting model for studying the biology of flashbacks and their relationship to panic. However, until patients with post-traumatic stress disorder without panic attacks are studied, the specificity of lactate-induced panic for panic disorder versus PTSD is not established.

Alcoholics without panic attacks have been shown to resemble controls in lactate sensitivity (Cowley et al., 1989). Two studies of alcoholics reporting panic attacks have come to different conclusions, however (Cowley et al., 1989; George, Nutt, Waxman, & Linnoila, 1989). In one study (Cowley et al., 1989), male alcoholics with panic attacks resembled male, nonalcoholic patients with panic disorder in lactate-induced anxiety, symptom ratings, and panic rates. In the other (George, Nutt, Waxman, & Linnoila, 1989), male alcoholics with panic attacks had significantly lower panic rates than female patients with panic disorder who were also adult children of alcoholics.

The difference between these studies may be primarily a function of criteria used for lactate-induced panic. Increases in anxiety and symptoms were comparable in the alcoholics in both studies, but George, Nutt, Waxman, and Linnoila (1989) required that the subject ask to stop the infusion in order to define the response as panic, while Cowley and associates (1989) assessed panic based on abrupt increases in anxiety or fear and DSM-III panic symptoms. Once more, subjective response criteria make comparisons between studies difficult.

The Axis I psychiatric disorder perhaps most closely related to panic disorder is generalized anxiety disorder. A study by Cowley, Dager, McClellan, Roy-Byrne, and Dunner (1988) of 12 patients with generalized anxiety disorder and no lifetime history of panic attacks suggests that these patients may be intermediate in lactate response between patients with panic disorder and control subjects. Although only one of the 12 generalized anxiety disorder patients panicked with lactate, these patients were significantly more likely than control subjects to report gradually increasing anxiety and panic symptoms over the course of the infusion, with peak scores indistinguishable from those of patients with panic disorder. This raises the question of whether generalized anxiety disorder is actually biologically closely related to panic disorder or whether lactate is generally anxiogenic with "panic" responses determined by the way in which patients with panic disorder experience anxiety.

Interestingly, Russell, Kushner, Beitman, and Bartels (1991) noted that 11 patients with nonfearful panic disorder, who experienced somatic symptoms of panic disorder but without subjective fear or anxiety, had reproduction of their symptoms or a typical panic attack accompanied by fear during lactate infusion and went on to respond to antipanic treatment.

TREATMENT EFFECTS AND
CLINICAL SIGNIFICANCE

Vulnerability to lactate-induced panic decreases significantly after treatment of panic attacks with imipramine and desipramine (Liebowitz et al.,

1984; Rifkin, Klein, Dillon, & Levitt, 1981; Yeragani, Pohl et al., 1988), monoamine oxidase inhibitors (Kelly, Mitchell-Heggs, & Sherman, 1971), alprazolam (Carr et al., 1986; Cowley et al., 1991), and valproic acid (Keck, Taylor, Tugrul, McElroy, & Bennett, 1993). Imipramine also appears to correct blood gas abnormalities and hyperventilation associated with lactate-induced panic attacks (Gorman et al., 1985c). In contrast, acute pretreatment with propranolol does not reverse lactate-induced panic symptoms (Gorman et al., 1983).

Antipanic medications may decrease lactate response as a result of improvement in clinical state or a direct effect of the medication. Fyer, Liebowitz, Gorman, Davies, and Klein (1985) reported results of lactate infusions performed in 13 panic patients before treatment, while panic-free on tricyclic antidepressants, and again while still in remission but medication-free for one to six months. Seven patients panicked before treatment, but none panicked while on medication. Three of 13 panicked once off the medication, despite continued clinical remission, suggesting in part a direct effect of medication on lactate response.

In another study by Cowley and coworkers (1991) of patients with panic disorder treated for eight weeks with alprazolam or placebo, patients on alprazolam who were not judged treatment responders nevertheless showed decreases in lactate response. In this study, patients were considered treatment responders if they were panic-free for at least a week at week 8 and were judged by themselves and the clinician as being very much or markedly improved. Many nonresponders, although not meeting these criteria, were nevertheless significantly improved at the end of the study.

Changes in clinical state without medication also appear to change lactate response. For example, successful cognitive behavioral therapy decreased lactate response in one case report (Guttmacher, 1984) and in four of six panic disorder patients treated by Shear and associates (1991). Patients who improved clinically on placebo in the study by Cowley and coworkers (1991) could tolerate higher lactate doses before developing symptoms. Thus, both medication treatment and clinical improvement without medication appear to lessen lactate response.

Does lactate vulnerability differentiate a distinct subgroup of patients with panic disorder? One study has examined the relationship between lactate response and clinical presentation (Cowley & Dunner, 1988). In this sample of 47 patients with panic disorder or agoraphobia with panic attacks, patients who panicked with lactate did not differ from those who did not panic in the duration or severity of panic disorder, age of onset of illness, frequency or spontaneity of panic attacks, self-rated disability or phobic avoidance, or the Symptom Check List-90 (SCL-90) and Hamilton rating scale scores for anxiety, depression, and somatization. For 44 patients, family history data were available. Lactate panickers were significantly more likely to have a family history of panic in at least one first-degree relative than were nonpanickers (10 of 19 panickers versus four of 25 nonpanickers). However, Fyer and associates (unpublished data) found no difference between lactate panickers and nonpanickers in the overall percentage of their relatives who had panic attacks.

A small group of patients with panic attacks following solvent exposure, who may thus differ from other panic patients in the pathophysiology of their attacks, exhibited typical panic responses to lactate infusion (Dager, Holland, Cowley, & Dunner, 1987). Although at one time mitral valve prolapse was thought to distinguish a subgroup of patients with panic disorder, panic patients with and without mitral valve prolapse were not found to differ in clinical presentation or lactate vulnerability (Dager, Cowley, & Dunner, 1987).

Overall, lactate response does not seem to identify a clinically distinct subgroup of patients with panic disorder, at least using the measures just mentioned. The relationship between lactate response and family history warrants further examination.

Lactate responsivity also does not seem to predict treatment response. In 86 patients undergoing lactate infusion before treatment with alprazolam or placebo, lactate response was not related to outcome with either treatment (Cowley et al., unpublished data).

MECHANISM OF ACTION

How does lactate infusion cause panic symptoms? Numerous studies have attempted to answer this question. Most have examined psychophysiological and peripheral blood tests in human subjects, using measures known to be affected by stress or anxiety in normal control subjects. Measures used have included heart rate; systolic and diastolic blood pressure; electromyography (EMG); finger temperature; electroencephalography (EEG); electro-oculographically recorded blink rate; brain stem auditory evoked potentials; cardiac output; peripheral vascular resistance; respiratory rate; ventilatory volumes; oxygen metabolism; electrodermal skin conductance; D- and L-lactate; pyruvate;

cortisol; beta-endorphin; calcium; electrolytes; hemoglobin; pH, partial pressure of carbon dioxide, and bicarbonate; phosphate; prolactin; epinephrine; norepinephrine; testosterone; vasopressin; human growth hormone; luteinizing hormone; 3-methoxy-4-hydroxyphenylethylene glycol (MHPG) levels; platelet factor 4; metabolites of plasma thromboxane B_2; prostacyclin; and urinary tribulin. (See, for example, Aronson et al., 1989; Bonn et al., 1971; Carr et al., 1986; Clow et al., 1988; Cowley, Hyde, Dager, & Dunner, 1987; Dager, Cowley, Dorsa, & Dunner, 1989; Den Boer et al., 1989; Ehlers et al., 1986; Fink et al., 1970; Freedman, Ianni, Ettedgui, Pohl, & Rainey, 1984; Fyer et al., 1984; Gaffney et al., 1988; Kelly et al., 1971; Lapierre et al., 1984; Liebowitz et al., 1985b; Rainey et al., 1985.)

Surprisingly, despite the impressive array of variables assessed, there appear to be few distinctive peripheral physiological responses or changes in blood characteristic of lactate-induced panic. In the majority of studies, lactate panickers are more likely than nonpanickers to develop greater or more rapid heart rate increases (Cowley et al., 1987a; Ehlers et al., 1986; Freedman et al., 1984; Gaffney et al., 1988; Lapierre et al., 1984; Liebowitz et al., 1985b), and higher diastolic blood pressures (Cowley, Hyde, Dager, & Dunner, 1987; Ehlers et al., 1986; Gaffney et al., 1988; Liebowitz et al., 1985a). Lactate panickers also display greater oxygen metabolism and ventilatory ratio for oxygen (Rainey et al., 1986), and lower bicarbonate and PCO_2 levels (Gaffney et al., 1988; Liebowitz et al., 1985b) during lactate infusion. In addition, EEG monitoring (Fink et al., 1970; Knott, 1990; Lapierre et al., 1984) shows decreased alpha activity, increased beta activity, and paradoxical increases in slow-wave delta activity only in panickers.

Other studies investigating the mechanism of lactate-induced panic have included attempts to block lactate response with pharmacological pretreatment; use of infusates such as bicarbonate or hyperosmolar saline, which isolate a single component of lactate such as osmolality or metabolic alkalosis; imaging studies; and examination of the central effects of lactate infusion in animals. Although we still do not know how lactate works, this research has yielded a great deal of information and several interesting theories to guide further investigation.

In the original study of lactate infusion by Pitts and McClure (1967), lactate-induced symptoms were attenuated by the addition of calcium to the sodium lactate. This led them to suggest that lactate caused anxiety by "the complexing of ionized calcium at the surface of excitable membranes" (p. 1335), with the resulting decrease in ionized calcium interfering with nerve conduction and activity. However, in a later study, Pitts and Allen (1979) showed that ethylenediaminetetracetic acid (EDTA), which binds calcium ions, did not produce panic. Grosz and Farmer (1969) argued that the amount of calcium ion bound by the time of onset of symptoms would be insufficient to produce significant hypocalcemia, while Fyer and associates (1984) showed that although calcium declines in all subjects undergoing lactate infusion, the extent of this decrease does not differentiate panickers from nonpanickers. However, a recent animal study showing increases in CSF calcium but decreases in plasma calcium during lactate infusion in rabbits (George, Glue, Bacher, Waxman, & Nutt, 1990), as well as the initial blockade of panic symptoms with pretreatment with calcium, leave open the possibility that calcium is involved in lactate-induced panic.

Many panic symptoms mimic those of hyperadrenergic states. Since stimulation of the locus coeruleus, a site which regulates central noradrenergic activity, produces fear responses in animals, investigators have long expected to find evidence of increased sympathetic nervous system function in lactate-induced panic attacks. As noted earlier, most lactate infusion studies have shown greater increases in heart rate and diastolic blood pressure in lactate panickers. However, larger rises in norepinephrine and epinephrine have been seen only at selected times in isolated studies (Liebowitz et al., 1985b). Plasma MHPG increases are not associated with lactate-induced panic (Den Boer et al., 1989; Pohl et al., 1987). Administration of propranolol either before the infusion or after the development of panic symptoms does not significantly alter lactate response (Aronson et al., 1989; Gorman et al., 1983), and the alpha-2 adrenergic agonist clonidine is only partially effective in blocking lactate-induced panic (Coplan et al., 1992a).

An alternative hypothesis, that panic is associated with decreased parasympathetic rather than increased sympathetic nervous system activity, has been tested in two lactate studies with mixed results. Both lactate and hyperventilation decreased vagal tone in normal volunteers in one report (George et al., 1989), while no increase in vagal tone was observed during lactate infusions in another sample of both controls and patients with panic disorder (Gorman et al., 1987).

One group has demonstrated increases in oxygen metabolism and the ventilatory ratio for oxygen in lactate-induced panic (Rainey et al., 1986). This, coupled with observations of greater increases in lactate levels in patients with panic disorder (Liebowitz et al., 1985b; Rainey et al., 1985), led them to propose that patients with panic disorder have a defect in aerobic metabolism (Rainey et al., 1985).

Lactate infusion has several different known effects, including the delivery of a large salt and osmotic load and the generation of a significant metabolic alkalosis. Until recently, the panicogenic effects of the osmotic load involved in lactate infusions had not been tested. However, a small pilot project from our center (Jensen et al., 1991) suggests that patients who panic with lactate also are likely to panic with hyperosmolar saline. Sodium lactate, normal saline, and 3 percent (hypertonic) saline solutions were given in randomized order on three separate days to five men with panic disorder. One patient panicked with hypertonic saline and refused subsequent infusions. Of the remaining four subjects, four panicked with lactate, three panicked with hypertonic saline, and none panicked with normal saline. Although preliminary, these results suggest that the effects of lactate may not be specific to lactate itself but may instead result from physiological changes accompanying the infusion.

Similarly, bicarbonate infusions produce symptoms similar to those seen with lactate infusion in both controls (Grosz & Farmer, 1972) and patients with panic disorder (Gorman et al., 1989). In the study by Gorman and associates (1989), 13 of 22 patients panicked with lactate. Twenty of these patients also underwent bicarbonate infusions, and nine of these panicked. Lactate seemed to be a stronger panicogenic stimulus, since time to panic was shorter with lactate than with bicarbonate. Interestingly, although this might seem to suggest that metabolic alkalosis can provoke panic, bicarbonate panickers showed a decrease in carbon dioxide pressure consistent with hyperventilation, while bicarbonate nonpanickers showed the expected rise in PCO_2, indicating hypoventilation and a normal compensation for the metabolic alkalosis produced by the infusion. As the authors point out, this suggests that the common factor between lactate- and bicarbonate-induced panic is hyperventilation and respiratory alkalosis.

In fact, hyperventilation is probably the most consistent physiological concomitant of lactate-induced panic (Gorman et al., 1986; Liebowitz et al., 1985b). Many lactate panickers show evidence of chronic hyperventilation at baseline. Lactate panickers also develop lower bicarbonate and PCO_2 levels during the infusion than do nonpanickers. Hypophosphatemia at baseline, which may predict subsequent lactate-induced panic, is also consistent with hyperventilation. Since hyperventilation can both result from and exacerbate anxiety states (Cowley & Roy-Byrne, 1987), the role of hyperventilation in lactate-induced panic is unclear, although a minority of patients studied by Gorman and associates (1986) showed acute hyperventilation before lactate was begun, indicating a possible panicogenic effect of hyperventilation in these subjects.

Given the paucity of peripheral biochemical or physiological manifestations of lactate-induced panic, it appears likely that lactate induces panic via central mechanisms. However, until lately lactate has not been thought to cross into the central nervous system in significant amounts. Theories of lactate's central actions have assumed an indirect effect through lactate metabolites such as bicarbonate, which crosses the blood brain barrier as carbon dioxide. Increasing CO_2 levels increase locus coeruleus activity, act as a respiratory stimulant, and have been shown to be panicogenic (Gorman et al., 1988). In addition, a hypersensitive central response to CO_2 or a specific defect of the redox system in the ventral medulla making patients more vulnerable to rising central CO_2 levels (Carr & Sheehan, 1984) have been proposed.

Two recent results argue, however, that the metabolism of lactate may be unnecessary for its panicogenic effects and that lactate may have direct effects on the central nervous system. First, D-lactate, which is poorly metabolized in humans, also produces panic and acts as a respiratory stimulant (Gorman et al., 1990). In addition, a study of lactate infusion in mechanically ventilated baboons demonstrated that CSF CO_2 did not change during or after the conclusion of the lactate infusion (Dager et al., 1990). These findings were subsequently replicated by Coplan and coworkers (1992b), confirming that lactate-induced panic is not precipitated by peripheral conversion of lactate to bicarbonate with resulting central hypercapnia.

In contrast to Coplan and associates (1992b), who sampled cisternal fluid lactate at only one time point immediately post-infusion, Dager and associates (1990) measured progressive increases in cisternal fluid lactate during lactate infusion. However, the use of anesthesia, mechanical ventilation, and delivery of a higher lactate load in the Dager study make the results difficult to generalize to human lactate studies. Subsequent magnetic resonance spectroscopy (MRS) studies, which can measure changes in brain lactate noninvasively (Dager & Steen, 1992), have demonstrated rises in brain lactate during lactate infusion in rodents (Dager, Marro, Richards, & Metzger, 1992a) and healthy human volunteers (Dager, Marro, Richards, & Metzger, 1992b). Furthermore, patients with panic disorder who panic with lactate have significantly higher rises in brain lactate levels than do normal controls or medicated patients who no longer panic with lactate infusion (Dager, Marro, Metzger, & Richards, 1994).

Several positron emission tomography (PET) studies by Reiman and others (1986, 1989; Reiman, Fusselman, Fox, & Raichle, 1989) sought to obtain neuroanatomic information about lactate-induced panic. Preliminary results were interpreted to show that at rest, patients with panic disorder who subsequently developed panic attacks with lactate had asymmetric (left less than right) parahippocampal gyrus blood flow, blood volume, and metabolic rate for oxygen (Reiman et al., 1986). Panic attacks during lactate infusion appeared to be associated with increased blood flow in both temporal poles and insular cortex (Reiman, Raichle et al., 1989). Increases in bilateral temporal pole blood flow seemed to occur in normal controls anticipating an electric shock (Reiman, Fusselman, Fox, & Raichle, 1989), suggesting a neuroanatomic association between lactate-induced anxiety and normal anticipatory anxiety. However, findings in patients with panic disorder were not replicated in a subsequent PET study (Binkelfat, personal communication). In addition, reassessment of Reiman and associates' findings indicated that problems in coregistration of PET data with anatomical location had resulted in extracranial signal being misinterpreted as intracranial, thus invalidating the conclusions (Drevets, Videen, MacLeod, Haller, & Raichle, 1992).

Some researchers (Ehlers et al., 1986) have suggested that panic symptoms during lactate infusion do not result from a specific effect of lactate in patients with panic disorder. Instead, they propose that lactate is equally anxiogenic in both patients and controls, but that patients with panic disorder are more anxious and aroused at baseline. Three other groups have shown that patient-control differences in lactate response are much greater than and are not attributable merely to baseline differences (Cowley, Hyde, Dager, & Dunner, 1987; Gorman et al., 1985a; Yeragani, Pohl, Balon, & Sherwood, 1987). However, baseline state clearly influences the nature and intensity of lactate response. Before the infusion starts, patients with panic disorder are more anxious and symptomatic than controls and, in most studies, have higher heart rates, systolic blood pressure, and forearm blood flow as well as showing signs of chronic hyperventilation (Cowley, Hyde, Dager, & Dunner, 1987;

Ehlers et al., 1986; Kelly et al., 1971; Liebowitz et al., 1984, 1985b; Yeragani, Pohl, Balon, & Sherwood, 1987). Both panic disorder patients and controls who go on to panic during the infusion have higher anxiety levels and panic symptom scores at baseline before the infusion starts (Cowley, Hyde, Dager, & Dunner, 1987; Den Boer et al., 1989; Liebowitz et al., 1984; Yeragani, Pohl, Balon, & Sherwood, 1987; Yeragani et al., 1987). Those patients with panic disorder falling in the upper quartile for baseline Acute Panic Inventory (API) scores are significantly more likely than those in the lower quartile to panic during the subsequent lactate infusion (Cowley, Hyde, Dager, & Dunner, 1987).

Lactate-induced panic also may be associated with biochemical indices of increased arousal or anticipatory anxiety at baseline. Aronson and associates (1989) demonstrated baseline beta-adrenergic receptor down-regulation, as measured by decreased lymphocyte ^{3}H-dihydroalprenolol binding, in nine panic patients, all of whom subsequently panicked during lactate infusion. Male panickers show greater baseline prolactin levels than male nonpanickers (Hollander et al., 1989a), and elevated baseline cortisol levels may be associated with panic responses late in the ensuing lactate infusion (Hollander et al., 1989b).

As noted, expectations and psychological factors are likely to affect lactate response. Several investigators have in fact espoused a cognitive theory of lactate-induced anxiety, postulating that the significant physiological changes accompanying lactate infusion remind patients of past panic attacks and induce anxiety and panic through a learned phobic response (Ackerman & Sachar, 1974; Margraf et al., 1986). Lactate itself would then be a nonspecific stimulus rather than provoking panic via a specific biological mechanism. Lactate infusion is associated in both patients and controls with a doubling of cardiac output, tachycardia, and metabolic alkalosis, all of which might produce physical symptoms reminiscent of panic attacks. Patients with panic disorder, who are more sensitive than controls to interoceptive cues, would then be more likely to interpret these sensations as being potentially dangerous and being signs of impending panic.

The role of such cognitive factors in lactate-induced panic is an area of ongoing debate. Panic disorder patients do not panic with a variety of other stressors, including such pharmacological stimuli as thyrotropin-releasing hormone (Stein & Uhde, 1991) and hypoglycemia (Uhde, Vittone, & Post, 1984), which create dramatic paniclike arousal or autonomic symptoms. Koenigsberg, Pollak, Fine, and Kakuma (1992) have administered lactate during sleep when, presumably, cognitive factors or expectancies have minimal effects. In their sample, patients with panic disorder were significantly more likely than control subjects to display lightening of sleep, arousal, or awakening in response to lactate, suggesting that panic disorder patients are biologically more sensitive at least to the arousing effects of lactate.

Nevertheless, a wide variety of challenges produce panic, and responses to challenge tests can be altered by giving patients with panic disorder false feedback about their heart rate response (Margraf, 1988) or by giving subjects an illusion of controlling the intensity of the stimulus delivered. For example, patients with panic disorder inhaling carbon dioxide are less likely to report panic responses and have less catastrophic thoughts when given a full explanation of possible effects of carbon dioxide rather than minimal information (Rapee, Mattick, & Murrell, 1986). Patients given an illusion of control (but no actual control) over the amount of carbon dioxide administered are also less likely to report anxiety, panic attacks, and panic symptoms than those patients without a sense of control (Sanderson, Rapee, & Barlow, 1989). Such findings clearly indicate that cognitive factors influence responses to challenge tests, but do not necessarily prove that the challenge is not intrinsically anxiogenic on a biological basis. Further work with physiologically active placebos may clarify this issue.

CONCLUSION

Lactate infusion studies have been performed by a large number of research groups over the past 25 years. Patients with current or recent panic attacks, regardless of coexisting psychiatric diagnosis, appear to develop more psychological and physiological symptoms of panic with lactate than do normal controls or psychiatric patients without panic attacks. Patients with generalized anxiety disorder without a history of panic attacks report similar symptoms to panic disorder patients but are less likely to describe sudden panic responses. The effect of lactate in alcoholics with panic attacks, patients with past panic attacks, and those with a family history of panic attacks remains an unresolved issue in the diagnostic specificity of the test.

The sensitivity of lactate-induced panic is only moderate, with 40 to 60 percent of patients with panic disorder panicking using strict response criteria. Both the specificity and sensitivity of this challenge test depend on the response criteria used. A major problem with lactate infusion remains the subjective assessment of panic responses. Heart rate response represents a promising objective measure, but the lack of clear, easily measured peripheral physiological or biochemical concomitants of lactate-induced panic is a major limitation in the use of this technique.

Despite extensive research efforts, the mechanism of lactate-induced panic is still unknown. The most promising leads generated by studies to date include the role of hyperventilation, calcium, and osmotic load in lactate effects. Parasympathetic nervous system effects of lactate await clarification. Given the surprising paucity of peripherally measurable changes unique to subjects panicking with lactate, the most attractive theories at present are those linking lactate's effects with central nervous system and cognitive factors. Recent studies suggest that CNS lactate increases during lactate infusion, that these rises are greater in patients panicking with the infusion, and that peripheral metabolism of lactate is unnecessary for its panicogenic actions. Animal studies and imaging techniques represent promising avenues for elucidating the general and regional effects of lactate within the central nervous system. Relating such findings back to human studies and developing an animal model of panic will be important challenges in the future.

Clinically, lactate infusion does not seem to delineate an important subgroup of patients with panic attacks. Preliminary data linking lactate-induced panic with a family history of panic require replication. Lactate response decreases with pharmacological and cognitive-behavioral treatment of panic. However, initial response to lactate does not appear to predict subsequent response to treatment, at least with alprazolam or placebo. In rare cases of diagnostic confusion, a panic response to lactate may be helpful in making a diagnosis. However, given the test's only moderate sensitivity, a negative response is uninformative and the best diagnosis for panic remains the clinical history.

The lactate infusion continues to be an intriguing challenge test. In contrast with many pharmacological challenges, where the mechanism of action of the stimulus is at least partially understood, lactate provides a fairly good model for spontaneous panic symptoms by still-unknown means. Despite the lack of clear-cut answers at present, continued efforts to understand how lactate works hold promise in clarifying the nature of both lactate-induced and spontaneous panic attacks.

REFERENCES

Ackerman, S. H., & Sachar, E. J. (1974). The lactate theory of anxiety: A review and reevaluation. *Psychosomatic Medicine, 36,* 69–79.

Aronson, T. A., Carasiti, I., McBane, D., & Whitaker-Azmitia, P. (1989). Biological correlates of lactate sensitivity in panic disorder. *Biological Psychiatry, 26,* 463–477.

Bonn, J. A., Harrison, J., & Rees, W. L. (1971). Lactate-induced anxiety: Therapeutic application. *British Journal of Psychiatry, 119,* 468–471.

Carr, D. B., & Sheehan, D. V. (1984). Panic anxiety: A new biological model. *Journal of Clinical Psychiatry, 45,* 323–330.

Carr, D. B., Sheehan, D. V., Surman, O. S., Coleman, J., Greenblatt, D., Heninger, G., Jones, K., Levine, P., & Watkins, W. D. (1986). Neuroendocrine correlates of lactate-induced anxiety and their response to chronic alprazolam therapy. *American Journal of Psychiatry, 143,* 483–494.

Clow, A., Glover, V., Weg, M. W., Walker, P. L., Sheehan, D. V., Carr, D. B., & Sandler, M. (1988). Urinary catecholamine metabolite and tribulin output during lactate infusion. *British Journal of Psychiatry, 152,* 122–126.

Cohen, M. E., Consalazio, F. C., & Johnson, R. E. (1947). Blood lactate response during moderate exercise in neurocirculatory asthenia, anxiety neurosis, or effort syndrome. *Journal of Clinical Investigation, 26,* 339–342.

Coplan, J. D., Liebowitz, M. R., Gorman, J. M., Fyer, A. J., Dillon, D. J., Campeas, R. B., Davies, S. O., Martinez, J., & Klein, D. F. (1992a). Noradrenergic function in panic disorder: Effects of intravenous clonidine pretreatment on lactate-induced panic. *Biological Psychiatry, 31,* 135–146.

Coplan, J. D., Sharma, T., Rosenblum, L. A., Friedman, S., Bassoff, T. B., Barbour, R. L., & Gorman, J. M. (1992b). Effects of sodium lactate infusion on cisternal lactate and carbon dioxide levels in nonhuman primates. *American Journal of Psychiatry, 149,* 1369–1373.

Cowley, D. S., & Arana, G. W. (1990). The diagnostic utility of lactate sensitivity in panic disorder. *Archives of General Psychiatry, 47,* 277–284.

Cowley, D. S., Dager, S. R., & Dunner, D. L. (1986). Lactate-induced panic in primary affective disorder. *American Journal of Psychiatry, 143,* 646–648.

Cowley, D. S., Dager, S. R., & Dunner, D. L. (1987). Lactate infusions in major depression without panic attacks. *Journal of Psychiatric Research, 21,* 243–248.

Cowley, D. S., Dager, S. R., Foster, S. I., & Dunner, D. L. (1987). Clinical characteristics and response to sodium lactate of patients with infrequent panic attacks. *American Journal of Psychiatry, 144,* 795–798.

Cowley, D. S., Dager, S. R., McClellan, J., Roy-Byrne, P. P., & Dunner, D. L. (1988). Response to lactate infusion in generalized anxiety disorder. *Biological Psychiatry, 24,* 409–414.

Cowley, D. S., Dager, S. R., Roy-Byrne, P. P., Avery, D. H., & Dunner, D. L. (1991). Lactate vulnerability after alprazolam versus placebo treatment of panic disorder. *Biological Psychiatry, 30,* 49–56.

Cowley, D. S., & Dunner, D. L. (1988). Response to sodium lactate in panic disorder: Relationship to presenting clinical variables. *Psychiatry Research, 25,* 253–259.

Cowley, D. S., Hyde, T. S., Dager, S. R., & Dunner, D. L. (1987). Lactate infusions: The role of baseline anxiety. *Psychiatry Research, 21,* 169–179.

Cowley, D. S., Jensen, C. F., Johannessen, D., Parker, L., Dager, S. R., & Walker, R. D. (1989). Response to sodium lactate infusion in alcoholics with panic attacks. *American Journal of Psychiatry, 146,* 1479–1483.

Cowley, D. S., & Roy-Byrne, P. P. (1987). Hyperventilation and panic disorder. *American Journal of Medicine, 83,* 929–937.

Dager, S. R., Cowley, D. S., Dorsa, D. M., & Dunner, D. L. (1989). Plasma beta-endorphin response to lactate infusion. *Biological Psychiatry, 25,* 243–245.

Dager, S. R., Cowley, D. S., & Dunner, D. L. (1987). Biological markers in panic states: Lactate-induced panic and mitral valve prolapse. *Biological Psychiatry, 22,* 339–359.

Dager, S. R., Holland, J. P., Cowley, D. S., & Dunner, D. L. (1987). Panic disorder precipitated by exposure to organic solvents in the workplace. *American Journal of Psychiatry, 144,* 1056–1058.

Dager, S. R., Marro, K. I., Richards, T. L., & Metzger, G. D. (1992a). MRS detection of whole brain lactate rise during 1M sodium lactate infusion in rats. *Biological Psychiatry, 32,* 913–921.

Dager, S. R., Marro, K. I., Richards, T. L., & Metzger, G. D. (1992b). Localized magnetic resonance spectroscopy measurement of brain lactate during intravenous lactate infusion in healthy volunteers. *Life Science, 51,* 973–985.

Dager, S. R., Marro, K. I., Metzger, G. D., & Richards, T. L. (1994). Preliminary applications of magnetic resonance spectroscopy to investigate lactate-induced panic. *American Journal of Psychiatry, 151,* 57–63.

Dager, S. R., Rainey, J. M., Kenny, M., Artru, A. A., Metzger, G. D., & Bowden, D. M. (1990). Central nervous system effects of lactate infusion in primates. *Biological Psychiatry, 27,* 193–204.

Dager, S. R., & Steen, R. G. (1992). Applications of magnetic resonance spectroscopy to the investigation of neuropsychiatric disorders. *Neuropsychopharmacology, 6,* 249–266.

Den Boer, J. A., Westenberg, H. G. M., Klompmakers, A. A., & van Lint, L. E. M. (1989). Behavioral, biochemical, and neuroendocrine concomitants of lactate-induced panic anxiety. *Biological Psychiatry, 26,* 612–622.

Dillon, D. J., Gorman, J. M., Liebowitz, M. R., Fyer, A. J., & Klein, D. F. (1987). Measurement of lactate-induced panic and anxiety. *Psychiatry Research, 20,* 97–105.

Drevets, W. C., Videen, T. O., MacLeod, A. K., Haller, J. W., & Raichle, M. E. (1992). PET images of blood flow changes during anxiety: Correction. *Science, 256,* 1696.

Ehlers, A., Margraf, J., Roth, W. T., Taylor, C. B., Maddock, R. J., Sheikh, J., Kopell, M. L., McClenahan, K. L., Gossard, D., Blowers, G. H., Agras, W. S., & Kopell, B. S. (1986). Lactate infusions and panic attacks: Do patients and controls respond differently? *Psychiatry Research, 17,* 295–308.

Facchinetti, F., Romano, G., Fava, M., & Genazzani, A. R. (1992). Lactate infusion induces panic attacks in patients with premenstrual syndrome. *Psychosomatic Medicine, 54,* 288–296.

Fink, M., Taylor, M. A., & Volavka, J. (1970). Anxiety precipitated by lactate. *New England Journal of Medicine, 281,* 1429.

Freedman, R. R., Ianni, P., Ettedgui, E., Pohl, R., & Rainey, J. M. (1984). Psychophysiological factors in panic disorder. *Psychopathology, 17*(Suppl. 1), 66–73.

Fyer, A. J., Gorman, J. M., Liebowitz, M. R., Levitt, M., Danielson, E., Martinez, J., & Klein, D. F. (1984). Sodium lactate infusion, panic attacks, and ionized calcium. *Biological Psychiatry, 19,* 1437–1447.

Fyer, A. J., Liebowitz, M. R., Gorman, J. M., Davies, S. O., & Klein, D. F. (1985). Lactate vulnerability of remitted panic patients. *Psychiatry Research, 14,* 143–148.

Gaffney, F. A., Fenton, B. F., Lane, L. D., & Lake, C. R. (1988). Hemodynamic, ventilatory, and biochemical responses of panic patients and normal controls with sodium lactate infusion and spontaneous panic attacks. *Archives of General Psychiatry, 45,* 53–60.

Ganellen, R., Matuzas, W., Uhlenhuth, E., Glass, R., & Easton, C. (1986). Panic disorder, agoraphobia, and anxiety-relevant cognitive style. *Journal of Affective Disorders, 11,* 219–225.

George, D. T., Brewerton, T. D., & Jimerson, D. C. (1987). Comparison of lactate-induced anxiety in bulimic patients and healthy controls. *Psychiatry Research, 21,* 213–220.

George, D. T., Glue, P., Bacher, J. D., Waxman, R. P., & Nutt, D. J. (1990). Lactate-induced electrolyte changes in the cerebrospinal fluid of rabbits. *Biological Psychiatry, 27,* 104–108.

George, D. T., Nutt, D. J., Walker, W. V., Porges, S. W., Adinoff, B., & Linnoila, M. (1989). Lactate and hyperventilation substantially attenuate vagal tone in normal volunteers. *Archives of General Psychiatry, 46,* 153–156.

George, D. T., Nutt, D. J., Waxman, R. P., & Linnoila, M. (1989). Panic response to lactate administration in alcoholic and nonalcoholic patients with panic disorder. *American Journal of Psychiatry, 146,* 1161–1165.

Goetz, R. R., Klein, D. F., Gully, R., Kahn, J., Liebowitz, M. R., Fyer, A., & Gorman, J. M. (1993). Panic attacks during placebo procedures in the laboratory. *Archives of General Psychiatry, 50,* 280–285.

Gorman, J. M., Battista, D., Goetz, R. R., Dillon, D. J., Liebowitz, M. R., Fyer, A. J., Kahn, J. P., Sandberg, D., & Klein, D. F. (1989). A comparison of sodium bicarbonate and sodium lactate infusion in the induction of panic attacks. *Archives of General Psychiatry, 46,* 145–150.

Gorman, J. M., Cohen, B. S., Liebowitz, M. R., Fyer, A. J., Ross, D., Davies, S. O., & Klein, D. F. (1986). Blood gas changes and hypophosphatemia in lactate-induced panic. *Archives of General Psychiatry, 43,* 1067–1071.

Gorman, J. M., Davies, M., Steinman, R., Liebowitz, M. R., Fyer, A. J., Coromilas, J., & Klein, D. F. (1987). An objective marker of lactate-induced panic. *Psychiatry Research, 22,* 341–348.

Gorman, J. M., Dillon, D., Fyer, A. J., Liebowitz, M. R., & Klein, D. F. (1985a). The lactate infusion model. *Psychopharmacology Bulletin, 21,* 428–433.

Gorman, J. M., Fyer, M. R., Goetz, R., Askanazi, J., Martinez, J., Liebowitz, M. R., Fyer, A. J., Kinney, J., & Klein, D. F. (1988). Ventilatory physiology of patients with panic disorder. *Archives of General Psychiatry, 45,* 31–39.

Gorman, J. M., Fyer, A. J., Ross, D. C., Cohen, B. S., Martinez, J. M., Liebowitz, M. R., & Klein, D. F. (1985c). Normalization of venous pH, pCO_2, and bicarbonate levels after blockade of panic attacks. *Psychiatry Research, 14,* 57–65.

Gorman, J. M., Goetz, R. R., Dillon, D., Liebowitz, M. R., Fyer, A. J., Davies, S., & Klein, D. F. (1990). Sodium D-lactate infusion of panic disorder patients. *Neuropsychopharmacology, 3,*(3), 181–190.

Gorman, J. M., Levy, G. F., Liebowitz, M. R., McGrath, P., Appleby, I. L., Dillon, D., Davies, S., & Klein, D. F. (1983). Effect of acute beta-adrenergic blockade on lactate-induced panic. *Archives of General Psychiatry, 40,* 1079–1082.

Gorman, J. M., Liebowitz, M. R., Fyer, A. J., Dillon, D., Davies, S. O., Stein, J., & Klein, D. F. (1985b). Lactate infusions in obsessive-compulsive disorder. *American Journal of Psychiatry, 142,* 864–866.

Grosz, H. J., & Farmer, B. B. (1969). Blood lactate in the development of anxiety symptoms. *Archives of General Psychiatry, 21,* 611–619.

Grosz, H. J., & Farmer, B. B. (1972). Pitts and McClure's lactate-anxiety study revisited. *British Journal of Psychiatry, 120,* 415–418.

Guttmacher, L. B. (1984). In vivo desensitization alteration of lactate-induced panic: A case study. *Behavior Therapy, 15,* 369–372.

Hollander, E., Liebowitz, M. R., Cohen, B. S., Gorman, J. M., Fyer, A. J., Papp, L. A., & Klein, D. F. (1989a). Prolactin and sodium lactate-induced panic. *Psychiatry Research, 28,* 181–191.

Hollander, E., Liebowitz, M. R., Gorman, J. M., Cohen, B. S., Fyer, A. J., & Klein, D. F. (1989b). Cortisol and sodium lactate-induced panic. *Archives of General Psychiatry, 46,* 135–140.

Holmgren, A., & Strom, G. (1959). Blood lactate concentration and relative workload in normal men and in mitral stenosis, atrial septal defect, and vasoregulatory asthenia. *Acta Medica Scandinavia, 163,* 183–184.

Jensen, C. F., Peskind, E., Veith, R., Hughes, J., Cowley, D. S., Roy-Byrne, P. P., & Raskind, M. (1991). Hypertonic saline infusion induces panic in patients with panic disorder. *Biological Psychiatry, 30,* 628–630.

Jones, M., & Mellersh, V. (1946). A comparison of the exercise response in anxiety states and normal controls. *Psychosomatic Medicine, 8,* 180–187.

Keck, P. E., Jr., Taylor, V. E., Tugrul, K. C., McElroy, S., & Bennett, J. A. (1993). Valproate treatment of panic disorder and lactate-induced panic attacks. *Biological Psychiatry, 33,* 542–546.

Kelly, D., Mitchell-Heggs, N., & Sherman, D. (1971). Anxiety and the effects of sodium lactate assessed clinically and physiologically. *British Journal of Psychiatry, 119,* 129–141.

Knott, V. J. (1990). Neuroelectrical activity related to panic disorder. *Progress in Neuropsychopharmacology and Biological Psychiatry, 14,* 697–707.

Koenigsberg, H. W., Pollak, C. P., Fine, J., & Kakuma, T. (1992). Lactate sensitivity in sleeping panic disorder patients and healthy controls. *Biological Psychiatry, 32,* 539–542.

Lapierre, Y. D., Knott, V. J., & Gray, R. (1984). Psychophysiological correlates of sodium lactate. *Psychopharmacology Bulletin, 20,* 50–57.

Liebowitz, M. R., Fyer, A. J., Gorman, J. M., Dillon, D., Appleby, I. L., Levy, G., Anderson, S., Levitt, M., Palij, M., Davies, S. O., & Klein, D. F. (1984). Lactate provocation of panic attacks, I: Clinical and behavioral findings. *Archives of General Psychiatry, 41,* 764–770.

Liebowitz, M. R., Fyer, A. J., Gorman, J. M., Dillon, D., Davies, S. O., Stein, J., Cohen, B. S., & Klein, D. F. (1985a). Specificity of lactate infusions in social phobia versus panic disorder. *American Journal of Psychiatry, 142,* 947–950.

Liebowitz, M. R., Gorman, J. M., Fyer, A. J., Levitt, M., Dillon, D., Levy, G., Appleby, I. L., Anderson, S., Palij, M., Davies, S. O., & Klein, D. F.

(1985b). Lactate provocation of panic attacks, II: Biochemical and physiological findings. *Archives of General Psychiatry, 42,* 709–719.

Lindy, D. C., Walsh, B. T., Gorman, J. M., Roose, S. P., Gladis, M., Devlin, M. J., & Glassman, A. H. (1988). Lactate infusions in patients with bulimia. *Psychiatry Research, 26,* 287–292.

Margraf, J. (1988, May 12). *Panic anxiety: Physiological or psychological?* Paper presented at the 141st annual meeting of the American Psychiatric Association. Montreal, Canada.

Margraf, J., Ehlers, A., & Roth, W. T. (1986). Biological models of panic disorder and agoraphobia: A review. *Behavior Research and Therapy, 24,* 553–567.

Mathews, A. (1986). Cognitive processes in anxiety and depression. *Journal of the Royal Society of Medicine, 79,* 158–161.

McGrath, P. J., Stewart, J. W., Liebowitz, M. R., Markowitz, J. M., Quitkin, F. M., Klein, D. F., & Gorman, J. (1988). Lactate provocation of panic attacks in depressed outpatients. *Psychiatry Research, 25,* 41–47.

Pitts, F. N., Jr. (1985, September). *Lactate infusion and panic attacks.* Paper presented at the World Congress of Biological Psychiatry. Philadelphia.

Pitts, F. N., Jr., & Allen, R. E. (1979). Biochemical induction of anxiety. In W. E. Fann, I. Karacan, A. D. Pokorny, & R. L. Williams (Eds.), *Phenomenology and treatment of anxiety* (pp. 125–146). New York: SP Medical and Scientific Books.

Pitts, F. N., Jr., & McClure, J. N., Jr. (1967). Lactate metabolism in anxiety neurosis. *New England Journal of Medicine, 277,* 1329–1336.

Pohl, R., Ettedgui, E., Bridges, M., Lycaki, H., Jimerson, D., Kopin, I., & Rainey, J. M. (1987). Plasma MHPG levels in lactate and isoproterenol anxiety states. *Biological Psychiatry, 22,* 1127–1136.

Rainey, J. M., Aleem, A., Ortiz, A., Yeragani, V., Pohl, R., & Berchou, R. (1987). A laboratory procedure for the induction of flashbacks. *American Journal of Psychiatry, 144,* 1317–1319.

Rainey, J. M., Frohman, C. E., Warner, K., Bates, S., Pohl, R. B., & Yeragani, V. (1985). Panic anxiety and lactate metabolism. *Psychopharmacology Bulletin, 21,* 434–437.

Rainey, J. M., Pohl, R., Ortiz, A., Yeragani, V., Jolly, S., & Berchou, R. (1986, May 9). *A shift from aerobic to anaerobic metabolism during lactate- and isoproterenol-induced panic anxiety.* Paper presented at the 41st annual meeting of the Society of Biological Psychiatry. Washington, DC.

Rainey, J. M., Pohl, R. B., Williams, M., Knitter, E., Freedman, R., & Ettedgui, E. (1984). A comparison of lactate and isoproterenol anxiety states. *Psychopathology, 17*(Suppl. 1), 74–82.

Rapee, R. M., Mattick, R., & Murrell, E. (1986). Cognitive mediation in the affective component of spontaneous panic attacks. *Journal of Behavior Therapy and Experimental Psychiatry, 17,* 243–253.

Reiman, E. M., Fusselman, M. J., Fox, P. T., Raichle, M. E. (1989). Neuroanatomical correlates of anticipatory anxiety. *Science, 243,* 1071–1074.

Reiman, E. M., Raichle, M. E., Robins, E., Butler, F. K., Herscovitch, P., Fox, P. T., & Perlmutter, J. (1986). The application of positron emission tomography to the study of panic disorder. *American Journal of Psychiatry, 143,* 469–477.

Reiman, E. M., Raichle, M. E., Robins, E., Mintun, M. A., Fusselman, M. J., Fox, P. T., Price, J. L., & Hackman, K. A. (1989). Neuroanatomical correlates of a lactate-induced anxiety attack. *Archives of General Psychiatry, 46,* 493–500.

Rifkin, A., Klein, D. F., Dillon, D., & Levitt, M. (1981). Blockade by imipramine or desipramine of panic induced by sodium lactate. *American Journal of Psychiatry, 138,* 676–677.

Russell, J. L., Kushner, M. G., Beitman, B. D., & Bartels, K. M. (1991). Nonfearful panic disorder in neurology patients validated by lactate challenge. *American Journal of Psychiatry, 148,* 361–364.

Sandberg, D., Endicott, J., Harrison, W., Nee, J., & Gorman, J. (1993). Sodium lactate infusion in late luteal phase dysphoric disorder. *Psychiatry Research, 46,* 79–88.

Sanderson, W. C., Rapee, R. M., & Barlow, D. H. (1989). The influence of an illusion of control on panic attacks induced via inhalation of 5.5% carbon dioxide-enriched air. *Archives of General Psychiatry, 46,* 157–162.

Shear, M. K., Fyer, A. J., Ball, G., Josephson, S., Fitzpatrick, M., Gitlin, B., Frances, A., Gorman, J., Liebowitz, M., & Klein, D. F. (1991). Vulnerability to sodium lactate in panic disorder patients given cognitive-behavioral therapy. *American Journal of Psychiatry, 148,* 795–797.

Stein, M. B., & Uhde, T. W. (1991). Endocrine, cardiovascular, and behavioral effects of intravenous protirelin in patients with panic disorder. *Archives of General Psychiatry, 48,* 148–156.

Targum, S. D. (1990). Differential responses to anxiogenic challenge studies in patients with major depressive disorder and panic disorder. *Biological Psychiatry, 28,* 21–34.

Uhde, T. W., Vittone, B. J., & Post, R. M. (1984). Glucose tolerance testing in panic disorder. *American Journal of Psychiatry, 141,* 1461–1462.

Van der Molen, G. M., & van den Hout, M. A. (1988). Expectancy effects on respiration during lactate infusion. *Psychosomatic Medicine, 50,* 439–443.

Van der Molen, G. M., van den Hout, M. A., Vroemen, J., Lousberg, H., & Griez, E. (1986). Cognitive factors in lactate-induced anxiety. *Behavior Research and Therapy, 24,* 677–680.

Yeragani, V. K., Balon, R., Rainey, J. M., Ortiz, A., Berchou, R., Lycaki, H., & Pohl, R. (1988a). Effects of laboratory-induced panic anxiety on subsequent provocative infusions. *Psychiatry Research, 23,* 161–166.

Yeragani, V. K., Pohl, R., Balon, R., Rainey, J. M., Berchou, R., & Ortiz, A. (1988b). Sodium lactate infusions after treatment with tricyclic antidepressants: Behavioral and physiological findings. *Biological Psychiatry, 24,* 767–774.

Yeragani, V. K., Pohl, R., Balon, R., & Sherwood, P. (1987). Lactate infusions: The role of baseline anxiety and autonomic measures. *Psychiatry Research, 22,* 263–264.

Yeragani, V. K., Pohl, R., Balon, R., Weinberg, P., Berchou, R., & Rainey, J. M. (1987). Preinfusion anxiety predicts lactate-induced panic attacks in normal controls. *Psychosomatic Medicine, 49,* 383–389.

10

Cholecystokinin and Panic Disorder

JACQUES BRADWEJN AND
DIANA KOSZYCKI

Cholecystokinin (CCK) is a peptide that was discovered in the gastrointestinal tract by Ivy and Oldberg in 1928 based on its ability to stimulate gall bladder contraction and pancreatic secretion. Almost 50 years later, Vanderhaeghen, Signeau, and Gepts (1975) reported that CCK was abundant in numerous regions of the mammalian central nervous system (CNS), where it is believed to serve a neurotransmitter or neuromodulator function. (For review, see Beinfield, 1988.) Molecular forms of varying amino acid lengths of CCK have been isolated in the brain (Miller, Jardine, Weissman, Go, & Speicher, 1984; Morley, Rehfeld, & Emson, 1984; Sauter & Frick, 1983). Of the various fragments identified, the C-terminal octapeptide (CCK_8) in the sulphated (CCK_{8S}) and unsulphated form (CCK_{8US}) appear to be most abundant (Goltermann, Rehfeld, & Roigaard-Petersen, 1980; Larsson & Rehfeld, 1979). Moreover, two principal CCK receptor types have been identified (Dourish and Hill, 1987; Moran, Robinson, Goldrich, & McHugh, 1986) the CCK_A ("peripheral") receptors, which have a higher affinity for CCK_{8S}

The studies reviewed in this chapter received financial support from the Fonds de la Recherche en Sante du Quebec, the Medical Research Council of Canada, and St. Mary's Hospital Foundation.

233

than for CCK_4 or gastrin, and the CCK_B ("brain") receptors, which have high affinity for all of these compounds. The distinction between CCK_A and CCK_B receptors, made mainly on the basis of different sensitivities to a variety of agonists and antagonists, has been supported by molecular cloning (Pisegna, DeWeerth, Huppi, & Wank, 1992; Wank, Pisegna, & DeWeerth, 1992). The majority of CCK receptors in the CNS belong to the B subtype, although CCK_A receptors are found in the area postrema, nucleus tractus solitarius, and interpeduncular nucleus (Dourish & Hill, 1987; Hill, Campbell, Shaw, & Woodruff, 1987; Moran et al., 1986; Vandijk, Richard, Trzeciak, Gillessen, & Mohler, 1984).

The discovery of CCK in mammalian brain naturally sparked interest in the potential contribution of this neuropeptide to CNS disorders. In particular, a large body of histochemical data describing the colocalization of CCK and dopamine in dopamine neuronal networks prompted several research groups to investigate the role of CCK in the genesis and treatment of schizophrenia in the early 1980s. Unfortunately, these studies produced variable results, primarily because of limited knowledge at the time of the CCK receptor system and the lack of investigative tools for human research. The recent characterization of different CCK receptor types as well as the availability of selective CCK receptor antagonists will certainly revive interest in this important area of research.

A number of studies conducted mainly in our laboratory have led recently to speculation that alterations in CCK activity might contribute to the pathophysiology of panic disorder. This chapter provides an overview of the clinical and animal data that support the CCK hypothesis of panic disorder and describes the research strategies that have been employed to confirm this hypothesis.

HISTORICAL PERSPECTIVE

The potential involvement of CCK in anxiety regulation was inferred initially from studies of Bradwejn and de Montigny (1984, 1985a, 1985b), which revealed that benzodiazepine receptor agonists, administered intravenously or microiontophoretically, antagonized the excitatory influence of CCK_{8S} on hippocampal pyramidal neurons in rats. This antagonism was selective for CCK_{8S}, as the excitatory effects of acetylcholine, metenkephalin, aspartate, or glutamate were not attenuated by benzodiazepines, and specific for benzodiazepines, as intravenous phenobarbital, haloperidol, or meprobamate had no effect on CCK_{8S}-induced excitation. In addition, the antagonistic action of benzodiazepine agonists on CCK_{8S} excitation was reversed by flumazenil, an antagonist of benzodiazepine receptors, suggesting a mediating role of benzodiazepine receptors.

While these experiments provided the first evidence that benzodiazepine receptor agonists could antagonize the central action of a neuropeptide, it remained to be verified whether this effect was attributed to the anxiolytic properties of benzodiazepines or to other pharmacological properties associated with these compounds. This question was investigated by examining whether microiontophoretically applied PK 8165, a partial benzodiazepine agonist with putative anxiolytic action but no appreciable sedative, anticonvulsant, or myorelaxant effects, could attenuate the excitatory influence of CCK_{8S} on rat hippocampal neurons. This study revealed that PK 8165 attenuated CCK_{8S}-induced excitation in a dose-dependent fashion, suggesting that the antagonistic action of benzodiazepines was indeed related to their anxiolytic effects (Bradwejn & de Montigny, 1985b). These results suggested that the antagonism of the excitation by CCK_{8S} of hippocampal neurons might constitute an important mechanism by which benzodiazepines exert their anxiolytic effects.

More important, the observation that anxiolytic molecules could antagonize the central action of an excitatory neuropeptide raised the question about whether CCK might be anxiogenic. Several research possibilities were considered in testing this hypothesis. For example, one potential strategy was to evaluate the effects of CCK_{8S} in patients with generalized anxiety disorder and healthy volunteers. However, an anecdotal report by the biochemist Jens Rehfeld during a CCK meeting held in Brussels in 1984 helped guide our research program. In the course of investigating the influence of exogenous CCK-tetrapeptide (CCK_4) on insulin secretion in human volunteers, Rehfeld noted a number of "side effects" following CCK_4 administration, including anxiety, choking, and feeling unreal. As these "side effects" were compatible with the symptoms profile of panic attacks, Bradwejn, Koszycki, and Meterissian (1990) and de Montigny (1989) independently conducted pilot studies to investigate the possible panicogenic effects of CCK_4 in patients with panic disorder and healthy volunteers. These studies revealed that CCK_4 produced "panic-like" attacks in healthy volunteers (de Montigny, 1989) and panic attacks, as described by criteria from the third edition of the *Diagnostic and Statistical Manual of Mental Disorders* (DSM-III) and patient self-report, in patients with panic disorder (Bradwejn et al.,

1990). These preliminary results were encouraging and led to a series of studies on the potential relationship between CCK neurotransmission and panic disorder.

VALIDATION OF CCK$_4$ AS A PANICOGENIC AGENT

Our work on CCK$_4$ has focused, to a large extent, on evaluating the validity of this peptide as a panicogenic agent for laboratory studies (Bradwejn, Koszycki, & Payeur, 1991) using the seven criteria for an "ideal" panicogenic agent described by Guttmacher, Murphy, and Insel (1983) and Gorman, Fyer, Liebowitz, and Klein (1987). In all of our studies, we have employed the following standard methodology. Subjects are comfortably seated and an intravenous line is installed into their right antebecubital vein through which sodium chloride is slowly dripped. Approximately 30 minutes after the intravenous line is installed, a standard dose of CCK$_4$ (or placebo) is injected in a bolus push (i.e., less than five seconds). Subjects are instructed to fully describe any symptom they experience since CCK administration, and one of the investigators records the onset, duration, and description of these symptoms. Once subjects indicate that the overall effects of CCK$_4$ have abated, they are asked to rate on a scale of 0 to 4 (not present to extremely severe) the intensity of 18 symptoms on a Panic Symptoms Scale (PSS) derived from the revised edition of DSM-III (DSM-III-R). Symptoms not appearing on the PSS but spontaneously reported by subjects also are rated.

The outcome of our studies indicate that CCK$_4$ satisfies all seven requirements for an ideal panicogenic agent:

1. *The agent should be safe.* CCK$_4$ is safe to administer to human subjects. We have injected CCK$_4$ to over 200 subjects, and with the exception of a brief vasovagal reaction occurring in less than 5 percent of subjects, no significant adverse effects have been observed.

2. *The agent should induce both physical and affective symptoms of panic.* CCK$_4$ elicits both emotional (e.g., anxiety, fear, apprehension) and somatic symptoms (e.g., dyspnea, palpitations/rapid heart, choking) that typically occur during a panic attack (Bradwejn & Koszycki, 1992). Moreover, in our studies, a panic attack is operationally defined as the occurrence of at least four DSM-III-R somatic symptoms plus a subjective sense of anxiety, fear, and/or apprehension.

3. *The agent should provoke attacks that resemble the patient's clinical panic attacks.* The panic attacks induced by CCK_4 have been appraised by patients to be identical or very similar to their spontaneous panic attacks in terms of the type and quality of symptoms (Bradwejn, Koszycki & Shriqui, 1991; Bradwejn et al., 1990). Moreover, CCK_4 does not induce a stereotyped response in patients. Rather it mimics the individual symptom profile each patient usually experiences. The majority of patients have reported that the main difference between the CCK_4-induced panic attack and their clinical attacks is that the symptoms induced with CCK_4 occur more abruptly and are generally of a shorter duration.

4. *The effects of the agent should be specific for patients with a history of panic attacks.* We have found that response to CCK_4 reliably differentiates panic disorder patients from healthy controls with no personal or family history of panic attacks. In a double-blind placebo-controlled study (Bradwejn, Koszycki, & Shriqui, 1991), we noted that patients with panic disorder experienced a greater number of symptoms and more intense symptoms following challenge with two doses of CCK_4 (25 and 50 μg). In addition, the incidence of panic attacks was markedly higher in patients than controls following injection of 25 μg (91 versus 17 percent) and 50 μg (100 versus 47 percent) of the peptide. Interestingly, we noted that the number and intensity of symptoms as well as the symptom profile were remarkably similar in both patients and normal subjects who panicked with the 50 μg dose of CCK_4, suggesting that the enhanced response to CCK in patients could not be readily attributed to a tendency to overendorse symptoms. The hypersensitivity to CCK in panic patients is corroborated by studies conducted by Abelson and Nesse (1990) and by Van Megen, Westenberg, Den Boer, Haigh, and Traub (1994). These authors found that panic attacks induced with pentagastrin, a CCK-B agonist, were reported to be similar to spontaneous panic attacks and had little or no effect in healthy subjects. Further studies are required to determine whether the effects of CCK_4 can differentiate patients suffering from panic disorder and those with other psychiatric syndromes.

5. *The effects of the agent should be reliable.* In order to determine whether the behavioral effects of CCK_4 could be replicated in the same individual we administered 25 μg of CCK_4 to 11 panic patients on two separate occasions in the absence of intervening treatment (Bradwejn, Koszycki, Payeur, Bourin, & Borthwick, 1992). Although the latency to effect symptoms with CCK_4 was significantly shorter on the second challenge day, the vulnerability of patients to the panicogenic properties

of CCK_4 was undiminished with repeated challenge. Panic attack frequency following the initial and subsequent challenge was 82 and 73 percent, respectively. In addition, the number and intensity of symptoms remained constant with rechallenge. This property of CCK_4 also has important implications in relation to testing the effectiveness of antipanic drugs in blocking CCK_4-induced panic.

The effectiveness of CCK_4 in provoking panic responses also appears to be dose dependent. In a double-blind dose response study of CCK_4 (0, 10, 15, 20, and 25 μg) in 29 patients with panic disorder, the panic attack rate was 17 percent (10 μg), 64 percent (15 μg), 75 percent (20 μg), and 75 percent (25 μg). None of the patients panicked with placebo (0 μg). Moreover, the behavioral effects of CCK_4 were associated with marked and dose-related increases in heart rate and blood pressure (Bradwejn, Koszycki, Annable et al., 1992). In another double-blind study of 36 healthy volunteers, CCK_4 (0, 9, 25, and 50 μg) also was found to induce panic in a dose-dependent manner. The panic attack rate was 11 percent (9 μg), 17 percent (25 μg), and 47 percent (50 μg). No panic attacks occurred with placebo injections (Bradwejn, Koszycki, & Bourin, 1991).

6. *Antipanic agents should block the effects of the agent.* Recently we have demonstrated that the panicogenic effects of CCK_4 can be antagonized by chronic treatment with imipramine (Bradwejn & Koszycki, 1994). Specifically, 11 patients with panic disorder who displayed a positive panicogenic response to CCK_4 were treated with imipramine on a chronic basis and rechallenged with CCK_4 after being free of both panic and agoraphobic symptoms for at least eight weeks. With rechallenge, patients displayed a marked reduction in the number and sum intensity of symptoms, duration of symptoms, and cardiovascular responsiveness. Moreover, only two of the 11 patients who previously panicked with CCK_4 experienced a panic attack when rechallenged. It is also notable that patients who consumed higher doses of imipramine experienced fewer and less intense panic symptoms at rechallenge, suggesting that the decreased sensitivity to CCK_4 following chronic imipramine therapy was most likely attributed to a drug effect rather than to other factors such as spontaneous remission of symptoms.

7. *The effects of the agent are not antagonized by drugs without anti-panic effects.* There is indirect evidence that CCK_4 also satisfies this criterion. In the context of investigating the effects of CCK_B receptor antagonists on CCK_4-induced panic symptoms, we observed

that pretreatment with placebo failed to antagonize CCK_4-induced panic symptoms in patients with panic disorder (Bradwejn, & Koszycki, 1992; Bradwejn, Koszycki, Couetoux du Tertre, van Megan et al., 1994). In another study that investigated the possible mediating role of benzodiazepine receptors in CCK_4-induced panic symptoms, pretreatment with the benzodiazepine receptor antagonist flumazenil, a compound without any known antipanic activity, failed to diminish response to CCK_4 challenge in healthy volunteers (Bradwejn, Koszycki, Couetoux du Tertre, Paradis, & Bourin, 1994).

Another research strategy that we have employed in evaluating whether CCK_4 is a valid panicogenic agent has been to compare its effects with those produced by other valid pharmacological models of panic. In this respect, we have compared response to a 25 μg dose of CCK_4 and a single inhalation of 35 percent carbon dioxide (CO_2) in patients with panic disorder (Bradwejn & Koszycki, 1991) and healthy volunteers (Koszycki, Bradwejn, & Bourin, 1991). In the study with patients, CCK_4 was found to be more effective in inducing panic attacks than 35 percent CO_2 (91 versus 45 percent), although the profile of symptoms that emerged in response to either agent was similar in patients who experienced a panic attack. By contrast, these concentrations of CCK_4 and CO_2 were equipotent in promoting panic attacks in healthy subjects (17 versus 21 percent).

Summarizing, our work has demonstrated that CCK_4 satisfies previously established criteria for an ideal panicogenic agent and that it compares well to at least one widely accepted pharmacologic model of panic. It also should be emphasized that CCK_4 is the only valid panicogen that fulfills criteria for a neurotransmitter. CCK is well characterized in the CNS and is abundant in brain regions implicated in the promotion of panic attacks, including the brainstem, hippocampus, amygdala, and cerebral cortex (Karkanias, Block, Reines, & Bradwejn, 1989). Moreover, biochemical and electrophysiological data suggest interactions between CCK and multiple neurotransmitter systems, including serotonin, noradrenaline, gamma-amenobutyric acid, and dopamine. As a panicogenic agent, therefore, CCK_4 provides an important opportunity to identify an endogenous anomaly associated with panic disorder and to enhance our understanding of the multiple neurotransmitter systems that potentially contribute to the generation of panic attacks.

Another important feature of CCK_4 is that it is simple to administer in a low-volume intravenous bolus infusion (in less than five seconds).

This method of administration has considerable advantage over the slow infusion procedures required to provoke panic attacks with other agents, such as sodium lactate. The relatively protracted infusion interval has been associated with physiologic alterations, such as volume overload, and metabolic changes that can introduce nonspecific psychological effects (Margraf, Ehlers, & Roth, 1986). Another technical advantage is that the latency to effect symptoms of panic with CCK_4 is rapid and predictable, permitting measurement of central and peripheral nervous system activity during the interval associated with peak panic symptoms. Considered together, the technical advantage of CCK_4 administration, coupled by its presence in the CNS, commends its use for research into the pathophysiology of panic disorder.

Finally, it is relevant to add that the behavioral effects of exogenous CCK_4 in clinical paradigms are paralleled by the data describing the effects of CCK_4 agonists in nonhuman primates. Ervin, Palmour, and Bradwejn (1991) reported that intravenous CCK_4 administration in the unrestrained green vervet monkey produced behavioral activation reminiscent of fear and defense posturing. The emergence of these behaviors appeared to be dose-related and largely influenced by the baseline behavioral profile of the individual animal in its social environment. For example, high CCK_4 doses produced immobilization and freezing in ordinarily anxious and fidgety monkeys but actually promoted mild restlessness and activation in naturally calm monkeys. Immobilization and freezing have been observed in monkeys in response to social stress or threat and are thought to be behavioral equivalents of human fear and panic (Friedman, Sunderland, & Rosenblaum, 1987). CCK agonists, including CCK_4, pentagastrin, and CCK_8, also have been reported to have potent anxiogenic effects in rodent models of anxiety. (For review see Harro, Vasar, & Bradwejn, 1993.)

CHOLECYSTOKININ'S
MECHANISM OF ACTION

The observation that challenge doses of CCK_4 have profound panicogenic effects in humans obviously raised questions about the specific mechanisms subserving these effects. In this respect, much of our recent research endeavors have focused on determining neurotransmitter mediation of CCK_4-induced panic. Studies are currently under way to evaluate whether pharmacological agents that act on specific neurotransmitter systems can either block or amplify the panicogenic effects of CCK_4. Moreover, because a number of researchers have advocated the importance of psychological variables to experimentally induced anxiety, we also have endeavored to assess the contribution of such variables in influencing panicogenic responses to CCK_4.

Fortunately, our clinical studies with CCK_4 have been paralleled by the development of CCK receptor antagonists with selectivity for central (CCK_B) and peripheral (CCK_A) receptor subtypes (Freidinger, 1989; Silverman, Greenberg, & Bank, 1987; Woodruff & Hugues, 1991). These antagonists can be grouped broadly into five classes: (1) derivatives of cyclic neucleotides; (2) derivatives of amino acids; (3) partial sequence and derivatives of the C-terminal sequence heptapeptides of CCK; (4) benzodiazepine derivatives; and (5) nonpeptide peptoids. A number of investigations have revealed that CCK_B but not CCK_A receptor antagonists are anxiolytic in rodent-based tests of anxiety. (For review see Harro et al., 1993.) Other studies also have shown that pretreatment with CCK_B antagonists (e.g., L-265,260, CI-988, LY262691) reduces the anxiogenic effects CCK agonists in rodents (Harro, Pold, & Vasar, 1990; Harro & Vasar, 1991; Harro et al., 1993; Rataud et al., 1991; Singh, Lewis, Field, Hugues, & Woodruff, 1991), and nonhuman primates (Palmour, Bradwejn, & Ervin, 1992).

In a study designed to evaluate the effects of CCK_B receptor antagonists on CCK_4-induced panic, 29 patients with panic disorder (with or without agoraphobia) were pretreated with L-365,260 (10 or 50 milligrams [mg] P.O.) or placebo 90 minutes prior to CCK_4 administration (Bradwejn, Koszycki, Coutetoux du Tertre, van Megan et al., 1994). A challenge dose of 20 μg of CCK_4 was used in this investigation since results from our dose-response study (Bradwejn & Koszycki, 1992; Bradwejn et al., 1992) showed that this dose precipitated a panic attack in 75 percent of patients. Thus, it was hypothesized that this dose would promote noticeable changes in behavior and other indices of anxiety without being potent enough to mask the effectiveness of L-365,260 to block the effects of CCK_4. The main finding of the study was that the 50 mg dose of L-365,260 was superior over placebo in reducing the number and intensity of symptoms and frequency of panic attacks induced with CCK_4. Moreover, both the 10 and 50 mg doses of L-365,260 were superior over placebo in reducing CCK_4-evoked increases in heart rate.

These preliminary data clearly demonstrate that CCK_B receptors mediate the panicogenic effects of CCK_4 in humans and that CCK_B antagonists may have therapeutic benefits in the treatment of panic disorder.

We also have determined whether the benzodiazepine receptors might be an important site of action the panicogenic effects of CCK_4. Benzodiazepine agonists selectively and specifically antagonized CCK-induced excitation of rat hippocampal neurons (Bradwejn & de Montigny, 1984). Moreover, neuronal responsivity to CCK_{8S} in rats decreases following long-term administration of benzodiazepine agonists (Bouthillier and de Montigny, 1988). There is also evidence that benzodiazepine agonists attenuate the anxiogenic effects of CCK_4 in nonhuman primates (Palmour et al., 1992) and healthy volunteers (de Montigny, 1989), although such data do not establish that benzodiazepine receptor activity invariably contributes to the panicogenic effects of CCK_4. Thus, to further explore the role benzodiazepines receptors in CCK_4-induced panic, we determined whether pretreatment with the benzodiazepine receptor antagonist flumazenil could affect response to CCK_4 using a double-blind, placebo-controlled, crossover design. Because flumazenil has inverse agonist properties in panic patients but no intrinsic behavioral effects in healthy subjects (Nutt, Glue, Lawson, & Wilson, 1990), and because there are no available benzodiazepine ligands that possess pure antagonistic action in patients, only healthy volunteers were selected for participation in this study.

In investigating the interaction between CCK and benzodiazepine receptors in CCK_4-induced panic, we proposed a model that was based on the concept that exogenous CCK_4, through actions on CCK_B receptors, might interact with benzodiazepine receptors in eliciting panic symptoms by indirectly acting like a benzodiazepine receptor inverse agonist. In other words, we postulated that CCK_4 might act as a endogenous "virtual" inverse agonist of benzodiazepine receptors. To support this hypothesis, it was necessary to determine whether flumazenil could antagonize the effects of CCK_4. Our findings indicated that CCK_4 does not produce its panicogenic effects via benzodiazepine receptors. In particular, we found no difference between flumazenil and placebo treatment for the number and sum intensity of symptoms induced with CCK_4, panic attack frequency, and increases in heart rate and blood pressure (Bradwejn, Koszycki, Couetoux du Tertre, Paradis, & Bourin, 1994).

There are rather limited behavioral data suggesting that noradrenergic, serotonergic, and adenosinergic receptors mediate the effects of

CCK agonists. Palmour and Ervin (personal communication) demonstrated that propranolol blocked the anxiogenic effects of CCK in nonhuman primates, and as previously mentioned, chronic imipramine treatment antagonized the panicogenic effects of CCK_4 in panic patients (Bradwejn and Koszycki, 1994). These data suggest that perhaps both alpha- and beta-norepinephrine receptor activation may be instrumental in interacting with endogenous CCK in promoting symptoms of panic anxiety. There is also some interesting data suggesting that serotonin ($5HT_3$) receptors are mediators of CCK-induced anxiety. In this respect, Vasar, Peuranen, Oopik, Harro, and Mannisto (1993) reported that the anxiogenic effect of caerulein, a CCK agonist, was prevented by prior treatment with the $5HT_3$ receptor antagonist odansetron. A possible interaction between CCK and adenosine receptors is supported by the finding that NECA (N-ethylcarboxamido-adenosine), an agonist of adenosine A_2 receptors, antagonized the anxiogenic effects of CCK_4 in nonhuman primates (Palmour et al., 1992). This latter finding is interesting in light of the hypothesis that the clinical effects of benzodiazepine agonists are mediated by adenosine receptors and that adenosine receptors mediate the panicogenic effects of caffeine and play a role in the pathophysiology of panic disorder (Phillis, 1984; Uhde, 1990).

Finally, we have recently assessed the potential contribution of psychological factors in influencing panicogenic response to CCK_4. In particular, we examined whether anxiety sensitivity (Reiss, Peterson, Gursky, & McNally, 1986) was an important determinant of panicogenic response to 50 µg challenge dose of CCK_4 in healthy volunteers with no personal history of panic attacks or family history of panic disorder (Koszycki, Cox, & Bradwejn, 1993). Anxiety sensitivity is a cognitive disposition to interpret arousal symptoms as threatening based on the belief that these symptoms have undesirable consequences. Previous studies employing voluntary hyperventilation as a challenge revealed that healthy volunteers with high levels of anxiety sensitivity displayed a greater anxiogenic response than subjects with low levels of anxiety sensitivity. In our study, individuals with a preexisting high level of anxiety sensitivity experienced significantly more catastrophic cognitions and fear of somatic symptoms, but they were not more susceptible to experiencing a panic attack following CCK_4 administration. Hence, anxiety sensitivity appears to play a negligible role in mediating panicogenic responses to CCK_4 challenge.

NEUROANATOMICAL CORRELATES
OF CCK$_4$-INDUCED PANIC

A question of central importance concerns the site(s) of panicogenic action of CCK$_4$ in humans. In this respect, our group, in collaboration with researchers at the Montreal Neurological Institute, investigated the neuroanatomical correlates of CCK$_4$ challenge in healthy subjects (Benkelfat et al., 1992). The effects of CCK$_4$ on cerebral blood flow (CBF) was measured with oxygen radiolabelled water (H$_2$^{15}O) positron emission tomogrophy (PET) scans, and magnetic resonance imaging (MRI) scans were obtained in all subjects for subsequent anatomical correlation of blood flow changes. The CBF images revealed significant extracranial CBF increases bitemporally and CBF increases in the anterior cingulate gyrus, the claustrum-insular-amygdala region, and the cerebellar vermis. Interestingly, subjects who did not experience a panic attack following CCK$_4$ challenge exhibited significantly greater CBF increases in the anterior cingulate gyrus than subjects who panicked following CCK$_4$ challenge.

The results of this study were intriguing for several reasons. First, blood flow changes in the vicinity of the poles of the temporal lobes during panic attacks induced with sodium lactate infusion were thought to represent central nervous system (CNS) activity (Reiman, Fusselman, Fox, & Raichle, 1989; Reiman et al., 1989). In these studies, MRI was not used for anatomical correlation of blood flow changes. The results obtained with CCK$_4$ suggested that the changes observed with lactate may have in fact reflected extracranial changes in blood flow. A technical comment in support of this interpretation was recently published (Drevets, Videen, Macleod, Haller, & Raichle, 1992). Second, the results with CCK$_4$ confirmed findings obtained with lactate challenge that the anterior cingulate gyrus may be an important central site underlying the expression of at least some of the symptoms of panic. Third, the apparent differences between panickers and nonpanickers suggested that panic disorder may be associated with a lack of CNS "panic control" mechanisms. Additional brain imaging studies evaluating the effects of CCK antagonists and antipanic agents on CCK$_4$-induced panic in panic disorder and normal control subjects will further elucidate the neuroanatomical basis of panic attacks and anxiety.

There is some indirect evidence that regions of the brainstem also may be important sites by which CCK$_4$ promotes its effects. A number of animal studies have implicated the brainstem regions in the control of sympathetic nerve discharge and vasomotor tone. Increases in blood pressure and heart rate have been observed following electrical or pharmacological stimulation of the nucleus tractus solitarius (NTS) (Jordan & Spyer, 1986; Kirchheim, 1976; Spyer, 1981), and medullary nuclei (Adair, Hamilton, Scappaticci, Helke, & Gillis, 1977; Dampney, Goodchild, Robertson, & Montgomery, 1982; Pilowsky, West, & Chalmers, 1985; Ross et al., 1984), and the parabrachial nucleus (Marovitch, Kumada, & Reis, 1982). These brainstem regions are interrelated by diverse neuronal projections and are connected to adrenergic structures (Chan, Chan, & Ong, 1986; Dampney, Czachurski, Dembowsky, Goodchild, & Seller, 1977; Dampney et al., 1982; Ross et al., 1984), such as the locus coeruleus, a brain nucleus implicated in panic attacks (Gorman, Liebowitz, Fyer, & Stein, 1989).

Our clinical studies with CCK_4 has revealed that this peptide has robust effects on heart rate and blood pressure. It is conceivable that CCK_4 produces these effects by a direct or indirect action on CCK receptors in and about the regions of the NTS and other brainstem nuclei. In this respect, it is notable that CCK immunoreactivity in cells and pathways have been identified in the NTS, the medullary nuclei, and the parabrachial nucleus (Kubota et al., 1983; Takagi et al., 1984; Mantyh & Hunt, 1984; Vanderhaeghen, 1981; Vanderhaeghen, Lotstra, DeMey, & Giles, 1980). Binding sites for CCK in these regions also have been reported to be distributed in a fashion that correlates with CCK immunoreactivity (Zarbin, Innis, Wamsley, Snyder, & Kuhar, 1983). Moreover, CCK_A and CCK_B receptors have been identified pharmacologically in the NTS (Branchereau et al., 1992). The emotional and psychosensorial alterations that follow CCK_4 challenge might result from action of this peptide on brainstem structures and subsequent activation/inhibitions of higher CNS regions mediated by neuronal projections. As these brainstem structures are not fully shielded by the blood/brain barrier, CNS penetration by CCK_4 might not even be necessary for this action. This also might explain the rapid (in less than one minute) onset of action of CCK_4 observed in both patients and normal subjects. Considering the animal and human data, one might propose that CCK is a normal endogenous anticipatory stress modulator, acting, at least in part, at the brainstem level, and that heightened sensitivity of the brain to its action leads to anxiety, fear, and panic attacks.

FUTURE RESEARCH

It will be interesting to determine whether CCK_4 could be used as a diagnostic tool in panic disorder. As previously noted, panic disorder and normal control subjects display marked differences in their sensitivity to the panicogenic effects of CCK_4. Between 75 and 90 percent of patients panic with a 25 μg challenge dose of CCK_4 compared to less than 20 percent of healthy volunteers. This represents a difference in panic rate ranging from 55 to 70 percent. Although we have yet to study the effects of CCK_4 in patients suffering from other psychiatric disorders, it is possible that lower doses of CCK_4 will differentiate panic patients from those with other pathological states. Provocation studies in patients with various psychiatric syndromes should help determine whether CCK_4 shows selectivity of action in panic and whether it could be used as a diagnostic tool.

Results from studies on the mechanism of action of CCK_4, on its site of action, and on its selectivity of action have identified mediators or target systems of CCK_4's anxiogenic effects. Several other systems will likely be recognized. Further, these systems could play a role in the neurobiology of panic disorder. Accordingly, future studies should focus on evaluating whether panic disorder is associated with an endogenous malfunction or anomaly of specific systems. Conventional approaches, such as the measurement of body fluid concentrations of metabolites, could be used in such investigations. Lydiard, Ballenger, Laraia, Payeur, and Beinfeld (1992), for example, found that panic patients exhibited decreased CSF concentrations of CCK_{8S} relative to normal controls and psychiatric patients who did not experience panic attacks. This suggests that panic disorder may be related to an abnormal turnover of CCK_{8S} or CCK_4. Moreover, the observation that patients have decreased concentrations of CCK_{8S}, a mixed CCK_A/CCK_B receptor agonist, and are hyperresponsive to the panicogenic effects of CCK_4, a selective CCK_B receptor agonist, raises the question of whether panic disorder is related to an imbalance between the CCK_A and CCK_B systems. This hypothesis is pertinent in the light of recent identification of both CCK_A and CCK_B receptor activity in the NTS. The development of more sensitive analytical techniques that permit measurement of shorter CCK fragments, such as CCK_4, might help determine whether panic disorder is associated with an abnormal CCK turnover rate.

An important step in testing the hypothesis of an endogenous anomaly of the CCK_B system in panic disorder will be pharmacological validation. If spontaneous panic attacks are the result of an enhanced activity of the CCK_B system, then CCK_B antagonists should have antipanic properties. Clinical trials with CCK_B antagonists in panic disorder are scientifically justified.

Fortunately, research on the role of CCK_4 in panic disorder has received considerable attention from industry. Many pharmaceutical companies have developed CCK_B antagonists and have put these agents on fast-track drug development programs with the intention of testing their efficacy in panic and other anxiety disorders. We might soon find out whether the hypothesis of an endogenous anomaly in panic disorder receives pharmacological validation.

It should be emphasized that even if the hypothesis of an endogenous anomaly of the CCK_B system in panic disorder does not receive pharmacological validation, CCK_4 could nevertheless remain a practical research tool that might lead to the discovery of other neuronal systems not previously known to play a role in panic disorder. This might result in a better understanding of the neurobiology of panic disorder and to novel treatments.

CONCLUSIONS

These studies support the validity of CCK_4 as a panicogenic agent and suggest that the CCK system might have a role to play in the neurobiology of panic disorder. Independent preclinical studies have supported the potential involvement of CCK in anxiety and panic attacks. In animal models of anxiety, CCK_B agonists and antagonists are anxiogenic and anxiolytic, respectively (Csonka et al., 1988; Deupree & Hsiao, 1987; Harro, Kiivet, Lang, & Vasar, 1990; Harro, Pold, & Vasar, 1990; Harro & Vasar, 1991; Hughes et al., 1990; Rataud et al., 1991; Singh et al., 1991). As the clinical specificity of animal models of anxiety is unclear, only clinical studies will delineate the role of the CCK system in panic disorder and other anxiety disorders. It is too early to tell whether the CCK system is a major player in the neurobiology of these disorders. If it is, exciting research lies ahead. The availability of selective CCK receptor ligands as well as the recent report of cloning of both CCK receptor subtypes provide tools for interesting pharmacological and molecular studies. These studies might have implications on the diagnosis, treatment, and prevention of anxiety disorders.

REFERENCES

Abelson, J. L., & Nesse, R. M. (1990). Cholecystokinin-4 and panic. *Archives of General Psychiatry, 47,* 395.

Adair, J. R., Hamilton, B. L., Scappaticci, K. A., Helke, C. J., & Gillis, R. A. (1977). Cardiovascular responses to electrical stimulation of the medullary raphe area of the cat. *Brain Research, 128,* 141–145.

Beinfeld, M. (1988). Cholecystokinin and gastrin chemistry, distribution, release and activity. In A. Negro-Vilan and P. M. Conn (Eds.), *Peptide hormones: Effects and mechanisms of action,* vol. 2 (pp. 41–47). Boca Raton, FL: CRC Press.

Benkelfat, C., Bradwejn, J., Meyer, E., Ellenbogen, M., Milot, S., Gjedde, A., & Evans, A. (1992). Neuro-anatomical correlates of CCK_4-induced-panic in normals. *Clinical Neuropharmacology, 15*(Suppl. 1), 233B.

Bouthillier, A., & de Montigny, C. (1988). Long term benzodiazepine treatment reduces neuronal responsiveness to cholecystokinin: An electrophysiological study in the rat. *European Journal of Pharmacology, 151,* 135–138.

Bradwejn, J., & Koszycki, D. (1991). Comparison of CO2-induced panic attacks with cholecystokinin-induced panic attacks in panic disorder. *Progress in Neuro-Psychopharmacology and Biological Psychiatry, 15,* 237–239.

Bradwejn, J., & Koszycki, D. (1992). CCK_4 and panic attacks in man. In S. Iversen, C. Dourish, & F. Cooper (Eds.), *Multiple cholecystokinin receptors in man* (pp. 121–131). Oxford: Oxford University Press.

Bradwejn, J., & Koszycki, D. (1994). Imipramine antagonism of the panicogenic effects of cholecystokinin-tetrapeptide in panic disorder patients. *American Journal of Psychiatry, 151,* 261–263.

Bradwejn, J., Koszycki, D., Annable, L., Couetoux du Tertre, A., Reines, S., & Karkanias, C. (1992). A dose-ranging study of the behavioral and cardiovascular effects of CCK-tetrapeptide in panic disorder. *Biological Psychiatry, 32,* 903–912.

Bradwejn, J., Koszycki, D., & Bourin, M. (1991). Dose-ranging study of the effects of cholecystokinin in healthy volunteers. *Journal of Psychiatry and Neuroscience, 16,* 91–95.

Bradwejn, J., Koszycki, D., Couetoux du Tertre, A., Paradis, M., & Bourin, M. (1994). Effects of flumazenil on cholecystokinin-tetrapeptide-induced panic symptoms in healthy volunteers. *Psychopharmacology, 114,* 257–261.

Bradwejn, J., Koszycki, D., Couetoux du Tertre, A., van Megan, H., Den Boer, J., Westenberg, H. G. M., & Annable, L. (1994). The panicogenic effects of cholecystokinin tetrapeptide are antagonized by L-365,260, a central cholecystokinin receptor antagonists, in patients with panic disorder. *Archives of General Psychiatry, 51,* 486–493.

Bradwejn, J., Koszycki, D., & Meterissian, G. (1990). Cholecystokinin-tetrapeptide induced panic attacks in patients with panic disorder. *Canadian Journal of Psychiatry, 35,* 83–85.

Bradwejn, J., Koszycki, D., & Payeur, R. (1991). Cholecystokinin-tetrapeptide: A provocation agent for research in panic disorders? In M. Briley & S. File (Eds.), *New concepts in anxiety* (pp. 313–319). London: Macmillan.

Bradwejn, J., Koszycki, D., Payeur, R., Bourin, M., & Borthwick, H. (1992). Study of the replication of action of cholecystokinin in panic disorders. *American Journal of Psychiatry, 149,* 962–964.

Bradwejn, J., Koszycki, D., & Shriqui, C. (1991). Enhanced sensitivity of cholecystokinin-tetrapeptide in panic disorder: Clinical and behavioral findings. *Archives of General Psychiatry, 48,* 603–607.

Bradwejn, J., & de Montigny, C. (1984). Benzodiazepines antagonize cholecystokinin-induced activation of rat hippocampal neurons. *Nature, 312,* 363–364.

Bradwejn, J., & de Montigny, C. (1985a). Antagonism of cholecystokinin-induced activation by benzodiazepine receptor agonists: Microintophoretic studies in the rat hippocampus. *Annals of the New York Academy of Sciences, 448,* 575–580.

Bradwejn, J., & de Montigny, C. (1985b). Effects of PK 8165, a partial benzodiazepine receptor agonist, on cholecystokinin-induced activation of hippocampal pyramidal neurons: A microiontophoretic study in the rat. *European Journal of Pharmacology, 112,* 415–418.

Branchereau, P., Böhme, G. A., Champagnat, J., Morin-Surun, M. P., Durieux, C., Blanchard, J. C., Roques, B. P., & Denavit-Saubie, M. (1992). Cholecystokinin$_A$ and cholecystokinin$_B$ receptors in neurons of the brainstem solitary complex of the rat: Pharmacological identification. *Journal of Pharmacology and Experimental Therapeutics, 260,* 1433–1440.

Chan, S. H., Chan, J. Y. H., & Ong, B. G. (1986). Anatomic connections between nucleus reticularis rostroventrolateralis and some medullary cardiovascular sites in the rat. *Neuroscience Letter, 71,* 277–282.

Csonka, E., Fekete, M., Nagy, G., Szanto-Fekete, M., Feledgy, G., Penke, B., & Kovaks, K. (1988). Anxiogenic effect of cholecystokinin in rats. In B. Penke & A. Torok (Eds.), *Peptides* (pp. 249–252). New York: Walter de Gruyter.

Dampney, R. A. L., Czachurski, J., Dembowsky, K., Goodchild, A. K., & Seller, H. (1977). Afferent connections and spinal projections of the pressor region in the rostral ventrolateral medulla of the cat. *Journal of Autonomic Nervous System, 20,* 73–86.

Dampney, R. A. L., Goodchild, A. K., Robertson, L. G., & Montgomery, W. (1982). Role of ventrolateral medulla in vasomotor regulation: A correlative anatomical and physiological study. *Brain Research, 249,* 223–235.

Deupree, D., & Hsiao, S. (1987). Cholecystokinin octapeptide, proglumide, and conditioned taste avoidance in rats. *Physiological Behaviour, 41,* 125–128.

Drevets, W. C., Videen, T. O., Macleod, A. K., Haller, J. W., & Raichle, M. E. (1992). PET images of blood flow changes during anxiety: Correction. *Science, 256,* 1696.

Dourish, C. T., & Hill, D. R. (1987). Classification and function of CCK receptors. *Trends in Pharmacological Science, 8,* 207–208.

Ervin, F., Palmour, R., & Bradwejn, J. (1991). A new primate model for PD. New Research Program and Abstracts, 144th meeting of the American Psychiatric Association, New Orleans, Louisiana.

Friedinger, R. M. (1989). Cholecystokinin and gastrin antagonists. *Medical Research Review, 9,* 271–290.

Friedman, S., Sunderland, G. S., & Rosenblaum, L. A. (1987). A non-human model for panic disorder. *Psychiatry Research, 23,* 65–75.

Goltermann, N. R., Rehfeld, J. F., & Roigaard-Petersen, H. (1980). In vivo biosynthesis of cholecystokinin in rat cerebral cortex. *Journal of Biological Chemistry, 255,* 6181–6185.

Gorman, J. M., Fyer, M. R., Liebowitz, M. R., & Klein, D. F. (1987). Pharmacologic provocation of panic attacks. In H. Y. Meltzer (Ed.), *Psychopharmacology: A third generation of progress* (pp. 980–983). New York: Raven Press.

Gorman, J. M., Liebowitz, M. R., Fyer, A. J., & Stein, J. (1989). Neuroanatomical hypothesis for panic disorder. *American Journal of Psychiatry, 146,* 148–161.

Guttmacher, L. B., Murphy, D. L., & Insel, T. R. (1983). Pharmacologic models of anxiety. *Comprehensive Psychiatry, 24,* 312–326.

Harro, J., Kiivet, R. A., Lang, A., & Vasar, E. (1990). Rats with anxious or non-anxious type of exploratory behaviour differ in their brain CCK-8 and benzodiazepine receptor characteristics. *Behavioral Brain Research, 39,* 63–71.

Harro, J., Pold, M., & Vasar, E. (1990). Anxiogenic-like action of caerulein, a CCK-8 receptor agonist, in the mouse: Influence of acute and subchronic diazepam treatment. *Naunyn-Schmideberg's Archives of Pharmacology, 341,* 62–67.

Harro, J., & Vasar, E. (1991). Evidence that CCK_B receptors mediate the regulation of exploratory behaviour in the rat. *European Journal of Pharmacology, 193,* 379–381.

Harro, J., Vasar, E., & Bradwejn, J. (1993). Cholecystokinin in animal and human research on anxiety. *Trends in Pharmacological Science, 14,* 244–249.

Hill, D. R., Campbell, N. J., Shaw, T. M., & Woodruff, G. N. (1987). Autoradiographic localization and biochemical characterization of peripheral type CCK receptors in rat CNS using highly selective non-peptide CCK agonists. *Journal of Neuroscience, 7,* 2967–2976.

Hughes, J., Boden, P., Costall, B., Domeney, A., Kelly, E., Horwell, D. C., Hunter, J. C., Pinnock, R. D., & Woodruff, G. N. (1990). Development of a class of selective cholecystokinin type B receptor antagonists having potent anxiolytic activity. *Proceedings of the National Academy of Science USA, 87,* 6728–6732.

Jordan, D., & Spyer, K. M. (1986). Brainstem integration of cardiovascular and pulmonary afferent activity. *Progress in Brain Research, 67,* 295–314.

Karkanias, C. D., Block, G. A., Reines, S., & Bradwejn, J. (1989). Neurobiology of panic disorder. *American Journal of Psychiatry, 146,* 1357.

Kirchheim, H. R. (1976). Systematic arterial baroreceptor reflexes. *Physiology Review, 56,* 100–176.

Koszycki, D., Bradwejn, J., & Bourin, M. (1991). Comparison of the effects of cholecystokinin and carbon dioxide in healthy volunteers. *European Neuropharmacology, 1,* 137–141.

Koszycki, D., Cox, B., & Bradwejn, J. (1993). Anxiety sensitivity and response to cholecystokinin tetrapeptide in healthy volunteers. *American Journal of Psychiatry, 150,* 1881–1883.

Kubota, Y., Inagaki, S., Shinosaka, S., Cho, H. J., Tateishi, K., Hashimura, E., Hamaoka, T., & Tohyama, M. (1983). The distribution of cholecystokinin octapeptide-like structures in the lower brainstem of the rat: An immunohistochemical study. *Neuroscience, 9,* 587.

Larsson, L. E., & Rehfeld, J. F. (1979). Localization and molecular heterogeneity of cholecystokinin in the central and peripheral nervous system. *Brain Research, 165,* 201–218.

Lydiard, B., Ballenger, J., Laraia, M., Payeur, R., & Beinfeld, M. (1992). CCK-8 concentrations in CSF of panic disorder and normal controls. *American Journal of Psychiatry, 149,* 691–693.

Mantyh, P. W., & Hunt, S. P. (1984). Evidence for cholecystokinin-like immunoreactive neurons in the rat medulla oblongata which project to the spinal cord. *Brain Research, 291,* 49.

Margraf, J., Ehlers, A., & Roth, W. T. (1986). Sodium lactate infusions and panic attacks: A review and critique. *Psychosomatic Medicine, 48,* 23–51.

Marovitch, S., Kumada, M., & Reis, D. J. (1982). Role of parabrachialis in cardiovascular regulation in the cat. *Brain Research, 232,* 57–75.

Miller, L. J., Jardine, I., Weissman, E., Go, V. L., & Speicher, D. (1984). Characterization of cholecystokinin from the human brain. *Journal of Neurochemistry, 43,* 835–840.

de Montigny, C. (1989). Cholecystokinin tetrapeptide induces panic-like attacks in healthy volunteers: Preliminary findings. *Archives of General Psychiatry, 46,* 511–517.

Moran, T. H., Robinson, P. H., Goldrich, M. S., & McHugh, P. R. (1986). Two brain cholecystokinin receptors: Implications for behavioral actions. *Brain Research, 362,* 175–179.

Morley, P. D., Rehfeld, J. F., & Emson, P. C. (1984). Distribution and chromatrographic characterization of gastrin and cholecystokinin in the rat central nervous system. *Journal of Neurochemistry, 42,* 1523–1535.

Nutt, D., Glue, P., Lawson, C., & Wilson, S. (1990). Flumazenil provocation of panic attacks. *Archives of General Psychiatry, 47,* 917–925.

Palmour, R., Bradwejn, J., & Ervin, F. (1992). The anxiogenic effects of CCK_4 in monkeys are reduced by CCK-B antagonists, benzodiazepines or adenosine A2 agonists. *Clinical Neuropharmacology, 15* (Suppl. 1), 489B.

Phillis, J. W. (1984). Adenosine's role in the central actions of the benzodiazepines. *Progress in Neuro-Psychopharmacology and Biological Psychiatry, 8,* 495–402.

Pilowsky, R., West, M., & Chalmers, J. (1985). Renal sympathetic nerve responses to stimulation, inhibition and destruction of the ventrolateral medulla in the rabbit. *Neuroscience Letter, 60,* 51–55.

Pisegna, J. R., DeWeerth, A., Huppi, K., & Wank, S. A. (1992). Molecular cloning of the human brain and gastric cholecystokinin receptor-structure, functional expression and chromosomal localization. *Biochemical & Biophysiology Research Committee, 189,* 296–303.

Rataud, J., Darche, F., Piot, O., Stutzmann, J. M., Böhme, G. A., & Blanchard, J. C. (1991). "Anxiolytic" effect of CCK-antagonists on plus-maze behaviour in mice. *Brain Research, 548,* 315–317.

Rehfeld, J. F. (1992). CCK and anxiety: Introduction. In S. Iversen, C. Dourish and F. Cooper (Eds.), *Multiple cholecystokinin receptors in man* (pp. 117–120). Oxford: Oxford University Press.

Reiman, E. M., Fusselman, M. J., Fox, P. T., & Raichle, M. E. (1989). Neuroantomical correlates of anticipatory anxiety. *Science, 243,* 1071–1074.

Reiman, E. M., Raichle, M. E., Robins, E., Mintun, M. A., Fusselman, M. J., Fox, P. T., Price, J. L., & Hackman, K. A. (1989). Neuroanatomical correlates of a lactate-induced panic attack. *Archives of General Psychiatry, 46,* 493–500.

Reiss, S., Peterson, R. A., Gursky, D. M., & McNally, R. J. (1986). Anxiety sensitivity, anxiety frequency and the prediction of fearfulness. *Behavioral Research Therapy, 24,* 1–8.

Ross, C. A., Ruggiero, D. A., Park, D. H., Joh, T. H., Sved, A. F., Fernandez-Pardal, J., Saaverda, J. M., & Reis, D. J. (1984). Tonic vasomotor control by the rostral ventrolateral medulla: Effect of electrical or chemical stimulation of the area containing C1 adrenaline neurons on arterial pressure, heart rate, and plasma catecholamines and vasopressin. *Journal of Neuroscience, 4,* 474–494.

Sauter, A., & Frick, W. (1983). Determination of cholecystokinin tetrapeptide and cholecystokinin octapeptide sulfate in different rat brain regions by high-pressure liquid chromatography with electrochemical detection. *Analytic Biochemistry, 133,* 307–313.

Silverman, M. A., Greenberg, R. E., & Bank, S. (1987). Cholecystokinin receptor antagonists: A review. *American Journal of Gastroenterology, 82,* 703–708.

Singh, L., Lewis, A. S., Field, M. J., Hugues, J., & Woodruff, G. N. (1991). Evidence for an involvement of the brain cholecystokinin B receptor in anxiety. *Proceedings of the National Academy of Science USA, 88,* 1130–1133.

Spyer, M. (1981). Neural organization and control of the baroreceptor reflex. *Review of Physiology, Biochemistry, and Pharmacology, 88,* 23–124.

Takagi, H., Kubota, Y., Mori, S., Tateishi, K., Hamaoka, T., & Tohyama, M. (1984). Fine structural studies of cholecystokinin-8-like immunoreactive neurons and axon terminals in the nucleus tractus solitarius of the rat. *Journal of Comprehensive Neurology, 227,* 369.

Uhde, T. W. (1990). Caffeine provocation of panic: A focus on biological mechanisms. In J. C. Ballenger (Ed.), *Neurobiology of PD, Frontiers of clinical neuroscience,* vol. 8. (pp. 219–242). New York: Wiley-Liss.

Vanderhaeghen, J. (1981). Gastrins and cholecystokinins in central nervous system and hypophysis. In J. E. Dumont & J. Nunez (Eds.), *Hormones and cell regulation* (vol. 5 pp. 149–152). Amsterdam: Elsevier.

Vanderhaeghen, J., & Crawley, J. (Eds.). (1985). Neuronal cholecystokinin. *Annals of the New York Academy of Science, 448,* 1–697.

Vanderhaeghen, J., Lotstra, F., DeMey, J., & Giles, C. (1980). Immunohistochemical localization of cholecystokinin- and gastrin-like peptides in the brain and hypophysis of the rat. *Proceedings of the National Academy of Science USA, 77,* 1190.

Vanderhaeghen, J., Signeau, J. C., & Gepts, W. (1975). New peptide in the vertebrate CNS reacting with antigastrin antibodies. *Nature, 257,* 604–605.

Vandijk, A., Richard, J. G., Trzeciak, A., Gillessen, D., & Mohler, H. (1984). Cholecystokinin receptors: Biochemical demonstration and autoradiographical localization in rat brain and pancreas using [3H] cholecystokinin as radioligand. *Journal of Neuroscience, 4,* 1021–1033.

Van Megan, H. J. G. M., Westenberg, H. G. M., Den Boer, J. A., Haigh, J. R. M., & Traub, M. (1994). Pentagastrin induced panic attacks: Enhanced sensitivity in panic disorder patients. *Psychopharmacology, 114,* 449–455.

Vasar, E., Peuranen, E., Oopik, T., Harro, J., & Mannisto, P. T. (1993). Ondansetron, an antagonist of 5-HT3-receptors, antagonizes the antiexploratory effects of caeurlein, an agonist of CCK-receptors, in the elevated plus maze. *Psychopharmacology, 110,* 213–218.

Wank, S. A., Pisgena, J. R., & DeWeerth, A. (1992). Brain and gastrointestinal cholecystokinin receptor family: Structure and functional expression. *Proceedings of the National Academy of Sciences, 89,* 8691–8695.

Woodruff, G. N., & Hugues, J. (1991). Cholecystokinin antagonists. *Annual Review of Pharmacology and Toxicology, 31,* 469–501.

Zarbin, M. A., Innis, R. B., Wamsley, J. K., Snyder, S. H., & Kuhar, M. J. (1983). Autoradiographic localization of cholecystokinin receptors in rodent brain. *Journal of Neuroscience, 3,* 877–906.

11

Respiratory Neurobiology of Panic

LASZLO A. PAPP AND
JACK M. GORMAN

Respiratory abnormalities are commonly associated with anxiety in general and with panic attacks in particular. Symptoms such as shortness of breath, choking sensation, rapid breathing, frequent sighing, and light-headedness have been repeatedly described throughout the psychiatric and respiratory physiology literature as well as in lay publications. Recent research data on respiratory psychophysiology along with increased understanding of the significance of the prominent respiratory symptoms in panic disorder now present an opportunity to advance an integrative explanation of the association between anxiety and respiration.

While the tendency of panic patients to hyperventilate in response to laboratory challenges and stress may be the most salient marker of a panic attack, we will argue that hyperventilation is neither a necessary nor a sufficient cause of panic disorder. Only a minority of panic patients are chronic hyperventilators.

Supported in part by MH-41778, MH-30906, Scientist Development Award for Clinicians MH-00585 (Dr. Papp) and Research Scientist Award MH-00416 (Dr. Gorman) from the National Institute of Mental Health.

255

We propose instead that hyperventilation during acute panic results from a stimulation of hypersensitive central nervous system respiratory regulators. Triggering this control mechanism will result in acute hyperventilation. The range of secondary, hyperventilatory symptoms such as chest pain, paresthesias, dizziness, nausea, and derealization may frighten some, perhaps psychologically vulnerable patients into catastrophic thinking, thus intensifying the experience of panic. Medications may work by normalizing the sensitivity of the brain stem, behavioral techniques may reduce the tendency to hyperventilate, and cognitive interventions may allay the fear associated with hyperventilation-induced physiologic changes. The primary abnormality in this view, however, is with the threshold for response of the central carbon dioxide (CO_2) detection system. Supplementing this theory, Klein (1993) proposed the existence of a "suffocation false alarm" mechanism. According to this theory, one of the mechanisms that signal suffocation is a rise in CO_2 concentration. This mechanism is activated more easily in panic patients than in normals. The suffocation false alarm as well as the CO_2 hypersensitivity mechanisms may act in conjunction with psychological factors to induce panic in panic disorder patients.

This chapter examines the data that link hyperventilation to panic; describes the respiratory changes that commonly accompany spontaneous and laboratory-induced panic attacks; reviews carbon dioxide challenge studies conducted in panic disorder patients; and finally shows the response of the respiratory system to antipanic treatments.

HYPERVENTILATION AND PANIC

The symptoms of the "hyperventilation syndrome" (Kerr, Dalton, & Gliebe, 1937)—dizziness, breathlessness, tingling in hands and feet, dry mouth, unsteady feeling, nausea, sense of lost reality, palpitations, and chest pain—overlap considerably with those found in panic disorder patients (Cowley & Roy-Byrne, 1987).

An increase in the amount of air inhaled and exhaled per minute (minute ventilation), calculated as the product of the rate of breathing (frequency) and the amount of air inhaled and exhaled at each breath (tidal volume), is properly called hyperventilation only if overall ventilation exceeds the demands of cellular metabolism. In this case more CO_2 is exhaled than is produced. The resulting drop in the partial pressure of CO_2 in arterial blood ($PaCO_2$) below 35 torr is called hypocapnia.

CO_2 exists in dynamic equilibrium with hydrogen ion according to the following equation:

$$H^+ + HCO_3{}^- = H_2CO_3 = CO_2 + H_2O$$

The conversion of carbonic acid (H_2CO_3) to carbon dioxide and back is catalyzed by the enzyme carbonic anhydrase. The loss of CO_2 through alveolar hyperventilation shifts the equilibrium, resulting in a reduction of free hydrogen ion. Thus, alkalosis develops and pH rises above 7.45. Because the increase in pH is caused by increase in ventilation, this shift is termed respiratory alkalosis. Hyperventilation results in the reduction of plasma phosphate level as well (Mostellar & Tuttle, 1964).

The hypocapnic, alkalotic state induces a number of important secondary physiological changes (Missri & Alexander, 1978). First, hemoglobin binds oxygen more tightly, a phenomenon known as the Bohr effect. This means that although the subject is breathing deeper and faster, resulting in higher than normal oxygen concentration, the tissues become relatively hypoxic. Second, the hypocapnia produced by acute hyperventilation produces a marked decrease in cerebral blood flow (Plum, Posner, & Smith, 1968), which may account for many of the symptoms reported by the hyperventilating subject, including lightheadedness, dizziness, derealization, and anxiety. Finally, the kidneys attempt to compensate for the alkalotic state by increasing the excretion of bicarbonate and decreasing the excretion of titratable acid (Gennari, Goldstein, & Schwartz, 1972). This tends to bring pH back toward the normal range of 7.35 to 7.45.

As hyperventilation increases, the reduction in cerebral blood flow creates a situation of relative cerebral hypoxia (Hauge, Thoresen, & Walloe, 1980; Kennealy, McLennan, London, & McLaurin, 1980). This stimulates dilatation of the cerebral vasculature and restores blood flow to nearly normal levels. The state of chronic hyperventilation, once in place, can be maintained by relatively few deep breaths per hour (Salzman, Heyman, & Sicker, 1963).

The chronic, compensated hyperventilator, then, will manifest decreased $PaCO_2$, HCO_3, and phosphate, but nearly normal pH and cerebral blood flow (Berger, Mitchell, & Severinghause, 1977). Urine pH also will return to normal since at the lower plasma HCO_3 level its reabsorption becomes complete (Gledhill, Beirne, & Dempsey, 1975). The acute alkalotic state, however, is rapidly reestablished by an even slight increase in ventilation (Kerr et al., 1937; Lum, 1976).

The significant symptomatic overlap between panic attacks and hyperventilation coupled with earlier claims that habitual hyperventilation-induced respiratory alkalosis is a common cause of panic disorder (Lum, 1981) generated a number of trials of hyperventilation. These uncontrolled trials simply required that the anxious subject voluntarily hyperventilate. Developing anxiety symptoms during the procedure was accepted as evidence that the pathophysiology underlying the anxiety disorder was hyperventilation (Compernolle, Hoogduin, & Joele, 1979). The presence of respiratory alkalosis during these trials was rarely documented.

Several studies have now failed to show that hyperventilation causes panic in panic disorder patients. Contrary to expectation, the initial results of a controlled study (Gorman et al., 1984) showed a panic rate of only about 25 percent to hyperventilation in panic disorder patients. The continuation and extension of this investigation (Gorman et al., 1988; Gorman et al., 1994), as well as a replication by another research group (Zandbergen, Lousberg, Pols, deLoof, & Griez, 1990), confirmed these findings. Bass, Leiliot, & Marks (1989) recently demonstrated in a controlled study that panic patients are no more reactive to standard hyperventilation tests than normal controls. The diagnostic nonspecificity of the hyperventilation test itself also has been documented (de Ruiter, Garssen, Rijken, & Kraaimaat, 1989). Hibbert and Pilsbury (1989), using ambulatory transcutaneous pCO_2 monitoring, found that only seven of 15 panic patients showed signs of hyperventilation during spontaneous panic attacks. It has thus been established through the work of many investigators that hyperventilation is a relatively weak panicogenic agent, neither a necessary nor a sufficient factor by itself to provoke panic in patients with panic disorder (Griez, Zandbergen, Lousberg, & van den Hout, 1988; Rapee, 1986).

A claim has also been made that panic patients are chronic hyperventilators who, when under stress, hyperventilate acutely and impose a state of hypocapnic alkalosis (Lum, 1981). However, a number of studies contributed to loosen the link between chronic hyperventilation and panic disorder. Venous blood gas assays demonstrated that at least 50 percent of panic patients show no evidence of chronic hyperventilation at baseline (Gorman et al., 1986a). Baseline arterial blood gas samples further confirmed that only those patients who subsequently panicked to lactate infusion were chronic hyperventilators as indicated by their significantly lower HCO_3 levels compared to controls (Papp et al., 1989a). Panic patients may not demonstrate lower end tidal CO_2 concentrations at rest, another sign of hyperventilation, than normal controls or patients with social phobia and generalized anxiety disorder (Holt & Andrews, 1989). Ambulatory transcutaneous pCO_2 monitoring in panic disorder patients failed to establish a correlation between CO_2 levels and symptoms of hyperventilation (Hibbert & Pilsbury, 1989). Urine pH measurements in unmedicated panic patients could only confirm the presence of acute hyperventilatory episodes (Papp & Gorman, 1990a).

Therefore, chronic hyperventilation, the phenomenon thought to be responsible for the claimed success of breathing retraining treatments of panic patients, may not be as common as originally thought. However, breathing retraining may correct respiratory abnormalities other than chronic hyperventilation. Specifically, acute hyperventilation that is frequently present during panic attacks may be the target for this type of behavioral intervention. Indeed, breathing retraining, when effective, seems to benefit panic patients even if they are not chronic hyperventilators (Hibbert & Chan, 1989).

Ambulatory monitoring of respiratory rate and tidal volume is technically difficult and not without controversies at present. It would be the ideal method to assess respiratory status and monitor treatment response. Our preliminary data with an ambulatory respiratory monitor, the Respitrace, show that while the overall minute ventilation of panic disorder patients and controls is similar, panic patients may be chest rather than abdominal breathers and that panic attacks are accompanied by significantly increased tidal volume rather than an increase in respiratory rate (Papp et al., unpublished data). Normal adult breathing is primarily abdominal. The tendency for chest breathing may be one of the many possible autonomic dysregulatory mechanisms predisposing to the development of panic disorder (Lum, 1981).

It seems clear that most panic disorder patients are not chronic hyperventilators and that hyperventilation does not cause panic attacks. Yet panic disorder patients prominently complain about respiratory symptoms, and, as described in the next section, respiratory stimulation is one of the most prominent physiologic changes during laboratory-induced panic.

RESPIRATORY ABNORMALITIES
DURING LABORATORY PANIC INDUCTION

Pharmacologic induction of panic attacks in the laboratory is one of the most successful strategies in panic research. Sodium lactate-induced attacks are similar to spontaneously occurring panics (Dillon, Gorman, Liebowitz, Fyer, & Klein, 1987). The only biophysiologic measures that show good correlation with lactate-induced panic attacks appear to be respiratory parameters (Den Boer, Westenberg, Klompmakers, & van Lint, 1989). In fact, the absence of good correlation between subjective anxiety and physiologic change is quite striking across the literature when respiratory parameters are not assessed during panic-inducing procedures (Aronson, Carasiti, McBane, & Whitaker-Azmitia, 1989). Respiratory parameters may be the best phychophysiologic correlates of subjective anxiety (Grossman, 1983; Papp et al., 1988b). Lactate metabolizes to bicarbonate, resulting in metabolic alkalosis. According to standard "textbook" physiology, the induction of metabolic alkalosis causes a compensatory reduction in overall ventilation so that CO_2 is retained, thereby returning pH back to normal (Javaheri, Shore, Rose, & Kazemi, 1982). Paradoxically, however, lactate-induced panic is accompanied by hyperventilation and hypocapnia (Gaffney, Fenton, Lane, & Lake, 1988; Gorman et al., 1986a; Papp et al., 1989a; Reiman et al., 1989), resulting in exaggerated rather than compensated alkalosis. Hypophosphatemia, another direct sign of hyperventilation, specifically identified patients who subsequently panicked to lactate (Balon, Yeregani, & Pohl, 1988; Gorman et al., 1986a). Panicking patients develop higher plasma lactate levels than normal controls during the infusion. It appears that the difference in lactate levels is due to hyperventilation-induced respiratory alkalosis (Gorman et al., 1986a). Similar findings were reported during glucose infusion when the subjects were instructed to hyperventilate simultaneously (Maddock & Mateo-Bermudez, 1990). Again, panic patients developed significantly higher plasma lactate levels than normal controls, suggesting more hyperventilation in patients than in controls.

We placed arterial lines in panic patients during lactate infusions and found that low arterial pCO_2 prior to the lactate infusion at baseline, indicating acute hyperventilation, predicted subsequent panic during the lactate infusion (Papp et al., 1989a). Acute hyperventilation just prior to the infusion may be necessary for lactate panic to occur.

Similar findings were reported by Reiman and coworkers (1986), who placed arterial lines prior to lactate infusions conducted with concomitant positron emission tomography (PET) scanning. Reiman and associates' (1989) next study again demonstrated the significance of respiratory stimulation during lactate-induced panic. In this PET scan study the biological correlates of lactate-induced panic included low arterial pCO_2 level, high systolic blood pressure, and increased blood flow in discrete brain regions. Stewart, Devous, Rush, Lane, & Bonte (1988) also found that lactate infusion resulted in increased total cerebral blood flow in all subjects. However, patients who panicked during lactate infusion exhibited less of an increase, a finding that suggests that panicking patients may have lowered their pCO_2 by hyperventilation.

Previously we had shown that pharmacologic treatment of panic normalized venous blood gases (Gorman et al., 1985) and also decreased hyperventilation-related complaints in patients during a second lactate infusion (Gorman et al., 1987).

Sodium bicarbonate infusion–induced panic attacks, also contrary to the usual physiologic response to metabolic alkalosis, are accompanied by a drop in arterial pCO_2 (Gorman et al., 1989). Sodium d-lactate, which is considered largely inert metabolically, seems nonetheless both a panicogen and a respiratory stimulant (Gorman et al., 1990a). Caffeine, another frequently used panicogen, also is known to stimulate ventilation. The ingestion of caffeine results in increased carbon dioxide (CO_2) sensitivity (D'Urzo et al., 1990) and caffeine-induced panic is associated with elevated lactate level (Uhde, 1990).

Marked hyperventilation (increased oxygen [O_2] consumption) was noted during isoproterenol-induced attacks (Rainey, Yeragani, & Pohl, 1986) as well as during spontaneous, placebo infusion–induced panic attacks (Goetz et al., 1993). These latter "spontaneous" panic attacks were accompanied by significantly greater increases in minute ventilation than seen during lactate-induced panic. The infusion of lactate, by producing metabolic alkalosis, actually may blunt the full expression of the acute hyperventilation that normally accompanies respiratory activation during panic attacks.

Taken together, these data strongly indicate that the impulse to increase ventilation is a powerful factor during panic attacks and may be a common denominator among the many methods of laboratory induction of panic. Hyperventilation does not cause panic but often accompanies it in a prominent position. Since disturbances in respiratory response seem critical components in the pathophysiology of panic, investigators turned to direct assessment of ventilation in panic patients. A primary strategy for this line of research is the carbon dioxide challenge test.

CARBON DIOXIDE AND PANIC DISORDER

The history of carbon dioxide inhalation in psychiatry has been reviewed elsewhere (Griez & van den Hout, 1984). After some initial attempts to use it for the treatment of "dementia precox," "manic depressive insanity," and "involutional melancholia" (Loevenhart, Lorenz, & Waters, 1929), CO_2 inhalation resurfaced again in the 1950s.

In 1951 Cohen and White studied patients with "neurocirculatory asthenia"—an earlier diagnostic category that shares many features with panic disorder. They found that rebreathing up to 4 percent CO_2 caused anxiety attacks in these patients. At around the same time Meduna (1950) reported that CO_2 inhalation resulted in significant clinical improvements in stutter and "anxiety neurosis."

Encouraged by these results, the American Psychiatric Association established the Carbon Dioxide Research Association. The initial enthusiasm for work with CO_2, however, quickly abated, and CO_2 treatment was abandoned by most psychiatrists. A few behavioral therapists continued to use repeated inhalation of CO_2 as a method of desensitization of phobias (Wolpe, 1973).

The unexpected rediscovery in 1984 that CO_2 inhalation is a powerful panicogenic agent in patients with panic disorder (Gorman et al., 1984) once again resulted in renewed interest in CO_2 research. Since then the inhalation of CO_2 has become a reliable and frequently used method of panic induction in patients with panic disorder (Carr et al., 1987; Fishman, Carr, Beckett, & Rosenbaum, 1994; Fyer et al., 1987; Gorman et al., 1988, 1994; Griez, Lousberg, van den Hout, & van der Molen, 1987; Sanderson & Wetzler, 1990; Woods et al., 1986).

Carbon dioxide is a powerful respiratory stimulus and a potent dilator of the cerebral vasculature. Normally, room air contains almost no CO_2. At least three highly developed and sensitive receptor systems in the body detect increases in CO_2 (hypercapnia): the intrapulmonary receptors, the peripheral chemoreceptors of the aortic arch and carotid bodies, and the chemosensitive areas of the medullary reticular activating system in the brainstem. Arterial CO_2 changes are detected by the peripheral chemo-receptors. They send efferent fibers via the vagus nerve to the nucleus solitarius in the medulla (Errington & Dashwood, 1979). Rostral and caudal medullary chemoreceptors detect increases in central CO_2 concentrations. The central chemoreceptors project to higher portions of the brain stem, including the pontine noradrenergic nucleus, the locus coeruleus.

If CO_2 is added to the inhaled air, the medullary chemoreceptors initiate a rapid, reflexive increase in minute ventilation. The increase in minute ventilation per unit of CO_2 concentration (delta VE/delta $PaCO_2$ or delta end tidal CO_2) is best characterized by a routine respiratory parameter, called CO_2 sensitivity. CO_2 sensitivity or ventilatory response is a trait characteristic measure, relatively unaffected by current state of anxiety.

CO_2 challenge studies have shown unequivocally that panic patients panic to CO_2 more often than normal controls. At various concentrations of CO_2, beginning at 4 percent and ranging as high as 50 percent, approximately 40 to 75 percent of panic patients experience panic attacks compared to less than 10 percent of the controls (Carr et al., 1987; Gorman et al., 1984; Gorman et al., 1990b, 1994; Griez et al., 1987; Griez, Zandbergen, Pols, & de Loof, 1990; Rapee, Mattick, & Murrell, 1986; Wolpe, 1973; Woods et al., 1986).

CO_2-induced panic attacks closely resemble the kind patients with panic disorder experience outside of the laboratory (Sanderson & Wetzler, 1990), and therefore CO_2 panic seems a valid analog of spontaneous panic attacks. Different anxiety disorder groups may demonstrate different dose-dependent responses to inhaled CO_2 (Gorman et al., 1988). Panic disorder patients appear to panic to lower doses of CO_2 than social phobics, who in turn respond to lower doses than controls. Thus, the panic-inducing dose of CO_2 may differentiate among DSM-III-R anxiety conditions and other diagnostic groups.

CO_2 challenge studies also have supported the possibility that panic patients have a biologically based hypersensitivity to the effects of CO_2 at the level of the central respiratory control system. CO_2 hypersensitivity is not due to baseline differences in anxiety level between panic patients and controls (Griez et al., 1990). Several studies now have found CO_2 hypersensitivity among panic patients as determined by formal CO_2 sensitivity measures. The two most frequently used clinical methods of CO_2 sensitivity determination are the complex, sophisticated, and probably more accurate steady-state canopy procedure (Kinney, Morgan, & Domingues, 1964) and the simple and considerably quicker rebreathing method (Read, 1967). With both methods the change in minute ventilation is measured in response to different CO_2 concentrations.

Because of its simplicity, most studies to date have utilized the Read rebreathing method. Four of the five rebreathing studies involving panic patients (Carr et al., 1987; Lousberg, Griez, & van den Hout, 1988; Pain, Biddle, & Tiller, 1988; Papp et al., 1990) found differences in CO_2 sensitivity between panic patients and controls. Two (Pain et al., 1988; Papp & Gorman, 1990b) found higher CO_2 sensitivity in patients than controls due to the respiratory frequency component of minute ventilation but, surprisingly, lower tidal volume response in patients than in controls. Two studies (Carr et al., 1987; Lousberg et al., 1988) reported overall higher CO_2 sensitivity in patients compared to controls, and one study (Woods et al., 1986), although they did not analyze the components separately, found no differences between patients and controls. The extension of the Papp study (Papp, Martinez, Coplan, & Gorman, 1994) also showed significant irregularities in respiratory rhythms in panic disorder patients.

The somewhat conflicting data may be explained by certain methodological problems with the rebreathing method. First, the concentration of CO_2 in the rebreathing bag usually reaches 9 percent during the test. This amount of CO_2 may be overwhelming for all subjects and therefore may obscure subtle differences between patients and controls. Second, the procedure itself seems anxiogenic for some patients. Unfortunately, none of these studies reported CO_2 sensitivity for panicking and nonpanicking subjects separately. Carr and associates (1987) reported that their findings applied only to panicking patients. Third, it is necessary to use a hyperoxic gas mixture for the rebreathing test in order to control for the hypoxic response and to achieve equilibrium among the various compartments quickly (Rebuck & Slutsky, 1981). This gas composition, however, does not simulate the normoxic condition that is theoretically the in vivo panicogenic climate for panic patients. Finally, due to the effects of high CO_2 concentration on cerebral blood flow during rebreathing, this method may not represent the ordinary steady-state CO_2 sensitivity (Berkenbosch, Bovill, Dahan, DeGoede, & Olievier, 1989). The rebreathing method may model the respiratory biology of fear rather than that of a panic attack (Papp et al., 1994).

To date few studies have used the steady-state method to assess CO_2 sensitivity in panic patients. In one, we found significantly higher CO_2 sensitivity in a small sample of patients compared to controls (Papp et al.,

1989b). These panic patients who did not panic to 5 percent CO_2 nonetheless showed more of an increase in minute ventilation than normals to CO_2 stimulation. In a related study, inspiratory drive, a measure believed to reflect the brain stem component of respiratory control (Milic-Emili & Grunstein, 1976), increased more quickly in panicking than in nonpanicking patients or controls undergoing 5 percent CO_2 inhalation (Gorman, Liebowitz, Fyer, Fyer, & Klein, 1986). The increase among the panicking patients reached maximum levels even before the actual attacks occurred.

The steady-state method, using lower CO_2 doses than that necessary in the rebreathing method, seems to differentiate better among diagnostic groups and yield more valuable information regarding the respiratory status of panic patients. In order to assess drug effects on respiration, for instance, the steady-state method may provide more reliable data than rebreathing (Bailey, Andriano, Goldman, Stanley, & Pace, 1986; Bourke & Warley, 1986). Of the two procedures, the steady-state method may better represent the in vivo ventilatory response to CO_2 (Berkenbosch et al., 1989).

A criticism of the CO_2 hypersensitivity theory is based on the finding that acetazolamide, a carbonic anhydrase inhibitor, does not induce panic in panic disorder patients (Mathew, Wilson, & Tant, 1989). However, the only evidence supporting the development of central hypercarbia in this experiment was increased cerebral blood flow. The vasodilatory effects of acetazolamide may be unrelated to carbonic anhydrase inhibition (Hauge, Nicolaysen, & Thoresen, 1983). The investigators measured only respiratory frequency—which did not increase—and not tidal volume. Therefore, it remains unknown whether acetazolamide produces enough CO_2 increase during the experiment to stimulate the chemoreceptors. This experiment therefore failed to address CO_2 anxiogenesis directly (Klein, Papp, & Gorman, 1990). The replication of the Mathew experiment indeed confirmed that acetazolamide is not panicogenic (Gorman et al., 1993). However, it also showed that acetazolamide had no effect on ventilation. The repeat experiment with acetazolamide did not include any instruction to the subjects concerning respiratory control, which was the explanation Mathew used for the lack of respiratory stimulation (Mathew, 1990).

The assumption underlying the CO_2 hypersensitivity theory of panic is that it represents an organic abnormality, probably at the level of the medullary chemoreceptor and other autonomic control loci in the brain stem. We propose that it is the stimulation of these hypersensitive loci that triggers hyperventilation and the other manifestations of panic. Biological treatments such as repeated pharmacological challenges and antipanic medications should have an effect on these loci.

RESPIRATORY CONTROL
AND ANTIPANIC MEDICATIONS

If our current model is correct in explaining the association between respiratory abnormalities and panic disorder, the antipanic effect of a medication should correlate with its effects on respiratory control. Antipanic drugs may re-regulate the hypersensitive CO_2 receptors in the brain and consequently blunt the exaggerated ventilatory response during panic attacks. Indirect evidence supporting this model comes from studies showing that successful pharmacological treatment of panic patients normalizes venous blood gases (Gorman et al., 1985) and reduces CO_2 sensitivity. There is a substantial literature demonstrating moderate respiratory depressant effects for benzodiazepines (Clergue, Desmonts, Duvaldestin, Delevault, & Saumon, 1981). Some—mostly high-potency—benzodiazepines, while traditionally used to control insomnia and generalized anxiety, are increasingly acknowledged as powerful antipanic agents as well (Ballenger et al., 1988). Ethanol, the most frequently used self-medication for anxiety, is a well-known respiratory depressant as well and shows cross-tolerance with most benzodiazepines. Fishman and associates (1994) showed that alprazolam, an antipanic drug, normalized CO_2 sensitivity in panic patients. Alprazolam (Woods et al., 1986) and clonazepam (Beckett, Fishman, & Rosenbaum, 1986) have been shown capable of blocking CO_2-induced panic attacks. Antipanic medications seem to decrease hyperventilation-related complaints in panic patients undergoing second lactate infusions even if there was no panic response during the first lactate infusion (Gorman et al., 1987).

Investigators have just begun to decipher the complexities of the serotonin (5HT) system in the brain. (See Chapter 7 for review.) If $5HT_{1A}$ receptor agonists indeed increase respiratory rate in humans as reported (Edwards, Whitaker-Azmitia, & Harkins, 1990), the lack of antipanic efficacy of buspirone, a $5HT_{1A}$ agonist (Sheehan, Raj, Sheehan, & Soto, 1990), is consonant with its respiratory stimulant effect. On the other hand, clomipramine, a tricyclic antidepressant with prominent serotonergic effects and documented antipanic efficacy (McTavish & Benfield, 1990), normalized the CO_2 sensitivity of panic patients in one experiment (Lousberg, Griez, Pols, & Zandbergen, N. D.) and improved hyperventilation syndrome in another (Hoes, 1983).

There is only very preliminary data regarding the respiratory effects of the commonly used predominantly noradrenergic antipanic medications (e.g., imipramine, desipramine). While its specific effect on CO_2 sensitivity has not been assessed, imipramine blocks CO_2-induced panic attacks in panic patients (Woods, Charney, Delgado, & Heninger, 1990), while in a sample of chronic obstructive pulmonary disease (COPD) patients desipramine did not affect respiration (Gordon, Michiels, Mahutte, & Light, 1985).

Repeated administration of panic-inducing agents may desensitize the respiratory control mechanism. Repeated CO_2 inhalation (van den Hout, van der Molen, Griez, Lousberg, & Nansen, 1987) leads to reduced, but not normalized, anxiogenic response among panic patients. Similar effect was found with repeated lactate infusions (Bonn, Harison, & Rees, 1973) and caffeine ingestion (Uhde, 1990). We speculate that the hypersensitive central chemoreceptors may become partially down-regulated after repeated stimulation by powerful panicogenic agents.

CONCLUSION

The data reviewed here show that panic disorder patients are not, by and large, chronic hyperventilators. Hyperventilation does not usually lead to panic attacks. Chronic hyperventilation is neither necessary nor sufficient in the development of panic disorder. The so-called hyperventilation syndrome and panic disorder are not the same condition.

Nevertheless, panic patients acutely hyperventilate during naturally occurring and laboratory-provoked panic, including lactate, bicarbonate, and isoproteronol infusions. Panic disorder patients panic to CO_2 inhalation and may have biologically based CO_2 hypersensitivity. Finally, preliminary evidence suggests that antipanic medications and repeated panicogenic challenges desensitize the hypersensitive respiratory control mechanism in panic disorder.

The presence of hypersensitive brainstem CO_2 receptors may represent one of the manifestations of a genetically mediated brain stem autonomic nervous system dysregulation in panic disorder. Inherited CO_2 hypersensitivity would support previous work suggesting a strong genetic basis to panic disorder (Burrows, Judd, & Hopper, 1989; Torgersen, 1983; Weissman, 1989). (See Chapter 3 for review.) It seems, however, that it is the tendency to have panic attacks, rather than the complete diagnostic category of panic disorder, that shows high familial pattern (Torgersen, 1983). Therefore, genetic studies looking for a chromosomal marker for panic disorder may be compromised if only the clinical picture of panic disorder is used to distinguish affected from unaffected family members of panic patients. Abnormal response to a biologic challenge test such as CO_2 inhalation may be a phenotype more useful in categorizing family members.

Our current model proposes that panic patients may have hypersensitive CO_2 chemoreceptors in the brain. Increasing the inhaled CO_2 concentration triggers these hypersensitive receptors, causing an inappropriately prolonged phase of hyperventilation even after the stimulus is stopped. Numerous other panicogens also stimulate respiration, although the precise mechanism of this effect has not been elucidated yet. According to one theory, this mechanism may be one of several to trigger a "false suffocation alarm" and induce a panic attack.

Future studies in the area should correlate the efficacy of antipanic treatment modalities with the specific effects of these treatments on ventilatory control; monitor respiratory parameters during panic-inducing laboratory procedures and compare these with the results of ambulatory monitoring of respiration; and involve the family members of panic disorder patients as well as other relevant diagnostic groups in respiratory studies.

REFERENCES

Aronson, T. A., Carasiti, I., McBane, D., & Whitaker-Azmitia, P. (1989). Biological correlates of lactate sensitivity in panic disorder. *Biological Psychiatry, 26*(5), 463–477.

Bailey, P. L., Andriano, K. P., Goldman, M., Stanley, T. H., & Pace, N. L. (1986). Variability of the respiratory response to diazepam. *Anesthesiology, 64*(4), 460–465.

Ballenger, J. C., Burrows, G. D., DuPont, R., Lesser, I. M., Noyes, R., Pecknold, J. C., Rifkin, A., & Swinson, R. P. (1988). Alprazolam in panic disorder and agoraphobia: results from a multicenter trial I: Efficacy in short-term treatment. *Archives of General Psychiatry, 45*, 413–422.

Balon, R., Yeragani, V. K., & Pohl, R. (1988). Relative hypophosphatemia in patients with panic disorder [letter]. *Archives of General Psychiatry, 45*, 294–295.

Bass, C., Lelliot, P., Marks, I. (1989). Fear talk versus voluntary hyperventilation in agoraphobics and normals: A controlled study. *Psychological Medicine, 19*(3), 669–676.

Beckett, A., Fishman S. M., & Rosenbaum, J. F. (1986). Clonazepam blockade of spontaneous and CO_2 inhalation-provoked panic in a patient with panic disorder. *Journal of Clinical Psychiatry, 47,* 475–476.

Berger, A. J., Mitchell, R. A., & Severinghause, J. W. (1977). Regulation of respiration. *New England Journal of Medicine, 297*(2), 292–297; *297*(3), 138–143; *297*(4), 194–201.

Berkenbosch, A., Bovill, J. G., Dahan, J., DeGoede, J., & Olievier, L. C. W. (1989). The ventilatory CO_2 sensitivities from Read's rebreathing method and the steady-state method are not equal in man. *Journal of Physiology, 411,* 367–377.

Bonn, J. A., Harison, J., & Rees, L. (1973). Lactate infusion in the treatment of "free-floating" anxiety. *Canadian Psychiatric Association Journal, 18,* 41–45.

Bourke, D. L., & Warley, A. (1986). The steady-state and rebreathing methods compared during morphine administration in humans. *Journal of Physiology* (London), *411,* 437–455.

Burrows, G. D., Judd, F. K., & Hopper, J. L. (1989). The biology of panic-genetic evidence. *International Journal of Clinical Pharmacology Research, 9*(2), 147–149.

Carr D. B., Fishman, S. M., Systrom, D., Beckett, A., Sheehan, D. V., & Rosenbaum, J. F. (1987, May). *Carbon dioxide in panic disorder and premenstrually normals.* Paper presented at the 140th annual meeting of the American Psychiatric Association, Chicago.

Clergue, F., Desmonts, P., Duvaldestin, P., Delevault, E., & Saumon, G. (1981). Depression of respiratory drive by diazepam as premedication. *British Journal of Anaesthesiology, 53,* 1059–1063.

Cohen, M. E., & White, P. D. (1951). Life situations, emotions and neurocirculatory asthenia. *Psychosomatic Medicine, 13,* 335–357.

Compernolle, T., Hoogduin, K., & Joele, L. (1979). Diagnosis and treatment of the hyperventilation syndrome. *Psychosomatics, 20,* 612–625.

Cowley, D. S., & Roy-Byrne, P. P. (1987). Hyperventilation and panic disorder. *American Journal of Medicine, 83*(5), 929–937.

Den Boer, J. A., Westenberg, H. G., Klompmakers, A. A., & van Lint, L. E. (1989). Behavioral, biochemical and neuroendocrine concomitants of lactate-induced panic anxiety. *Biological Psychiatry 26*(6), 612–622.

Dillon, D. J., Gorman, J. M., Liebowitz, M. R., Fyer, A. J., & Klein, D. F. (1987). The measurement of lactate induced panic and anxiety. *Psychiatry Research, 20,* 97–105.

D'Urzo, A. D., Jhirad, R., Jenne, H., Avendano, M. A., Rubenstein, I., D'Costa, M., & Goldstein, R. S. (1990). Effect of caffeine on ventilatory responses to hypercapnia, hypoxia, and exercise in humans. *Journal of Applied Physiology,, 68*(1), 322–328.

Edwards, E., Whitaker-Azmitia, P. M., & Harkins, K. (1990). 5-HT$_{1A}$ and 5-HT$_{1B}$ agonists play a differential role in the respiratory frequency in rats. *Neuropsychopharmacology, 3,* 129–136.

Errington, M. L., & Dashwood, M. R. (1979). Projections to the ventral surface of the cat brainstem demonstrated by horseradish peroxidase. *Neuroscience Letters, 12,* 153–158.

Fishman, S. M., Carr, D. B., Beckett, A., & Rosenbaum, J. F. (1994). Hypercaneic ventilatory response in patients with panic disorder before and after alprazolam treatment and in pre- and postmenstrual women. *Journal of Psychiatric Research, 28*(2), 165–170.

Fyer, M. R., Uy, J., Martinez, J., Goetz, R., Klein, D. F., Fyer, A., Liebowitz, M. R., & Gorman, J. (1987). Carbon dioxide challenge of patients with panic disorder. *American Journal of Psychiatry, 144*(8), 1080–1082.

Gaffney, F. A., Fenton, B. J., Lane, L. D., & Lake, C. R. (1988). Hemodynamic, ventilatory and biochemical responses of panic patients and normal controls with sodium lactate infusion and spontaneous panic attacks. *Archives of General Psychiatry, 45,* 53–61.

Gennari, F. J., Goldstein, M. B., & Schwartz, W. B. (1972). The nature of renal adaptation to chronic hypocapnia. *Journal of Clinical Investigations, 51,* 1722–1730.

Gledhill, N., Beirne, G. J., & Dempsey, J. A. (1975). Renal response to hypocapnia in man. *Kidney International, 8,* 376–386.

Goetz, R. R., Gully, R., Dillon, D. J., Kahn, J., Liebowitz, M. R., Fyer, A. J., Klein, D. F., & Gorman, J. M. (1993). Panic attacks during laboratory placebo procedures; Physiology and symptomatology. *Archives of General Psychiatry, 50,* 280–285.

Gordon, G. H., Michiels, T. M., Mahutte, C. K., & Light, R. W. (1985). Effect of desipramine on control of ventilation and depression scores in patients with severe chronic obstructive pulmonary disease. *Psychiatry Research, 15,* 25–32.

Gorman, J. M., Askanazi, J., Liebowitz, M. R., Fyer, A. J., Stein, J., Kinney, J., & Klein, D. F. (1984). Response to hyperventilation in a group of patients with panic disorder. *American Journal of Psychiatry, 141*(7), 857–861.

Gorman, J. M., Battista, D., Goetz, R. R., Dillon, D. J., Liebowitz, M. R., Fyer, A. J., Kahn, J. P., Sandberg, D., & Klein, D. F. (1989). A comparison of sodium bicarbonate and sodium lactate infusion in the induction of panic attacks. *Archives of General Psychiatry, 46,* 145–150.

Gorman, J. M., Cohen, B. S., Liebowitz, M. R., Fyer, A. J., Ross, D., Davies, S. O., & Klein, D. F. 1986a). Blood gas changes and hypophosphatemia in lactate-induced panic. *Archives of General Psychiatry, 43,* 1067–1071.

Gorman, J. M., Fyer, M. R., Goetz, R., Askinazi, J., Liebowitz, M. R., Fyer, A. J., Kenny, J., & Klein, D. F. (1988). Ventilatory physiology of patients with panic disorder. *Archives of General Psychiatry, 45,* 31–39.

Gorman, J. M., Fyer, A. J., Ross, D. C., Cohen, B. S., Martinez, J., Liebowitz, M. R., & Klein, D. F. (1985). Normalization of venous pH, pCO_2 and HCO_3 levels after blockade of panic attacks. *Psychiatry Research, 14,* 57–65.

Gorman, J. M., Goetz, R. R., Dillon, D., Liebowitz, M. R., Fyer, A. J., Davies, S., & Klein, D. F. (1990). Sodium D-Lactate infusion of panic disorder patients. *Neuropsychopharmacology, 3*(3), 181–189.

Gorman, J. M., Liebowitz, M. R., Dillon, D., Fyer, A. J., Cohen, B. S., & Klein, D. F. (1987). Anti-panic drug effects during lactate infusion in lactate refractory panic patients. *Psychiatry Research, 21*(3), 205–212.

Gorman, J. M., Liebowitz, M. R., Fyer, A. J., Fyer, M. R., & Klein, D. F. (1986b). Possible respiratory abnormalities in panic disorder. *Psychopharmacology Bulletin, 22,* 797–801.

Gorman, J. M., Liebowitz, M. R., Fyer, A. J., & Stein, J. (1989). A neuroanatomical hypothesis for panic disorder. *American Journal of Psychiatry, 146,* 148–161.

Gorman, J. M., Papp, L. A., Coplan, J. D., Klein, D. F., Martinez, J., Lennon, S., Goetz, R. R., & Ross, D. (1994). Anxiogenic effects of CO_2 with panic disorder and hyperventilation in panic patients. *American Journal of Psychiatry, 151,* 547–553.

Gorman, J. M., Papp, L. A., Coplan, J., Martinez, J., Liebowitz, M. R., & Klein, D. F. (1993). The effect of acetazolamide on ventilation in panic disorder patients. *American Journal of Psychiatry, 150,* 1480–1484.

Gorman, J. M., Papp, L. A., Goetz, R., Martinez, J., Hollander, E., & Jordan, F. (1990b). High dose carbon dioxide challenge test in anxiety disorder patients. *Biological Psychiatry, 28,* 743–757.

Griez, E., Lousberg, H., van den Hout, M. A., & van der Molen, M. (1987). CO_2 vulnerability in panic disorder. *Psychiatry Research, 20,* 490–497.

Griez, E., & van den Hout, M. A. (1984). *Carbon dioxide and anxiety: An experimental approach to a clinical claim.* Unpublished doctoral dissertation, Rijksuniversiteit te Maastricht, The Netherlands.

Griez, E., Zandbergen, J., Lousberg, H., & van den Hout, M. (1988). Effects of low pulmonary CO_2 on panic anxiety. *Comprehensive Psychiatry, 29*(5), 490–497.

Griez, E., Zandbergen, J., Pols, H., & de Loof, C. (1990). Response to 35% CO_2 as a marker of panic in severe anxiety. *American Journal of Psychiatry, 145,* 795–796.

Grossman, P. (1983). Respiration, stress and cardiovascular function. *Psychophysiology, 20*(3), 284–300.

Hauge, A., Thoresen, M., & Walloe, L. (1980). Changes in cerebral blood flow during hyperventilation and CO_2 rebreathing in humans by a bidirectional, pulsed ultrasound doppler blood velocity meter. *Acta Psychiatrica Scandanavia, 110,* 167–173.

Hauge, A., Nicolaysen, G., & Thoresen, M. (1983). Acute effects of acetazolamide on cerebral blood flow in man. *Acta Psychiatrica Scandanavia, 117,* 233–239.

Hibbert, G., & Pilsbury, D. (1989). Hyperventilation: Is it a cause of panic attacks? *British Journal of Psychiatry, 155,* 805–809.

Hibbert, G. A., & Chan, M. (1989). Respiratory control: Its contribution to the treatment of panic attacks. *British Journal of Psychiatry, 154,* 232–236.

Hoes, J. J. (1983). Pharmacotherapy of the hyperventilation syndrome. *Annals of Medical Psychology, 141*(8), 859–874.

Holt, P. E., & Andrews, G. (1989). Hyperventilation and anxiety in panic disorder, social phobia, GAD and normal controls. *Behaviour Research and Therapy, 27*(4) 453–460.

Javaheris, S., Shore, N. J., Rose, B., & Kazemi, H. (1982). Compensatory hypo-ventilation in metabolic alkalosis. *Chest, 81,* 296–301.

Kennealy, J. A., McLennan, J. E., London, R. G., & McLaurin, R. L. (1980). Hyperventilation-induced cerebral hypoxia. *American Review of Respiratory Diseases, 122,* 407–411.

Kerr, W. J., Dalton, J. W., & Gliebe, P. A. (1937). Some physical phenomena associated with the anxiety states and their relation to hyperventilation. *Annals of Internal of Medicine, 11,* 961–992.

Kinney, J. M., Morgan, A. P., & Domingues, F. J. (1964). A method for continuous measurement of gas exchange and expired radioactivity in acutely ill patients. *Metabolism, 13,* 205–211.

Klein, D. F. (1993). False suffocation alarms spontaneous panics and related conditions: On integrative hypothesis. *Archives of General Psychiatry, 50,* 306–317.

Klein, D. F., Papp, L. A., & Gorman, J. M. (1990). Acetazolamide as a control for CO_2 induced panic [letter]. *American Journal of Psychiatry, 147,*675–676.

Loevenhart, A. S., Lorenz, W. F., & Waters, R. (1929). Cerebral stimulations. *Journal of the American Medical Association, 11,* 880–883.

Lousberg, H., Griez, E., & van den Hout, M. A. (1988). Carbon dioxide chemosensitivity in panic disorder. *Acta Psychiatrica Scandanavia, 77,* 214–218.

Lousberg, H. H. A., Griez, E. J. L., Pols, H., & Zandbergen, J. (N. D.) *Effect of clomipramine on carbon dioxide chemoreactivity in panic disorder patients.* Unpublished manuscript.

Lum, L. C. (1976). The syndrome of habitual chronic hyperventilation. In O. W. Hill (Ed.), *Modern trends in psychosomatic medicine*, (Vol. 3. pp. 1–4). London: Buttersworths.

Lum, L. C. (1981). Hyperventilation and anxiety state. *Journal of the Royal Society of Medicine, 74*, 1–4.

Maddock, R. J., & Mateo-Bermudez, J. (1990). Elevated serum lactate following hyperventilation during glucose infusion in panic disorder. *Biological Psychiatry, 27*, 411–418.

Mathew, R. J. (1990). Acetazolamide as a control for CO_2 induced panic. (Response to Klein et al.) *American Journal of Psychiatry, 147*, 676.

Mathew, R. J., Wilson, H. W., & Tant, S. (1989). Responses to hypercarbia induced by acetazolamide in panic disorder patients. *American Journal of Psychiatry, 146*, 996–1000.

McTavish, D., & Benfield, P. (1990). Clomipramine. An overview of its pharmacological properties and a review of its therapeutic use in obsessive-compulsive disorder and panic disorder. *Drugs, 39*, 136–153.

Meduna, L. J. (1950). *Carbon dioxide therapy: A neurophysiological treatment of nervous disorders,* Springfield, IL: Charles C. Thomas.

Milic-Emili, J., Grunstein, M. M. (1976). Drive and timing components of ventilation. *Chest, 70*(Suppl. 1), 131–133.

Missri, J. C., & Alexander, S. (1978). Hyperventilation syndrome. *Journal of the American Medical Association, 240*(19), 2093–2096.

Mostellar, M. E., & Tuttle, E. P. (1964). Effects of alkalosis on plasma concentration and urinary excretion of inorganic phosphate in man. *Journal of Clinical Investigation, 13*, 138–234.

Pain, M. C. F., Biddle, N., & Tiller, J. W. G. (1988). Panic disorder, ventilatory response to carbon dioxide's respiratory variables. *Psychosomatic Medicine, 50*, 541–548.

Papp, L. A., & Gorman, J. M. (1990a). Urine pH in panic: A possible screening device. *Lancet, 335*, 355.

Papp, L. A., Gorman, J. M. (1990b, December). *Respiratory neurobiology of panic.* Paper presented at the annual meeting of the American College of Neuropsychopharmacology, San Juan, P.R.

Papp, L. A., Goetz, R., Cole, R., Liebowitz, M. R., Fyer, A. J., Klein, D. F., Jordan, F., & Gorman, J. M. (1989b). Hypersensitivity to carbon dioxide in panic disorder. *American Journal of Psychiatry, 146*, 779–781.

Papp, L. A., Gorman, J. M., Goetz, R., Liebowitz, M., Fyer, A. J., & Klein, D. F. (1988b, May). *Carbon dioxide sensitivity in panic disorder.* Paper presented at the 141st annual meeting of the American Psychiatric Association. Montreal, Canada.

Papp, L. A., Gorman, J. M., Liebowitz, M. R., Fyer, A. J., Cohen, B., & Klein, D. F. (1988a). Epinephrine infusions in patients with social phobia. *American Journal of Psychiatry, 145*, 733–736.

Papp, L. A., Martinez, J. M., Coplan, J., & Gorman, J. M. (in press). Rebreathing tests in panic disorder. *Biological Psychiatry*

Papp, L. A., Martinez, J. M., Klein, D. F., Liebowitz, M. R., Fyer, A. J., Hollander, E., & Gorman, J. M. (1989a). Arterial blood gas changes in panic disorder and lactate-induced panic. *Psychiatry Research, 28,* 171–180.

Plum, F., Posner, J. B., & Smith, W. W. (1968). Effect of hyperbaric-hypoxic hyperventilation on blood, brain and CSF lactate. *American Journal of Physiology, 15*(5), 1240–1244.

Rapee, R. (1986). Differential response to hyperventilation in panic disorder and generalized anxiety disorder. *Journal of Abnormal Psychology, 95*(1), 24–28.

Rapee, R., Mattick, R., & Murrell, E. (1986). Cognitive mediation in the affective component of spontaneous panic attack. *Journal of Behavior Therapy and Experimental Psychiatry, 17*(4), 245–253.

Rainey, J. M., Yeragani, V., & Pohl, R. (1986, May). *The relationship of minute ventilation to oxygen consumption during lactate and isoproterenol induced panic anxiety.* Paper presented at the meeting of the Society of Biological Psychiatry. Washington, DC.

Read, D. J. C. (1967). A clinical method for assessing the ventilatory response to carbon dioxide. *Australian Annals of Medicine, 16,* 20.

Rebuck, A. S., & Slutsky, A. S. (1981). Measurement of ventilation responses in hypercapnia and hypoxia. In T. F. Hornbein (Ed.), *Regulation of breathing,* part 2. New York: Marcel Dekker.

Reiman, E. M., Raichle, M. E., Robins, E., Butler, F. K., Herscovitch, P., Fox, P., & Perlmutter, J. (1986). The application of positron emission tomography to the study of panic disorder. *American Journal of Psychiatry, 143,* 469–477.

Reiman, E. M., Raichle, M. E., Robins, E., Mintun, M. A., Fusselman, M. J., Fox, P. T., Price, J. L., & Hackman, K. A. (1989). Neuroanatomical correlates of lactate-induced anxiety attack. *Archives of General Psychiatry, 46,* 493–500.

Ruiter, C. de, Garssen, B., Rijken, H., & Kraaimaat, F. (1989). The hyperventilation syndrome in panic disorder, agoraphobia, and generalized anxiety disorder. *Behaviour Research and Therapy, 27*(4), 447–452.

Salzman, H. A., Heyman, A., & Sicker, H. J. (1963). Correlation of clinical and physiological manifestations of sustained hyperventilation. *New England Journal of Medicine, 286,* 1431–1436.

Sanderson, W. C., & Wetzler, S. (1990). Five percent carbon dioxide challenge: Valid analogue and marker of panic disorder? *Biological Psychiatry, 27,* 689–701.

Sheehan, D. V., Raj, A. B., Sheehan, K. H., & Soto, S. (1990). Is buspirone affective for panic disorder? *Journal of Clinical Psychopharmacology, 10*(1), 3–11.

Stewart, R. S., Devous, M. D., Rush, A. J., Lane, L., & Bonte, F. J. (1988). Cerebral blood flow changes during sodium-lactate-induced panic attacks. *American Journal of Psychiatry, 145,* 442–449.

Torgersen, S. (1983). Genetic factors in anxiety disorders. *Archives of General Psychiatry, 40*(10), 1085–1089.

Uhde, T. W., (1990). Caffeine provocation of panic: A focus on biological mechanisms. In J. C. Ballenger (Ed.), *Neurobiology of panic disorder* (p. 226). New York: Alan R. Liss.

van den Hout, M. A., van der Molen, G. M., Griez, E., Lousberg, H., & Nansen, A. (1987). Reduction of CO_2-induced anxiety in patients with panic attacks after repeated CO_2 exposure. *American Journal of Psychiatry, 144,* 788–791.

Weissman, M. M. (1989). The eqidemiology of anxiety disorders: Rates, risks and familial patterns. *Journal of Psychiatric Research, 22*(1), 99–114.

Wolpe, J. (1973). *The practice of behavior therapy,* 2nd ed. New York: Pergamon Press.

Woods, S. W., Charney, D. S., Delgado, P. L., & Heninger, G. R. (1990). The effect of long-term imipramine treatment on carbon dioxide-induced anxiety in panic disorder patients. *Journal of Clinical Psychiatry, 51,* 505–507.

Woods, S. W., Charney, D. S., Lake, J., Goodman, W. K., Redmond, D. E., & Heninger, D. R. (1986). Carbon dioxide sensitivity in panic anxiety: Ventilatory and anxiogenic response to carbon dioxide in healthy subjects and panic anxiety patients before and after alprazolam treatment. *Archives of General Psychiatry, 43,* 900–909.

Zandbergen, J., Lousberg, H., Pols, H., deLoof, C., & Griez, E. (1990). Hypercarbia versus hypocarbia in panic disorder. *Journal of Affective Disorders, 18,* 75–81.

PART III
Treatments of
Panic Disorder

12

Somatic Treatment Strategies in Panic Disorder

B. ASHOK RAJ AND
DAVID V. SHEEHAN

In the United States, by the end of World War II, psychoanalytic psychotherapy had become the standard treatment for anxiety states. Biological treatments introduced into psychiatry by that time, such as insulin coma, electroshock therapy, and lobotomy, were ineffective in managing the severe anxiety disorders. Bromides, chloral hydrate, and paraldehyde had been in use since the mid-1800s. Barbiturate, with its anticonvulsant, sedative, and hypnotic properties, was synthesized in 1903. Pharmacotherapy of anxiety centered around these highly sedating drugs until the introduction of meprobamate in the 1950s. The benzodiazepine era began when chlordiazepoxide was introduced in 1960, and it continues to some degree to this day. A new dimension was added to the pharmacotherapy of anxiety disorders when Klein (1964) observed that imipramine, introduced in 1957 for the treatment of depression, blocked "spontaneous panic attacks."

Panic disorder, with or without agoraphobia, is a severe anxiety state that is characterized by panic attacks, anticipatory anxiety, phobic avoidance behavior, somatization-hypochondriasis, obsessional features, and depression. This complex disorder with its multiple dimensions is very responsive to pharmacotherapy. In this chapter we examine the clinical characteristics, differential effects, and issues concerning the four classes of antipanic drugs available to us at this time. These four classes are: the benzodiazepines, cyclic antidepressants, selective serotonin uptake inhibitors, and monoamine oxidase inhibitors.

BENZODIAZEPINES

Historically, benzodiazepines were considered ineffective in treating panic disorder. This perception changed when Sheehan, Uzogara, and Coleman (1982) and Chouinard, Annable, Fontaine, and Solyom (1982) reported that alprazolam, a triazolobenzodiazepine, was effective in panic disorder. Since that observation, several other benzodiazepines have been shown to be effective antipanic drugs. Studies documenting antipanic efficacy have been reported for diazepam by Noyes and associates (1984) and Dunner, Ishiki, Avery, Wilson, and Hyde (1986), for clonazepam by Beaudry, Fontaine, Chouinard, and Annable (1985), Svebak, Camron, and Levande (1990), and Tesar and coworkers (1991); and for lorazepam by Charney and Woods (1989), Schweizer, Fox, and Case (1987), Howell, Laraia, and Ballenger (1987), and Rickels and Schweizer (1986). A report by Schweizer and Rickels (1988) and a study by Rickels, Fox, Greenblatt, Sandler, and Schless (1988) found that clorazepate also has antipanic properties.

Antipanic properties have been reported for bromazepam by Beaudry, Fontaine, and Chouinard (1984); for the standard formulation of adinazolam by Pyke and Greenberg (1989); and for the sustained release formulation of adinazolam by Sheehan, Raj, and Sheehan (1990). These benzodiazepines are not currently available in the United States.

The number of available and effective drugs presents the clinician with a pleasant problem: Which drug to use?

Choice of Benzodiazepine

A conservative approach would dictate that alprazolam be the initial choice in most cases, since it has been extensively studied, found consistently effective, has low toxicity, and is the only drug approved by the Food and Drug Administration for panic disorder. A more complex approach will consider differential clinical effects of the various benzodiazepines, their pharmacokinetic and pharmacodynamic characteristics, concomitant medications, and patient characteristics, such as age and medical status.

The most frequently prescribed benzodiazepines for panic disorder are alprazolam and clonazepam. In a double-blind, placebo-controlled study by Tesar and associates (1991), both drugs were found equally effective. Patients who suffer from frequent acute panic attacks prefer benzodiazepines that are rapidly absorbed. Alprazolam, clonazepam, diazepam, and clorazepate are rapidly absorbed, while lorazepam is intermediate. Rapid onset of action is not always desirable, because it also may be accompanied by rapid onset of side effects.

From a practical standpoint, the most important factors to consider are duration of therapeutic action and rate of elimination. Greenblatt (Greenblatt, Shader, & Abernathy, 1983; Greenblatt et al., 1979) found that duration of action depends more on the volume of distribution than the half-life of the drug. The volume of distribution is dependent on lipophilicity. Abernathy, Greenblatt, Divoll, & Shader (1983) found diazepam to be the most lipophilic, lorazepam the least, and alprazolam intermediate. The more lipophilic the drug, the more rapidly it crosses the blood/brain barrier, and the more likely it is to produce "a buzz" after ingestion. The more lipid soluble the drug, the more rapidly it moves out of the brain and blood into inactive peripheral sites, such as fatty tissue. This is why diazepam, which has a longer half-life than lorazepam, has a shorter duration of action, and alprazolam with a half-life of 12 hours provides relief from anxiety for about four to six hours. Clonazepam has a six- to eight-hour duration of action. Sustained release preparations of clorazepate (Tranxene-SD), diazepam (Valrelease), and adinazolam (Deracyn SR) have durations of action of about 12 hours and may be ideal for some patients. Obesity increases the volume of distribution and elimination half-life of these drugs, but decreases the duration of action.

Benzodiazepines are metabolized in the liver either by oxidation or conjugation. The oxidative system is impaired by aging, hepatic disease, and drugs such as cimetidine, estrogens, and the hydrazine monoamine oxidase inhibitors. In these situations the toxic effects of benzodiazepines are increased. Lorazepam and oxazepam are metabolized by conjugation and may be the drugs of choice in these cases.

Dosage and Schedule

When starting with alprazolam, generally begin with 0.5 milligrams (mg) three times a day, then titrate the dose over time. A schedule as in Table 12–1 may be provided to the patient.

TABLE 12–1
Directions for Taking Benzodiazepines[a]

Breakfast	Lunch	Evening Meal Tablets	Bedtime	Day
½	½	½	0	1–2
1	½	½	0	3–4
1	½	1	0	5–6
1	1	1	0	7–8
1½	1	1	0	9–10
1½	1	1½	0	11–12
1½	1½	1½	0	13–14
2	1½	1½	0	15–16
2	1½	2	0	17–18
2	2	2	0	19–20
2	2	2	1	21–22
2	2	2	2	23–24

Source: D. V. Sheehan, 1985, Department of Psychiatry and Behavioral Medicine, University of South Florida, College of Medicine, Tampa, Florida. Copyright 1985 D. V. Sheehan. Reproduced with permission.
[a]If no side effects (drowsiness) or benefit occurs with medication, increase dose to next level every two days. When coming off the medicine, do not reduce the dose for any reason at a rate faster than ½ a tablet every four days. The above directions are for 1 mg tablets of alprazolam or clonazepam. Doses should be reduced more cautiously in the elderly. There are no food or drug restrictions with benzodiazepines. Use caution when driving and operating high-speed equipment. Avoid alcohol consumption.

If sleep (nocturnal) panic attacks or insomnia are a problem, a bedtime dose should be prescribed. The dosage range is between 4 to 6 mg per day. Some patients will tolerate and need 9 mg, and others may require only 2 mg. The large phase I Cross National Collaborative Study, which evaluated 540 patients with alprazolam vs. placebo in an eight-week trial, found that the mean effective and tolerated dose of alprazolam was approximately 5.5 mg (Ballenger et al., 1988). Although a wide dose range exists for alprazolam in the treatment of panic disorder, higher doses frequently are more effective than lower doses. Lydiard and associates (1992) demonstrated in a fixed-dose, double-blind, placebo-controlled study evaluating alprazolam that although a lower dose, 2 mg, is effective on panic attacks, the high dose, 6 mg, was significantly more effective in panic attack as well as on the other core symptoms of panic disorder—anticipatory anxiety and phobic avoidance. Doses higher than those just recommended seldom produce dramatic additional benefit, and thus, the patient may do better on an antidepressant.

Two kinds of dose adjustment problems may be observed with alprazolam in the early weeks of treatment. First, after an initial good antipanic effect, the patient's anxiety suddenly returns. This apparent loss of effectiveness is due to the phenomenon of tolerance. Instead of switching drugs at this point, the correct response is to recommend an increase in dosage to recapture benefit. Second, in a small number of patients, interdose anxiety may be experienced on alprazolam. This is compensated for by increasing the dose or taking it after a meal. If this fails, clonazepam or sustained-release preparations of clorazepate or diazepam can be used. Despite claims of 24-hour efficacy, it is our experience that usually two doses a day, 12 hours apart, are required for these sustained-release products. The antipanic dosage range for clonazepam is 2 to 6 mg per day. Charney and Woods (1989) found that the antipanic dose of lorazepam is between 4 and 8 mg a day.

Duration of Initial Therapeutic Trial

Benzodiazepines have a rapid onset of action, with significant therapeutic benefits observable as early as the first week of treatment. If properly titrated, maximum effect is seen by four to six weeks of treatment. If benefit is not seen by week 10, then an antipanic drug from a different class is indicated.

Adverse Effects

In general, these medications are well tolerated, with minimal side effects and a wide margin of safety in case of overdose.

Sedation

Sedation is the commonest initial side effect, noted in 4 to 9 percent of patients. Tesar and Rosenbaum (1986) report rates as high as 20 percent for clonazepam. This drowsiness tends to disappear with time or reduction in dosage.

Intoxication

Intoxication is clinically manifested by ataxia and slurred speech. It is dose related and easily managed by dose adjustment.

Amnesia

Amnesia is now noted to occur even with oral dosing. It is anterograde in nature, due to disrupted consolidation and not impairment of memory retrieval. Morris and Estes (1987) have shown amnesia is more likely to occur when alcohol is used along with the benzodiazepine. Larson, Kukull, Buchner, and Reifler (1987) report that the elderly are at risk especially when using anxiolytics with long half-lives. Scharf, Saskin, and Fletcher (1987) have found the highest risk to be with the use of high-potency benzodiazepines.

Psychomotor Impairment

Direct and indirect evidence document the potential of these drugs to cause psychomotor impairment. Oster, Russell, Huse, Adams, and Imbimbo (1987) studied members of a health maintenance organization and found that benzodiazepine users were more likely to receive accident-related health care than nonusers. Skegg, Richards, and Doll (1979) found benzodiazepine users were five times more likely to experience serious motor vehicle accidents than nonusers, and Smiley (1987) observed that behavioral tolerance does not occur with chronic use. Therefore, patients should be warned about avoiding alcohol and being extra careful when performing skilled tasks.

Other Side Effects

Treatment-emergent hostility has been noted in 10 percent of patients by Rosenbaum, Woods, Groves, and Klerman (1984). Increased independence and assertiveness are often positive effects associated with successful treatment and should not be interpreted as undesirable drug-induced hostility. Sexual side effects such as loss of libido, ejaculatory inhibition, erection failure, and inhibition of female orgasm have been reported but are infrequent. Unusual side effects such as reversible hepatitis and mania have been noted in the literature. Even with adequate control of panic, depression may emerge during the course of treatment. If depression persists even after drug reduction, it can be managed by adding an antidepressant. For alprazolam, rates of depression as low as 2.7 percent have been reported by Tesar and coworkers (1991) and as high as 33 percent by Lydiard, Laraia, Ballenger, and Howell (1987).

Issues in Benzodiazepine Therapy

Prior to initiating or renewing a prescription for benzodiazepines, patients should be assessed for risk of abusing this class of drug. They should be informed of the potential for dependence and cautioned never to discontinue the medication abruptly.

Abuse

Despite popular perception of widespread benzodiazepine abuse, this is not supported by the literature. Ladewig and Grossenbacher (1988), in a study of patients in Basle, found the prevalence of benzodiazepine abuse to be one in 10,000. In a prospective study of 71 patients with major depression or anxiety disorder treated with benzodiazepines, Garvey and Tollefson (1986) did not find any cases of abuse; about 7 percent misused their medication, and all had a diagnosis of depression. In a study of 5426 randomly sampled physicians from the American Medical Association physician data base, Sheehan, Hughes, and Storr (1991) found that while 11.9 percent of physicians have used benzodiazepines during the past year, only 0.6 percent of those users met criteria of the third revised edition of the *Diagnostic and Statistical Manual of Mental Disorders* (DSM-III-R) for benzodiazepine abuse, and 0.5 percent of the users met criteria for benzodiazepine dependence during the past year.

Patients will often increase the dose of medication over time, but the increases usually are small and should not be misinterpreted as abuse. This behavior most often is the consequence of subtherapeutic doses of drug being prescribed and not patient craving. Svenson, Persson, and Sjoberg (1980) report that normal and low-anxiety subjects find these drugs dysphoric, and Johanson and Uhlenhuth (1980) found they may actually prefer placebo to diazepam. Studies of populations that abuse alcohol and other drugs suggest that they are at higher risk. Busto, Simpkins, Sellers, Sisson, and Segal (1983) found 17 percent of alcoholics abused benzodiazepines, and in polydrug abusers, Busto and coworkers (1986) report abuse by 33 percent. In a study of admissions to an alcohol treatment unit, Ashley and associates (1978) identified 35 percent as users of benzodiazepine, but only 10 percent were considered abusers. Perera, Tulley, and Jenner (1987) observed that self-treatment of withdrawal symptoms and potentiation of street drug effects were the principal reasons for benzodiazepine use by drug addicts. This suggests that the clinician should screen for present or past alcohol or drug abuse prior to starting treatment. A positive history of substance abuse is not an absolute contraindication for therapy with benzodiazepines, provided great caution is exercised with this population. Rothstein, Cobble, and Sampson (1976), in a study of 108 alcoholics whose anxiety was treated for a year with benzodiazepines, observed that 94 percent felt that it helped them function and remain out of hospital, while abuse was noted for 5 percent.

Dependence

The consequence of dependence is the emergence of withdrawal symptoms on discontinuation. The longer the use of benzodiazepines, the greater the likelihood of physical dependence, although this phenomenon has been noted after only one week of treatment by Kales and associates (1986). As dependence often is confused with addiction, it is important to inform and discuss the consequences of long-term use with patients and educate them never to discontinue these drugs abruptly.

Discontinuation

All benzodiazepines have anticonvulsant properties. Therefore, abrupt termination or rapid taper can lead to severe withdrawal symptoms, including seizures. In addition, during the discontinuation phase, patients may experience "rebound anxiety" (anxiety symptoms even worse than prior to treatment) usually peaking within the first week of discontinuation. Relapse (recurrence of symptoms that patients had at baseline) also can occur during this phase with rates higher than 50 percent (Versiani, Costa, Silva, & Klerman, 1987). A slow taper can minimize these withdrawal symptoms and help decipher rebound anxiety from relapse. To minimize the discomfort of withdrawal, we now taper our patients no faster than a half tablet every one to two weeks.

CYCLIC ANTIDEPRESSANTS

Klein (1964) used imipramine successfully to treat a number of anxious patients with spontaneous panic attacks. Since then at least 15 controlled studies have been reported supporting this observation. At this time, the consensus is that this class of drug exerts its antipanic action even in the absence of comorbid depression.

Choice of Drug

Imipramine is the most widely studied of this class. It is available in generic form, making it very affordable. Clinical experience suggests that most cyclic antidepressants provide long-term antipanic effects, except perhaps amoxapine. Liebowitz and coworkers (1984), Lydiard (1987), and Kalus, Asnis, van Praag, and Friedman Harkavy (1991) have found desipramine to be effective in panic disorder. Given the large number of medications in this class with comparable efficacy, choice of drug should be based on side effects profile and whether it is predominantly noradrenergic or serotonergic. Patients with panic disorder are sensitive to the activating and anticholinergic effects of these drugs. Imipramine and desipramine are the least anticholinergic and most noradrenergic; amitriptyline is the most anticholinergic and serotonergic, with doxepin in between these extremes. It makes sense to begin with a drug from the end of the spectrum that is least anticholinergic and, if this is ineffective, moving to one farther up.

Dosing Schedule and Duration of Initial Trial

Rapid increase in dose during the early part of treatment does not shorten the time required for a clinical response. It may cause intolerable activation and side effects, leading to premature discontinuation and future phobic responses to medication. To avoid this we suggest starting with 25 mg of the tricyclic at bedtime, increasing by 25 mg every third day. Therapeutic dosage is usually at the point when the patient begins to experience side effects. The range is from 150 mg to 300 mg for these drugs, except nortriptyline, which should be adjusted to stay within its therapeutic window—a plasma level of 50 to 140 nanograms per milliliter (ng/ml). Compliance is better if the patient is told prior to starting therapy that side effects occur early and that it may take several weeks before therapeutic benefit is experienced. Plateaus of tolerance may occur during the initial weeks of treatment, indicated by loss of benefit and side effects. Increasing the dosage at that point will restore benefit. Some patients will show no benefit and no side effects even after four weeks at 300 mg. Prior to initiating higher doses, it is prudent to advise patients that further increases are beyond those recommended, to get an electrocardiogram to ensure that there is no preexisting atrioventricular block, and perhaps to get a blood level. Blood pressure, sitting and standing, should be taken at each visit to rule out postural hypotension.

The advantage of a single dose at bedtime is that it encourages compliance, and the patient is less disrupted subjectively when panic attacks occur during the hours of sleep. The dangers include an increased risk for a fall if the person gets up to go to the toilet at night, and peak blood levels increase the risk for cardiac arrhythmias or seizures. We recommend giving a third of the total dosage as a daytime dose and the rest at bedtime. The initial trial should be at least eight to 10 weeks at therapeutic dosage; some may take as long as 12 weeks to respond.

Blood Levels

The usefulness of blood level monitoring of tricyclic antidepressants in the treatment of panic disorder has been studied only minimally in contrast to that for major depression. Those few studies in panic disorder have focused on imipramine, suggesting that a minimal serum imipramine/desipramine level (main metabolite of imipramine) of 150 ng/ml appears to be a threshold level for response (Ballenger et al., 1984; Mavissakalian, 1990). In addition, although lower doses and blood levels were effective for panic attacks, higher doses and levels were necessary to treat phobic avoidance (Mavissakalian, 1990).

Adverse Effects

Richelson (1983) has shown that cyclic antidepressants have varying receptor affinity profiles, and their side effects can be related to these affinities.

Anticholingeric Effects

Dry mouth and constipation are almost universal with these drugs. In patients who exhibit loose bowels or frequency due to anxiety, this may be a desirable side effect. Impaction, obstruction, and paralytic ileus are rare. Urinary hesitancy occurs, sometimes to the point of retention. Blurred vision or inability to focus on fine print may be a problem.

Nonadrenergic Effects

Nonadrenergic effects include tremor, jitteriness, and tachycardia. Pulse rate can go up by as much as 15 beats per minute. Orthostatic hypotension occurs in 5 to 24 percent; it is an early side effect. Roose and Glassman (1989) observed that tolerance does not usually develop during the first six weeks of treatment.

Antihistaminic Effects

Sedation is common in the initial weeks, and weight gain may be a major problem during long-term therapy.

Other Side Effects

A variety of sexual problems, including erectile impotence and inhibited or delayed ejaculation, have been reported. Treatment may increase the intraocular pressure in those patients with narrow angle glaucoma potentially resulting in loss of visual acuity.

Issues in Antidepressant Therapy

It must be recognized that tricyclic antidepressants may have toxic effects on the cardiovascular and central nervous systems and be potentially lethal in the event of an overdose.

Central Nervous System Toxicity

These compounds have the potential to induce delirium or seizures. Delirium occurs in less than 5 percent of cases and is more likely to occur at higher doses, in the elderly, and with polypharmacy. Seizures occur at a frequency of 0.4 to 0.8 percent and are more likely in the presence of predisposing factors, such as a history of head injury, previous seizures, or central nervous system disease.

Cardiovascular System Toxicity

The cyclic agents are markedly cardiotoxic in an overdose, but relatively benign in physically healthy individuals. In the presence of preexisting cardiac disease, they present varying degrees of risk. They tend to slow conduction, causing patients with bundle branch block to be at risk of developing significant conduction complications. This problem can be avoided by obtaining an electocardiogram prior to starting therapy in order to identify patients with atrioventricular conduction delays.

Lethality

The clinical picture of toxicity or overdose is coma, seizures, blood pressure drop, and conduction delays. A variety of ventricular dysrhythmias can occur and cause death. About 70 to 80 percent of tricyclic overdoses do not reach the hospital alive, according to Callahan and Kassel (1985). A fatal dose may be as little as a two-week supply of medicine. Therefore, in all cases, a careful assessment of suicide potential must be made prior to prescribing these medications and at the time of each follow-up visit.

MONOAMINE OXIDASE INHIBITORS

Arnot (1960) was the first to describe the anxiolytic effect of a monoamine oxidase (MAO) inhibitor. Over the years, MAO inhibitors were branded as drugs of questionable efficacy by the Medical Research Council Study on Depression (1965). When Sheehan, Ballenger, and Jacobson (1980) showed that phenelzine was superior to imipramine on several panic disorder measures, including reduction of disability, renewed interest developed in this class of drug for panic disorder and agoraphobia.

Choice of Drug

The MAO inhibitors in psychiatric use in the United States are phenelzine and isocarboxazid (hydrazines) and tranylcypromine (a nonhydrazine). Controlled studies by Sheehan (Sheehan et al., 1980; Sheehan, Claycomb, & Surman, 1984) have shown phenelzine to be effective in panic disorder, while the evidence for isocarboxazid and tranylcypromine is anecdotal. Tranylcypromine may be the MAO inhibitor of choice in elderly patients, as it is less likely to decrease blood pressure and its MAO inhibition is more rapidly reversible.

Dosage, Schedule, and Duration of Initial Treatment

Prior to starting treatment, the patient should be given written instructions about the diet and drug restrictions to be followed. A low-tyramine diet should be started two days prior to initiation of medication. The starting dose with phenelzine is 15 mg, increasing by 15 mg every four days to about 60 mg a day. Beyond this level, increments are made on a weekly basis to 90 mg a day. The therapeutic dose usually coincides with the onset of mild postural hypotension as measured by the sphygmomanometer. For tranylcypromine, the effective dose ranges from 40 to 60 mg a day. The daily dose should be given in divided doses during the day. Bedtime dosing should be avoided as it tends to disrupt sleep. The initial trial is for at lease eight weeks after therapeutic dose has been reached.

Adverse Effects

Adverse effects are similar to those described for the cyclic agents. The MAO inhibitors are not particularly anticholinergic, but they do cause mild dry mouth, constipation, and even urinary retention. Unlike the tricyclics, they usually cause a slowing of the pulse and are even more hypotensive. The onset of hypotension is sometimes a late event, occurring a few weeks into treatment. Weight gain and delayed or inhibited orgasm or ejaculation are even greater with phenelzine than the tricyclics. Several months into treatment, the patient may experience electric shock sensations or carpal tunnel syndrome. This is treated with 100 to 300 mg pyridoxine (Vitamin B_6) a day and a modest lowering of the dose. Nighttime insomnia is common and can be minimized by avoiding dosing after 5 P.M. Liver toxicity is more common with phenelzine and isocarboxazid than with tranylcypromine, and liver enzymes should be checked every six to 12 months.

Issues in Therapy

Issues in therapy include the risks of hypertensive crisis and lethality in overdose. Prior to starting MAO inhibitors, the risks, benefits, and alternate treatments available should be explained in great detail to the patient and significant other.

Hypertensive Crisis

Hypertensive crisis is a potentially lethal event, occurring when tyramine is absorbed from the gastrointestinal tract or the patient receives a drug that cannot be metabolized due to inhibition of the MAO system. Its clinical features are a sudden onset, with increase in heart rate and pounding in the blood vessels, followed by headache, initially in the occipital or temporal regions, later spreading all over the head. The person is flushed, sweats profusely, and may have nausea, vomiting, and elevated temperature. Neck stiffness and photophobia also may occur. The headache may persist for several days after the blood pressure returns to normal. The risk of hypertensive episodes is reduced by adequate education and providing patients with written drug and diet restrictions. The hypertension may be treated with several different medications, but Haft and Litterer (1984) suggest that nifedipine is probably the drug of choice, as blood pressure is lowered in direct proportion to the increase, cardiac output is maintained, coronary vasodilation protects against angina, and it does not worsen any congestive failure that may accompany the hypertensive crisis. Nifedipine may be given sublingually or orally, the former route having a more rapid effect. The initial dose is 10 to 20 mg and may be repeated in 30 minutes if necessary. We do not recommend that patients carry an antihypertensive with them, since in our experience many misinterpret a hypotensive episode as a hypertensive crisis. Patients taking a hypotensive agent under those circumstances could seriously worsen their hypotension. Prior to starting treatment, diet restrictions should be observed for about two days and should be followed for two weeks after discontinuation. A schedule as in Table 12–2 may be provided to the patient.

Lethality

The mortality in MAO inhibitor overdoses is unfortunately over 50 percent. The therapeutic index is low, with deaths reported from as little as six times the usual dose of tranylcypromine, according to Tucker and

TABLE 12–2
Directions for Taking MAO Inhibitors[a,b]

Breakfast	Lunch	Evening Meal Tablets	Bedtime	Day
0	0	1	0	1–3
1	0	1	0	4–7
1	1	1	0	8–12
1	1	2	0	13–19
2	1	2	0	20–26
2	2	2	0	27–33
2[c]	2	3	0	34–40
3[c]	2	3	0	41–47

Source: "Monoamine Oxidase Inhibitors" by D. V. Sheehan and B. A. Raj, 1988. In *Handbook of Anxiety Disorders*, by C. G. Last and M. Hersen (Eds.), p. 506. New York: Pergamon Press. Copyright 1985 by D. V. Sheehan. Reproduced with permission.
[a]10 mg tablets of Parnate or Marplan or 15 mg tablets of Nardil.
[b]If no side effects (drowsiness) or benefit occurs with medication, increase dose to next level. When coming off the MAO inhibitors, do not reduce the dose suddenly at a rate faster than 1 tablet every three days, ideally 1 tablet every two weeks. There are food or drug restrictions with MAO inhibitors. Use caution when driving and operating high-speed equipment. Avoid alcohol consumption.
[c]For Parnate and Marplan only, not Nardil.

Sirisinha (1965). Typically, after an overdose, there is a lag period of eight to 12 hours before signs of central nervous system overstimulation are seen. These are thrashing movements, profuse sweating, restlessness, irrational behavior, convulsions, and coma. There may be hypertension or hypotension; hyperpyrexia is common and is the usual cause of death. Specific antidotes are not available; however, aggressive management of hyperpyrexia and supportive medical treatment are often helpful and has been elaborated on by Sheehan and Raj (1988).

New MAO Inhibitors

Recently there has been interest in developing MAO inhibitors that are safer with less side effects. Moclobemide and brofaromine are examples of "reversible MAO inhibitors." If enough dietary tyramine is present, tyramine will displace the MAO inhibitor from the MAO enzyme and be metabolized. This reversibility is associated with no cheese reactions or hypertensive crisis. Currently these medications are being evaluated for panic disorder.

SELECTIVE SEROTONIN UPTAKE INHIBITORS

The possible role of serotonin in panic disorder has been reviewed by Sheehan, Zak, Miller, and Fanous (1988); Charney, Krystal, and Southwick (1990); and Sheehan, Raj, Trehan, and Knapp (1993). The number of drugs that selectively influence serotonin uptake is growing, with evidence from open and controlled studies that they are effective in panic disorder. Trazodone, fluoxetine, sertraline, paroxetine, and clomipramine are currently available to clinicians in the United States. Charney and associates (1986) found 150 mg of imipramine and 8 mg of alprazolam to be superior to 250 mg of trazodone on measures of panic, phobic avoidance, and global outcome. Mavissakalian, Perel, Bowler, and Dealy (1987) found 300 mg of trazodone to be superior to placebo in agoraphobic patients with panic attacks. These doses are low, and increased efficacy may need higher doses. Our own experience is that this drug has moderate power with minimally disruptive side effects, the major concerns being priapism in men, and sedation.

Controlled studies of fluoxetine in panic disorder are lacking. In an open trial, Gorman and coworkers (1987) observed that seven of 16 patients experienced cessation of panic attacks; doses ranged from 10 mg to 70 mg a day. In an open-label study, Schneier and associates (1990) reported significant improvement in 19 of 25 (76 percent) of the panic disorder patients treated with fluoxetine. Our clinical experience with this drug is that is has moderate antipanic properties in doses of 20 to 60 mg a day. It has a desirable side effect profile and is well tolerated if starting doses are as low as 5 mg and titration upward is done slowly. Studies are lacking for sertraline, but clinical experience supports antipanic properties for this compound in standard antidepressant dosages. Ohrstrom, Judge, and Manniche (1992) have reported efficacy for paroxetine compared to placebo in a 12-week, flexible-dose, double-blind study. Effective dosage was 20 to 60 mg, the most common adverse reaction being nausea, sweating, and dry mouth. In this study, 8 percent of the paroxetine group withdrew because of adverse events, as compared to 5 percent of the placebo group, suggesting that it is well tolerated. Fluvoxamine is a selective serotonin uptake inhibitor. Its efficacy has been documented relative to placebo and cognitive therapy by Black, Wesner, and Gable (1993), to ritanserin by Den Boer and Westenberg (1990), to maprotiline by Den Boer and Westenberg (1988), and to clomipramine by Kahn, Westenberg, Verhoeven, Gispen-de Wied, and Kamerbeek (1987) and Den Boer, Westenberg, Kamerbeek, Verhoeven, and Kahn (1987). These selective serotonin uptake inhibitors are very desirable drugs because of their side effect profile and relatively low lethality in overdose. Lack of weight gain make them particularly attractive for the already obese patient, and lack of cardiotoxic effects make them attractive for the elderly patient with panic disorder.

Clomipramine, a tricyclic, is a specific inhibitor of serotonin uptake in the synaptic cleft. It has been found effective in five open trials comparing it to placebo reviewed by Modigh (1987) and four controlled trials conducted by Escobar and Landbloom (1976); Karabanow (1977); Pecknold, McClure, Appeltauer, Allan, and Wrzesinski (1982); and Johnston, Troyer, and Whitsett (1988). Waxman (1977) and Allsop, Cooper, and Poole (1984) found it superior to diazepam, and Kahn and associates (1987) report that it is superior to 5-hydroxytryptophan and placebo. Den Boer and Westenberg (1988) found clomipramine to be equal to fluvoxamine and superior to maprotiline. In these studies, effective doses ranged from 25 mg to 200 mg a day. Our clinical experience is consistent with this reported efficacy, and it is our impression that clomipramine may be qualitatively more effective than other tricyclics. The side effects experienced with this drug are similar to that described for tricyclic antidepressants. The risk of seizures increases with doses greater than 250 mg.

COMBINATIONS AND ALTERNATE CHOICES

If a patient is resistant or gets only a partial response after trials of drugs from the previously described groups, it may be time to try combinations or agents less systematically and more anecdotally studied in panic disorder.

Combinations

The most common combination seen in clinical practice is that of a benzodiazepine with an antidepressant. In general, this is safe, and as the drugs have different effects on the dimensions of panic disorder, such as anticipatory anxiety or depression, it is usually of benefit. There are two problems: The first is in deciding the source or proportion of side effect from the drugs in the combination. For example, sedation or headaches can occur both with benzodiazepines and antidepressants. Second, it may be difficult to push either drug to its maximum potential due to synergistic effects.

When MAO inhibitors are added to previously well tolerated doses of clonazepam or alprazolam, the patient may experience new onset sedation or signs of benzodiazepine toxicity. This is because, with progressive inhibition of the oxidase system in the liver, metabolism of benzodiazepine is decreased. This is adjusted for by lowering the dose of benzodiazepine or switching to one that is mostly metabolized by conjugation in the liver, such as lorazepam or oxazepam. MAO inhibitors and tricyclics can be used in combination if both are started simultaneously or if the MAO inhibitor is added to a tricyclic regimen already in place. Tricyclics generally should not be added to an ongoing trial of a MAO inhibitor. The selective serotonin uptake inhibitors (SSUIs) and MAO inhibitors should not be used in combination since a serotonin syndrome is a possibility. After fluoxetine monotherapy is discontinued, the clinician should wait four to six weeks before starting a MAO inhibitor and two to three weeks for the other SSUIs.

Adding fluoxetine to ongoing tricyclic therapy will lead to a threefold or greater increase in tricyclic plasma levels and possible clinical toxicity. The tricyclic dose should be decreased by 50 percent before adding fluoxetine. In our experience, adding a tricyclic to ongoing fluoxetine therapy also results in high levels of tricyclic; consequently, add only small doses and proceed cautiously. Plasma levels of the tricyclic increase less when paroxetine is added and least with sertraline.

Alternate Agents

Two new psychotropic agents have been introduced in the last three years: buspirone, a nonbenzodiazepine anxiolytic, and the antidepressant bupropion.

Buspirone

In two double-blind, placebo-controlled studies, in patients with panic disorder and agoraphobia, Sheehan (Sheehan, Raj, & Sheehan, 1991; Sheehan, Raj, Sheehan, & Soto, 1990); compared buspirone to imipramine and to alprazolam respectively. In both studies, it was not better than placebo, even in doses as high as 100 mg per day.

Bupropion

Sheehan, Davidson, Manschreck, and Van Wyck Fleet (1983) reported that bupropion was not effective in panic disorder.

Clonidine

Liebowitz, Fyer, and McGrath (1981), in an eight-week open clinical trial of patients with panic disorder, noted some antipanic efficacy for clonidine. Doses were started at 0.1 mg twice daily and increased by 0.1 mg a week up to a maximum of 1 mg a day. Of the 11 subjects, four had a good response on 0.2 to 0.5 mg per day. Four other subjects had initial benefit, which wore off despite dosage increase to 0.7 mg or 1 mg a day. Hoehn-Saric, Merchant, Keyser, and Smith (1981) treated 14 panic disorder patients in a double-blind crossover design with clonidine and placebo over a four-week period. Three patients improved and three worsened in comparison to previous treatment. Eight subjects had a moderate anxiolytic response, but less than with previous anxiolytic therapy. With clonidine, anxiolytic effect begins in the first week, with some additional gains in the second week and a tendency to relapse after three to four months. Average dose is 0.2 to 0.5 mg per day, and the common side effects are drowsiness, sedation, fatigue, and loss of motivation. A 10 to 20 mm drop in blood pressure may occur, causing dizziness or weakness.

Calcium Channel Blockers

Goldstein (1985) treated seven treatment-resistant patients, four of whom improved with either 80 mg of verapamil or 60 mg of diltiazem given three times a day. In a 16-week double-blind, crossover trial of verapamil in 11 patients, Klein and Uhde (1988) reported marked benefit in four and marginal response in three subjects. With these drugs, electrocardiogram, blood pressure, and pulse should be monitored. When used concomitantly with other psychotropics, additive effects should be kept in mind, such as bradycardia with lithium or elevation of serum carbamazepine levels.

Anticonvulsants

Uhde, Stein, and Post (1988), in a double-blind, placebo-controlled study of 14 panic patients, found minimal improvement with carbamazepine. The mean dose was 697 mg, with a range of 200 mg to 1,200 mg per day and a duration of treatment of 22 to 188 days. Tondo and coworkers (1989) reported improvement in 20 of 34 patients treated with carbamazepine in doses of 170 to 500 mg per day for two to 12 months. Case reports have suggested some efficacy for valproic acid in doses of 1,000 to 2,250 mg per day with anxiolysis in one to two weeks. A recent six-week open trial of valproic acid in 12 patients with panic disorder found that all experienced significant improvement with minimal side effects (Woodman & Noyes, 1994).

SPECIAL POPULATIONS

The Pregnant Patient

Panic disorder is primarily an illness of women of childbearing age. Therefore, very likely clinicians will have to advise a patient who is on medication and planning pregnancy or announces that she is pregnant.

Teratogenic effects for diazepam and its metabolite have been documented by some studies but not in others. Until proven otherwise, it should be presumed that even those benzodiazepines that are not metabolized to desmethyldiazepam (such as alprazolam) are potentially teratogenic. The reported defects are cleft palate, inguinal hernia, pyloric stenosis, cardiovascular defects, and occasionally skeletal problems such as spina bifida and syndactyly. At the time of delivery, there is danger of withdrawal syndrome and central nervous system depression in the child. It remains unclear to what extent teratogenic effects are direct toxic effects of the drug or effects of the drug in preventing spontaneous abortions that might otherwise occur in a fetus with an abnormality.

Cyclic antidepressants have been associated with an increased risk for teratogenicity in some studies but not others. Infants born to women taking tricyclics may show signs of heart failure, tachycardia, myoclonus, and urinary retention. While teratogenic effects have not been reported, they may occur with MAO inhibitors. It is possible that a hypertensive episode may be harmful to the fetus.

The patient planning pregnancy should be advised to slowly taper her medications. For those unable or unwilling to discontinue due to recurrence of severe panic, a prn schedule of the lowest possible dose of medication might be employed. Clinicians should document that a risk benefit discussion has been held. The medications may be restarted after the child's birth, provided breastfeeding is not planned.

The patient on medication who announces she is pregnant should be reassured and called in for a discussion of the risks. Rapid taper of drug is not warranted, as the period of maximum risk for teratogenicity usually has passed by the time the patient discovers she is pregnant. Furthermore, abrupt withdrawal may increase the risk of miscarriage. Amniocentesis and/or abortion are not indicated as the abnormalities, if they occur, usually are not life-threatening. The patient can be told that her risk of having a child with an abnormality is not much higher than the 3 percent risk inherent in all pregnancies. A taper schedule should be worked out, and the patient should be offered support and reassurance through the rest of her pregnancy. The risk-benefit discussion should be well documented in the patient's chart.

The Substance Abuser

In a study of alcoholics, Mullaney and Trippet (1979), noted that 60 percent had panic symptoms and about half had diagnosable panic disorder. Watson and Gold (1984) found cocaine produces anxiety in 83 percent and panic attacks in 50 percent of those studied. Aronson and Logue (1988), in a study of panic patients, observed secondary alcohol abuse in 27 percent and secondary sedative abuse in 32 percent. Consequently, substance abusers may have underlying panic disorder, and panic disorder patients may have underlying substance abuse.

All panic disorder patients should have a full substance use history taken prior to initiation of treatment. The physical exam should look for evidence of needle marks, skin changes, and enlarged liver. Generally, benzodiazepines should not be the drug of first choice in this population.

Gawin and Kleber (1986) have suggested that tricyclic antidepressants may decrease the craving for cocaine. The cyclic antidepressants and the selective serotonin uptake inhibitors are the drugs of initial choice. Patients in treatment who show signs of abuse of alcohol and drugs may need to be hospitalized for detoxification and stabilization on a regime that combines drug therapy, group and other psychotherapies, along with enrollment in Alcoholics Anonymous and Narcotics Anonymous.

The Geriatric Patient

Panic disorder is a chronic condition, and as the graying of America occurs, we are likely to see more elderly with this disorder. Panic disorder can occur *de novo* in the elderly, and it is our experience that it responds to standard antipanic medications. In treating the elderly patient, it is important to keep in mind that major pharmacokinetic changes occur with age. First-pass metabolism in the liver is decreased due to lowered function of the oxidase system; drug transport is altered due to changes in albumin fraction; and storage is affected by changes in the muscle-to-fat ratio. All of this translates into higher blood levels for a given dose, prolonged half-life, and longer duration of therapeutic action for most antipanic drugs. All the different classes of drugs can be used safely if the axiom "Start low and go slow" is scrupulously followed.

We have used alprazolam effectively in the elderly panic patient (unpublished data), with a mean dose of 2.5 mg and a range of 0.5 to 5.5 mg ($N = 18$). Nortriptyline, a secondary amine tricyclic, is one of the better-tolerated antidepressants in the treatment of elderly depression. We found it both effective and well tolerated in the treatment of panic disorder, with a mean dose of 55 mg and a range of 25 to 100 mg ($N = 8$). Georgotas and associates (1986) have documented the safety and efficacy of MAO inhibitors in treating elderly depression. They also should be considered in treating panic disorder in the elderly. Tranylcypromine may be the preferred drug as it is less hypotensive, and its MAO inhibition is more rapidly reversible. The side effects of all these drugs in the elderly are similar to those seen in young adults.

Prior to starting treatment, ask patients about concomitant and over-the-counter medications. Elderly patients should have a baseline EKG prior to starting antidepressants; blood pressure and pulse should be taken sitting and standing at each visit.

ISSUES IN THE SOMATIC TREATMENT OF PANIC DISORDER

The main issues in the somatic treatment of panic disorder are choice of drug and duration of treatment. Here we provide clinicians with an approach that they can use in their practice. This is schematically presented in Figure 12–1.

Choice of Drug

Clinicians have a smorgasbord of medications to pick from. Usually the initial choice is from one of four classes of drug: benzodiazepines, cyclic antidepressants, selective serotonin uptake inhibitors, and MAO inhibitors. This initial choice should be arrived at after considering these three factors: the dominant clinical picture, the side effect profile, and patient preference.

Dominant Clinical Picture

A thorough evaluation of the patient with panic disorder will reveal multiple dimensions of psychopathology: panic attacks, anticipatory anxiety, phobic avoidance, depression, obsessional features, somatization, and secondary disability. One or more of these dimensions may dominate the clinical picture and dictate the choice of drug. The differential effects of these drugs on the dimensions of panic disorder are shown in Table 12–3.

Sheehan and coworkers (1982, 1984) found the benzodiazepine alprazolam to be effective in controlling all the dimensions of panic disorder except depression. It was second to the MAO inhibitor phenelzine with regard to its effect on overall disability. This was corroborated by results from the Cross-National Collaborative Panic Study by Ballenger and associates (1988). In that study, 31 percent of the subjects had secondary major depression. Lesser and others (1988) found that these patients responded well to alprazolam, with significant reduction both in panic and depression. Clonazepam has not been studied as extensively, but Tesar and coworkers (1991) found it to be as effective as alprazolam.

DOMINANT CLINICAL PICTURE   INITIAL DRUG CHOICE & TREATMENT FLOW

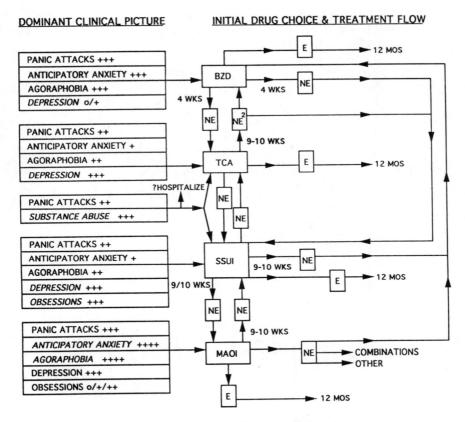

Figure 12–1. Medication treatment strategies in panic disorder.

(Key: 0 = none; + = mild; ++ = moderate; +++ = severe; ++++ = very severe; WKS = Weeks; MOS = Months; E = Effective; NE = Not effective; NE^2 = If depression clears but anxiety remains, okay to add benzodiazepine. If depression does not clear, not okay.; BZD = Benzodiazepine; TCA = Tricyclic antidepressant; SSUI = Selective serotonin uptake inhibitor; MAOI = Monoamine oxidase inhibitor.)

Treatment-emergent depression has been observed with both drugs. Given these findings, benzodiazepines are a good initial choice for the patient with moderate to severe panic disorder and agoraphobia with only mild levels of depression. Their weakness lies in their failure to adequately control the depression dimension in panic disorder.

It is now accepted that tricyclic antidepressants exert their antipanic effect, even in the absence of clinical depression. They decrease panic, somatization, and depression, but are less effective in controlling

TABLE 12–3
Comparative Drug Effects on Dimensions of Panic Disorder

Name of Drug	Panic Attacks	Anticipatory Anxiety	Phobia	Depression	Obsessions	Relative Side Effects	Overall Efficacy	Concerns
Alprazolam	3.5	4	3	0 to 1	0 to 1	1 to 2	3.5	
Clonazepam	3.5	4	3	0 to 1	0 to 1	1 to 2	3.5	Dependence, withdrawal syndrome
Lorazepam	3	3	2	0 to 1	0 to 1	1 to 2	2 to 3	
Imipramine	3	2	2	3	1	3	2 to 3	
Desipramine	3	2	2	3	1	2	2 to 3	Anticholinergic effects, hypotension, weight gain
Clomipramine	3.5	2	3	3	3	3.5	3.5	
Trazadone	2	1	2	2.5	1	1 to 2	2	Priapism in mass (1/6000 cases), sedation
Fluoxetine	2	1	2	2.5	2.5	1 to 2	3	
Sertraline	2	1	2	2.5	2.5	1 to 2	3	Activating effects initially, sexual dysfunction
Paroxetine	2	1	2	2.5	2.5	1 to 2	3	
Phenelzine	4	3	3	4	2.5	3.5	4	Hypotension, hypertensive reaction, drug and diet restrictions, weight gain
Tranylcypromine	3	2	3	3	2.5	2 to 3	3	

Key: 0 = No effect, 1 = Mild, 2 = Moderate, 3 = Moderate plus, 4 = Severe or Maximum.

anticipatory anxiety and phobic avoidance, according to Klein (1964). These are the drugs of initial choice when panic is accompanied by moderate to severe depression or is complicated by substance abuse.

An increasing number of drugs are serotonin selective, including fluoxetine, trazodone, sertraline, and paroxetine. Several, such as fluvoxamine and citalopram, are undergoing clinical trials and should be available in the near future. At this time, they appear to have two advantages over the cyclic agents. Their side effects are less disruptive, and all appear to have antiobsessional effects. It is not established that they have the same power with regards to the other dimensions of this disorder. Therefore, these drugs are the initial choice in patients who have panic disorder with a moderate degree of depression and/or obsessional features.

Sheehan and associates (1984), in a double-blind, placebo-controlled study, compared phenelzine, alprazolam, and imipramine in patients with panic disorder and agoraphobia. In the mild to moderately ill patient, all three drugs were equally effective. In severely ill patients, the MAO inhibitor was clearly superior in increasing confidence, motivation, and decreasing disability. It has been suggested that phenelzine may be superior to imipramine in the management of atypical depression with panic attacks, but this was not confirmed in a replication study by Quitkin and coworkers (1990). The MAO inhibitor phenelzine appears to be the drug of initial choice in the severely ill patient and in those who have failed trials of the other classes of compounds.

Side Effect Profile

The side effect profile influences the decision-making process in two ways. First, is the drug's side effect medically dangerous in certain situations? If the patient, for example, already has hypotension or a bundle branch block, adding a tricyclic may be unwise. Second, what side effect is acceptable to the patient? Several patients who responded very well to a cyclic antidepressant or MAO inhibitor discontinued their drug due to excessive weight gain or sexual difficulties. A computer operator stopped taking imipramine because of difficulty focusing on the screen. Noyes, Garvey, Cook, and Samuelson (1989), in a study of 107 patients treated with tricyclic antidepressants, found that 35 percent discontinued their drug because of side effects. Overall, benzodiazepines are not disruptive, but persistent sedation or subjective impairment of mentation may result in premature discontinuance. Girdwood (1974) notes that of all the options currently available, benzodiazepines appear to have the lowest mortality and morbidity per million prescriptions.

Patient Preference

This is the era of informed consent and educated consumers of health care. Prior to initiating treatment, the risks and benefits of each class of drug should be discussed with the patient. This may provoke initial anxiety with refusal to try one or more drugs. A fairly common scenario is one in which the patient comes in with preconceived ideas about certain treatments. Fear of "addiction" to benzodiazepines is common, and more recently patients have refused a trial of fluoxetine based on unjustified negative information publicized in the media. Usually, education and reassurance will overcome these resistances.

Duration of Treatment

The questions regarding treatment duration are: Is long-term drug treatment necessary or important, and if so, for how long? Several studies by Coryell, Noyes, and Clancy (1983); Uhde and associates (1985); and Breier, Charney, and Heninger (1986) have all documented that panic disorder is a chronic illness, with the vast majority of patients exhibiting disability 20 years later.

It is becoming clearer that untreated or inadequately treated panic disorder has serious consequences. Coryell, Noyes, and Clancy (1982) reported higher rates of mortality from cardiovascular disease and suicide. Kahn, Drusin, and Klein (1987) found a high rate of panic disorder among patients with idiopathic cardiomyopathy presenting for cardiac transplant. Weissman, Klerman, Markowitz, and Ouellette (1990), examining data from the Epidemiologic Catchment Area Study, found that the risk for suicide attempt by patients with panic disorder is comparable to that observed for depression. Twenty percent of patients with panic disorder made suicide attempts, and 12 percent of patients with panic attacks not yet meeting criteria for panic disorder made suicide attempts. (See chapter 5). All of this strongly suggests that panic disorder is a serious, chronic, and disabling disorder that demands aggressive and, if necessary, prolonged treatment.

Zitrin, Klein, Woerner, and Ross (1983) observed that when imipramine was discontinued after six months of treatment, less than a third of the patients relapsed over a two-year period. Fyer, Liebowitz, and Gorman (1989) reported relapse in 44 percent of patients on imipramine and 55 percent of those on alprazolam over an eight-week period following discontinuation. Sheehan (1986) reported relapse rates of 92 percent for those on alprazolam, 86 percent for imipramine, and 71 percent for phenelzine within three months of stopping these medications after one year of therapy. The overall relapse rate was approximately 80 percent. In a follow-up of 423 patients three to six years after they had been treated with alprazolam or imipramine, Katschnig, Stolk, and Klerman (1989) note that only 55 percent were still taking their medication, 18.2 percent had been continuously well, 12.7 percent recovered during follow-up and remained well, and the rest were symptomatic. The evidence seems to support chronic treatment beyond one year. There is no reliable way of determining who will relapse after discontinuation. Some clues might be persistence of limited symptom attacks, high levels of anticipatory anxiety, and an early age of onset. Pollack and associates (1993) have reported poor outcome at follow-up was associated with total duration of the disorder, agoraphobic subtype, and the presence of comorbid social phobia. It is our policy to maintain therapy for at least six months, preferably for one year, before attempting slow taper. In the event of relapse, medication is restarted and maintained for another 12-month period.

CONCLUSION

There has been tremendous expansion in our knowledge of pharmacological interventions in panic disorder over the last decade. Not only have new drugs been introduced, but we have learned to use the old drugs more safely and effectively. We hope the protocols, strategies, and individual drug characteristics described in this chapter will help guide clinicians safely through the maze of pharmacotherapy. It should help them make treatment choices based on existing knowledge, which will translate into a beneficial experience for patients, whose lasting gratefulness is our reward.

REFERENCES

Abernathy, D. R., Greenblatt, D. J., Divoll, M., & Shader, R. I. (1983). Pharmacokinetics of alprazolam. *Journal of Clinical Psychiatry, 44*, 45–47.

Allsopp, L. F., Cooper, G. L., & Poole, P. H. (1984). Clomipramine and diazepam in the treatment of agoraphobia and social phobia in general practice. *Current Medical Research Opinion, 9*, 64–70.

Arnot, R. (1960). Calming effects of the monoamine oxidase inhibitors. *Disorders of the Nervous System, 11*, 448.

Aronson, T. A., & Logue, C. M. (1988). Phenomenology of panic attacks: A descriptive study of panic disorder patients self reports. *Journal of Clinical Psychiatry, 49*(1), 8–13.

Ashley, M. J., LeRiche, W. H., Olin, G. S., Hatcher, J., Kornaczewski, A., Schmidt, W., & Rankin, J. G. (1978). "Mixed" (drug abusing) and "pure" alcoholics: A socio-medical comparison. *British Journal of Addiction, 73*, 19–34.

Ballenger, J. C., Burrows, G. D., Dupont, R. L., Lesser, I. M., Noyes, R., Pecknold, J. C., Rifkin, A., & Swinson, R. P. (1988). Alprazolam in panic disorder and agoraphobia: Results from a multicenter trial. I: Efficacy in short-term treatment. *Archives of General Psychiatry, 45*(5), 413–422.

Ballenger, J. C., Howell, E. F., & Laraia, M. (1987, May). *Comparison of four medicines in panic disorder.* Paper presented at the annual meeting of the American Psychiatric Association. Chicago.

Ballenger, J. C., Peterson, G. A., Laraia, M., Hucek, A., Lake, C. R., Jimerson, D., Cox, D., & Trockman, C. (1984). A study of plasma catecholamines in agoraphobia and the relationship of serum tricyclic level to treatment response. In J. C. Ballenger (Ed.), *Biology of agoraphobia* (pp. 27–63). Washington, DC: American Psychiatric Press.

Beaudry, P., Fontaine, R., & Chouinard, G. (1984). Bromazepam, another high potency benzodiazepine for panic attacks [letter]. *American Journal of Psychiatry, 141*, 464–465.

Beaudry, P., Fontaine, R., Chouinard, G., & Annable, L. (1985). An open clinical trial of clonazepam in the treatment of patients with recurrent panic attacks. *Progress in Neuropsychopharmacological and Biological Psychiatry, 95*–6, 589.

Berwish, N. J., & Amsterdam, J. D. (1989). An overview of investigational antidepressants. *Psychosomatics, 30*, 1–18.

Black, D. W., Wesner, R., & Gabel, J. (1993). A comparison of fluvoxamine, cognitive therapy and placebo in the treatment of panic disorder. *Archives of General Psychiatry, 50*, 44–50.

Breier, A., Charney, D. S., & Heninger, G. R. (1986). Agoraphobia with panic attacks: Development, diagnostic stability and course of illness. *Archives of General Psychiatry, 43*, 1029–1036.

Busto, U., Sellers, E. M., Naranjo, C. A., Campbell, H. D., Sanchez-Craig, H., & Simpkins, J. (1986). Patterns of benzodiazepine abuse and dependence. *British Journal of Addiction, 81*, 87–94.

Busto, U., Simpkins, J., Sellers, E. M., Sisson, B., & Segal, R. (1983). Objective determination of benzodiazepine use and abuse in alcoholics. *British Journal of Addiction, 78*, 429–435.

Callahan, M., & Kassel, D. (1985). Epidemiology of fatal tricyclic antidepressant ingestion: Implications for management. *Annals of Emergency Medicine, 14,* 1–9.

Charney, D. S., Krystal, J. J., & Southwick, S. M. (1990). Serotonin function in panic and generalized anxiety disorders. *Psychiatric Annals, 10,* 593–602.

Charney, D. S., & Woods, S. W. (1989). Benzodiazepine treatment of panic disorder: A comparison of alprazolam and lorazepam. *Journal of Clinical Psychiatry, 50,* 418–423.

Charney, D. S., Woods, S. W., Goodman, W. K., Rifkin, B., Kinch, M., Aiken, B., Quadrino, L. M., & Heninger, G. R. (1986). Drug treatment of panic disorder: The comparative efficacy of imipramine, alprazolam and trazadone. *Journal of Clinical Psychiatry, 47,* 580–586.

Chouinard, G., Annable, L., Fontaine, R., & Solyom, L. (1982). Alprazolam and the treatment of generalized anxiety and panic disorders: A double-blind placebo-controlled study. *Psychopharmacology, 77*(3), 229–233.

Clinical Psychiatry Committee of the British Medical Research Council. (1965). Clinical trial of the treatment of depressive illness. *British Medical Journal, 1,* 881–886.

Coryell, W., Noyes, R., & Clancy, J. (1982). Excess mortality in panic disorders. *Archives of General Psychiatry, 39,* 701–703.

Coryell, W., Noyes, R., & Clancy, J. (1983). Panic disorder and primary unipolar depression: A comparison of background and outcome. *Journal of Affective Disorder, 5,* 311–317.

Den Boer, J. A., & Westenberg, H. G. (1988). Effect of a serotonin and noradrenaline uptake inhibitor in panic disorder: A double-blind comparative study with fluvoxamine and maprotiline. *International Clinical Psychopharmacology, 3*(1), 59–74.

Den Boer, J. A., & Westenberg, H. G. (1990). Serotonin function in panic disorder: A double-blind placebo-controlled study with fluvoxamine and ritanserin. *Psychopharmacology, 102*(1), 85–94.

Den Boer, J. A., Westenberg, H. G., Kamerbeek, W. D., Verhoeven, V. M., & Kahn, R. S. (1987). Effect of serotonin uptake inhibitors in anxiety disorders: A double-blind comparison of clomipramine and fluvoxamine. *International Clinical Psychopharmacology, 2,* 21–32.

Dunner, D. L., Ishiki, D., Avery, D. H., Wilson, L. G., & Hyde, T. S. (1986). Effect of alprazolam and diazepam on anxiety and panic attacks in panic disorder: A controlled study. *Journal of Clinical Psychiatry, 47,* 458–460.

Escobar, J. I., & Landbloom, R. P. (1976). Treatment of phobic neurosis with chlorimipramine: A controlled clinical trial. *Current Therapeutics and Research, 20*(5), 680–685.

Fyer, A. J., Liebowitz, M. R., & Gorman, J. M. (1989, December). *Comparative discontinuation of alprazolam and imipramine in panic patients.*

Paper presented at the 27th annual meeting of the American College of Neuropsychopharmacology. San Juan, PR.

Garvey, M. J., & Tollefson, G. D. (1986). Prevalence of misuse of prescribed benzodiazepines in patients with primary anxiety disorder or major depression. *American Journal of Psychiatry, 143*(12), 1601–1603.

Gawin, F. H., & Kleber, H. D. (1986). Pharmacologic treatment of cocaine abuse. *Psychiatric Clinics of North America, 9*(Suppl. 3), 573–583.

Georgotas, A., McCue, R. E., Hapworth, W., Friedman, E., Kim, O. M., Welkowitz, J., Chang, I., & Cooper, T. B. (1986). Comparative efficacy and safety of MAOI's versus TCA's in treating depression in the elderly. *Biological Psychiatry, 21,* 1155–1166.

Girdwood, R. H. (1974). Death after taking medicaments. *British Medical Journal, 1*(106), 501–504.

Goldstein, J. A. (1985). Calcium channel blockers in the treatment of panic disorder [letter]. *Journal of Clinical Psychiatry, 46*(12), 546.

Gorman, J. M., Liebowitz, M. R., Fyer, A. J., Goetz, D., Campeas, R. B., Fyer, M. R., Davies, S. O., & Klein, D. F. (1987). An open trial of fluoxetine in the treatment of panic attacks. *Journal of Clinical Psychopharmacology, 7,* 329–332.

Greenblatt, D. J., Shader, R. I., & Abernathy, D. R. (1983). Current status of benzodiazepines. *New England Journal of Medicine, 6,* 354.

Greenblatt, D. J., Shader, R. I., Franke, K., MacLaughlin, D. S., Harmatz, J. S., Allen, M. D., Werner, A., & Woo, E. (1979). Pharmacokinetics and bioavailability of intravenous, intramuscular and oral lorazepam in humans. *Journal of Pharmaceutical Sciences, 68,* 57–63.

Haft, J. L., & Litterer, W. E., III (1984). Chewing nifedipine to rapidly treat hypertension. *Archives of Internal Medicine, 144,* 2357–2359.

Hoehn-Saric, R., Merchant, A. F., Keyser, M. L., & Smith, V. K. (1981). The effects of clonidine on anxiety disorders. *Archives of General Psychiatry, 38,* 1278–1282.

Howell, E. F., Laraia, M., & Ballenger, J. C. (1987, May). *Lorazepam treatment of panic disorder.* Paper presented at the new research session of the 140th annual meeting of the American Psychiatric Association. Chicago.

Johanson, C. E., & Uhlenhuth, E. H. (1980). Drug preference and mood in humans: Chazepam. *Psychopharmacology, 71,* 269–273.

Johnston, D. G., Troyer, I. E., & Whitsett, S. F. (1988). Clomipramine treatment of agoraphobic women. *Archives of General Psychiatry, 45,* 453–459.

Kahn, J. F., Drusin, R. E., & Klein, D. F. (1987). Idiopathic cardiomyopathy and panic disorder: Clinical association in cardiac transplant candidates. *American Journal of Psychiatry, 144,* 1327–1330.

Kahn, R. S., Westenberg, H. G. M., Verhoeven, W. M. A., Gispen-de Wied, C. C., & Kamerbeek, W. D. (1987). Effect of a serotonin precursor and uptake inhibitor in anxiety disorders: A double-blind comparison of 5-hydroxytryptohan, clomipramine and placebo. *International Clinical Psychopharmacology, 2,* 33–45.

Kales, A., Bixler, E. O., Vela-Bueno, A., Soldatos, C. R., Niklaus, D. E., & Manfredi, R. L. (1986). Comparison of short and long half-life benzodiazepine hypnotics: Triazolam and quazepam. *Clinical Pharmacological Therapy, 40,* 378–386.

Kalus, O., Asnis, G. M., van Praag, H. M., & Friedman Harkavy, J. M. (1991). Desipramine treatment in panic disorder. *Journal of Affective Disorders, 21,* 239–244.

Karabanow, O. (1977). Double-blind controlled study in phobias and obsessions. *Journal of International Medical Research, 5*(Suppl. 5), 42–48.

Katschnig, H., Stolk, J., & Klerman, G. L. (1989, December). *Long-term follow up of panic disorder: I: Clinical outcome of a large group of patients participating in an international multicenter clinical drug trial.* Paper presented at the 27th annual meeting of the American College of Neuropsychopharmacology. San Juan, PR.

Klein, D. F. (1964). Delineation of two drug responsive anxiety syndromes. *Psychopharmocologia, 5,* 397–408.

Klein, E., & Uhde, T. W. (1988). Controlled study of verapamil for treatment of panic disorder. *American Journal of Psychiatry, 145,* 431–434.

Ladewig, D., & Grossenbacher, H. (1988). Benzodiazepine abuse in patients of doctors in domicilary practice in the Basle area. *Pharmacopsychiatry, 21*(2), 104–108.

Larson, E. B., Kukull, W. A., Buchner, D., & Reifler, B. V. (1987). Adverse drug reactions associated with global cognitive impairment in elderly persons. *Annals of Internal Medicine, 107,* 169–173.

Lesser, I. M., Rubin, R. T., Pecknold, J. C., Rifkin, A., Swinson, R. P., Lydiard, R. B., Burrows, G. D., Noyes, R., & DuPont, R. L. (1988). Secondary depression in panic disorder and agoraphobia. *Archives of General Psychiatry, 45*(5), 437–443.

Liebowtiz, M. R., Fyer, A. F., Gorman, J. M., Dellon, D., Appleby, I. L., Levy, G., Anderson, S., Levitt, M., Paly, M., Davies, S. D., & Klein, D. F. (1984). Lactate provocation of panic attacks. I: Clinical and behavioral findings. *Archives of General Psychiatry, 41,* 764–770.

Liebowitz, M. R., Fyer, A. J., & McGrath, P. (1981). Clonidine treatment of panic disorder. *Psychopharmacology Bulletin, 17,* 122–123.

Lydiard, R. B. (1987). Desipramine in agoraphobia with panic attacks: An open fixed-dose study. *Journal of Clinical Psychopharmacology, 7,* 258–260.

Lydiard, R. B., Laraia, M. T., Ballenger, J. C., & Howell, E. F. (1987). Emergence of depressive symptoms in patients receiving alprazolam for panic disorder. *American Journal of Psychiatry, 144,* 664–665.

Lydiard, R. B., Lesses, I. M., Ballenger, J. C., Rubin, R. T., Laraia, M., & DuPont, R. (1992). A fixed-dose study of alprazolam 2 mg, alprazolam 6 mg, and placebo in panic disorder. *Journal of Clinical Psychopharmacology, 12*(2), 96–103.

Mavissakalian, M. (1990). Relationship of dose/plasma concentrations on imipramine to the treatment of panic disorder with agoraphobia. In J. C. Ballenger (Ed.), *Clinical aspects of panic disorder* (pp. 211–218). New York: Wiley-Liss.

Mavissakalian, M., Perel, J., Bowler, K., & Dealy, R. (1987). Trazadone in the treatment of panic disorder and agoraphobia with panic attacks. *American Journal of Psychiatry, 144*, 785–787.

Medical Research Council Clinical Psychiatry Committee (1965). Clinical trial of the treatment of depressive illness. *British Medical Journal, 1*, 881–886.

Modigh, K. (1987). Antidepressant drugs in anxiety disorders. *Acta Psychiatrica Scandinavia, 76*(Suppl. 335), 57–71.

Morris, H. H., & Estes, M. L. (1987). Traveler's amnesia: Transient global amnesia secondary to triazolam. *Journal of the American Medical Association, 258*, 945–946.

Mullaney, J. A., & Trippet, C. J. (1979). Alcohol dependence and phobias: Clinical descriptions and relevance. *British Journal of Psychiatry, 135*, 565–573.

Noyes, R., Anderson, D. J., Clancy, J., Crowe, R. R., Slymen, D. J., Ghoneim, M. M., & Hinrichs, J. V. (1984). Diazepam and propranolol in panic disorder and agoraphobia. *Archives of General Psychiatry, 41*(3), 287–292.

Noyes, R., Jr., Garvey, M. J., Cook, B. L., & Samuelson, L. (1989). Problems with tricyclic antidepressant use in patients with panic disorder or agoraphobia: Results of a naturalistic follow-up study. *Journal of Clinical Psychiatry, 50*, 163–169.

Ohrstrom, J. K., Judge, R., & Manniche, P. M. (1992, December). *Paroxetine in the treatment of panic disorder.* Paper presented at the annual meeting of the American College of Neuropsychopharmacology, San Juan, PR.

Oster, G., Russell, M. W., Huse, D. M., Adams, S. F., & Imbimbo, J. (1987). Accident- and injury-related health care utilization among benzodiazepine users and nonusers. *Journal of Clinical Psychiatry, 48*(Suppl. 12), 17–21.

Pecknold, J. C., McClure, D. J., Appeltauer, L., Allan, T., & Wrzesinski, L. (1982). Does tryptophan potentiate clomipramine treatment of agoraphobic and social phobic patients? *British Journal of Psychiatry, 140*, 464–490.

Perera, K. M. H., Tulley, M., & Jenner, F. A. (1987). The use of benzodiazepines among street drug addicts. *British Journal of Addiction, 82*, 511–515.

Pollack, M. H., Otto, M. W., Tesar, G. E., Cohen, L. S., Meltzer-Brody, S., & Rosenbaum, J. F. (1993). Long-term outcome after acute treatment with alprazolam or clonazepam for panic disorder. *Journal of Clinical Psychopharmacology, 13*(4), 257–263.

Pyke, R. E., & Greenberg, H. S. (1989). Double-blind comparison of alprazolam and adinazolam for panic and phobic disorders. *Journal of Clinical Psychopharmacology, 9,* 15–21.

Quitkin, F. M., McGrath, P. J., Stewart, J. W., Harrison, W., Tricamo, E., Wager, S. G., Ocepek-Welikson, K., Nunes, E., Rabkin, J. G., & Klein, D. F. (1990). Atypical depression, panic attacks, and response to imipramine and phenelzine: A replication. *Archives of General Psychiatry, 47*(10), 935–941.

Richelson, E. (1983). Are receptor studies useful for clinical practice? *Journal of Clinical Psychiatry, 44*(9, Sec. 2), 4–9.

Rickels, K., Fox, I. L., Greenblatt, D. J., Sandler, K. R., & Schless, A. (1988). Clorazepate and lorazepam: Clinical improvement and rebound anxiety. *American Journal of Psychiatry, 145*(3), 312–317.

Rickels, K., & Schweizer, E. E. (1986). Benzodiazepines for treatment of panic attacks: A new look. *Psychopharmacology Bulletin, 22,* 93–99.

Roose, S. P., & Glassman, A. H. (1989). Cardiovascular effects of tricyclic antidepressants in depressed patients. *Journal of Clinical Psychiatry,* Monograph Series 7(2), 1–18.

Rosenbaum, J. F., Woods, S. W., Groves, J. E., & Klerman, G. L. (1984). Emergence of hostility during alprazolam treatment. *American Journal of Psychiatry, 141*(6), 792–793.

Rothstein, E., Cobble, J. C., & Sampson, N. (1976) Chlordiazepoxide: Long-term use in alcoholism. *Annals of the New York Academy of Sciences, 273,* 381–384.

Scharf, M. B., Saskin, P., & Fletcher, K. (1987). Benzodiazepine induced amnesia: Clinical and laboratory findings. *Journal of Clinical Psychiatry Monograph 5*(1), 14–17.

Schneier, F. R., Liebowitz, M. R., Davies, S. O., Fairbanks, J., Hollander, E., Campeas, R., & Klein, D. F. (1990). Fluoxetine in panic disorder. *Journal of Clinical Psychopharmacology, 10*(2), 119-121.

Schweizer, E. E., Fox, I., & Case, W. G. (1987, May). *Alprazolam versus lorazepam in the treatment of panic disorder.* Paper presented at the New Clinical Drug Evaluation Unit meeting. Key Biscayne, FL.

Schweizer, E. E., & Rickels, K. (1988). Buspirone in the treatment of panic disorder: A controlled pilot comparison with clorazepate. *Journal of Clinical Psychopharmacology, 8*(4), 303.

Sheehan, D. V. (1986, April). *One year follow up of patients with panic disorder after withdrawal from long-term antipanic medication.* Paper presented at the Conference on Biological Research in Panic Disorder. Washington, DC.

Sheehan, D. V., Ballenger, J., & Jacobson, G. (1980). Treatment of endogenous anxiety with phobic, hysterical and hypochondriacal symptoms. *Archives of General Psychiatry, 37,* 51–59.

Sheehan, D. V., Claycomb, J. B., & Surman, O. S. (1984). The relative efficacy of alprazolam, phenelzine and imipramine in treating panic attacks and phobias. *Abstracts of 137th Annual Meeting of the American Psychiatric Association,* 83.

Sheehan, D. V., Davidson, J., Manschreck, T. C., & Van Wyck Fleet, J. (1983). Lack of efficacy of a new antidepressant (bupropion) in the treatment of panic disorder with phobias. *Journal of Clinical Psychopharmacology, 31*(1), 28–31.

Sheehan, D. V., Hughes, P., & Storr, C. (1991, May). *Benzodiazepine use by physicians.* Paper presented at the annual meeting of the American Psychiatric Association. New Orleans.

Sheehan, D. V., & Raj, B. A. (1988). Monoamine oxidase inhibitors. In C. G. Last & M. Hersen (Eds.), *Handbook of Anxiety Disorders* (pp. 478–503). New York: Pergamon Press.

Sheehan, D. V., Raj, B. A., & Sheehan, K. H. (1990). Adinazolam sustained release formulation in the treatment of panic disorder: A pilot study. *Irish Journal of Psychological Medicine, 7*(2), 24–128.

Sheehan, D. V., Raj, B. A., & Sheehan, K. H. (1991, May). *The relative efficacy of high dose buspirone and alprazolam in the treatment of panic disorder: A double-blind placebo-controlled study.* Paper presented at the 144th annual meeting of the American Psychiatric Association. New Orleans.

Sheehan, D. V., Raj, B. A., Sheehan, K. H., & Soto, S. (1990). Is buspirone effective for panic disorder? *Journal of Clinical Psychopharmacology, 10*(1), 3–11.

Sheehan, D. V., Raj, B. A., Trehan, R. R., & Knapp, E. J. (1993). Serotonin in panic disorder and social phobia. *International Clinical Psychopharmacology, 8*(Suppl. 2), 63–77.

Sheehan, D. V., Uzogara, E., & Coleman, J. H. (1982, May). *The treatment of panic attacks with agoraphobia with alprazolam and ibuprofen: A controlled study.* Paper presented at the annual meeting of the American Psychiatric Association. Toronto.

Sheehan, D. V., Zak, J. P., Miller, J. A., & Fanous, B. S. (1988). Panic disorder: The potential role of serotonin reuptake inhibitors. *Journal of Clinical Psychiatry, 49*(Suppl. 8), 30–36.

Skegg, D. C. G., Richards, S. M., & Doll, R. (1979). Minor tranquilizers and road accidents. *British Medical Journal, 1,* 917–919.

Smiley, A. (1987). Effects of minor tranquilizers and antidepressants on psychomotor performance. *Journal of Clinical Psychiatry, 48* (Suppl. 12), 22–28.

Svebak, S., Camron, A., & Levande, S. (1990). Clonazepam and imipramine in the treatment of panic attacks: A double-blind comparison of efficacy and side effects. *Journal of Clinical Psychiatry, 51*(Suppl.), 7–14.

Svenson, E. M., Persson, L., & Sjoberg, L. (1980). Mood effects of diazepam and caffeine. *Psychopharmacology, 62,* 73–80.

Tesar, G. E., & Rosenbaum, J. F. (1986). Successful use of clonazepam in patients with treatment-resistant panic disorder. *Journal of Nervous and Mental Disorders, 174,* 477–482.

Tesar, G. E., Rosenbaum, J. F., Pollack, M. H., Otto, M. W., Sachs, G. S., Herman, J. B., Cohen, L. S., & Spier, S. A. (1991). Double-blind placebo-controlled comparison of clonazepam and alprazolam for panic disorder. *Journal of Clinical Psychiatry, 52*(2), 69–76.

Tondo, L., Burrai, C., Scamonatti, L., Toccafondi, F., Poddighe, A., Minnai, G., Tundo, A., & Floris, G. (1989). Carbamazepine in panic disorder [letter]. *American Journal of Psychiatry, 146,* 558.

Tucker, E., & Sirisinha, I. (1965). Toxicity of monoamine oxidase inhibitors: Report of a fatal case with histochemical findings and a review of the literature. *Alabama Journal of Medicine, 2,* 301–304.

Uhde, T. W., Boulenger, J. P., Roy-Byrne, P. P., Geraci, M. F., Vittone, B. J., & Post, R. M. (1985). Longitudinal course of panic disorder: Clinical and biological considerations. *Progress in Neuropsychopharmacological and Biological Psychiatry, 9,* 39–51.

Uhde, T. W., Stein, M. B., & Post, R. M. (1988). Lack of efficacy of carbamazepine in the treatment of panic disorder. *American Journal of Psychiatry, 145,* 1104–1109.

Versiani, M., Costa, E., Silva, J. A., & Klerman, G. L. (1987, December 7–11). *Treatment of panic disorder with alprazolam, clomipramine, imipramine, tranylcypromine or placebo.* Paper presented at the annual meeting of the American College of Neuropsychopharmacology. San Juan, PR.

Watson, A. M., & Gold, M. S. (1984). Chronic cocaine abuse: Evidence for adverse effects on health and functioning. *Psychiatric Annals, 14,* 733–743.

Waxman, D. (1977). A clinical trial of clomipramine and diazepam in the treatment of phobic and obsessional illness. *Journal of International Medical Research, 5,* 99–110.

Weissman, M. M., Klerman, G. L., Markowitz, J. S., & Ouellette, R. (1990). Suicidal ideation and suicide attempts in panic disorder and panic attacks. *New England Journal of Medicine, 321*(18), 1209–1214.

Woodman, C. L., & Noyes, R., Jr. (1994). Panic disorder: Treatment with valproate. *Journal of Clinical Psychiatry, 55,* 134.

Zitrin, C. M., Klein, D. F., Woerner, M. G., & Ross, D. C. (1983). Treatment of phobias 1: Comparison of imipramine hydrochloride and placebo. *Archives of General Psychiatry, 40,* 125–138.

13

Cognitive Behavioral Treatment of Panic Disorder

WILLIAM C. SANDERSON AND
SCOTT WETZLER

Nowhere have cognitive behavioral therapies (CBTs) achieved greater success than in the treatment of panic disorder. CBT is considered the psychotherapy of choice for anxiety disorder patients and is often administered conjointly with pharmacological treatment. According to conventional wisdom, CBT addresses the agoraphobic avoidance associated with panic disorder, whereas medications ameliorate the panic attacks themselves as well as the anticipatory anxiety. This would suggest that multimodal treatments, combining drugs and CBT, are indicated for most cases of panic disorder, and that CBT may be unnecessary for those patients who do not suffer from agoraphobia. In this chapter we plan to debunk such "conventional wisdom" and treatment recommendations. Rather, we demonstrate that CBT is an effective treatment for *all* components of panic disorder. We then describe in detail a version of CBT that combines cognitive and behavioral principles, identify the underlying mechanism of action of CBT, and indicate how and when medication may be prescribed along with CBT.

EFFICACY OF CBT
IN PANIC DISORDER

Several recent reports investigated the efficacy of CBT in the treatment of panic disorder (with and without agoraphobia). In all studies, CBT was proven to be an effective treatment. The first CBT study of panic disorder was conducted by Barlow and his colleagues (1984) ($N = 9$). After receiving CBT, patients had significantly fewer panic attacks, less anticipatory anxiety, and less agoraphobic avoidance according to all indices (i.e., self-report questionnaires, psychophysiological measures, and clinical ratings) than did wait-list controls. A 14-week open trial of CBT by Gitlin and associates (1985) ($N = 11$) found that 91 percent (10/11) of panic disorder patients were not panicking at posttreatment and that these gains were maintained at a five-month follow-up assessment. Two open trials by Clark and his colleagues (Clark, Salkovskis, & Chalkley, 1985; Salkovskis, Jones, & Clark, 1986) ($N = 27$) also found that CBT substantially reduced the number of panic attacks, both at posttreatment and at follow-up assessments. A naturalistic study of the efficacy of CBT by Sokol, Beck, Greenberg, Wright, and Berchick (1989) ($N = 17$) found that patients were panic-free at the end of treatment (mean number of individual sessions $= 18$) and at a 12-month follow-up assessment. Finally, Michelson and his colleagues (1990) found that a 12-week trial of CBT ($N = 10$) resulted in complete remission of spontaneous panic attacks.

Although these preliminary studies in which a total of 70 panic disorder patients received various forms of CBT all found that CBT was an effective treatment, Barlow and his colleagues decided to conduct two large controlled trials. The first study (Barlow, Craske, Cerny, & Klosko, 1989) contrasted different components of CBT—exposure to somatic cues plus cognitive therapy, relaxation training, and exposure plus cognitive therapy plus relaxation training—to a wait-list control group. All forms of CBT were proven superior to the wait-list control group. Treatments containing exposure plus cognitive therapy (Groups 1 and 3) were the most effective, inasmuch as 85 percent of these patients were panic-free at posttreatment. Gains were maintained at a two-year follow-up assessment (Brown, Craske, & Barlow, 1990).

The second study (Klosko, Barlow, Tassinari, & Cerny, 1990) contrasted CBT to alprazolam, placebo, and a wait-list control group. CBT was significantly more effective than placebo and the wait-list on most measures, but not different from alprazolam (although alprazolam was not significantly more effective than placebo). Eighty-seven percent of panic disorder patients receiving CBT were panic-free at posttreatment assessment, compared to 50 percent for alprazolam, 36 percent for placebo, and 33 percent for wait-list controls.

In summary, these studies all demonstrate that CBT is an effective treatment for panic disorder. When CBT directly targets the panic attacks themselves, it significantly reduces the number of spontaneous panic attacks, and the majority of panic disorder patients will be panic-free by the end of treatment. CBT is also an effective treatment for the anticipatory anxiety, agoraphobic avoidance, and secondary depression frequently associated with panic disorder. CBT is equally effective as alprazolam in the treatment of panic disorder and may, in fact, be superior to medication or other forms of psychotherapy (Clum, 1989). Moreover, the beneficial effects of CBT appear to be lasting, which is to say that patients remain symptom-free for as long as two years posttreatment.

COMPONENTS OF CBT
FOR PANIC DISORDER

Forms of CBT for panic disorder vary according to their emphasis on the "cognitive" side or the "behavioral" side. The comprehensive cognitive behavioral treatment approach for panic disorder we advocate is an amalgam of the behavioral approach described by David Barlow (1988; Barlow & Cerny, 1988) and the cognitive approach described by Aaron Beck (1988; Beck & Emery, 1985). This strategy addresses the entire configuration of panic disorder: (1) the panic attacks themselves with their cognitive, affective, and somatic symptomatology; (2) the anticipatory anxiety (the so-called fear of fear); (3) the agoraphobic avoidance that often is present to varying degrees; and (4) the sense of hopelessness that develops as the disorder becomes chronic and debilitating. The treatment approach consists of six components (see Table 13–1), including psychoeducation, cognitive restructuring, respiratory control, relaxation training, visualization/imagery exercises, and exposure. An effort is made to administer these components in sequential order, focusing on coping techniques in the early sessions, which the patient then applies during later sessions when he or she confronts panic-provoking situations and stimuli. However, the various components are highly interrelated, and

TABLE 13–1
Cognitive Behavioral Treatment Components

I. *Coping Techniques*
  1. Psychoeducation
  2. Cognitive Restructuring
  3. Respiratory Control
  4. Relaxation Training
II. *Affective Therapy: Provoking Anxiety and Panic*
  1. Visualization/Imagery Exercises
  2. Exposure
      a. interoceptive
      b. situational

in later sessions reference is often made back to information and skills learned during earlier sessions.

Psychoeducation

By the time panic disorder patients consult with a mental health professional, they typically have been to many different doctors without receiving a clear diagnosis and explanation of panic disorder. In the absence of such information, these patients often imagine that they are going to die, go crazy, or lose control. In almost all cases, they suspect that the doctor has overlooked some *life-threatening* physical condition that would account for their symptomatology. Therefore, the psychoeducation phase consists of a didactic presentation about panic disorder, within the framework of the cognitive behavioral model of panic. (See Rapee, Craske, & Barlow, 1989.)

During the initial session(s), anxiety, panic, and agoraphobia are defined. Each symptom is identified as a feature of panic disorder and shown to be harmless. Common myths about the danger of panic attacks (e.g., panic attacks are a sign of an undetected brain tumor, palpitations cause heart attacks, hyperventilation leads to fainting, etc.) are debunked. The development of the disorder is understood as a psychological response to stress, and avoidance behavior and anticipatory anxiety are viewed as ways to ward off a recurrence of the panic attacks.

Written materials, such as pamphlets and books, are valuable educational tools since they may be reread whenever the patient desires. We recommend several excellent "self-help" books that offer simple, supportive information about panic disorder (Barlow & Craske, 1989; Burns,

1989; Weekes, 1972; Wilson, 1987). In addition, we encourage patients to join the Anxiety Disorders Association of America (6000 Executive Blvd, Rockville, MD 20852). For a nominal fee, patients receive a bimonthly newsletter providing self-help tips and educational information (e.g., latest research findings) and have access to many other valuable resources. In this way, psychoeducation may become an ongoing venture for the patient, not just one component of the therapy.

Cognitive Restructuring

The cognitive restructuring component of CBT derives from Beck's seminal work on how faulty information processing may underlie affective disturbances and dysfunctional behaviors (Beck, 1988; Beck & Emery, 1985). Therapeutic change is achieved as these faulty cognitions (i.e., thoughts, beliefs, and assumptions) are identified and then subjected to rigorous reality-testing.

The first step is to help patients identify how certain cognitions accentuate or provoke panic. This is done by retrospectively examining the thoughts, beliefs, and assumptions elicited during a typical panic or anxiety episode. The first and most recent panic attacks are vividly remembered, and a detailed discussion of the last two attacks is a useful place to begin this examination. Through a series of questions, the therapist tries to determine each patient's idiosyncratic panic sequence and to uncover unrealistic catastrophic thoughts. Under such questioning, the validity of these cognitions is implicitly and explicitly challenged.

A typical panic sequence follows this line:

1. I was sitting in a meeting at work.
2. I noticed my heart began to beat faster (physical symptom).
3. I assumed these palpitations were the early signs of a panic attack and that I would lose control and start to yell. Everyone would think I was crazy (catastrophic thought).
4. I became even more anxious, worried about losing control, and started to perspire profusely (escalation).
5. I excused myself from the meeting (escape and avoidance).
6. I felt depressed and discouraged because I couldn't even handle an innocuous work meeting (hopelessness).

This description of a typical panic sequence reveals the panic disorder patient's interior monologue. In therapy, it is necessary to make these private thoughts explicit, since most patients are unaware of their own thinking. For the most part, people process information automatically, and stimuli are interpreted rapidly. There is also a tendency to deny catastrophic ways of thinking because these beliefs seems so incredible once the panic attack has subsided. The therapeutic setting should promote the patient's sense of comfort and acceptance in order to facilitate disclosure. But in addition, we recommend that patients self-monitor their cognitions *during* episodes of panic. A written numbered format may be used, as in the example just given. After several sessions of reviewing these panic-related cognitions, a clear panic sequence emerges, and patients begin to appreciate the role cognitions play.

Once patients become aware of the importance of their cognitions in eliciting and fueling their panic attacks, then they are in a position to reevaluate the validity of these cognitions and ultimately to challenge them. In particular, catastrophic misinterpretations of panic-related somatic cues are targeted (Clark, 1986). But other common misinterpretations include the overestimation of the consequences of panic (e.g., public humiliation, losing one's job, interpersonal rejection).

We use a "thought record" to quickly identify patients' thoughts, examine their validity, and challenge patients to respond with more rational thoughts. Patients are provided with a list of 10 cognition distortions, misinterpretations, or types of illogic as defined by Burns (1989). For example, in Figure 13–1, the thought record indicates that automatic thought #1 is an instance of "jumping to conclusions" (making a negative interpretation without definitive evidence in support of one's conclusion). By recognizing this distortion for what it is, patients are able to correct the conclusion by substituting a more rational response. It is important to note that cognitive restructuring is not "positive thinking." Rather, it is realistic thinking.

The final phase of cognitive restructuring is to *decatastrophize* the situation with patients, especially when dealing with agoraphobic avoidance. This is easily accomplished through a series of questions: What if your worst fears come true, would it really be as bad as you imagine? Consider patients who believe they will have a panic attack on a plane, causing them to scream wildly and try to escape. In fact, if their worst fears were realized and they did have a panic attack, the most likely outcome would be a feeling of great discomfort, not screaming, attempts to escape, and embarrassment. Decatastrophizing greatly reduces the patient's need to avoid panic-related situations.

I. Describe the situation: sitting in a meeting at work, began experiencing palpitations

II. Specify feelings/emotion(s) and rate the intensity of each from 1 (just present) to 100 (very intense) (Example: 20 may equal mild, 50 may equal moderate).

1. anxious (90)   2. frustrated (40)

III. Complete the 3 columns.

AUTOMATIC THOUGHT(S) List your thoughts	COGNITIVE DISTORTION	RATIONAL RESPONSES Respond to each thought you listed
1. These palpitations are going to lead to a panic attack!	jumping to conclusions	1. Having palpitations is not necessarily a sign that I will have a panic attack. I have had palpitations many times without experiencing panic. The palpitations are probably a result of the two cups of coffee I had earlier. If I maintain a realistic perspective, I can avoid worsening the symptoms.
2. If I have a panic attack I will lose control, start yelling and run out of the room. Everyone will think I am crazy!	jumping to conclusions	2. I always fear losing control during panic, but I have had hundreds of attacks and never even came close to actually losing control. When I have had a panic attack in public, no one has ever noticed, even when I asked them afterward.
3. I am sick and tired of dealing with my anxiety. I will never get over this—my life is ruined!	overgeneralization, disqualifying the positive	3. I am tired of dealing with this problem and wish I didn't have it, and it has affected my life, but my life is not ruined, I have many positive things going on. I have made progress dealing with this problem and am confident that I will continue to improve.

IV. Outcome: Describe how you feel after completing the above.

I felt much better because I realized that I will not necessarily experience a panic attack during the meeting, and even if I do, I will be uncomfortable but I have always handled panic attacks in the past and no one has noticed.

Figure 13–1. Thought Record

320

Respiratory Control

Respiratory control helps the patient regain a sense of control over the somatic features of panic and anxiety. They are taught a method of breathing that increases relaxation and prevents hyperventilation (Clark et al., 1985). Hyperventilation initiates a cascade of somatic symptoms such as dizziness, chest pain, breathlessness, and parasthesias, which culminate in panic. These symptoms instill a frightening sense that one's body is out of control.

Under stress and anxiety, respiration rate often increases, characterized by the use of chest muscles and short, shallow breaths. To combat this tendency, patients are taught diaphragmatic breathing (i.e., breathing that involves in and out movement of the abdomen, not chest) at a regular rate (approximately 12 breaths per minute). This exercise is then practiced outside of the session in many different situations. Patients learn to quickly control their breathing, and come to recognize that this is an effective strategy that they can rely on in panic-provoking situations.

Relaxation Training

Relaxation training is a progressive muscle exercise also intended to help patients gain a greater sense of control over their bodies. It is practiced daily as a way to decrease tension that might otherwise escalate into a full-blown panic attack. The basic technique involves tensing and relaxing muscles to achieve a more serene state. Specific step-by-step details regarding this exercise may be found in an excellent text by Barlow and Cerny (1988).

Visualization

In therapy, discussion of anxiety-provoking situations and experiences is all too often devoid of the vivid images, associations, and emotion necessary to foster real change. Visualization is meant to enhance this dialogue. When patients close their eyes and imagine such situations, they are often flooded with anxiety. By confronting such anxiety-provoking situations in their mind's eye, patients learn how to cope before they have to confront them for real.

The therapist helps patients to visualize the situation in as much detail as possible. As patients describe the image, the therapist asks relevant questions about the associated thoughts and feelings. This is meant to elaborate the image, but it is also a useful assessment. (Reporting on cognitions and emotions in an imagined situation in the present is usually more accurate than recalling cognitions and emotions in a real situation from the past.) In time, patients are asked to visualize effective coping techniques and responses. In this way, visualization serves as an inoculation—if patients can handle small amounts of manufactured anxiety, they will be better prepared to handle anxiety in a naturalistic setting.

Exposure

Exposure is the final component of CBT in which patients confront anxiety- and panic-provoking stimuli. These phobic stimuli may be *external situations* or *internal sensations*. By repeatedly facing their anxiety in a structured situation, patients learn to develop appropriate coping mechanisms and become further inoculated.

Based on patients' individualized hierarchy of feared situations (see Figure 13–2), the therapy exposes them to each of these situations. Similarly, interoceptive exposure is based on patients' individualized hierarchy of feared internal sensations (e.g., dizziness, palpitations). Exposure to these sensations may be achieved using idiosyncratic methods, such as overbreathing, spinning, and physical exertion.

The use of a hierarchy of least feared to most feared stimuli allows the therapy to progress and build on past accomplishments. Patients first learn to cope with mildly anxiety-provoking situations and later face the more difficult situations. Facing anxiety within a supportive therapeutic setting helps patients to utilize their newly developed coping skills. Patients learn to tolerate anxiety without the need to escape. This lesson is passed on from one anxiety-provoking situation to the next.

As always, practice between sessions is expected. We encourage patients to expose themselves to phobic stimuli at least three times during the week between sessions. First, patients complete the exposure exercise with the assistance of the therapist, such as inducing heart palpitations by walking up and down stairs for three minutes, and later they practice this exercise at home. Patients' self-confidence soar as they realize that the therapist has confidence that they can handle this formerly anxiety-provoking experience on their own.

Case Example. Mr. D is a 30-year-old excessively hardworking lawyer with daily panic attacks and moderate agoraphobia. He was referred for

Name _____ Date _____

Rate the degree to which you currently FEAR and AVOID the situations listed below.

FEAR/ANXIETY:

0......1......2......3......4......5......6......7......8

none   mild   moderate   severe   very
                                               severe

AVOIDANCE:

0......1......2......3......4......5......6......7......8

do not   rarely   sometimes   usually   always
avoid   avoid   avoid   avoid   avoid

Description of Situation	Fear	Avoid
take shuttle from NY to Boston—alone	8	8
take shuttle from NY to Boston—with wife	7	8
drive through Midtown Tunnel—alone	6	8
drive through Midtown Tunnel—with wife	5	6
drive alone: exit 17–30 on the highway	5	4
go through Midtown Tunnel as a passenger	4	4
drive alone: exit 17–24 on the highway	3	2
drive alone: exit 17–20 on the highway	2	1

Figure 13–2. Fear and Avoidance Hierarchy

CBT. During the initial sessions, Mr. D received an individualized evaluation, which revealed that his greatest concern was fear of having a heart attack. He was greatly reassured by the psychoeducational information about the physiological arousal occurring during panic. Specifically, he learned that his palpitations were benign and not indicative of impending heart failure; in fact, as he well knew, his heart rate increased dramatically during sex, an activity he enjoyed. Although Mr. D felt that the panic attacks were inexplicable and unpredictable, a careful review of his history revealed that the origin of his panic attacks was tied to increased stress regarding his performance at work. This understanding made the panic attacks less mysterious and overwhelming as well as more predictable.

Mr. D was asked to monitor all of his panic attacks on an ongoing basis by recording the situation in which they occurred, and his thoughts and physical symptoms. This homework assignment was designed to help him focus on the connection between his cognitions and the ensuing panic. It became clear to him that the deadline pressure he faced on the job (e.g., to prepare a legal document) led to increased arousal (e.g., palpitations, muscle tension), which he then interpreted in a catastrophic way (e.g., belief that he was having a heart attack), leading to a full-blown panic attack. The act of monitoring his thoughts during the panic attack was itself anxiety-reducing. In the therapy sessions, the logic of Mr. D's automatic thoughts and catastrophic thinking was examined and challenged. He was encouraged to reexamine outside of the therapy session the validity of his thoughts during panic episodes. In addition, Mr. D was given relaxation exercises and breathing retraining to mitigate the somatic symptoms of anxiety and panic. He was taught these exercises by the therapist, but then practiced them at home on a daily basis.

While the cognitive restructuring and relaxation training were quite effective, Mr. D continued to use avoidance as a strategy to decrease anxiety. For example, he would not ride his exercycle because he found the palpitations too uncomfortable. Thus, in the exposure phase of treatment, Mr. D developed a plan to progressively increase his tolerance of these sensations. Homework assignments consisted of using the exercycle for an increasing amount of time each day. The coping methods he had already learned proved to be especially useful in this context, and Mr. D's association between somatic arousal and panic was extinguished. This sense of control over panic attacks quickly generalized to other agoraphobic situations. His heart no longer started palpitating when he heard the senior partner's footsteps coming down the hall. Mr. D terminated after 16 sessions feeling much more hopeful and in control of his panic response.

THE MECHANISM OF ACTION OF CBT

Despite its established efficacy, the precise mechanism of action of CBT is still not well understood. Speculations abound, however, based more on ideological preconceptions than scientific examination (Barlow, 1988; Beck, 1985; Foa & Kozak, 1985; Gray, 1982, 1985; Rachman, 1985).

The two most comprehensive explanations for the efficacy of CBT with panic disorder patients (as well as patients with other anxiety disorders) are "emotional processing" (Foa & Kozak, 1985) and "toughening up" (Gray, 1982, 1985). While these two theories may be understood as alternatives, we have observed a common thread running between them both. According to our reading of the literature, both "emotional processing" and "toughening up" make reference to the evocation of anxiety and panic under controlled conditions that eventually results in an amelioration of the symptomatology (Barlow, 1988; Foa & Kozak, 1985; Gray, 1985; Rachman, 1985). While the elicitation of anxiety and panic may appear to be counterproductive, it is only once they are present that CBT may become effective (Barlow, 1988; Craske, Sanderson, & Barlow, 1987; Foa & Kozak, 1985; Gray, 1985; Rachman, 1980, 1985). How does this essential mechanism of action of CBT produce therapeutic benefits?

A panic attack is composed of somatic, cognitive, and affective features. According to most cognitive behavioral theories of panic disorder, as the panic attacks recur, these components become so interwoven that the presence of any single feature is likely to trigger the entire configuration of panic features. For example, physical arousal (e.g., palpitations, light-headedness, etc.) may trigger a panic attack, including cognitive and affective symptoms. But it is equally likely that the fear of loss of control (a cognitive feature) precipitated by a phobic situation may trigger a panic attack, including somatic and affective symptoms.

The aim of CBT for panic disorder is to extinguish the association between the full-blown panic attack and each of these components. For example, the recovered panic disorder patient is able to experience physical arousal without provoking the whole panic response (e.g., its cognitive and affective features). Or the recovered panic disorder patient may be able to feel a loss of control (e.g., in inescapable situations such as airplanes, elevators, and public meetings) without experiencing physical arousal and anxiety requiring a phobic response.

Simply stated, CBT works by exposing panic disorder patients to specific stimuli that usually trigger panic attacks and anxiety. Since this exposure is done in a systematic fashion under controlled conditions, it becomes less anxiety-provoking. The association between the triggering stimuli and the panic attack is extinguished. While cognitive behavioral therapies may differ with regard to their emphasis on the importance of cognition (Beck, 1985, 1988; Clark, 1986) versus behavior (Barlow, 1988) in this fear-reduction process, all theories of CBT are based to some degree on the principle that repeated exposure to anxiety-provoking stimuli in a systematic fashion results in anxiety reduction.

This explanation of the mechanism of action of CBT may seem paradoxical. How could the evocation of anxiety ultimately lead to anxiety-reduction? Usually, one would think, the less anxiety the better. In contrast, CBT cannot be effective without a certain degree of anxiety present.

We should note, however, that the rationale for evoking anxiety during CBT is different from the rationale for evoking anxiety during psychodynamic therapies. In psychodynamic approaches, the analyst's withholding demeanor recapitulates childhood frustrations for the patient and often elicits anxiety, which motivates the patient to make important changes (Meninger, 1958; Zetzel, 1978). Thus, anxiety is a *motivating* force pushing the patient toward change. By way of comparison, in CBT, anxiety is not viewed as a motivating factor—in our opinion, panic disorder patients require no additional motivation to engage in treatment. Rather, the evocation of anxiety in controlled circumstances is necessary to extinguish prior maladaptive responses. As patients develop effective coping skills in real-life situations, they attribute this success to themselves and not to some external factor (i.e., taking a pill or avoidance of an anxiety-provoking stimulus). Thus, the evocation of anxiety in CBT is related to *exposure* and *cognitive restructuring,* not to motivation.

MULTIMODAL TREATMENT
OF PANIC DISORDER

Several medications, including tricyclic antidepressants (TCA), MAO inhibitors, and the high-potency benzodiazepine alprazolam (Xanax) have been shown to be effective treatments for panic disorder (cf. Fyer

& Sandberg, 1988). As a therapeutic agent, alprazolam has several advantages over TCAs and MAO inhibitors, most notably a rapid onset of action and fewer side effects (Charney et al., 1986). For this reason, benzodiazepines in general, and alprazolam in particular, are the most commonly prescribed antipanic medications, according to surveys (Breir, Charney, & Heninger, 1986; Markowitz, Weissman, Ouellette, Lish, & Klerman, 1989; Taylor et al., 1989; Wardle, 1990).

Although alprazolam and CBT both have been demonstrated to be effective, no controlled study has reported on the relative efficacy of the combined treatment of alprazolam and CBT. This is a glaring omission considering the observation that many panic disorder patients receive combined treatment with benzodiazepines and psychotherapy (Nagy, Krystal, Woods, & Charney, 1989; Wardle, 1990).

Based on our work at two anxiety disorder clinics (Phobia and Anxiety Disorders Clinic, University at Albany, Albany, New York, and Center for Cognitive Therapy, University of Pennsylvania School of Medicine, Philadelphia, Pennsylvania), we have found that nearly half of all panic disorder patients presenting for psychological treatment were currently using a benzodiazepine: 60 percent (12 out of 20) in Sanderson, Rapee, & Barlow (1989); 46 percent (18 out of 39) in Sanderson and Beck (1989); 49 percent (27 out of 55) in Sanderson, DiNardo, Rapee, & Barlow (1990). Alprazolam was by far the most commonly used benzodiazepine: 83 percent (10 out of 12) in Sanderson and coworkers (1989); 67 percent (12 out of 18) in Sanderson and Beck (1989); and 85 percent (23 out of 27) in Sanderson and associates (1990). Despite their proven efficacy, only a small minority of patients were treated with TCAs: 0 percent in Sanderson and associates (1989); 5 percent in Sanderson and Beck (1989); 15 percent in Sanderson and coworkers (1990).

Rationale for Multimodal Treatment

A multimodal treatment approach for panic disorder has been advocated in several recent publications distributed to clinical psychiatrists (Marriott, Judd, Jeffreys, & Burrows, 1989; "Treatment of Panic Disorder," 1988). These publications claim that psychotherapy plus medication is the most effective treatment for panic disorder, better than either treatment alone. The rationale was clearly stated in *Current Therapeutics:* "Once panic is controlled with medication, maximum progress is made if various psychological techniques for anxiety control are used concomitantly" (Marriott et al., 1989, p. 111). These well-publicized recommendations are based on the assumption that two independent treatments will work synergistically.

Although there is no empirical support for this recommendation regarding panic disorder, many studies support the combined treatment of other psychiatric disorders with psychotherapy and medication. For example, the literature on the multimodal treatment of depression with TCAs plus psychotherapy suggests that combined treatment is generally *more* effective than either treatment alone (Elkin, Pilkonis, Docherty, & Sotsky, 1988; Karasu, 1990; Shea, Elkin, & Hirschfeld, 1988; Weissman, 1979).* Similarly, evidence suggests that the combined treatment of schizophrenia with neuroleptics plus psychosocial intervention results in a better outcome than medication alone (Frank & Gunderson, 1990; Wallace, Boone, & Donahoe, 1985).

Based on these data, it has become axiomatic that combined treatment of most psychiatric disorders is preferable when effective medications and psychotherapies are available. Once each has been proven effective, it is widely assumed that the treatment with the combination of medication and psychotherapy should be more effective than, or at least equivalent to, treatment with either modality alone.

The rationale for the combined treatment of panic disorder is clearly stated. Each modality is intended to compensate for limitations in the other modality. Since panic attacks are particularly terrifying for the panic disorder patient, the main treatment goal is symptom relief, which is best achieved in the short-term with alprazolam. Thus, alprazolam holds a strong appeal for all panic disorder patients, even for those who enter psychotherapy. The development of medication-free coping skills may be a long-term goal, but of secondary importance.

However, alprazolam does not offer a long-term solution, unless the patient was to be maintained continuously on the medication. Even then, alprazolam usually is not considered an effective treatment to eliminate agoraphobic avoidance (Ballenger, Burrows, & Dupont, 1988). Once the panic disorder patient is tapered off medication, the panic symptoms

---

*Although not all studies demonstrate increased efficacy of multimodal treatment of depression, no studies suggest that the combination of pharmacological and psychological treatment results in a poorer outcome than either treatment alone. The observation of increased efficacy of combined treatments in comparison to single treatments may be hampered by ceiling effects (i.e., patients receiving maximum benefit from one treatment would not be expected to improve further with the addition of a second treatment).

tend to return (Fyer et al., 1987; Pecknold, Swinson, Kuch, & Lewis, 1988; Roy-Byrne, Dager, Cowley, Vitaliano, & Dunner, 1989). Yet keeping the patient on alprazolam indefinitely is not a practical treatment strategy due to side effects (i.e., drowsiness), a fear of becoming dependent, or a wish to get pregnant. Thus, combined treatment of CBT and alprazolam makes common sense and has become accepted clinical wisdom. We, however, disagree.

The Negative Impact of Benzodiazepines on CBT

We have observed that the use of alprazolam during CBT, especially during the later sessions, undermines its efficacy (Sanderson & Wetzler, 1993). This clinical observation is counterintuitive because two treatments generally are viewed as better than one. Our claim is based on our clinical experience and our understanding of the mechanism of action of CBT; this question has never been scientifically examined and, thus, pertinent research data do not exist.

If the central mechanism of action of CBT is the evocation of anxiety and panic in a systematic fashion within the therapeutic context, then anything that interferes with the evocation of anxiety would be expected to diminish its therapeutic benefits. Since alprazolam and other benzodiazepines diminish anxiety and panic, even at subtherapeutic doses, it is impossible to elicit sufficient anxiety and panic to make the exposure component of CBT effective.*

Our observation of the interfering effects on CBT of anxiety-reducing mechanisms is not limited to medication. For example, we have observed that continued avoidance of anxiety-producing stimuli (e.g., leaving a phobic situation) or reliance on "safety signals" (e.g., going out only in the company of a spouse) also reduces the efficacy of CBT because it circumvents the aim of exposure. Thus, it is a general principle that anything

---

*Our observation is based on the combined treatment of panic disorder with CBT plus benzodiazepines. Since tricyclic antidepressants are much less frequently prescribed for panic disorder (Markowitz et al., 1989; Taylor et al., 1989), we have been unable to determine whether they also interfere with the efficacy of CBTs developed to ameliorate panic. Tricyclic antidepressants and benzodiazepines have different pharmacological effects, and therefore, there is no reason to speculate that tricyclic antidepressants (or any other class of medications shown to be effective for panic disorder) would interfere with CBT. In fact, Telch, Agras, Taylor, Roth, and Gallen (1985) found that the combined treatment of imipramine and intensive in vivo exposure was superior to either treatment alone with agoraphobic patients.

which interferes with the evocation of anxiety during CBT diminishes its efficacy.*

In our clinical experience, almost all patterns of alprazolam use diminish the efficacy of CBT. Therefore, the medication must be discontinued during CBT. As stated earlier, chronic use at a therapeutic dose interferes with CBT, but even a subtherapeutic dose of alprazolam also will reduce anxiety and therefore interfere with CBT. For example, prn use of alprazolam, especially if used during exposure exercises, has this effect. As many panic disorder patients attest, alprazolam has a "placebo effect." They report anxiety reduction seconds after taking minuscule doses, and attribute the benefits to the medication. For example, a patient may take half of a 0.25 mg tablet of alprazolam just prior to a public speech and experience no anxiety—a situation that would engender significant anxiety without the medication. Other panic disorder patients merely have to have an alprazolam tablet in their pocket or purse to feel its "effects."

Considering the potential advantages and pitfalls of using a multimodal treatment for panic disorder, we have several recommendations that maximize the efficacy of CBT:

1. For patients with moderate to severe panic disorder, alprazolam is a useful treatment in that it provides immediate relief of panic symptoms, thereby making certain patients who would otherwise be inaccessible amenable for psychotherapy. Without medication, CBT and other psychotherapeutic treatments often are insufficient. Although CBT may have a lasting impact on the patient's functioning, it will take longer to be effective than alprazolam. Many panic disorder patients cannot tolerate their symptomatology or cannot afford to wait until the therapy will become effective (e.g., cannot miss any more days at work), and therefore require immediate, symptom-oriented treatment with alprazolam.

---

*Although valid treatment studies are lacking, a few analog experiments with phobic patients (i.e., agoraphobia, social phobia, simple phobia) bear on this issue. Two studies found that anxiolytic medications interfered with the fear-reduction process of exposure (Hafner & Marks, 1976) and imaginal flooding (Chambless, Foa, Groves, & Goldstein, 1979). In contrast, two other studies found that anxiolytic medications enhanced the fear-reduction process of flooding (Hussain, 1971; Marks, Viswanathan, & Lipsedge, 1972). These inconsistencies make it all the more apparent that a definitive comparative treatment study is necessary.

2. For patients entering CBT, alprazolam is best used during the first month of therapy (i.e., during psychoeducation and relaxation training phases).

3. Patients should slowly be weaned off the medication during the beginning of cognitive restructuring and exposure phases. Although alprazolam enables patients to tolerate more exposure, alprazolam must be discontinued for them to derive maximum benefit from CBT. Therapists should expect to see increased anxiety as alprazolam is withdrawn, and many patients still may request medication because they do not realize that this anxiety is transient. But therapists should insist on complete discontinuation at this point, and patients' anxiety may be addressed using the CBT approach. Having developed new coping skills, patients will be better able to tolerate anxiety.

4. By the end of treatment, further use of alprazolam (i.e., on a prn basis) should still be discouraged. Continued reliance on the medication, even as a "safety signal" (i.e., carrying a tablet in one's purse), indicates that patients have made only a partial recovery, and requires further psychotherapeutic intervention.

CONCLUSION

In summary, cognitive behavioral therapy is an effective and long-lasting treatment for all features of panic disorder. Although CBT may be administered in conjunction with alprazolam during the early phase of treatment, in the later stages the medication interferes with the mechanism of action underlying CBT. An understanding and thorough training in the cognitive and behavioral principles and techniques is necessary to become a skilled practitioner.

REFERENCES

Ballenger, J. C., Burrows, G. D., & Dupont, R. L., Jr. (1988). Alprazolam in panic disorder and agoraphobia: Results from a multicenter trial. I: Efficacy in short-term treatment. *Archives of General Psychiatry, 45,* 423–428.

Barlow, D. H. (1988). *Anxiety and its disorders: The nature and treatment of anxiety and panic.* New York: Guilford Press.

Barlow, D. H., & Cerny, J. (1988). *Psychological treatment of panic.* New York: Guilford Press.

Barlow, D. H., Cohen, A. S., Waddell, M. T., Vermilyea, B. B., Klosko, J. S., Blanchard, E. B., & DiNardo, P. A. (1984). Panic and generalized anxiety disorders: Nature and treatment. *Behavior Therapy, 15,* 431–449.

Barlow, D. H., & Craske, M. G. (1989). *Mastery of your anxiety and panic.* Albany, NY: Graywind Publications.

Barlow, D. H., Craske, M. G., Cerny, J. A., & Klosko, J. S. (1989). Behavioral treatment of panic disorder. *Behavior Therapy, 20,* 261–282.

Beck, A. T. (1985). Theoretical perspectives on clinical anxiety. In A. H. Tuma & J. D. Maser (Eds.), *Anxiety and the anxiety disorders* (pp. 183–196). Hillsdale, NJ: Lawrence Erlbaum Associates.

Beck, A. T. (1988). Cognitive approaches to panic disorder: Theory and therapy. In S. Rachman & J. D. Maser (Eds.), *Panic: Psychological perspectives* (pp. 91–108). Hillsdale, NJ: Lawrence Erlbaum Associates.

Beck, A. T., & Emery, G. (1985). *Anxiety disorders and phobias: A cognitive perspective.* New York: Basic Books.

Breir, A., Charney, D. S., & Heninger, G. R. (1986). Agoraphobia with panic attacks: Development, diagnostic stability, and course of illness. *Archives of General Psychiatry, 43,* 1029–1036.

Brown, T. A., Craske, M. G., & Barlow, D. H. (1990, November). *Behavioral treatment of panic disorder: A two-year follow-up.* Paper presented at the annual meeting of the Association for the Advancement of Behavior Therapy. San Francisco.

Burns, D. D. (1989). *The feeling good handbook: Using the new mood therapy in every day life.* New York: Morrow.

Chambless, D. L., Foa, E. B., Groves, G. A., & Goldstein, A. J. (1979). Flooding with brevital in the treatment of agoraphobia: Countereffective? *Behaviour Research & Therapy, 17,* 243–251.

Charney, D. S., Woods, S. W., Goodman, W. K., Rifkin, B., Kinch, M., Aiken, B., Quadrino, L. M., & Heninger, G. R. (1986). Drug treatment of panic disorder: The comparative efficacy of imipramine, alprazolam, and trazodone. *Journal of Clinical Psychiatry, 47,* 580–586.

Clark, D. M. (1986). A cognitive approach to panic. *Behaviour Research and Therapy, 24,* 461–471.

Clark, D. M., Salkovskis, P. M., & Chalkley, A. J. (1985). Respiratory control as a treatment for panic attacks. *Journal of Behavior Therapy & Experimental Psychiatry, 16,* 23–30.

Clum, G. A. (1989). Psychological interventions vs. drugs in the treatment of panic. *Behavior Therapy, 20,* 429–457.

Craske, M. G., Sanderson, W. C., & Barlow, D. H. (1987). How do desynchronous response systems relate to the treatment of agoraphobia: A follow-up evaluation. *Behaviour Research and Therapy, 25,* 117–122.

Elkin, I., Pilkonis, P. A., Docherty, J. P., & Sotsky, S. M. (1988). Conceptual and methodological issues in studies of psychotherapy and pharmacotherapy, I: Active ingredients and mechanisms of change. *American Journal of Psychiatry, 145,* 909–917.

Foa, E. B., & Kozak, M. S. (1985). Treatment of anxiety disorders: Implications for psychopathology. In A. H. Tuma & J. D. Maser (Eds.), *Anxiety and the Anxiety Disorders* (pp. 421–452). Hillsdale, NJ: Lawrence Erlbaum Associates.

Frank, A. T., & Gunderson, J. G. (1990). The role of the therapeutic alliance in the treatment of schizophrenia. *Archives of General Psychiatry, 47,* 228–236.

Fyer, A. J., Liebowitz, M. R., Gorman, J., Compeas, R., Levin, A., Davies, S. O., Goetz, D., & Klein, D. F. (1987). Discontinuation of alprazolam treatment in panic patients. *American Journal of Psychiatry, 144,* 303–308.

Fyer, A. J., & Sandberg, D. (1988). Pharmacologic treatment of panic disorder. In A. J. Frances & R. Hales (Eds.), *American Psychiatric Press Review of Psychiatry* (Vol. 7, pp. 88–120). Washington, DC: American Psychiatric Press.

Gitlin, B., Martin, M., Shear, K., Frances, A., Ball, G., & Josephson, S. (1985). Behavior therapy for panic disorder. *Journal of Nervous and Mental Disease, 173,* 742–743.

Gray, J. A. (1982). *The neuropsychology of anxiety.* Oxford: Oxford University Press.

Gray, J. A. (1985). Issues in the neuropsychology of anxiety. In A. H. Tuma & J. D. Maser (Eds.), *Anxiety and the Anxiety Disorders* (pp. 5–25). Hillsdale, NJ: Lawrence Erlbaum Associates.

Hafner, R. J., & Marks, I. M. (1976). Exposure in vivo of agoraphobics: Contributions of diazepam, group exposure and anxiety evocation. *Psychosomatic Medicine, 7,* 419–425.

Hussain, M. Z. (1971). Desensitization and flooding (implosion) in treatment of phobias. *American Journal of Psychiatry, 127,* 1509–1514.

Karasu, T. B. (1990). Toward a clinical model of psychotherapy for depression, II: An integrative and selective treatment approach. *American Journal of Psychiatry, 147,* 269–278.

Klosko, J. S., Barlow, D. H., Tassinari, R., & Cerny, J. A. (1990). A comparison of alprazolam and behavior therapy in treatment of panic disorder. *Journal of Consulting and Clinical Psychology, 58,* 77–84.

Markowitz, J. S., Weissman, M. M., Ouellette, R., Lish, J. D., & Klerman, G. L. (1989). Quality of life in panic disorder. *Archives of General Psychiatry, 46,* 984–992.

Marks, I. M., Viswanathan, R., & Lipsedge, M. S. (1972). Enhanced extinction of fear by flooding during waning diazepam effect. *British Journal of Psychiatry, 121,* 493–505.

Marriott, P., Judd, F., Jeffreys, D., & Burrows, G. (1989, April). Panic and phobic disorders. Part I: Problems associated with drug therapy. *Current Therapeutics,* 107–121.

Meninger, K. (1958). *Theory of psychoanalytic technique.* New York: Basic Books.

Michelson, L., Marchione, K., Greenwald, M., Glanz, L., Testa, S., & Marchione, N. (1990). Panic disorder: Cognitive behavioral treatment. *Behaviour Research and Therapy, 28,* 141–151.

Nagy, L. M., Krystal, J. H., Woods, S. W., & Charney, D. S. (1989). Clinical and medication outcome after short-term alprazolam and behavioral group treatment in panic disorder. *Archives of General Psychiatry, 46,* 993–999.

Pecknold, J. C., Swinson, R. P., Kuch, K., & Lewis, C. P. (1988). Alprazolam in panic disorder and agoraphobia: Results from a multicenter trial. III. Discontinuation effects. *Archives of General Psychiatry, 45,* 429–436.

Rachman, S. (1980). Emotional processing. *Behaviour Research and Therapy, 18,* 51–60.

Rachman, S. (1985). The treatment of anxiety disorders: A critique of the implications for psychopathology. In A. H. Tuma & J. D. Maser (Eds.), *Anxiety and the Anxiety Disorders* (pp. 453–462). Hillsdale, NJ: Lawrence Erlbaum Associates.

Rapee, R. M., Craske, M. G., & Barlow, D. H. (1989). Psychoeducation. In C. Lindemann (Ed.), *Handbook of phobia therapy: Rapid symptom relief in anxiety disorders* (pp. 223–236). Northvale, NJ: Jason Aronson, Inc.

Roy-Byrne, P. P., Dager, S. R., Cowley, D. S., Vitaliano, P., & Dunner, D. L. (1989). Relapse and rebound following discontinuation of benzodiazepine treatment of panic attacks: Alprazolam versus diazepam. *American Journal of Psychiatry, 146,* 860–865.

Salkovskis, P. M., Jones, D. R., & Clark, D. M. (1986). Respiratory control in the treatment of panic attacks: Replication and extension with concurrent measurement of behaviour and pCO^2. *British Journal of Psychiatry, 148,* 526–532.

Sanderson, W. C., & Beck, A. T. (1989, November). The efficacy of cognitive therapy for panic disorder in medication-free and medication-withdrawal populations. In W. C. Sanderson (Chair), *Cognitive therapy of panic disorder.* Symposium conducted at the meeting of the Association for the Advancement of Behavior Therapy. Washington, DC.

Sanderson, W. C., DiNardo, P. A., Rapee, R. M., & Barlow, D. H. (1990). Syndrome comorbidity in patients diagnosed with a DSM-III-Revised anxiety disorder. *Journal of Abnormal Psychology, 99,* 308–312.

Sanderson, W. C., Rapee, R. M., & Barlow, D. H. (1989). The influence of an illusion of control on panic attacks induced via inhalation of 5.5% carbon dioxide-enriched air. *Archives of General Psychiatry, 46,* 157–162.

Sanderson, W. C., & Wetzler, S. (1993). Observations on the cognitive behavioral treatment of panic disorder: Impact of benzodiazepines. *Psychotherapy, 30,* 125–132.

Shea, M. T., Elkin, I., & Hirschfeld, R. M. A. (1988). Psychotherapeutic treatment of depression. In A. J. Frances & R. Hales (Eds.), *American Psychiatric Press Review of Psychiatry* (Vol. 7, pp. 235–255). Washington, DC: American Psychiatric Press.

Sokol, L., Beck, A. T., Greenberg, R. L., Wright, F. D., & Berchick, R. J. (1989). Cognitive therapy of panic disorder: A non-pharmacological alternative. *Journal of Nervous and Mental Disease, 177,* 711–716.

Taylor, C. B., King, R., Margraf, J., Ehlers, A., Telch, M., Roth, W. T., & Agras, W. S. (1989). Use of medication and in vivo exposure in volunteers for panic disorder research. *American Journal of Psychiatry, 146,* 1423–1426.

Telch, M. J., Agras, W. S., Taylor, C. B., Roth, W. T., & Gallen, C. (1985). Combined pharmacological and behavioral treatment for agoraphobia. *Behaviour Research & Therapy, 23,* 325–335.

The treatment of panic disorder. (1988, November). *Psychiatric Times* (Suppl.), 1–8.

Wallace, C. J., Boone, S. E., & Donahoe, C. P. (1985). The chronically mentally disabled: Independent living skills training. In D. H. Barlow (Ed.), *Clinical handbook of psychological disorders* (pp. 462–501). New York: Guilford Press.

Wardle, J. (1990). Behaviour therapy and benzodiazepines: Allies or antagonists? *British Journal of Psychiatry, 156,* 163–168.

Weekes, C. (1972). *Peace from nervous suffering.* New York: Hawthorne Books.

Weissman, M. M. (1979). The psychological treatment of depression: Evidence for the efficacy of psychotherapy alone, in comparison with, and in combination with pharmacotherapy. *Archives of General Psychiatry, 36,* 1261–1269.

Wilson, R. R. (1987). *Breaking the panic cycle.* Rockville, MD: Phobia Society of America.

Zetzel, E. (1978). *The capacity for emotional growth.* New York: International Universities Press.

Author Index

Ackerman, S. H., 222
Adair, J. R., 245
Adams, P. B., 73, 76, 90
Adams, S. F., 284
Adinoff, B., 121, 227
Aghajanian, G. K., 169
Agras, W. S., 19, 22, 41, 124, 208, 209, 210, 217, 221, 222, 327, 329
Aguera, M., 170
Aiken, B., 158, 293, 327
Akiskal, H. S., 34, 90
Albrecht, R. F., 197
Albus, M., 138, 139, 140
Aleem, A., 137, 194, 212, 213
Alexander, S., 257
Allan, T., 294
Allen, M. D., 197, 281
Allen, R. E., 218
Alling, C., 122, 123, 124, 125, 157, 164
Allsop, L. F., 294
Amin, M., 169
Amsterdam, D., 130
Amsterdam, J. D., 306
Anderson, D. J., 101, 110, 111, 112, 138, 280
Anderson, K., 42
Anderson, P., 42
Anderson, S., 194, 207, 208, 210, 214–215, 217, 218, 219, 222, 287
Andreasen, N. C., 75, 76, 84, 88, 89
Andrews, G., 67, 68, 259
Andrews, J. A., 100, 104
Andriano, K. P., 265

Annable, L., 238, 239, 241, 280
Annau, Z., 197
Anthony, J. C., 51, 60–61, 64, 100, 105, 106
Appeltauer, L., 294
Appleby, I. L., 194, 207, 208, 210, 211, 214–215, 217, 218, 219, 222, 287
Arana, G. W., 209, 212
Arnot, R., 290
Aro, H. M., 100, 108
Aronowitz, B., 101, 105, 109
Aronson, T. A., 39, 138, 194, 206, 208, 217, 218, 222, 260, 298
Artru, A. A., 220
Asberg, M., 165, 166
Asher, R., 22
Ashley, M. J., 285
Askanazi, J., 194, 220, 258, 262, 263
Asmundson, G. J. G., 27
Asnis, G. M., 92, 100, 102, 104, 106, 111, 124, 133, 134, 142, 144, 158, 159, 162, 163, 164, 175, 287
Avendano, M. A., 261
Avery, D. H., 211, 215, 280
Axelrod, J., 138

Bacher, J. D., 218
Badal, D. W., 67, 68, 69, 75
Bailey, P. L., 265
Bajwa, W. K., 124
Baker, L. A., 19

Ball, G., 215, 315
Ballenger, J. C., 17, 26, 37, 198, 246, 266, 280, 282, 284, 288, 290, 300, 306, 328
Balon, R., 137, 158, 161, 167, 211, 215, 221, 222, 260
Bank, S., 241
Banki, C. M., 166
Baraban, F. M., 169
Barbour, R. L., 220
Barlow, D. H., 16–17, 18, 19, 20, 21, 22, 23, 24, 41, 42, 82, 83, 85, 87, 100, 110, 223, 315, 316, 317, 321, 325, 326, 327, 332
Barr, G., 175
Bartels, K. M., 214
Basha, I., 16
Bass, C., 258
Bassoff, T. B., 220
Bates, S., 217, 219
Battig, K., 197
Battista, D., 219, 261
Baugh, S. J., 165
Beaudry, P., 280
Beck, A. T., 81, 82, 87, 88, 92, 93, 99, 100, 104, 106, 315, 316, 318, 325, 326, 327
Beck, J., 81, 82, 87, 88
Beckett, A., 262, 263, 264, 266
Beinfeld, M., 233, 246
Beirne, G. J., 257
Beitman, B. D., 16, 41, 91, 110, 214

337

Belardinelli, L., 197
Belin, M. F., 170
Benfield, P., 267
Benkelfat, C., 244
Bennett, J. A., 15
Bennett, W. M., 198
Berchick, R. J., 106, 315
Berchou, R., 137, 194, 211, 212, 213, 215, 217, 218, 222
Berg, C. J., 197
Berg, J., 122
Berger, A. J., 257
Berger, B. D., 154, 155
Berkenbosch, A., 264, 265
Berne, R. M., 197
Bervish, N., 130
Berwish, N. J., 306
Best, J. D., 122
Betz, F., 92, 93
Biddle, N., 264
Bidzinski, A., 154
Birbaumer, N., 24
Bishop, S. B., 106
Bixler, E. O., 286
Black, B., 199
Black, D., 158, 159, 294
Blanchard, E. B., 16–17, 21, 82, 85, 87, 332
Blanchard, J. C., 154, 241, 245, 247
Bland, R. C., 47
Blaschke, D., 133
Blazer, D. G., 51
Block, G. A., 239
Blowers, G. H., 208, 209, 210, 217, 221, 222
Blum, K., 154
Boden, P., 247
Böhme, G. A., 241, 245, 247
Bond, A. J., 197
Bondy, B., 138, 139, 140
Bone, G., 121
Bonn, J. A., 193, 206, 208, 210, 211, 217, 267
Bonte, F. J., 261
Boone, S. E., 328
Bothwick, H., 200, 237
Botsis, A. J., 42

Boulenger, J.-P., 132, 133, 184, 188, 189, 190, 198, 304
Bourin, M., 200, 237, 238, 239, 242
Bourke, D. L., 265
Bouthillier, A., 242
Bovill, J. G., 264, 265
Bowden, D. M., 220
Bower, B., 99
Bowler, K., 293
Boyd, J. H., 16, 82
Bradwejn, J., 200, 234, 235–236, 237, 238, 239, 240, 241, 242, 243, 244
Braestrup, C., 133
Branchereau, P., 245
Breier, A., 23–24, 88, 89, 127, 167, 304, 327
Brewerton, T. D., 208, 212
Brezinova, V., 197
Bridges, M., 218
Briley, M., 154
Broadhurst, P. L., 54, 155
Brocco, K. J., 82
Brocco, M. J., 154
Brockington, I. F., 106
Broekkamp, C. L., 154, 155
Bronzo, M., 122, 123, 125, 130, 132, 133
Brouillard, M., 22
Brown, F. W., 67, 68
Brown, G. W., 23, 106
Brown, H., 106
Brown, S., 42, 138, 139, 158, 159
Brown, T. A., 315
Bruinvels, J., 154
Bruns, R. F., 197
Bucher, K. D., 72, 73, 74
Buchner, D., 284
Buchsbaum, M. S., 197
Buda, A. J., 120, 122, 123, 125
Bunney, W. E., 120
Burke, J. D., 10, 51, 52, 82
Burnam, A., 51
Burns, D. D., 317, 318, 319
Burns, L. E., 21
Burrai, C., 297

Burrows, G. D., 17, 67, 68, 88, 89, 140, 266, 268, 282, 300, 327, 328
Bushnell, J. A., 27
Busto, U., 285
Butler, F. K., 221, 261
Buxton, D. A., 54, 155
Buzzi, R., 197

Cahn, W., 92
Calev, A., 197
Callahan, M., 289
Cameron, O. G., 22, 120, 122, 123, 124, 125, 130, 132, 133, 136, 137, 139, 140, 141, 184, 189
Campbell, H. D., 285
Campbell, N. J., 234
Campeas, R. B., 160, 218, 293
Camron, A., 280
Carasiti, I., 138, 206, 208, 217, 218, 222, 260
Carlsson, A., 154
Carr, D. B., 168, 194, 215, 217, 220, 262, 263, 264, 266
Carter, C. S., 138, 139
Case, W. G., 280
Casper, R., 166
Cassano, G. B., 90, 158, 159
Cerny, J. A., 16–17, 20, 21, 315, 316, 321
Ceulemans, D. L. S., 167
Chahal, R., 106
Chalkley, A. J., 315, 321
Chalmers, J., 245
Chambers, W. J., 104
Chambless, D. L., 20, 330
Champagnat, J., 245
Chan, J. Y. H., 245
Chan, M., 259
Chan, S. H., 245
Chang, D. S., 16, 20
Chang, I., 299
Chapman, T., 101, 105, 109
Charles, G., 130, 133
Charney, D. S., 23–24, 76, 88, 89, 90, 120, 121, 122, 123, 125, 126, 127,

128, 129, 130, 131, 132, 133, 138, 139, 140, 141, 143, 145, 158, 162, 163, 164, 167, 168, 169, 170, 190, 194, 262, 263, 264, 266, 267, 280, 283, 293, 304, 327

Chaudhry, D. R., 67, 68, 69, 75, 76

Chen, C., 42

Chernan, L., 100, 110

Chignon, J. M., 101, 103, 105, 108

Cho, H. J., 245

Choi, O. H., 198

Chopin, P., 154

Chouinard, G., 280

Christiansen, J., 22, 88, 89, 91, 92

Christianson, J., 101, 110, 111, 112

Chu, N. J., 197

Clancy, J., 67, 68, 69, 100, 101, 108, 110, 111, 112, 138, 280, 304

Clark, D. M., 315, 319, 321, 326

Clarke, A., 155

Claycomb, J. B., 290, 300, 303

Clayden, A. D., 165

Clayton, P. J., 67, 68, 69, 75, 76, 81, 84, 88, 89

Clergue, F., 266

Cliffe, I. A., 156

Clifford, J. N., 121

Cloninger, C. R., 81

Cloninger, R. L., 47, 67, 68, 69

Clothier, J., 42

Clow, A., 217

Clubb, M. M., 35

Clum, G. A., 316

Cobb, S., 198

Cobble, ! C., 286

Coccaro, F., 151

Coffey, C. E., 197

Coffin, V. L., 198

Cohen, ! S 332

Cohen, B. S., 212, 217, 219, 220, 222, 258, 260, 261, 266, 273

Cohen, E. W., 67, 68, 69, 75

Cohen, L. S., 280, 281, 284, 300, 305

Cohen, M. E., 67, 68, 206, 262

Cohen, R. M., 169

Cole, R., 264–265

Coleman, J., 168, 194, 215, 217, 280, 300

Colpaert, F. C., 154

Commissaris, R. L., 155

Compeas, R., 329

Compernolle, T., 258

Consalazio, F. C., 206

Cook, B. L., 20, 303

Cook, D., 122

Cook, J. M., 169

Cooper, A. M., 92

Cooper, G. L., 294

Cooper, M. F., 198

Cooper, T. B., 124, 165, 299

Coplan, J. D., 218, 220, 258, 262, 263, 264, 265

Cordon, J. J., 155

Coromilas, J., 210, 218

Coryell, W., 75, 76, 84, 88, 89, 91, 92, 97, 100, 108, 304

Costa, E., 169, 286

Costall, B., 154, 247

Cottler, L. B., 52

Couetoux du Tertre, A., 238, 241, 242

Cowley, D. S., 206, 208, 209, 211, 212, 213, 214, 215, 216, 217, 219, 220, 221, 222, 256, 329

Cox, B. J., 39, 91, 100, 103, 109, 243

Cox, D., 288

Coyrell, W. A., 22

Craig, T. J., 39

Craske, M. G., 20, 21, 22, 23, 41, 315, 317, 325

Crawley, J., 121, 152, 197, 253

Cress, M., 197

Croughan, J., 29, 103, 106

Crowe, R. R., 60, 67, 68, 69, 72, 73, 74, 75, 76, 138, 280

Csonka, E., 247

Cull, J. G., 106

Curtis, G. C., 22, 91, 92, 120, 122, 123, 124, 125, 130, 132, 133, 136, 137, 139, 140, 141

Curzon, G., 155

Czachurski, J., 245

Dackis, C. A., 122, 123, 124, 125

Dager, S. R., 206, 208, 209, 211, 212, 213, 214, 215, 216, 217, 220, 221, 222, 329

Dahan, J., 264, 265

Dahm, F. P., 101, 104, 106

Dalton, J. W., 256, 258

Daly, J. W., 197, 198

Dampney, R. A. L., 245

Danielson, E., 217, 218

Darche, F., 154, 241, 247

Darwin, C. R., 15

Dashwood, M. R., 263

Daughtry, G., 197

Davidson, J., 296

Davies, M., 210, 218

Davies, S., 124, 160, 194, 207, 208, 210, 211, 212, 214–215, 217, 218, 219, 220, 222, 258, 260, 261, 287, 293, 329

Davis, C. M., 122, 123, 124, 125

Davis, J. M., 166

Davis, M., 152

Davis, W. W., 25, 26

D'Costa, M., 261

Dealy, R., 293

DeGoede, J., 264, 265

Degryse, A. D., 154

Delevault, E., 266

Delgado, P. L., 267

Dellon, D., 287

de Loof, C., 258, 263

de Mayo, R., 24

Dembowsky, K., 245
DeMey, J., 245
de Montigny, C., 234, 235,
    242
Dempsey, J. A., 257
Denavit-Saubie, M., 245
Den Boer, J. A., 156, 158,
    159, 160, 162, 163, 164,
    167, 206–207, 208, 217,
    218, 222, 237, 239, 241,
    260, 294
Depauw, Y., 130, 133
Depeu, R. A., 24
Derogatis, L. R., 189
Derrick, P. L., 67, 68
DeRuiter, C., 82, 85, 87
Descarries, L., 168
Desmonts, P., 266
Deupree, D., 247
Devlin, M. J., 212
Devous, M. D., 261
DeWeerth, A., 234
Didier, M. I., 170
Dillon, D., 121, 194, 207,
    208, 209, 210, 211, 212,
    214–215, 217, 218, 219,
    220, 221, 222, 260, 261,
    266
Di Marco, J. P., 197
DiNardo, P. A., 16–17, 21,
    82, 84, 85, 87, 327, 332
Divoll, M., 281
Docherty, J. P., 328
Doctor, R. M., 23
Dogloo, L., 23
Doll, R., 284
Domeney, A. M., 154, 247
Domingues, F. J., 263
Donahoe, C. P., 328
Doran, A. R., 139
Doreen, B., 198
Doremfeld, D. M., 100, 103,
    109
Dorow, R., 169
Dorsa, D. M., 217
Dorward, J., 91
Dourish, C. T., 156, 233, 234
Dow, M. G., 106
Dragunow, M., 197
Drevets, W. C., 221, 244

Drexler, H., 197
Drusin, R. E., 304
Dryman, A., 53, 56, 59, 62,
    64
Duman, R. S., 139, 140
Dunner, D. L., 206, 208,
    209, 211, 212, 213, 214,
    215, 216, 217, 221, 222,
    280, 329
Dupont, R. L., 17, 88, 89,
    266, 282, 300, 328
Durieux, C., 245
D'Urzo, A. D., 261
Dustan, H. P., 136
Duvaldestin, P., 266

Easton, C., 209
Easton, J. D., 136
Eaton, W. W., 17, 50, 51, 53,
    54, 55, 56, 59, 60, 61,
    62, 64, 72, 73
Eaves, L. J., 70, 71, 76
Eckardt, M., 121
Ediger, J. M., 27
Edlund, M. J., 42, 122, 123,
    124,
    125
Edwards, E., 266
Egan, G., 141
Ehlers, A., 19, 41, 124, 191,
    208, 209, 210, 217, 221,
    222, 240, 327, 329
Elkin, I., 328
Elkins, R., 197
Ellenbogen, M., 244
Elsworth, J. D., 121, 125,
    126, 141
Emery, G., 316, 318
Emson, P. C., 233
Endicott, F., 165
Endicott, J., 1, 29, 75, 76,
    84, 88, 89, 103, 134,
    165, 213
Endler, N. S., 39, 91
Engel, J. A., 154
Eon, B., 154
Eriksen, E., 157, 164
Eriksson, C. E., 197
Eriksson, E., 122, 123, 124,
    125

Errington, M. L., 263
Ervin, F., 240, 241, 242, 243
Escobar, J. I., 294
Eshleman, S., 51
Estes, M. L., 284
Ettedgui, E., 194, 207, 208,
    217, 218
Evans, A., 244
Evans, L., 158, 159, 160
Everitt, B. J., 154
Extein, J., 139

Facchinetti, F., 213
Fagrell, B., 198
Fairbanks, J., 293
Fanous, B. S., 293
Faravelli, C., 23
Farmer, A., 106
Farmer, B. B., 219, 228
Fava, M., 42, 213
Fawcett, J., 89, 158, 159
Feighner, J. P., 1
Fekete, M., 247
Feldman, R. D., 139
Feledgy, G., 247
Fenton, B., 207, 208, 217,
    260
Fergusson, P. A., 91
Fernandez-Pardal, J., 245
Field, M. J., 241, 247
File, S. E., 152, 154, 155,
    197
Fine, J., 222
Finesinger, J., 135–136
Fink, M., 207, 208, 217
Finlay-Jones, R., 23
First, M. B., 25, 26, 106
Fishman, S. M., 262, 263,
    264, 266
Fitzpatrick, M., 215
Flaker, G., 16
Fletcher, A., 156
Fletcher, K., 284
Flor, H., 24
Floris, G., 297
Flowers, D., 121
Foa, E. B., 325, 330
Folstein, M., 106
Fontaine, R., 280
Forchetti, C. M., 170

Foster, S. I., 212
Fox, I. L., 280
Fox, K., 167
Fox, P. T., 221, 244, 260, 261
Frances, A., 25, 26, 92, 215, 315
Frank, A. T., 328
Franke, K., 281
Fraser, S., 140
Fredholm, B. B., 198
Freedman, R., 194, 207, 208, 217
Frick, W., 233
Friedinger, R. M., 241
Friedman Harkavy, J. M., 287
Friedman, C. J., 92
Friedman, E., 299
Friedman, S., 100, 110, 220, 240
Friedman, T., 100, 102, 104, 106, 111
Frohlich, E. D., 136
Frohman, C. E., 217, 219
Frosch, E., 76, 90
Fubizer, H. C., 148
Fusselman, M. J., 221, 244, 260, 261
Fyer, A. J., 26, 29, 39, 61, 83, 101, 103, 105, 109, 121, 160, 194, 207, 208, 209, 210, 211, 212, 214–215, 217, 218, 219, 220, 221, 222, 245, 258, 259, 260, 261, 262, 263, 264–265, 266, 271, 273, 287, 293, 296, 304, 326, 327, 329
Fyer, M. R., 39, 160, 182, 192, 193, 195, 220, 236, 258, 262, 263, 265, 293

Gabel, J., 294
Gaffney, F. A., 207, 208, 217, 260
Gallaway, M. P., 145
Gallen, C., 329
Gammon, G. D., 76, 89
Ganellen, R., 209

Gans, B. J., 197
Garrison, R., 56
Garside, R. F., 167
Garssen, B., 82, 85, 87, 258
Garvey, M. J., 20, 101, 110, 111, 112, 120, 285, 303
Gawin, F. H., 299
Gelders, Y. G., 167
Geller, I., 152, 154
Genazzani, A. R., 213
Gennari, F. J., 257
George, D. T., 42, 208, 212, 213, 214, 218, 227
George, L. K., 82
George, T., 121
Georgotas, A., 299
Gepts, W., 233
Geraci, F., 162, 163
Geraci, M. F., 186, 187, 304
German, D. C., 121
Germanson, T., 87, 91
Gerrard, P. A., 154
Gershon, S., 127, 158, 161, 167
Geyer, M. A., 155
Ghoneim, M. M., 138, 280
Gibbon, M., 106
Gibson, F. L., 155
Gietzen, D. W., 138, 139, 140
Gilboa, D., 197
Giles, C., 245
Gill, W. S., 106
Gillessen, D., 234
Gillis, R. A., 245
Gilmore, M. M., 92
Girdwood, R. H., 303
Gispen-de-Wied, C. C., 157, 159, 160, 294
Gitlin, B., 215, 315
Gittelman, R., 22
Gittelman-Klein, R., 22
Gittleson, N., 167
Gjedde, A., 244
Gladis, M., 212
Glanz, L., 315
Glaser, F. B., 87, 91
Glass, R., 209
Glassman, A. H., 212, 288
Glazer, W. M., 120, 128

Gledhill, N., 257
Gliebe, P. A., 256, 258
Glitz, D., 122, 123, 125, 130, 132, 133
Glover, V., 217
Glue, P., 120, 170, 218, 242
Go, V. L., 233
Goddard, A. W., 158, 159, 164, 169
Goddard, G. V., 197
Goetz, D., 160, 293, 329
Goetz, R. R., 39, 211, 219, 220, 258, 260, 261, 262, 263, 264, 265
Gold, M. S., 122, 123, 124, 125, 132, 298
Goldman, M., 265
Goldrich, M. S., 233, 234
Goldstein, A. J., 20, 330
Goldstein, J. A., 297
Goldstein, L., 138
Goldstein, M. B., 257
Goldstein, R. S., 261
Goleman, D., 99
Goltermann, N. R., 233
Gommeren, W., 167
Goodchild, A. K., 245
Goodman, R. R., 198
Goodman, T. A., 139, 140
Goodman, W. K., 127, 128, 158, 162, 163, 164, 168, 194, 262, 263, 264, 266, 293, 327
Goodwin, F. K., 10, 120, 139, 152
Gordon, E. K., 121
Gordon, G. H., 267
Gorman, J. M., 21, 28, 39, 61, 121, 158, 159, 160, 182, 192, 193, 194, 195, 207, 208, 209, 210, 211, 212, 213, 214–215, 217, 218, 219, 220, 221, 222, 236, 245, 258, 259, 260, 261, 262, 263, 264–265, 266, 271, 273, 287, 293, 304, 329
Gorsuch, R. L., 190
Gossard, D., 19, 41, 208, 209, 210, 217, 221, 222

Gradman, A. H., 122, 123, 125, 126, 141
Graeff, F. G., 155
Grande, T. P., 82
Grant, S. J., 120, 136
Gray, J. A., 325
Gray, R., 207, 208, 217
Greden, J. F., 183, 184, 189
Green, A. R., 154
Green, M. A., 91, 92
Greenberg, H. S., 136, 280
Greenberg, R. E., 241
Greenberg, R. L., 315
Greenblah, D. J., 194
Greenblatt, D., 168, 215, 217, 280, 281
Greenblatt, E. N., 154
Greenwald, M., 315
Greenwald, S., 1, 16, 17, 19, 20
Griez, E., 22, 161, 193, 194, 209, 258, 262, 263, 264, 267
Grossenbacher, H., 285
Grossman, P., 260
Grosz, D., 42
Grosz, H. J., 219, 228
Grove, W. M., 89
Groves, G. A., 330
Groves, J. E., 284
Gruenberg, E., 82, 106
Grunhaus, L., 89
Grunstein, M. M., 265
Guidotti, A., 169
Gully, R., 211, 261
Gunderson, J. G., 328
Gurguis, G. N. M., 128
Gurney, C., 167
Gursky, D. M., 243
Guttmacher, L. B., 182, 192, 193, 195, 215, 236
Guze, S. B., 1, 67, 68, 69, 81, 110

Haack, D., 139
Hackman, K. A., 221, 244, 260, 261
Hafner, R. J., 330
Haft, J. L., 291
Haigh, J. R. M., 237

Halbreich, U., 133, 134, 142
Haller, J. W., 221, 244
Halter, J., 122, 197
Hamann, M. S., 92
Hamaoka, T., 245
Hameede, F., 158, 159
Hamilton, B. L., 245
Hamlin, C. L., 122, 123, 124, 125
Hammen, C., 24
Hampa, B. J., 67, 68, 69, 75, 76
Hapworth, W., 299
Harding, P. S., 50
Harison, J., 267
Harkavy-Friedman, J. M., 100, 104, 106, 124, 142
Harkins, K., 266
Harmatz, J. S., 281
Harper, M., 61
Harris, E. L., 67, 68, 69, 75, 76
Harrison, J., 193, 206, 208, 210, 211, 217
Harrison, W., 213, 303
Harro, J., 240, 241, 243, 247
Hashimura, E., 245
Hatcher, J., 285
Hattox, S. E., 121
Hauge, A., 257, 265
Heath, A., 70, 71, 76
Heikkinen, M. E., 100, 108
Helke, C. J., 245
Helzer, J. E., 29, 51, 103, 106
Heninger, D. R., 262, 263, 264, 266
Heninger, F. R., 145
Heninger, G. R., 23–24, 88, 89, 120, 121, 122, 123, 125, 126, 127, 128, 129, 130, 131, 132, 133, 138, 139, 140, 141, 143, 158, 162, 163, 164, 167, 168, 169, 170, 190, 194, 215, 217, 267, 293, 304, 327
Henriksson, M. M., 100, 108
Henry, J. P., 198
Herman, J. B., 280, 281, 284, 300

Herscovitch, P., 221, 261
Heyden, J., 154
Heyman, A., 257
Hibbert, G., 258, 259
Hill, D. R., 233, 234
Hill, E. M., 122, 123, 125, 140, 141
Hinkle, P. E., 197
Hinricks, J. V., 138, 280
Hirschfeld, R. M. A., 10, 75, 76, 84, 88, 89, 328
Hjemdahl, B., 198
Hjorth, S., 154
Hoare, R. C., 121
Hodge, S. E., 73
Hoehn-Saric, R., 158, 159, 296
Hoenk, P. R., 67, 68, 69
Hoes, J. J., 267
Hoffman, W. E., 197
Holland, J. P., 216
Hollander, E., 222, 259, 260, 263, 293
Hollingsworth, P. J., 122, 123, 125, 140, 141
Holmberg, G., 160
Holmberg, J., 127
Holmgren, A., 206
Holt, P. E., 259
Hoogduin, K., 258
Hoppenbrouwers, M. L., 167
Hopper, J. L., 67, 68, 268
Hornblow, A. R., 27
Hornig, C. D., 28–29
Horowski, R., 169
Horwath, E., 28–29, 90, 76
Horwell, D. C., 247
Hory, H., 158, 159
Hoszer, C. E., 82
House, J. D., 100, 108
Howell, E. F., 280, 284, 306
Hsiao, S., 247
Huang, Y. H., 119, 124, 136, 168
Huber-Smith, J., 122
Huber-Smith, M. J., 120, 122, 123, 124, 125, 136, 137, 139
Hucek, A., 288
Hughes, J., 208, 219, 247

Hughes, M., 51
Hughes, P., 285
Hugues, J., 241, 247
Hunt, S. P., 245
Hunter, J. C., 247
Huppi, K., 234
Huse, D. M., 284
Hussain, M. Z., 330
Hyde, J. R. G., 154
Hyde, T. S., 206, 208, 209, 217, 221, 222, 280

Ianni, P., 217
Imbimbo, J., 284
Inagaki, S., 245
Innis, R. B., 139, 140, 245
Insel, T. R., 34, 130, 151, 169, 182, 192, 193, 195, 236
Iqbal, N., 124
Ishiki, D., 280
Isometsa, E. T., 100, 108
Itil, T. M., 197
Iversen, S. D., 154
Ivy, A., 233

Jacobsen, G., 37
Jacobson, G., 290
Jardine, I., 233
Jatlow, P. I., 121, 190
Javaheris, S., 260
Jeffreys, D., 327
Jenck, F., 154, 155
Jenkins, S., 161
Jenne, H., 261
Jenner, F. A., 285
Jennings, M., 121
Jensen, C. F., 208, 212, 213, 219
Jensvold, M., 197
Jhirad, R., 261
Jimerson, D. C., 120, 121, 122, 123, 125, 130, 190, 198, 208, 212, 218, 288
Joele, L., 258
Joffe, R. T., 122, 123, 125, 198
Joh, T. H., 245
Johannessen, D., 212, 213
Johanson, C. E., 285

Johnson, J., 1, 16, 17, 19, 20, 28–29, 83, 101, 103, 112
Johnson, R. E., 206
Johnston, A. L., 154
Johnston, D. G., 158, 159, 294
Jolly, S., 217, 218
Jones, B. J., 154
Jones, D. R., 315
Jones, J. C., 100, 110
Jones, K., 168, 194, 215, 217
Jones, M., 206
Jordan, D., 245
Jordan, F., 263, 264–265
Josephson, S., 215, 315
Joyce, P. R., 27
Judd, F. K., 67, 68, 140, 268, 327
Judd, L. L., 10
Judge, R., 294
Julius, S., 141

Kahn, J. F., 304
Kahn, J. P., 211, 219, 261
Kahn, R. S., 92, 144, 151, 157, 158, 159, 160, 162, 163, 164, 165, 175, 176, 294
Kakuma, T., 222
Kales, A., 286
Kalus, O., 124, 287
Kamerbeek, W. D., 157, 158, 159, 160, 294
Kaplan, M., 102, 100, 104, 106, 111
Kaplan, R. D., 92
Karabanow, O., 294
Karasu, T. B., 328
Karkanias, C., 238, 239, 241
Karno, M., 82
Kassel, D., 289
Katerndahl, D. A., 53
Kathol, R. G., 138
Katims, J. J., 197
Katschnig, H., 305
Katz, M. M., 166
Kaye, W. H., 130, 133
Kazemi, H., 260
Keane, P., 168

Keck, P. E., Jr., 215
Keefe, P., 21, 22
Keller, M. B., 19, 75, 76, 84, 88, 89, 101, 109
Kellner, R., 22, 81, 82, 86
Kelly, D., 194, 207, 208, 210, 215, 217, 222
Kelly, E., 247
Kenardy, J., 158, 159
Kendler, K. S., 51, 70, 71, 76
Kennealy, J. A., 257
Kennedy, A. J., 155
Kennett, G. A., 155
Kenny, J., 258, 262, 263
Kenny, M., 220
Kerber, R. E., 60, 138
Kerr, T. A., 167
Kerr, W. J., 256, 258
Kessler, L. G., 51
Kessler, R. C., 51, 53, 54, 70, 71, 72, 73
Ketelaars, C. E., 154
Keyl, P. M., 17, 55, 60, 61
Keyser, M. L., 296
Kidd, K. K., 67
Kiivet, R. A., 247
Kilfoil, T., 154
Kilpatrick, A., 67, 68, 69, 75
Kilts, C. D., 155
Kim, O. M., 299
Kimber, N. M., 140
Kincaid-Smith, P., 198
Kinch, M., 158, 293, 327
King, D. L., 39
King, M. E., 60
King, R., 327, 329
Kinney, J., 194, 220, 258, 262, 263
Kirchheim, H. R., 245
Klabunde, R. E., 198
Kleber, H. D., 132, 145, 299
Klein, D. F., 1, 21, 22, 23, 28, 29, 39, 83, 101, 103, 105, 109, 121, 160, 182, 192, 193, 194, 195, 207, 208, 209, 210, 211, 212, 213, 214–215, 217, 218, 219, 220, 221, 222, 236, 256, 258, 259, 260, 261, 262, 263, 264–265, 266,

Klein, D. F. (*Continued*)
273, 279, 286, 287, 293,
303, 304, 329
Klein, E., 132, 133, 162,
163, 186, 187, 297
Klein, H. M., 28
Klerman, G. L., 1, 16, 17,
19, 20, 27, 61, 83, 99,
101, 102, 103, 110, 111,
112, 284, 286, 304, 305,
327, 329
Klerman, J. L., 167
Klompmakers, A. A.,
206–207, 208, 217, 218,
222, 260
Klosko, J. S., 20, 315, 332
Knapp, E. J., 293
Knitter, E., 194, 207, 208
Knoff, R. F., 122
Knott, V. J., 207, 208, 211,
217
Ko, G. N., 125, 126, 141
Koek, W., 154
Koenigsberg, H. W., 92, 222
Kokzacks, S., 160
Kopell, B. S., 208, 209, 210,
217, 221, 222
Kopell, M. L., 208, 209,
210, 217, 221, 222
Kopin, I. J., 121, 218
Koranyi, E. K., 37
Korf, J., 151, 167
Korn, M., 42
Kornaczewski, A., 285
Kostopoulos, G. K., 197
Kostowski, W., 154
Koszycki, D., 200, 235–236,
237, 238, 239, 241, 242,
243
Kotler, M., 42
Kovaks, K., 247
Kozak, M. S., 325
Kraaimaat, F., 82, 85, 87,
258
Kramer, M., 64, 106
Krystal, J. H., 16, 20, 170,
327
Krystal, J. J., 293
Kubota, Y., 245
Kuch, K., 329

Kugelmass, S., 197
Kuhar, M. J., 245
Kukull, W. A., 284
Kumada, M., 245
Kuoppasalmi, K. I., 100, 108
Kushner, M. G., 41, 91, 110,
214

Laakman, G., 133
Lader, M., 20
Ladewig, D., 285
Laduron, P. M., 154
Lake, C. R., 120, 207, 208,
217, 260, 288
Lake, J., 262, 263, 264, 266
Lamerti, J. W., 41
Landbloom, R. P., 294
Landis, D. H., 120
Lane, J. D., 198
Lane, L. D., 207, 208, 217,
260, 261
Lang, A., 247
Lapierre, Y. D., 207, 208,
217
Laraia, M., 246, 280, 282,
284, 288, 306
Larsen, D. K., 27
Larson, E. B., 284
Larsson, L. E., 233
Last, C. G., 23
Latimer, P., 194
Laverty, R., 197
Lawson, C., 120, 170, 242
Lazar, J. B., 10
Leaf, P. J., 23
Leckman, J. F., 35, 75, 76,
89
Lee, M. A., 122, 123, 125,
130, 132, 133, 140, 141,
184, 189
Leeman, E., 76, 90
Leff, J. P., 49
Leger, L., 168
Leigh, H., 125, 126, 141
Lelliot, P., 28, 258
Lemus, C. Z., 157
Lennon, S., 258, 262, 263
Lepine, J. P., 101, 103, 105,
108
Lerer, B., 197

LeRiche, W. H., 285
Lesser, I. M., 39, 88, 89,
266, 282, 300
Lesses, I. M., 282
Levande, S., 280
Levin, A., 329
Levine, P., 168, 194, 215,
217
Levitt, M., 121, 194, 207,
208, 210, 214–215, 217,
218, 219, 222, 287
Levy, G., 194, 207, 208,
210, 211, 214–215, 217,
218, 219, 222, 287
Lewinsohn, P. M., 100, 104
Lewis, A. S., 241, 247
Lewis, B. D., 168
Lewis, C. P., 329
Lewis, N., 170
Leysen, J. E., 167
Liberthson, R. R., 60
Lieb, J., 16
Liebowitz, M. R., 23, 25, 31,
39, 61, 83, 121, 159,
160, 182, 192, 193, 194,
195, 207, 208, 209, 210,
211, 212, 213, 214–215,
217, 218, 219, 220, 221,
222, 236, 245, 258, 259,
260, 261, 262, 263, 264,
265, 266, 271, 273, 287,
293, 296, 304, 329
Liek, J., 1
Light, R. W., 267
Liljequist, S., 154
Lima, D. R., 138, 139
Lindemann, E., 135–136,
135
Lindy, D. C., 212
Linnoila, M., 121, 213, 214,
218, 227
Lippa, A. S., 154
Lipsedge, M. S., 330
Lish, J. D., 28–29, 73, 76,
90, 103, 110, 111, 112,
327, 329
Lister, R. G., 197
Litterer, W. E., III, 291
Locke, B. Z., 50, 64
Loevenhart, A. S., 262

Logue, C. M., 194, 298
Loke, J., 194
London, R. G., 257
Londos, C. D., 198
Lonnqvist, J. K., 100, 108
Lopatka, C., 22
Lorenz, W. F., 262
Lotstra, F., 245
Lousberg, H., 194, 209, 258, 262, 263, 264, 267
Lubetsky, M., 189
Lucas, J. A., 27
Lucas, M., 154
Ludlow, C., 197
Lukach, B. M., 33
Lum, L. C., 258, 259
Lundy, M. S., 33
Lushene, R. E., 190
Luthe, L., 161
Luy, B., 101, 110
Lycaki, H., 137, 211, 218
Lydiard, B., 246
Lydiard, R. B., 39, 88, 89, 122, 123, 124, 125, 282, 284, 287, 300

Maas, J. W., 121, 136, 166
MacLaughlin, D. S., 281
MacLeod, A. K., 221, 244
Macleod, N. K., 154
Maddock, R. J., 19, 41, 124, 138, 139, 140, 208, 209, 210, 217, 221, 222, 260
Magee, W. J., 53, 54, 72, 73
Magliozzi, J. R., 138, 139
Mahutte, C. K., 267
Maisling, G., 130
Maitre, M., 170
Manfredi, R. L., 286
Mann, S. A., 49
Manniche, P. M., 294
Mannisto, P. T., 243
Mannuzza, S., 29, 101, 103, 105, 109
Mansbach, R. S., 155
Manschreck, T. C., 296
Mantyh, P. W., 245
Mao, C. C., 169
Marangos, P. J., 169, 197, 198

Marchione, K., 315
Marchione, N., 315
Margraf, J., 19, 41, 124, 191, 208, 209, 210, 217, 221, 222, 223, 240, 327, 329
Marion, T., 101, 110
Markowitz, J. M., 212, 213
Markowitz, J. S., 1, 16, 27, 61, 99, 102, 103, 110, 111, 112, 304, 327, 329
Marks, I. M., 20, 24, 28, 50, 258, 330
Marks, J. M., 17, 28
Marovitch, S., 245
Marriott, P., 327
Marro, K. I., 220, 221
Marshall, L. E., 163, 164
Martin, D., 122, 123, 124, 125
Martin, M., 315
Martin, N. G., 76
Martin, P., 121
Martin, R. L., 81
Martin, R. N., 67, 68, 69
Martinez, J. M., 212, 217, 218, 220 258, 259, 260, 261, 262, 263, 264, 265, 266
Marttunen, M. J., 100, 108
Marwaha, J., 169
Maser, J. D., 47, 184, 189
Mason, S. T., 148
Massion, A. O., 101, 109
Mateo-Bermudez, J., 260
Mathew, R. J., 265
Mathews, A., 209
Mattick, R., 223, 263
Matuzas, W., 209
Mavissakalian, M., 92, 160, 288, 293
Mayes, D., 122
Mayol, A., 24
McBane, D., 138, 206, 208, 217, 218, 222, 260
McCann, D. S., 120, 122, 123, 124, 125, 136, 137, 139
McCauley, P. A., 84
McChesney, C. M., 67, 68, 69, 75, 76

McClellan, J., 214
McClenahan, K. L., 208, 209, 210, 217, 221, 222
McClure, D. J., 294
McClure, J. N., 7, 194, 206, 207, 208, 210, 217
McCue, R. E., 299
McElroy, S., 15
McEvoy, L. T., 82, 106
McGonagle, K. A., 51
McGrath, P., 42, 211, 212, 213, 215, 217, 296, 303
McHugh, P. R., 233, 234
McInnes, R., 67, 68
McIntyre, L. M., 140
McLaurin, R. L., 257
McLennan, J. E., 257
McMillen, B. A., 121
McNair, D. M., 158, 159
McNally, R. J., 33, 243
McNamee, G., 28
McPherson, C. A., 122, 123, 125, 126, 141
McRae, A., 168
McTavish, D., 267
Meduna, L. J., 262
Meek, J. L., 170
Meissner, R., 133
Mellersh, V., 206
Mellman, T. A., 41, 132, 133, 184, 194
Meltzer-Brody, S., 22, 305
Mendel, J. G. C., 28
Mendlewicz, J., 67, 68, 75, 76
Mengali, F., 158, 159
Meninger, K., 326
Merchant, A., 106, 296
Merikangas, K. R., 67, 75, 76, 89
Mesters, P., 130, 133
Meterissian, G., 235–236, 237
Metzger, G. D., 220, 221
Meyer, E., 244
Michel, A., 154
Michelson, L., 315
Michenfelder, J. D., 197
Michiels, T. M., 267
Milde, J. W., 197

Miletich, D. J., 197
Milic-Emili, J., 265
Miller, I. W., 106
Miller, J. A., 293
Miller, L. J., 233
Miller, O. A., 133
Miller, P. P., 23
Milot, S., 244
Minnai, G., 297
Mintun, M. A., 221, 244, 260, 261
Missri, J. C., 257
Mitchell, R. A., 257
Mitchell-Heggs, N., 194, 207, 208, 210, 215, 217, 222
Modigh, K., 122, 123, 124, 125, 157, 164, 294
Mohler, H., 234
Molcho, A., 42
Monroe, S. M., 24
Montgomery, D., 154
Montgomery, K. C., 153
Montgomery, S. A., 165
Montgomery, W., 245
Moore, G., 160
Moran, C., 67, 68
Moran, T. H., 233, 234
Moret, C., 154
Morgan, A. P., 263
Mori, S., 245
Morin-Surun, M. P., 245
Morley, P. D., 233
Morris, H. H., 284
Mos, J., 154, 156
Mostellar, M. E., 257
Mukerji, V., 41
Mullaney, J. A., 298
Muller, P. J., 198
Munjack, D. J., 158, 159
Munoz, C., 138
Munoz, R., 1
Murberg, M., 145
Murphy, D. L., 162, 163, 182, 186, 187, 192, 193, 195, 236
Murphy, G. E., 110
Murrell, E., 223, 263
Musser, B., 197
Mussetti, L., 158, 159

Mutchler, K., 75
Myers, J. K., 50

Nagy, G., 247
Nagy, L. M., 16, 20, 327
Nanopoulos, D., 170
Nansen, A., 267
Naranjo, C. A., 285
Nash, P. A., 154
Nashold, B. S., Jr., 153
Naylor, R. J., 154
Neale, M., 70, 71
Nee, J., 213
Neese, R. M., 120, 122, 123, 124, 125, 136, 137, 139
Neims, A. H., 197
Nelson, B., 133, 134, 142
Nelson, C. B., 51
Nelson, P., 27
Nemiah, J., 181
Nesse, R. M., 22, 140, 141, 237
Nestadt, G., 82, 106
Neubig, R., 141
Newberg, L. A., 197
Newman, S. C., 47
Nichols, J. D., 121
Nickell, P. V., 187
Nicolaysen, G., 265
Niklaus, D. E., 286
Ninan, P. T., 169
Nishikawa, T., 170
Nisita, C., 158, 159
Nixon, J. M., 49
Norman, T. R., 140
Norman, W. H., 106
Norstad, N., 167
Norton, G. R., 39, 100, 101, 103, 109, 110
Novacenko, H., 133, 134, 142
Noyes, R., 17, 20, 22, 67, 68, 69, 72, 73, 74, 75, 76, 88, 89, 91, 92, 97, 100, 101, 108, 110, 111, 112, 138, 266, 280, 282, 297, 300, 303, 304
Nunes, E., 303
Nutt, D. J., 42, 120, 121, 122, 123, 124, 125, 130,

131, 132, 133, 140, 170, 213, 214, 218, 227, 242

Oakley, N. R., 154
Oakley-Browne, M. A., 27
O'Brien, D. W., 23
O'Brien, G. T., 23
Ocepek-Welikson, K., 303
O'Connell, M. T., 155
O'Gorman, T. W., 97
Ohrstrom, J. K., 294
Oldberg, 233
Olievier, L. C. W., 264, 265
Olin, G. S., 285
Olivier, B., 156
Olivier, J., 154
O'Neil, C., 22
Ong, B. G., 245
Oopik, T., 243
Oppenheimer, B. J., 67, 68
Orenstein, H., 39
Orsulak, P. J., 120
Ortiz, A., 137, 194, 211, 212, 213, 215, 217, 218
Orvaschel, H., 51
Oster, G., 284
Ostergren, J., 198
Otto, M. W., 22, 280, 281, 284, 300, 305
Ouellette, R., 1, 16, 17, 19, 20, 61, 99, 102, 103, 110, 111–112, 304, 327, 329
Ouellette, S., 1, 27
Ozaki, L., 197

Pace, N. L., 265
Padgett, W. L., 198
Pain, M. C. F., 264
Palejko, W., 154
Palij, M., 194, 207, 208, 210, 214–215, 217, 218, 219, 222
Pallanti, S., 23
Palmour, R., 240, 241, 242, 243
Paly, M., 287
Panagiotis, N., 122

Papadimitriou, G., 67, 68, 75, 76
Papp, L. A., 222, 258, 259, 260, 262, 263, 264–265, 273
Paradis, M., 239, 242
Park, D. H., 245
Parker, L., 212, 213
Parma, A. M., 198
Paschelke, G., 169
Patel, J., 197, 198
Pathak, D., 22, 81, 82, 86
Patterson, M. B., 82
Paul, S. M., 169
Pauls, D. L., 35, 60, 67, 68, 69, 72, 73, 74, 75, 76
Payeur, R., 200, 236, 237, 246
Pecknold, J. C., 17, 88, 89, 161, 266, 282, 294, 300, 329
Pellow, S., 154
Pendleton, L., 82
Penke, B., 247
Perel, J., 293
Perera, K. M. H., 285
Perlmutter, J., 221, 261
Persson, L., 285
Persson, M., 168
Perugi, G., 90, 158, 159
Peskind, A., 39
Peskind, E., 208, 219
Peterson, G. A., 288
Peterson, R. A., 243
Petracca, A., 158, 159
Petronis, K. R., 60, 61, 100, 105
Peuranen, E., 243
Pfeifer, P. N., 122
Pfohl, B., 22, 88, 89, 91, 92
Phil, M., 61
Phillis, J. W., 197, 252
Pickel, V. M., 168
Pierce, C. M., 198
Pilkonis, P. A., 328
Pilowsky, R., 245
Pilsbury, D., 258, 259
Pincus, H. A., 25, 26
Pinnock, R. D., 247
Piot, O., 154, 241, 247

Pisgena, J. R., 234
Pitts, F. N., Jr., 7, 194, 206, 207, 208, 210, 217, 218
Platt, J. E., 140
Plaznik, A., 154
Plum, F., 257
Plutchik, R., 42
Poddighe, A., 297
Pohl, R., 137, 158, 161, 167, 194, 207, 208, 211, 212, 213, 215, 217, 218, 219, 221, 222, 260, 274
Pold, M., 241, 247
Polinsky, R. J., 121
Pollack, M. H., 22, 280, 281, 284, 300, 305
Pollak, C. P., 222
Pols, H., 161, 258, 263, 267
Poole, P. H., 294
Popkin, M. K., 198
Porges, S. W., 227
Posner, J. B., 257
Post, R. M., 120, 122, 123, 125, 130, 133, 188, 189, 190, 198, 222, 297, 304
Potkin, S., 158, 159
Pottash, A. C., 122, 123, 124, 125
Price, J. L., 221, 244, 260, 261
Price, L. H., 128
Prusoff, B. A., 67, 75, 76, 89
Puig-Antioch, J., 104. 133, 134, 142
Pujol, J. F., 168, 170
Pyke, R. E., 136, 280

Quadrino, L. M., 158, 293, 327
Quitkin, F. M., 212, 213, 303

Rabinovich, H., 133, 134, 142
Rabkin, J. G., 303
Rachman, S., 22, 325
Rae, D. S., 82
Raichle, M. E., 221, 244, 260, 261

Rainey, J. M., 137, 194, 207, 208, 211, 212, 213, 215, 217, 218, 219, 220, 222, 274
Raj, A. B., 133, 134, 142, 158, 161, 266
Raj, B. A., 121, 280, 292, 293, 296
Rajab, H. M., 101, 104, 106
Rall, T. W., 197, 198
Randrup, A., 133
Rankin, J. G., 285
Rapee, R. M., 21, 22, 82, 84, 85, 87, 223, 258, 263, 317, 327
Rapoport, J. L., 197
Raskind, M., 39, 208, 219
Rasmussen, S. A., 128
Rataud, J., 154, 241, 247
Ratcliff, K. S., 29, 103, 106
Ravitz, B., 121
Read, D. J. C., 264
Realini, J. P., 53
Rebuck, A. S., 264
Rech, R. H., 155
Redmond, D. E., 119, 120, 121, 124, 129, 132, 136, 145, 166, 168, 194, 262, 263, 264, 266
Redmond, E., 125, 126, 141
Reed, E. W., 67, 68, 69, 75
Reenan, A., 122
Rees, L., 193, 267
Rees, W. L., 206, 208, 210, 211, 217
Regier, D. A., 10, 50, 52
Rehfeld, J. F., 233, 235
Reich, J., 22, 88, 89, 91, 92, 97
Reifler, B. V., 284
Reiman, E. M., 221, 244, 260, 261
Reines, S., 238, 239, 241
Reis, D. J., 168, 245
Reiss, S., 243
Renaud, B., 168
Reyntgens, A. J., 167
Richard, J. G., 234
Richards, S. M., 284
Richards, T. L., 220, 221

Richelson, E., 288
Rickels, K., 167, 280
Rifkin, A., 17, 88, 89, 215, 266, 282, 300
Rifkin, B. G., 125, 126, 141, 158, 293, 327
Rijken, H., 258
Riskind, J. H., 106
Ritter, C., 60
Rivot, J. P., 170
Robertson, L. G., 245
Robins, E., 1, 110, 134, 165, 221, 244, 260, 261
Robins, L. N., 29, 51, 52, 103, 106
Robinson, D., 42
Robinson, P. H., 233, 234
Rockman, G. E., 101, 110
Roigaard-Petersen, H., 233
Romano, G., 213
Romanoski, A. J., 106
Ron Norton, G., 91
Roose, S. P., 212, 288
Roques, B. P., 245
Rose, B., 260
Rose, R. M., 120
Rosenbaum, J. F., 22, 41, 42, 262, 263, 264, 266, 280, 281, 283, 284, 300, 305
Rosenblum, L. A., 220, 240
Ross, C. A., 245
Ross, D., 212, 219, 220, 258, 260, 261, 262, 263, 266, 304
Ross, H. E., 87, 91
Roth, M., 23, 24, 61, 167
Roth, R. H., 121, 125, 126, 141, 145
Roth, W. T., 19, 41, 124, 191, 208, 209, 210, 217, 221, 222, 240, 327, 329
Rothchild, M. A., 67, 68
Rothstein, E., 286
Rotunda, R., 23
Roy-Byrne, P. P., 158, 159, 170, 190, 193, 208, 211, 214, 215, 219, 220, 256, 304, 329
Rubenstein, I., 261

Rubin, R. T., 17, 39, 88, 89, 282, 300
Rubinson, E., 124
Rudd, D. M., 101, 104, 106
Ruggiero, D. A., 245
Ruiter, C. de, 258
Ruken, H., 82, 85, 87
Rush, A. J., 261
Russell, J. L., 214
Russell, M. W., 284
Ryan, N. D., 133, 134, 142
Rydin, E., 166

Saaverda, J. M., 245
Sachar, E. J, 222
Sachar, E. J., 133, 134
Sachs, G. S., 22, 280, 281, 284, 300
Saletu, B., 197
Salkovskis, P. M., 315, 321
Salzman, H. A., 257
Sampson, N., 286
Samuelson, L., 303
Sanchez-Craig, H., 285
Sandberg, D., 213, 219, 261, 326, 327
Sanderson, W. C., 21, 81, 82, 83, 84, 85, 87, 88, 92, 93, 99, 100, 102, 104, 106, 111, 133, 134, 144, 223, 262, 263, 325, 327, 329
Sandler, K. R., 280
Sandler, L. S., 27
Sandler, M., 217
Sanghera, M. K., 121
Sartorius, N., 52
Saskin, P., 284
Satinover, I., 197
Sattin, A., 197
Saumon, G., 266
Sauter, A., 233
Savino, M., 90
Scamonatti, L., 297
Scappaticci, K. A., 245
Scatton, B., 170
Schalling, D., 166
Scharf, M. B., 284
Scheftner, W. A., 84, 88, 89
Schittecatte, M., 130, 133

Schless, A., 280
Schmidt, W., 285
Schneider, P., 158, 159
Schneier, F. R., 293
Schoenfeld, R. I., 155
Schön, H. W., 133
Schreiber, R., 156
Schubert, D. S. P., 82
Schwartz, W. B., 257
Schweizer, E. E., 280
Scott-Fleurie, M. H., 161
Scupi, B. S., 184, 189, 190
Segal, M., 168, 169
Segal, R., 285
Seifter, J., 152
Seller, H., 245
Sellers, E. M., 285
Sellers, T. D., 197
Serrano, A., 170
Severinghause, J. W., 257
Seyfried, W., 106
Shader, R. I., 281
Shah, K., 155
Shalomskas, D. E., 23, 169
Shamin, M. T., 198
Shapira, B., 197
Shapiro, S., 64, 106
Sharma, T., 220
Shaw, T. M., 234
Shea, M. T., 328
Shear, K., 315
Shear, M. K., 92, 215
Sheehan, D. V., 37, 38, 60, 121, 158, 161, 168, 194, 215, 217, 220, 262, 263, 264, 266, 280, 282, 285, 290, 292, 293, 296, 300, 303, 305
Sheehan, H., 158, 161
Sheehan, K. H., 121, 266, 280, 296
Sheikh, J., 19, 41, 208, 209, 210, 217, 221, 222
Shephard, R. A., 154, 155
Sher, K. J., 91, 110
Sherman, D., 136, 194, 207, 208, 210, 215, 217, 222
Sherwood, P., 221, 222
Shields, J., 70
Shinosaka, S., 245

Shore, N. J., 260
Shriqui, C., 237
Sicker, H. J., 257
Siever, L. J., 130, 132, 133, 190
Signeau, J. C., 233
Silva, J. A., 286
Silver, J. M., 170
Silverman, M. A., 241
Simonini, E., 90
Simpkins, J., 285
Singh, H., 137
Singh, L., 241, 247
Sirisinha, I., 292–293
Sisson, B., 285
Sjoberg, L., 285
Skegg, D. C. G., 284
Skeie, T. M., 99, 100, 104
Skolnick, B., 130
Skolnick, P., 169
Slater, E., 70
Slaughter, D. G., 153
Slutsky, A. S., 264
Slymen, D. J., 138, 280
Smiley, A., 284
Smith, C. B., 122, 123, 125, 140, 141
Smith, C. C., 139
Smith, V. K., 296
Smith, W. W., 257
Snaith, R. P., 165
Snyder, S. H., 197, 245
Sokol, L., 315
Soldatos, C. R., 286
Sollevi, A., 198
Solyom, L., 280
Soriani, A., 90
Soto, S., 121, 158, 161, 266, 296
Sotsky, S. M., 328
Southwick, S. M., 293
Sowers, J. R., 122
Spealman, R. D., 198
Speicher, D., 233
Spielberger, C. D., 190
Spier, S. A., 280, 281, 284, 300
Spitzer, R. L., 1, 103, 106, 134, 165
Spitznagel, E. L., 106

Spyer, K. M., 245
Spyer, M., 245
Stalla, G. K., 133
Stanley, T. H., 265
Starcevic, V., 22, 81, 82, 86
Steen, R. G., 220
Steer, R. A., 99, 100, 104, 106
Stefanski, R., 154
Stein, J., 61, 194, 212, 217, 245, 258, 262, 271
Stein, L., 154, 155
Stein, M. B., 85, 88, 89, 132, 133, 199, 222, 297
Stein, M. D., 130, 133
Steinbusch, H., 170
Steinman, R., 210, 218
Stene, M., 122
Stephens, P. M., 198
Sternberg, D. E., 120, 127
Stewart, J. W., 42, 212, 213, 303
Stewart, R. S., 261
Stillner, V. M., 198
Stolk, J., 305
Stoltzman, R., 82, 106
Stone, E. A., 140
Stone, T. W., 197
Storr, C., 285
Strauman, T., 163, 164
Strom, G., 206
Stutzmann, J. M., 154, 241, 247
Suckow, R. F., 165
Suelzer, M., 22, 88, 89, 91, 92, 101, 110, 111, 112
Sunderland, G. S., 240
Surman, O. S., 168, 194, 215, 217, 290, 300, 303
Sutherland, E. W., 198
Svebak, S., 280
Sved, A. F., 245
Svenson, E. M., 285
Svensson, K., 154
Swann, A. C., 42, 122, 123, 124, 125, 166
Sweeney, D., 122, 123, 124, 125

Swinson, R. P., 17, 39, 88, 89, 91, 100, 103, 109, 266, 282, 300, 329
Sylmen, D., 67, 68, 69, 73, 75
Synder, S. H., 198
Systrom, D., 262, 263, 264
Szanto-Fekete, M., 247

Takagi, H., 245
Tallman, J., 138, 139
Tancer, M. E., 85, 88, 89, 182, 191, 195, 196
Tant, S., 265
Tarazi, R. C., 136
Targum, S. D., 163, 164, 212
Tassinari, R., 315
Tateishi, K., 245
Taube, C. A., 50
Taylor, B., 124
Taylor, C. B., 19, 22, 41, 208, 209, 210, 217, 221, 222, 327, 329
Taylor, M. A., 207, 208, 217
Taylor, V. E., 15
Tearnan, B. H., 21, 22
Teherani, M., 101, 103, 105, 108
Telch, C., 22
Telch, M. J., 21, 22, 27, 327, 329
Tesar, G. E., 280, 281, 283, 284, 300, 305
Testa, S., 315
Thoresen, M., 257, 265
Thorpe, G. L., 21
Thuresson, K., 122, 123, 124, 125, 157, 164
Thyer, B. A., 22, 122
Tien, A. Y., 60–61
Tiller, J. W. G., 264
Tobena, A., 28
Toccafondi, F., 297
Tohyama, M., 245
Tollefson, G. D., 120, 285
Tomchick, R., 138
Tondo, L., 297
Tong, H. J., 168
Torgersen, S., 70, 268
Traub, M., 237

Trehan, R. R., 293
Tricamo, E., 303
Trippet, C. J., 298
Trockman, C., 288
Troughton, E., 92, 97
Troyer, I. E., 158, 159, 294
Trzeciak, A., 234
Tuck, M. L., 122
Tucker, E., 292–293
Tugrul, K. C., 15
Tulley, M., 285
Tundo, A., 297
Turk, D. C., 24
Turner, P., 138, 139
Tuttle, E. P., 257
Tye, N. C., 154
Tyers, M. B., 154

Uhde, T. W., 39, 40, 41, 85,
    88, 89, 122, 123, 125,
    128, 130, 132, 133, 162,
    163, 181, 182, 183, 184,
    186, 187, 188, 189, 190,
    191, 193, 194, 195, 196,
    198, 199, 222, 243, 261,
    267, 297, 304
Uhlenhuth, E. H., 22, 81, 82,
    86, 209, 285
Uy, J., 262
Uzogara, E., 280, 300

Valzelli, L., 167
Van Delft, A. M., 154, 155
van den Hout, M. A., 22,
    193, 194, 209, 258, 262,
    263, 264, 267
Vanderhaeghen, J., 233, 245,
    253
Van der Molen, G. M., 22,
    194, 209, 262, 263, 267
Van Dieren, A. C., 22
Vandijk, A., 234
van Gompel, P., 167
van Lint, L. E. M., 206–207,
    208, 217, 218, 222, 260
van Megan, H., 237, 239,
    241
van Praag, H. M., 42, 92,
    100, 104, 106, 124, 133,

    134, 144, 151, 157, 162,
    163, 164, 167, 175, 287
van Schaik, A., 82, 85, 87
Van Wyck Fleet, J., 296
Vasar, E., 240, 241, 243, 247
Veith, R., 208, 219
Vela-Bueno, A., 286
Verburg, C., 161
Verhoeven, V. M., 158, 159,
    160, 294
Verhoeven, W. M. A., 157,
    159, 160, 294
Verhofstad, A., 170
Vermilyea, B. B., 16, 17, 21,
    82, 85, 87, 332
Vermilyea, J., 16–17, 21, 82,
    85, 87
Vernikos-Danellis, J., 198
Versiani, M., 286
Vestal, R. E., 197
Victor, B., 189
Videen, T. O., 221, 244
Vieland, J. E., 73
Villacres, E., 170
Vincendon, G., 170
Viswanathan, R., 330
Vitaliano, P., 329
Vittone, B. J., 130, 132, 133,
    190, 222, 304
Volavka, J., 207, 208, 217
Von Korff, M. R., 17, 55,
    106
Vroemen, J., 209
Vry, J. de, 156

Waddell, M. T., 332
Wager, S. G., 303
Walker, J. R., 27
Walker, P. L., 217
Walker, R. D., 212, 213
Walker, R. G., 198
Walker, W. V., 227
Wallace, C. J., 328
Walloe, L., 257
Walsh, B. T., 212
Wamsley, J. K., 245
Wang, Z., 75
Wank, S. A., 234
Wardle, J., 327

Warley, A., 265
Warner, K., 217, 219
Warshaw, M. G., 101, 109
Waters, R., 262
Watkins, W. D., 168, 194,
    215, 217
Watson, A. M., 298
Waxman, D., 294
Waxman, R. P., 213, 214,
    218
Wedin, L., 160
Weekes, C., 318
Weg, M. W., 217
Weil-Malherbe, N., 138
Weiler, P. G., 139
Weinberg, C. R., 122
Weinberg, P., 137, 222
Weiner, R. D., 197
Weingartner, H., 197
Weisman, K., 167
Weiss, A., 133
Weissman, E., 233
Weissman, M. J., 67
Weissman, M. M., 1, 16,
    17, 19, 20, 27, 28–29,
    50, 53, 56, 59, 61, 62,
    73, 75, 76, 83, 89, 90,
    99, 101, 102, 103, 110,
    111, 112, 112, 167,
    268, 304, 327, 328,
    329
Welkowitz, J., 299
Wells, J. E., 27
Werner, A., 281
Wesner, R. W., 75, 294
West, G. A., 197
West, M., 245
Westberg, P., 122, 123, 124,
    125, 157, 164
Westenberg, H. G. M., 156,
    157, 158, 159, 160, 162,
    163, 164, 167, 176, 206,
    207, 208, 217, 218, 222,
    237, 239, 241, 260, 264
Wetzel, R. D., 110
Wetzler, S., 84, 92, 93, 102,
    111, 144, 162, 163, 164,
    168, 175, 262, 263, 329
Weyman, A. E., 60
Wheeler, E. D., 67, 68

Whitaker-Azmitia, P., 138, 206, 208, 217, 218, 222, 260, 266
White, P. D., 67, 68, 69, 75, 262
Whiting, R. L., 154
Whitsett, S. F., 158, 159, 294
Whitton, P., 155
Wickramaratne, P., 23, 67, 76, 90
Widiger, T. A., 25, 26
Wiklund, L., 168
William, P. W., 153
Williams, J. B., 103, 106
Williams, M., 194, 207, 208
Wilmotte, J., 67, 68, 75, 76, 130, 133
Wilson, H. W., 265
Wilson, K. G., 27
Wilson, L. G., 280
Wilson, R. R., 318
Wilson, S., 170, 242
Wilson, W. H., 197
Wing, J. K., 49
Winokur, A., 130
Winokur, G., 1, 84, 88, 89

Winter, J. C., 155
Wise, C. D., 154, 155
Wittchen, H.-U., 16, 27, 51, 52, 53, 54, 72, 73
Wittman, M., 133
Woerner, M. G., 304
Wolf, A. W., 82
Wolff, E. A., 188, 189
Wolff, J., 198
Wolkow, R., 158, 159
Wolpe, J., 262, 263
Woo, E., 281
Wood, J. H., 120
Wood, P., 67, 68
Woodman, C. L., 297
Woodruff, G. N., 234, 241, 247
Woodruff, R. A., 1
Woods, S. W., 16, 20, 23, 76, 90, 122, 123, 125, 126, 127, 128, 138, 139, 140, 141, 158, 159, 162, 163, 164, 168, 169, 170, 194, 262, 263, 264, 266, 267, 280, 283, 284, 293, 327
Wright, F. D., 315

Wrzesinski, L., 294
Wu, P. H., 197

Yarnell, P. R., 197
Yeragani, V., 137, 158, 161, 167, 211, 212, 213, 215, 217, 218, 219, 221, 222, 260, 274
Yergamio, V., 194

Zahn, T. P., 197
Zak, J. P., 293
Zandbergen, J., 258, 263, 267
Zarbin, M. A., 245
Zeigler, M. G., 120
Zetzel, E., 326
Zhao, S., 51
Zitrin, C. M., 304
Zohar, J., 151, 162, 163, 186, 187
Zung, W. W. K., 190
Zygan, K., 13

Subject Index

Acetazolamide, 265
Adrenergic receptors, 74–75
Agoraphobia, 20–22
  and caffeine, 188
  defined, 20
  without panic attacks, 28–29
Alcohol and panic, 39
Alprazolam, 195
Amphetamines and panic, 39
Atypical presentations, 40–43

Benzodiazepines, 280–286
  adverse effects, 283–284
  choice of, 280–281
  dosage, 281–286
  issues, 285–286
  trail duration, 283
Biopsychosocial model, 22

Caffeine-induced anxiety, 39–40, 181–199
  clinical validation, 192–193
  replicability, 193–195
  specificity, 188–192
  symptom convergence, 182–188
Carbon dioxide and panic disorder, 262–266
Cardiac arrhythmias, 38
Cardiovascular diseases and panic disorder, 38
Childhood separation anxiety, 22
Cholecystokinin (CCK), 233–248
  future research, 246–247
  historical perspective, 234–236
  mechanism, 240–243
  neuroanatomical correlates, 244–245
  validation of, 236–240
Clonidine, 129–133

Cognitive behavioral treatment (CBT), 315–331
  components of, 316–325
  efficacy, 315–316
  mechanism of action, 325–326
  multimodal treatment, 326–331
Cognitive restructuring, 318
Comorbidity, 75–76, 80–95
  anxiety disorders and panic, 90
  depression disorders and panic, 88–90
  exclusion rules and, 81
  frequency of, 83–88
  personality disorders and panic, 91–94
  significance of, 82–83
Course of attack, 19–22
Cyclic antidepressants, 286–290
  adverse effects, 288–289
  blood levels, 288
  choice, 287
  dose schedule, 287–288
  issues, 289–290
  toxic effects, 290–291
  trial duration, 287–288

Delusional disorder, 36
Depression and panic, 75
Desipramine, 133–135
Diagnosing, 17–19
Differential diagnosis, 25–35
  changes in DSM-IV, 25–27
  generalized anxiety disorder, 29–30
  major depression, 34–35
  nonclinical panic attacks, 27
  obsessive compulsive disorder, 33–34
  phobia:
    social, 31–32

Differential diagnosis (*Continued*)
   specific, 30–31
   post-traumatic stress disorder, 32

Endocrine diseases, 38
Epidemiologic Catchment Area (ECA)
   Program, 50–51
Epidemiology of panic, 50–63
   course, 61–63
   description, 52–57
   incidence, 57–59
   risk factors, 59–63
   sequelae, 62–63
Exposure, 322

Frequency of attacks, 19–20

Genetic modeling, 73
Genetics, 66–77
   clinical-implications, 76–77
   comorbidity, 75–76
   epidemiology, 66–67
   family studies, 67–69
   inheritance mode, 71–73
   modeling, 73
   twin studies, 69–71
Genome research, 74–75
Geriatric patients, 299–300

Hypchondriases, 35–36
Hyperventilation, 219, 256–259
Hypocapnia, 256–257

Imipramine, 195
Impairment, 16–17
Irritable panic, 42–43
Isoproterenol infusions, 136–138

Lactate infusion, 206–224
   assessment of responses, 208–212
   clinical significance, 214–216
   cognitive factors, role of, 222
   diagnostic specificity, 212–214
   mechanism of action, 216–223
   methods, 207–208
   treatment effects, 214–216
Life events, as stressors, 22–24
Limited symptom attacks, 19
Locus coeruleus, 119-121
Lymphocyte beta-adrenoceptor, 138–140

Medical illnesses, 37–39
Medications, *see* specific symptoms
Mendelian inheritance, 72
Monoamine oxidase inhibitors, 290–293
   adverse effects, 291
   choice, 290
   dosage, 290
   reverse MAO inhibitors, 293
   risks, 291–293
   trail duration, 290

National Comorbidity Survey (NCS), 51
Neurologic diseases, 38
Nocturnal panic, 41–42
Nonfearful panic, 40–41
Norepinephrine system, 119–143
   challenges, 126–138
   functioning baseline, 122–125
   functioning during panic, 125–126
   noradrenergic probes, 126–138
   peripheral receptors, 138–141

Origins of, 22–24

Panic disorder:
   biological basics, 4–8
   clinical aspects, 2–4
   defined, 1
   origins, 22–24
   see specific entries
   treatment of, 9–10
Physical disorders and anxiety, 38
Platelet alpha-2-adrenoceptor, 140–141
Polygenic transmission, 72
Postpartum stress, 23
Precursors:
   childhood separation anxiety, 22
Pregnancy, 297–298
Presenting problem, 16
Prevalence, 16–17
Prevalence of panic symptoms, 53
Psychoactive substances, 39–40
Psychoeducation, 317–318

Relaxation training, 321
Respiratory alkalosis, 257
Respiratory control, 321
Respiratory diseases, 38
Respiratory neurobiology, 255–268
   abnormalities, 260–262

Respiratory neurobiology (*Continued*)
  carbon dioxide and panic disorder,
    262–266
  control medications, 266–267
  hyperventilation, 256–259
Reverse MAO inhibitors, 293
Reverse-step chemical model, 197

Segregation analysis, 72
Separation anxiety:
  childhood, 22
  parental, 22
Serotonin, 293–295
Serotonin function and panic, 151–171
  animal anxiety models, 152–153
  anxiety and 5HT, 165–168
  assessment of 5HT function, 157–162
  behavioral effects, 155–157
  challenge studies, 162–165
  decreasing 5HT function, 153–155
  increasing 5HT function, 155
  theories, other, 168–171
Sex distribution, 73
Somatic treatment, 279–305
  benzodiazepines, 280–286

combination treatment, 295–296
cyclic antidepressants, 286–290
history of, 279–280
issues, 300–303
monoamine oxidase inhibitors, 290–295
serotonin, 293–295
side effects, 303–305
types of patients, 296–300
Somatization disorder, 36
Substance-induced anxiety, 38–40
Substance related disorders, 38, 90–91
Suicidal behaviors, 99–113
  assessment methods, 105–108
  factors associated with, 109–112
  studies summary, 100–102
Symptoms:
  limited, 19
  summary, 18
Symptoms of panic attacks, 55

Visualization, 321–322

Yohimbine, 126–129

Zung Anxiety Scale, 192